PATRIOTIC CORRECTNESS

Cultural Politics & the Promise of Democracy
A Series from Paradigm Publishers
Edited by Henry A. Giroux

꧁

Empire and Inequality: America and the World Since 9/11 (2004), Paul Street

Caught in the Crossfire: Kids, Politics, and America's Future (2005), Lawrence Grossberg

Reading and Writing for Civic Literacy: The Critical Citizen's Guide to Argumentative Rhetoric (2005), Donald Lazere

Why Are We Reading Ovid's Handbook on Rape? Teaching and Learning at a Women's College (2005), Madeleine Kahn

Schooling and the Struggle for Public Life, Updated Edition (2005), Henry A. Giroux

Listening Beyond the Echoes: Media, Ethics, and Agency in an Uncertain World (2006), Nick Couldry

Michel Foucault: Materialism and Education, Updated Edition (2006), Mark Olssen

Pedagogies of the Global: Knowledge in the Human Interest (2006), Arif Dirlik

Not Only the Master's Tools: African American Studies in Theory and Practice (2006), edited by Lewis R. Gordon and Jane Anna Gordon

The Giroux Reader (2006), Henry A. Giroux, edited and introduced by Christopher G. Robbins

Patriotic Correctness: Academic Freedom and Its Enemies (2008), John K. Wilson

Against the Terror of Neoliberalism (2008), Henry A. Giroux

Thinking Queerly: Posthumanist Essays on Ethics and Identity (2008), David Ross Fryer

PATRIOTIC CORRECTNESS

ACADEMIC FREEDOM
AND ITS ENEMIES

JOHN K. WILSON

Paradigm Publishers
Boulder • London

Copyright © 2008 Paradigm Publishers

Published in the United States by Paradigm Publishers, 3360 Mitchell Lane Suite E, Boulder, CO 80301 USA.

Paradigm Publishers is the trade name of Birkenkamp & Company, LLC, Dean Birkenkamp, President and Publisher.

Library of Congress Cataloging-in-Publication Data

Wilson, John K., 1969–
    Patriotic correctness : academic freedom and its enemies / John K. Wilson.
        p. cm. — (Cultural politics and the promise of democracy)
    Includes bibliographical references and index.
    ISBN 978-1-59451-193-6 (hc)
    ISBN 978-1-59451-194-3 (pbk)
        1. Academic freedom—United States.   2. Freedom of speech—United States.
3. Patriotism—United States.   I. Title.
    LC72.2.W55 2007
    378.1'213—dc22

                                                                            2007015062

Printed and bound in the United States of America on acid-free paper that meets the standards of the American National Standard for Permanence of Paper for Printed Library Materials.

Designed and typeset by Straight Creek Bookmakers.

12 11 10 09 08   1 2 3 4 5

Contents

✧

INTRODUCTION
The Rise of Patriotic Correctness

⊷

Academic freedom is always one of the first casualties of war. Like other civil liberties, academic freedom is seen as dangerous because it protects dissent at a time when national unity is demanded by those in power. The attacks of September 11, 2001, evoked calls for suppression of free thought, and academic freedom has been put in jeopardy at colleges around the country. Most alarmingly, the attacks on academic freedom are increasing, not abating. As 9/11 becomes a historic event rather than an immediate memory, the movement against academic freedom keeps growing in influence.

The post-9/11 attack on academic freedom is also alarming because it represents the first major setback for academic freedom in a half-century. The history of academic freedom in the United States has been largely a story of continual improvement in civil liberties on college campuses. For the past century, with few exceptions, the protection of dissent in American higher education has steadily increased. Today, the idea of academic freedom is under a new assault.

The Meaning of Academic Freedom

Academic freedom, as defined by the American Association of University Professors (AAUP) in its 1915 and 1940 Statements of Principles, traditionally refers to the freedom of faculty to research, to teach, and to speak out like any other person.[1] This means that all faculty (not merely those who hold tenure) have the right to choose their own research, to choose their own teaching approaches, and to speak for themselves in public about anything.

None of these rights are unlimited: A researcher isn't allowed to embezzle research funds; a teacher of a calculus class isn't allowed to devote all of the class time to teaching the works of Shakespeare to puzzled students expecting to learn math; and a professor who writes a letter to the newspaper proclaiming that he always fails students from a particular ethnic group should quickly be out of a job.

But professors must have an enormous amount of latitude to determine their research topics and teaching techniques, leaving it to qualified faculty to judge the quality of their work and whether it is deserving of tenure or promotion. For extramural utterances (the term for speaking in public or writing a letter to the newspaper), the principles of academic freedom provide a near-absolute protection.

In a free university, academic freedom belongs to students, too. Although student academic freedom originally referred only to the right to choose one's classes, its meaning was transformed during the twentieth century to encompass a broad range of civil liberties, including the right to speak freely, the right to protest peaceably, the right to a free press, the right to due process, and the right to invite any speakers to campus. Academic freedom is not some obscure idea invented by professors to protect themselves. It is a human right belonging to everyone, because academia provides us with a model for encouraging freedom and dissent throughout society.

The meaning of academic freedom is still disputed. Many conservative critics of academe cling to an archaic form of academic freedom abandoned long ago, which asserts that professors have only the freedom to express scholarly views, and not controversial political viewpoints. Others would give professors the freedom to express their views in public, but not in a classroom. But restricting academic freedom in the classroom is a dangerous principle. Whom can we trust to monitor ideas? The history of higher education is full of examples where the power to constrain controversy is abused to silence dissent.

Throughout most of the history of American higher education, there was no academic freedom. When Harvard College was founded in 1636, the teachers had no rights, and the students had no freedoms. The 1646 Statutes of Harvard imposed sharp restrictions on the freedom of students, forcing them to read the Bible twice a day and severely regulating expression: "They shall eschew all profanation of God's holy name, attributes, word, ordinances, and times of worship." Even the speaking of English was largely banned: "The Scholars shall never use their Mother tongue except that in public exercise of oratory or such like."[2] Harvard president Henry Dunster was forced to resign in 1654 because he refused to have his fourth child baptized.[3] In 1723, Cotton Mather led the first campus witch-hunt at Harvard, warning that students were privately reading "plays, novels, empty and vicious pieces of poetry, and Ovid's Epistles, which have a vile tendency to corrupt good manners" and worrying that the theology books of tutors "have rank poison in them."[4]

Right-wing activist David Horowitz declared about today's colleges, "Never has there been a time in American history where academics have been so repressive. Even when Cotton Mather was on faculty at Harvard and they were burning witches."[5] Many conservatives long for the good old days, but few openly wish that we could return to the age of witch burning as an improvement on current conditions.

Perhaps the best example of the importance of academic freedom, and what happens when we fail to defend it, is the story of left-wing economist Scott Nearing a century ago. While a lecturer at the Wharton School of Business at the University of Pennsylvania, Nearing was denied promotions despite the recommendations of the faculty and the Academic Council. Dean Robert Young warned him, "Mr. Nearing, if I were in your place I would do a little less speaking about child labor."[6]

Nearing's firing in 1915 was explicitly due to his political views. Trustee George Pepper said he supported free speech only if "free speech means the right to proclaim views not discordant with the ethical sense of the community."[7] Another trustee said that Nearing was a problem because "he advocated the ruthless redistribution of property."[8] One trustee noted that Nearing was accused of "economic heterodoxy."[9] Ralph Easley, head of the National Civic Federation, assured a trustee that "there will be no trouble to prove that Nearing is a socialist and a man whose utterances are of such a character as to make him unworthy of being connected with an institution like the University of Pennsylvania."[10] The *New York Times* applauded Nearing's dismissal in 1915 and declared, "when Trustees conscientiously endeavor to carry out the purposes of the founder by taking proper measures to prevent misuse of the endowment, we always hear a loud howl about academic freedom."[11] The conservative *New York Times* sarcastically urged "the upholders of academic freedom" to "establish a university of their own" where professors "could teach Socialism and shiftlessness until Doomsday without restraint."[12]

After Scott Nearing's firing from the University of Pennsylvania, he received an offer from Toledo University to teach. Upon reaching Toledo, Nearing was greeted warmly by the local newspaper: "Dr. Nearing can express whatever views he has, suggest any progressive reform he believes in, and there will be no reactionary, medieval-brained trustees attempting to muffle him."[13]

But Nearing didn't keep his mouth shut and didn't limit his criticism to child labor. As World War I became imminent, Nearing spoke out in opposition to U.S. intervention. Within a year and a half, the local newspaper had changed its position: "As long as Nearing stays at the University, the School will be under fire." According to the paper, "free speech is not involved," but rather "the peace and the future of T.U. and the community [are] at stake."[14] Nearing, once again, was fired for his views.

The newly formed AAUP quickly backed off from its commitment to academic freedom when America went to war. Arthur Lovejoy, one of the AAUP founders, declared that "such a war as this, in which the entire world is involved and the future character of human life and relations upon this planet is at issue, alters many things and suspends some of the rules of less critical and perilous times."[15] The AAUP issued a report revoking academic freedom for anyone opposing the draft, anyone who tried to "dissuade others" from helping the war effort, and any Germans who made "hostile or offensive expressions" about the government in private conversations.[16]

There were few legislative efforts to target college professors during World War I. Instead, it was the academics themselves who led the attack on academic freedom. In 1917, Columbia University president Nicholas Murray Butler expressed the wartime change in academic freedom: "What had been tolerated before becomes intolerable now. What had been wrongheadedness was now sedition. What had been folly was now treason. " Butler announced that anyone critical of the war would be fired: "This is the University's last and only warning."[17]

Richard Ely, the liberal economist whose case at the University of Wisconsin became one of the hallmark defenses of academic freedom, wrote to a friend: "We cannot take the same position in time of war as we take in time of peace.... A man who gives utterance to opinions which hinder us in this awful struggle deserves to be fired."[18]

At the University of Michigan, C. E. Eggert, W. W. Florer, E. A. Boucke, John Dieterle, W. W. Kusterman, Herman Wiegand, and Richard Ficken were fired for crimes such as a "pro-German attitude."[19] At the University of Illinois in 1917, President Edmund James noted that one sacrifice in war was "that you keep your mouth shut while we are in a fight."[20] Three faculty members at Illinois were dismissed after refusing to buy Liberty Bonds.[21]

Many liberals were willing to compromise academic freedom during wartime because they believed it would be a unique war, and the restrictions would soon disappear. Instead, the Red Scare followed, which would carry on the repression in academia for more than a decade.

McCarthyism on Campus

During the late 1940s and early 1950s, the McCarthy crusade led to hundreds of faculty being fired from their jobs, and many more intimidated into silence. It remains the most shameful period in the history of American higher education, as administrators and sometimes even faculty actively joined in the purges and blacklists.

J. Edgar Hoover noted in 1953, "No element of academic freedom is involved in the question of barring Communists from teaching jobs. A person, in order to be a teacher, ought to have a free intellect. You cannot have a free intellect if you are a Communist."[22] Hoover ordered FBI field offices to launch an immediate investigation of "Communist subversion" at fifty-five colleges and universities.[23]

According to David Horowitz, "The McCarthy 'witch-hunt' targeted members of a conspiratorial Communist Party, which is now known ... to have been conducting extensive espionage against the United States."[24] Contrary to common belief, the academic witch-hunt of the McCarthy era was not directed primarily at Communists and never involved espionage. Most of the professors dismissed by colleges and universities were not Communists, and many of them never had been Communists. Professors were fired for being summoned before legislative investigating committees, for participating in the 1948 Wallace campaign, for refusing to sign a loyalty oath, and even for signing petitions asking amnesty for Communists convicted under the Smith Act.[25]

University of Chicago president Robert Hutchins noted in 1951, "Everywhere in the U.S. university professors, whether or not they have tenure, are silenced by the general atmosphere of repression that now prevails."[26] Not only did McCarthyism attack academics who posed no danger to anyone, remarkably few of the victimized professors were active Communist Party members. One study noted, "almost all such incidents involved charges of past Party membership, most often in the 1930s."[27] And not one professor fired during the McCarthy era was ever found guilty of endangering national security.

Lionel Lewis studied 126 cases on 58 campuses where professors were investigated for their beliefs and concluded that "academic authorities were as much a threat to faculty and to their academic freedom as were the ominous political forces off campus."[28] Less than 20 percent of the professors still had their jobs after the investigation was complete; the rest were fired or resigned under the pressure.[29]

David Horowitz urged a return to the McCarthy era when professors were afraid to express political views: "My goal with the Academic Bill of Rights is to bring the university back to where Columbia was when I went there. When I was an undergraduate at Columbia it was the McCarthy era. I entered in 1955, but the atmosphere was there. None of my professors ever uttered a political comment in the classroom.... I would like to see politics taken out of the university classroom, period."[30]

Despite the end of the cold war, conservatives invoke the specter of communism to call for suppression on campus. Televangelist Pat Robertson, the founder of Regent University, declared about the professors featured in Horowitz's book, "[T]hese guys are out-and-out communists, they are radicals, you know some of them killers [*sic*], and they are propagandists of the first order and they don't want anybody else except them. That's why Regent University for example is so terrifically important."[31]

Ann Coulter, one of the far right's shining stars, wrote a best-selling book praising Joseph McCarthy and declared, "Liberals like to scream and howl about McCarthyism, I say let's give them some ... it's time for a new McCarthyism."[32] To conservatives like Coulter, the McCarthy era repression of liberal ideas and firing of hundreds of faculty was not a dark age of censorship, but a model of right-wing triumph they seek to re-create today on American campuses.

The Conservative Attack on Academic Freedom

Many conservatives are quite open about their desire to silence the left on campus. Sean Hannity declared that "fear is a great motivator" and told students, "I want you to start recording these left wingers."[33] Daniel Pipes, the founder of Campus Watch, stated: "I want Noam Chomsky to be taught at universities about as much as I want Hitler's writing or Stalin's writing. ... These are wild and extremist ideas that I believe have no place in a university."[34]

The war on Iraq and the war on terror are the excuse for the attacks on academic freedom by conservatives demanding allegiance to the president. David Horowitz claimed that 30,000 to 50,000 professors in America "are supporting the other side in the war on terror."[35] According to Horowitz, "We have now in this country a large community of people who are rooting for the enemy in America's war against terror. And many of them got the idea to root for them sitting in indoctrination courses in American universities."[36] Far-right extremists like Horowitz imagine that a "fifth column" in America, based at colleges, is supporting terrorism against America.[37] These conservative hallucinations, imitating the similar fears from the McCarthy era, form the basis of a new wave of attacks on academic freedom.

Unfortunately, the public perception of higher education is that "political correctness" dominates college campuses and conservatives are the only victims of censorship.[38] The impact of "patriotic correctness" on suppressing academic freedom is either ignored or actually celebrated as a way to restrain liberals on campus.

While right-wing pundits regularly publicize (and sometimes exaggerate) the threats to academic freedom for conservatives, liberal thinkers rarely focus on the current hazards posed to academic freedom. Matthew Streb concluded that "almost all" academic freedom problems "were handled in a satisfactory manner."[39]

Robert O'Neil, who led an AAUP committee examining higher education after 9/11, also gave an optimistic conclusion about the state of academic freedom. But O'Neil's view through rose-colored glasses was based on inadequate information (for example, he incorrectly claimed there was only one speaker disinvited from a college campus since September 11).[40] O'Neil also had low expectations for the fate of academic freedom. According to O'Neil, "it would be startling" if the protection of academic freedom had not declined after September 11.[41]

Yet why should we expect (or accept) that academic freedom must suffer because of a terrorist attack? America has witnessed terrorist attacks from antigovernment lunatics like Timothy McVeigh or antiabortion fanatics, but no one demanded a crackdown in academia on right-wing critics of government or prolife advocates. Some of the greatest advances in campus liberty took place in the late 1960s, when some of the worst campus violence was happening. Academic freedom is not a dangerous liberty that must be sacrificed in a time of terror; academic freedom is essential to a free society that resists the totalitarian impulses of homicidal religious fanatics. Silencing dissent on college campuses is not like searching bags at the airport; it makes no one safer when we restrict academic freedom.

There is no need to balance national security and academic freedom, because free universities do not threaten anyone. One can imagine impossible fantasies from the TV show *24*, where torturing a terrorist will save us all from a dirty bomb. But not even the most delusional opponent of civil liberties can explain how firing a professor will save us from a ticking time bomb.

Compared to earlier "wartime" situations, academic freedom is far better protected today than at any time in the past. However, the danger posed to academic freedom cannot be ignored. Efforts to silence faculty and students, even when they fail, can make others around the country more reluctant to speak openly. So it is not enough to stop the most extreme attacks on academic freedom; we must also develop a system to promote liberty as a core value of our colleges and our society. The very fact that politicians are so willing to call for censorship of professors or students is a disturbing reflection of how easily Americans will embrace repression. Academic freedom, like other kinds of freedom, is not some normal state of affairs only occasionally violated in extreme circumstances. Instead, freedom is the aberration from the historical norm, and it takes a great deal of work and constant vigilance for liberty to be maintained and expanded.

The theory of the right wingers who want to destroy academic freedom seems to be this: if only all Americans would stand together, put on a flag lapel pin, and support George W. Bush, the suicidal fundamentalist terrorists would shake in fear at our stern determination and give up. And since academia is the last major institution where dissent is permitted and even encouraged, the far right sees this as a treasonous enemy that must be put in its place.

7

Yet there are not al Qaeda supporters employed on college campuses. There is not one professor, out of more than a million in America, who came out publicly to support the 9/11 attacks. Such unanimity is unprecedented in the contemporary American university. Yet it is not enough to satisfy those on the right who imagine that criticizing the Bush administration is tantamount to treason during the war on terror.

Those who try to impose this narrow-minded patriotic correctness on academia misunderstand not only academia and how essential dissent is in the university, but they also misunderstand the nature of patriotism. It is perfectly patriotic for liberals or conservatives to criticize their government, past or present. The only genuinely un-American position is to denounce someone as "anti-American" if he or she critiques the government, because there is nothing more quintessentially American than attacking our own government for its failings.

In the past, the enemies of academic freedom were forthright about their opposition to free expression at colleges. But today's opponents of academic freedom have become much more savvy in their attacks on intellectual liberty. David Horowitz, the former leftist radical turned right-winger who runs his own David Horowitz Freedom Center, has begun a campaign against academic freedom in the name of "Students for Academic Freedom," hoping to use legislation and public pressure in the age-old conservative dream to bar politics from the classroom and stop dissent in the university. This Orwellian attack on academic freedom by invoking the name of academic freedom is dangerous precisely because it uses deception so effectively. Horowitz is not only threatening the practice of academic freedom, he is trying to cut the heart out of its meaning and turn the concept into the opposite of its true definition. It is disturbing enough to see politicians trying to banish criticism of the government from higher education, but when they do so in the name of saving academic freedom, it is perverse.

CHAPTER ONE
Academic Freedom in America after 9/11

⤫

The attacks of September 11, 2001, shocked America and the world. College campuses reacted to the terrorist acts with rallies, vigils, discussions, and a wide range of debates about the causes and cures for terrorism. Sometimes the reaction included threats and hatred toward Arabs and Muslims. Sometimes those who denounced the Bush administration's "war on terror" faced death threats and censorship. And for the first time in fifty years, academic freedom in the United States took a clear step backward.

Of course, leftists were not the only victims of repression on college campuses in the wake of 9/11. In rare cases, administrators with a misguided sense of protecting Muslim students from criticism targeted right-wingers. While conservatives contended that a few cases of censorship proved that left-wing thought police rule over college campuses, extensive analysis of academic freedom and civil liberties at American universities indicates that the opposite was true: Left-wing critics of the Bush administration suffered by far the most numerous and most serious violations of their civil liberties. Censorship of conservatives was rare and almost always overturned in the few cases where it occurred. Patriotic correctness, not political correctness, reigned supreme after 9/11.

Many conservative groups denounced academic freedom after 9/11. Winfield Myers of the right-wing Intercollegiate Studies Institute declared, "Uttering irresponsible phrases may not raise an eyebrow in the perpetually adolescent land inhabited by too many academics, but in the world where most people live, such language is unwise at best, traitorous at worst."[1] The American Council of Trustees and Alumni (ACTA) presented a list of 117 statements made by scholars the group deemed unpatriotic, such as New York University professor Todd Gitlin's comment: "There is a lot of skepticism about the administration's policy of going to war."[2] While not censorship in itself, the list raised alarms because ACTA helps to influence and train trustees who could attempt to censor these academics. "No one should have the license to hunt unpatriotic speech," noted George Borts, an economics professor at Brown University whose positive comment about the CIA was misinterpreted by ACTA and listed in its report.[3]

Conservatives attacked academia because at a time of flag waving and national unity, colleges were often the one institution in American society where a substantive debate about public policy occurred and dissent from the Bush administration's foreign policy was permitted. After 9/11, academic freedom in the United States encountered some of the most serious threats in a generation. It is only by denouncing these efforts at censorship, and vigorously defending the right of freedom on college campuses, that we can continue to protect academic freedom.

Academic Freedom after 9/11

The cliché of our times, constantly repeated but often true, is that "September 11 changed everything." One thing that changed for the worse was academic freedom. The dust of the World Trade Center was still thick in the air of New York City when opponents began calling for more limits on free speech at college campuses across the country.

On the morning of September 11, 2001, University of New Mexico history professor Richard Berthold told his class what he thought to be a joke, "Anyone who would blow up the Pentagon would have my vote."[4] Berthold received death threats, keeping him off campus. Berthold was threatened in front of his home by a biker who came at him screaming obscenities, and he also received several angry e-mails and letters with messages such as "I'd like to blow you up." He agreed to stay away from campus for a week for safety reasons while campus police investigated the threats.[5]

State politicians demanded Berthold's dismissal. New Mexico state representative William Fuller declared, "Treason is giving aide or comfort to the enemy. Any terrorist who heard Berthold's comment was comforted." According to Fuller, "If you read the Constitution, you'll see that the freedom of speech, what it says is that you cannot be imprisoned for what you say. And it doesn't say a thing about you can't be fired. We encourage you to continue to fight for this professor's termination."[6] An alumnus sued the university, claiming Berthold violated a state law that forbids government employees from teaching or advocating "sabotage, force and violence, sedition, or treason." Berthold declared, "I was a jerk," but noted that the U.S. Constitution's guarantee of free speech "protects my right to be a jerk."[7]

University President William Gordon promised to "vigorously pursue" disciplinary action against the professor.[8] Brian Foster, university provost, noted: "There are a lot of things you can't say with impunity, even on a college campus."[9] A letter of reprimand was placed in Berthold's personnel file, and he was forced to undergo an in-depth post-tenure review. Berthold was also ordered to follow a specific plan for complying with the standards of professional behavior. Gordon declared, "Our decision to take action in this case was based on our conclusion that Professor Berthold had, indeed, failed to carry out his responsibility to his students, when he made gratuitous remarks that were needlessly offensive and potentially hurtful in the classroom."[10] In the end, Berthold was pressured to retire from his job because of those eleven words he spoke on September 11, although in retrospect Berthold regretted that he gave in to demands for him to leave his job.[11] Even conservative academic groups recognized the need to protect Berthold's right to speak freely. "Academic freedom requires a free exchange of ideas—no matter how controversial," said Anne Neal of ACTA, opposing the university's investigation.[12] The conservative National Association of Scholars—in which Berthold once actively participated—wrote, "We strongly urge you to protect Professor Berthold's freedom of speech from any and all efforts to impose official censure of any kind on him."[13] But most conservative groups failed otherwise to defend the academic freedom of liberals after 9/11.

It was not conservatives who usually suffered on campus for their opinions in the wake of 9/11. Mohammad Rahat, an Iranian citizen and University of Miami medical technician who turned twenty-two years old on September 11, 2001, declared in a meeting that day, "Some birthday gift from Osama bin Laden."[14] Although Rahat plainly meant it "in a sarcastic way," he was suspended and then fired on September 25, 2001, for his words. Vice President of University Relations Paula Musto declared that Rahat's "comments were deeply disturbing to his coworkers and superiors at the medical school. They were inappropriate and unbecoming for someone working in a research laboratory. He was fired because he made those comments, certainly not because of his ethnic background."[15] Rahat had received only positive evaluations in thirteen months working in the lab, but his free speech got him fired by one of the leading universities in the country.[16]

At the University of California at Los Angeles, library assistant Jonnie Hargis was suspended without pay for one week after sending an e-mail response criticizing American policies in Iraq and Israel. On September 12, one of Hargis's colleagues sent around an e-mail titled "America: The Good Neighbor." Hargis replied: "This is all well and good but avoids the fact that U.S. taxpayers fund and arm an apartheid state called Israel, which is responsible for untold thousands upon thousands of deaths of Muslim Palestinian children and civilians. So, who are the 'terrorists' anyway?"[17] For criticizing Israel, Hargis was charged with "contribut[ing] to a hostile and threatening environment" for his colleagues who have "ethnic, religious, and family ties to Israel."[18] The staff was also told library policy forbids using its e-mail to send unsolicited political messages. Fortunately, Hargis had a union to defend his rights, and he successfully pursued a grievance. Hargis was repaid for his lost income, the incident was stricken from his job record, and the university has been forced to clarify its e-mail policies.[19] But for faculty and staff who lacked protection from unions and tenure, the climate of patriotic correctness silenced dissent.

Certainly, liberals and conservatives alike said some very stupid things after 9/11. The dumbest comment of them all was uttered on September 13, 2001, when Jerry Falwell, the founder of Liberty University in Lynchburg, Virginia, proclaimed that 9/11 was caused by the "pagans, and the abortionists, and the feminists, and the gays and the lesbians who are actively trying to make that an alternative lifestyle, the ACLU, People for the American Way, all of them who have tried to secularize America."[20] When the head of a university declares on national television that gay and feminist and prochoice views helped to make the worst terrorist attack in American history happen, will there be academic freedom on his campus to espouse those ideas?

Numerous college presidents and administrators denounced professors for expressing views deemed too left-wing or controversial after 9/11 and sought to discourage any similar sentiments. On September 13, 2001, two resident assistants (RAs) in Minnesota complained to the dean of students that undergraduates felt fearful and uneasy because some professors questioned the competence of the Bush administration. According to the RAs, "The recent attacks extend beyond political debate, and for professors to make negative judgments on our government before any action has taken place only fosters a cynical attitude in the classroom."[21] The administration asked faculty to think hard about what they said. Greg Kneser, dean of students, declared: "There were students who were just scared, and an intellectual discussion of the political ramifications of this was not helpful for them. They were frightened, and they look to their faculty not just for intellectual debate" but as "people they trust." According to Kneser, "Students spent the morning watching planes hitting buildings and blowing up. They weren't prepared for this political analysis critical of the U.S. government."[22] But the job of professors is to challenge students' ideas, not to refrain from criticizing the U.S. government in order to soothe the feelings of students.

City University of New York (CUNY) faculty who participated in an October 2, 2001, forum criticizing U.S. foreign policy for the attacks were denounced by CUNY chancellor Matthew Goldstein for making "lame excuses" for the terrorists, and condemned as seditious by the CUNY board of trustees. Math lecturer Walter Daum called the September 11 killers "mass murderers," but added: "The ultimate responsibility for the attacks lies with the rulers of this country, the capitalist ruling class of this country."[23] In response, CUNY trustee Jeffrey Wiesenfeld said: "These people should be ashamed of themselves. While recognizing their right to be stupid, their opinions render ill repute to the university. They're fortunate it's not up to me. I would consider that behavior seditious at this time."[24]

Even hypothetical discussions were suspicious. In Oregon, Portland Community College philosophy professor Stephen Carey challenged students in his critical thinking class to consider an extreme rhetorical proposition that would cause great emotion, like "Bush should be hung, strung up upside down, and left for the buzzards." One student's mother, misunderstanding the example, called the FBI and accused Carey of threatening to kill the president.[25]

Those who opposed U.S. military action in response to 9/11 found themselves under attack, sometimes literally. At Ohio State University on November 10, 2001, a Peace Camp protest against war was attacked by football fans who destroyed tents and injured one protestor.[26] At the University of Wisconsin at Stevens Point, a peace camp was attacked by homemade bombs made with drain cleaner and aluminum foil.[27] At Indiana University, a peace camp was attacked repeatedly, with protestors shot at with BB guns and tents vandalized; a peace symbol was set on fire and destroyed.[28]

Some campuses even banned the media from covering antiwar protests. At Washington University in St. Louis a week after 9/11, campus officials prohibited the news media and any outsiders from attending an antiwar protest on campus. Administrators claimed that they closed the campus to protect "nervous and concerned" students and were acting "in their best interest."[29]

When four leftist faculty at the University of North Carolina criticized U.S. foreign policy at a teach-in, Scott Rubush, associate editor of David Horowitz's *FrontPage Magazine,* told National Public Radio, "They're using state resources to the practical effect of aiding and abetting the Taliban"—and Rubush argued that they should be fired: "Tell the good folks at UNC–Chapel Hill what you think of their decision to allow anti-American rallies on their state-supported campus."[30] The administration received hundreds of angry e-mails and was denounced on the floor of the North Carolina legislature. Several antiwar faculty members received death threats.[31]

Attacking Arabs and Muslims

Anti-Arab and anti-Muslim violence and discrimination was one consequence of the terrorist attacks on 9/11. At the University of Michigan, Brenda Abdelall, president of the Arab Students Association, received a death threat within two hours of the attack. First-year student Areej El-Jawahri received threatening e-mail on September 11, including one message that said, "We will fuck you bastards for doing this."[32] Attacks on Arab and Muslim college students occurred across the country in the wake of 9/11.[33]

Arab and Muslim students also faced enormous scrutiny from authorities. An October 2001 survey by the American Association of Collegiate Registrars and Admissions Officers, "Campus Consequences of the September 11 Attacks," found that at least 220 colleges had been contacted by law enforcement in the weeks after September 11, 2001.[34] Police or FBI agents made 99 requests for private "nondirectory" information, such as course schedules, that under law cannot be released without student consent, a subpoena, or a pending danger (only 12 of the requests had a subpoena, although the Immigration and Naturalization Service doesn't require consent for information on foreign students). Most requests were for individual students, although 16 requests for student records were "based on ethnicity." Law enforcement received the information from 159 schools, and only 8 denied any requests.[35] At the University of Colorado at Denver, federal agents visited at least 5 times, interviewed at least 50 Arab students, and detained 2 of them briefly because they had been observed taking photographs of an arena for a photography class.[36]

A Saudi Arabian student at San Diego State, Yazeed al-Salmi, spent seventeen days in custody in San Diego, Oklahoma, and New York, even though he was not a suspect. He was held as a material witness because he had once lived in the same house as one of the terrorist attackers. He was denied contact with his family and attorney, held in solitary confinement, and prevented from washing or brushing his teeth. Al-Salmi said he was strip-searched twice a day while officers videotaped the procedure, and couldn't take a shower for nine days. When he was in New York, he said, "They don't call you by name, they call you 'fucking terrorist.'"[37]

Osama Awadallah, a Jordanian college student at Grossmont College in California, was held as a material witness for a month and then charged October 19, 2001, with lying to a grand jury about whether he knew one of the hijackers. His attorney reported that guards kept him from sleeping and "roughed him up."[38] In a Mississippi jail, a twenty-year-old student from Pakistan said he was stripped and beaten in his cell by inmates who were angry about the attacks while jail guards failed to intervene.[39]

Censorship of Prowar Views

In response to the violence and persecution against Muslim and Arab students, some colleges did try to restrict offensive speech in ways that threatened academic freedom.

At Orange Coast Community College in California on September 20, 2001, government professor Ken Hearlson was suspended for eleven weeks after Muslim students accused him of being biased against them and calling them "terrorists." Hearlson started his lecture on September 18 with an intentionally provocative question, "Why do Muslims condemn the terrorist attacks in New York and at the Pentagon but never denounce terrorist attacks in Israel?" Hearlson was immediately suspended with pay pending an investigation of the racial harassment charges. President Margaret Gratton said, "Under normal conditions, there would have been more extensive consultation" before placing a professor on leave, but because of the terrorist attacks, "this occurred in an exceptional environment."[40] Ruth Flower of the American Association of University Professors noted, "The process appears to be severely flawed."[41] More than 340 of Hearlson's students signed a petition calling for his reinstatement. College officials denied that academic freedom was involved. "This is not an academic freedom issue. It is an issue of classroom comportment and how he treats students," said spokesperson Jim Carnett. "It is beyond the bounds of academic freedom."[42] Hearlson did apparently point a finger at Middle Eastern students while he blamed Arab countries for fomenting terrorism, but tapes of the class cleared Hearlson of the Muslim students' claims that Hearlson had told them, "You killed 5,000 people" and "You drove two planes into the World Trade Center."[43]

In a case at Johns Hopkins University, Charles H. Fairbanks Jr., director of the Central Asia–Caucasus Institute at the Paul H. Nitze School of Advanced International Studies (SAIS), was demoted (but later reinstated) after a September 14 panel discussion on terrorism in which he criticized Iraq, Pakistan, and Palestinians. Fairbanks said, "Unfortunately, Palestinians hate us and that's a painful fact." A woman in the crowd accused Fairbanks of "innuendos intended to encourage and to assist people in conducting hate crimes ... toward Muslims." Fairbanks apologized, but after she interrupted him twice, he called for her to be removed. Stephen Szabo, interim dean of SAIS, got Fairbanks to agree to write a letter of regret about what he said. Two days later, Szabo decided to eliminate Fairbanks's administrator position (although he remained a research professor), claiming that the chaos of the panel showed that Fairbanks couldn't do a good job. After publicity about the dismissal, Szabo gave Fairbanks his job back.[44]

Columbus State Community College in Ohio temporarily barred Christian evangelist Jed Smock from speaking on campus because of concern that his criticism of the Koran would lead to violence. Columbus State police cut short Smock's appearance in a designated free speech area on campus after an argument with one of the students started heating up. Smock also lacked a speaking permit that campus authorities say is required, but that was denied by Columbus State president Val Moeller out of concerns for Smock's safety.[45]

At San Diego State University, an Arabic-speaking Ethiopian student, Zewdalem Kebede, claimed that he overheard three Saudi Arabian students in the library expressing their support for the September 11 attacks in Arabic.

Kebede angrily confronted them in Arabic: "You are proud of them. You should have to feel shame." After a "heated exchange," the Saudi Arabian students summoned the university police, who cautioned both parties. After being ordered to an informal meeting with the university judicial officer, Kebede received an October 5 letter that declared: "No disciplinary action will be taken by this office at this time, but you are admonished to conduct yourself as a responsible member of the campus community in the future. Specifically, confronting members of the campus community in a manner that is found to be aggressive or abusive is serious. Consider this letter to be your only warning that future incidents, where your involvement is proven, will result in you facing serious disciplinary sanctions."[46]

However, even open bigotry against Muslims was typically protected on college campuses. Indrek Wichman at Michigan State University wrote an e-mail in 2006 to Muslim students declaring, "I counsul [*sic*] you dissatisfied, agressive [*sic*], brutal and uncivilized slave-trading Moslems to be very aware of this as you proceed with your infantile 'protests.' If you do not like the values of the West—see the 1st Ammendment [*sic*]—you are free to leave. I hope for God's sake you choose that option. Please return to your ancestral homelands and build them up yourselves instead of troubling Americans. Cordially, I.S. Wichman, Professor of Mechanical Engineering."[47] Even though the e-mail revealed a bigoted (and barely literate) tenured professor, Muslim students asked only that he should be reprimanded. Michigan State's provost merely sent Wichman a note stating that his views did not reflect the university's position, and if Wichman expressed those views again, he should disassociate himself from the university.[48]

Watch What You Transmit: E-mail in an Age of Censorship

Websites and e-mail also prompted concerns from the left and the right, although the cases involving conservatives were typically resolved quickly and free speech was strongly upheld.

At Penn State University, some students complained about math professor Stephen Simpson's personal website urging America to "destroy all branches of the Iranian and Afghani governments, regardless of the suffering and death this will bring to the many innocents caught in the line of fire." Vice provost Robert Secor told Simpson that some students found his site "insensitive and perhaps even intimidating."[49] But Secor noted, "There's no action, there's no reprimand. We have to be very careful about protecting the rights of free speech, and we do."[50] After Duke University professor Gary Hull posted an article on his website titled "Terrorism and Its Appeasement," calling for a military response to the attacks, the website was shut down, but it was allowed back up with a requirement to include a disclaimer stating that it did not reflect Duke's views.[51] The University of North Carolina at

Wilmington cleared professor Mike Adams (but did read his personal e-mail) after a student complained that he sent an abusive e-mail in response to the student's antiwar e-mail.[52]

Leftist students and faculty, by contrast, faced more severe threats to their free expression on the web. University of California at San Diego officials ordered the Che Café student cooperative that operates the website burn.ucsd.edu to remove a link to the website of FARC (the Revolutionary Armed Forces of Colombia). Gary Ratcliff, the director of university centers, stated in the letter sent September 16, 2002, "Providing material support or resources to a designated [terrorist organization] is a violation of federal law. Using UCSD computing resources to violate federal laws is against UCSD Policies." University officials backed down after public complaints. In addition, UCSD had previously ordered the removal of the Groundwork Collective's link to an alleged terrorist group (the Kurdistan Workers Party) and placed the organization on probation for having this weblink.[53]

The law was even more harsh in dealing with a webmaster for Muslim websites that included views advocating violence. At the University of Idaho, on February 26, 2003, law enforcement agents raided graduate student housing and arrested Sami Omar Al-Hussayen, a Ph.D. computer science student from Saudi Arabia, while also interrogating twenty international students for more than four hours.[54] Government prosecutors charged Al-Hussayen for lying on his visa application (because they claimed studying was not his "sole" reason for coming to America) and illegally earning money (because he was paid $200 for working on a website). Al-Hussayen, a former president of the Muslim Students Association at the University of Idaho, was also accused of helping to raise money and providing computer services for the Islamic Assembly of North America (a legal organization still operating in the United States). Under the PATRIOT Act, providing "expert advice or assistance" to terrorists is a serious crime. Al-Hussayen's crime was creating a website and an e-mail listserv that included postings by other people advocating jihad and suicide bombings (although Al-Hussayen opposes suicide bombings, and the websites included a range of different views). Kim Lindquist, lead prosecutor in the Al-Hussayen case, noted: "Under student visas, young people are allowed to stay here, and they can make that transition fairly subtly and fairly quietly from appropriate student activities to a manifestation of things that are inappropriate, including advocacy of radical Islam."[55] The fact that prosecutors condemned him for "advocacy of radical Islam" rather than actual crimes indicates that Al-Hussayen was persecuted for his beliefs (which are not illegal) and the radical views (which he did not control) posted on websites he worked on. Al-Hussayen was never accused of plotting or committing any terrorist acts of any kind. Al-Hussayen, who faced 240 years in prison from the various counts, was found not guilty, but the U.S. government ordered him deported anyway and banned him from the country.[56]

Antimilitary views expressed in an e-mail could put a professor's job at risk. In New Jersey, Warren Community College adjunct English instructor John Daly resigned under pressure in 2005 because he wrote an e-mail to a student saying that he would urge his students to boycott an event featuring Lieutenant Colonel Scott Rutter. Daly urged that American soldiers should "turn their guns on their superiors." Daly was suspended from his classes, and the board of trustees held an emergency meeting to react to his e-mail.[57]

At St. Xavier University in Chicago, after Robert Kurpiel, a cadet at the U.S. Air Force Academy in Colorado, sent a form e-mail to St. Xavier University history professor Peter Kirstein, asking him to help promote an air force event, Kirstein wrote back on October 31, 2002: "You are a disgrace to this country and I am furious you would even think I would support you and your aggressive baby-killing tactics of collateral damage. Help you recruit. Who, top guns to reign death and destruction upon nonwhite peoples throughout the world? Are you serious sir? Resign your commission and serve your country with honour. No war, no air force cowards who bomb countries with AAA, without possibility of retaliation. You are worse than the snipers. You are imperialists who are turning the whole damn world against us. September 11 can be blamed in part for what you and your cohorts have done to Palestinians, the VC, the Serbs, a retreating army at Basra. You are unworthy of my support."[58]

When Kurpiel forwarded this message around, Kirstein and St. Xavier quickly received a large number of denunciations for his comments. Although Kirstein apologized for his e-mail, many called for his dismissal. On November 15, 2002, St. Xavier president Richard Yanikoski announced that Kirstein would be immediately suspended, receive a reprimand, and undergo a post-tenure review during a sabbatical in spring 2003. Yanikoski added, "Any future faculty contract(s) extended to Professor Kirstein will include a binding addendum specifically requiring him to adhere both to institutional policies and to the norms of the American Association of University Professors in matters relating to the proper exercise of academic freedom and extramural activities."[59]

A tenured professor was suspended for responding rudely to an unsolicited e-mail and expressing his view that killing is wrong. Nothing is more alien to the idea of academic freedom than this. To make matters worse, President Yanikoski claimed to be following the academic freedom standards of the AAUP and even required Kirstein to sign a statement pledging to follow them before reinstatement. Yanikoski failed to understand the basic meaning of academic freedom. The AAUP, in its "Statement on Extramural Utterances," clearly protects Kirstein's right to his ideas and his method of expression.[60] While the AAUP urges professors to exercise their academic freedom rights in a responsible manner, it does not give universities the power to punish irresponsible speech unless it clearly proves that an individual is "unfit" to teach. No one has accused Kirstein of any unprofessional conduct in his teaching, and to suspend a "professor of the year" for his beliefs is wrong. One may certainly disagree with Kirstein's belief that the air force is cowardly and engaged in "baby-killing tactics," and Kirstein apologized for the tone of his e-mail. But sometimes moral arguments are impolite. According to Yanikoski, no one at St. Xavier is allowed to make "demeaning, degrading statements as a professor in or outside the classroom."[61] But virtually all moral judgments can be viewed as demeaning or degrading to someone.

Waving the American Flag

Flags also sparked several campus free speech controversies after 9/11. But it is notable that in every instance where an administrator's bad judgment led to a flag being removed from those with conservative sentiments, the decision was quickly overturned. However, the use of American flags by liberals was much more likely to be banned.

At Central Michigan University on October 8, 2001, four roommates in Emmons Hall placed an American flag and prowar pictures and articles on the front of their door. Resident assistant Kari Buchanan told them to remove the items because it might be "offensive" to some students. After an article about the incident appeared in the campus newspaper, on October 10, residence hall director Albert Nowak and two other administrators told the four students that they could repost all their images (including the flags) except for things deemed "hate-related items and ... profanity." These banned items included a column in the *San Francisco Chronicle* headlined "Bastards!" and a picture of the Statue of Liberty "giving terrorists the finger." President Michael Rao reversed the decision, declaring students could post anything on their doors. Rao wrote: "The university's removal of any items considered offensive or vulgar by some is not condoned. The university is taking steps to assure students in the residence halls that their right to post materials and express opinion on their room doors is protected.... I value everything the American flag stands for. To request its removal from any place on our campus would violate my personal standards and the values of the university."[62]

At Lehigh University in Pennsylvania, vice provost of student affairs John Smeaton publicly apologized for "a momentary lapse of judgment" on September 13, 2001, when he ordered removal of the American flag from the campus bus for one hour.[63] At the College of the Holy Cross in Massachusetts, Sociology Department chair Royce Singleton told a secretary to take down a flag she had hung in the office in honor of a friend who died on one of the hijacked airliners. After the incident became public, the flag was moved to the Psychology Department and the secretary was allowed to put a flag on her desk.[64] Florida Gulf Coast University dean of library services Kathleen Hoeth reversed a "bad decision" she made in telling employees to remove stickers saying "Proud to be an American" from their workspace.[65]

John Leo proclaimed, "Colleges and schools frequently resist the flying of the flag or simply ban it as narrow or too provocative."[66] Yet in contrast to the strong defense of American flag wavers immediately after 9/11, students critical of Bush administration policy faced a much harsher response when they sought to use the American flag for their cause. At Wheaton College in Massachusetts, antiwar students who put an upside-down American flag in their home received death threats, a brick through their window, and a small fire set on their lawn.[67] At Yale University, prowar students broke into the suite of antiwar activist Katherine Lo on March 27, 2003, a day after she hung an American flag upside down from her bedroom window to protest the war. The students tried unsuccessfully to break into her bedroom and then wrote a note on her message board calling for the killing of Iraqis and Muslims, ending with the message, "I hate you, GO AMERICA."[68] At Grinnell College in Iowa, two students were threatened with arrest for flying the American flag upside down from their dormitory window.[69]

In the wake of 9/11, patriotic fervor was so strong that the failure to show patriotic sentiments was suspect. In some cases, politicians literally forced colleges to engage in patriotic flag waving. Florida's Carey Baker Freedom Flag Act requires all public schools and colleges to do fund-raising to purchase flags and to display a flag in every single classroom.[70]

On September 17, 2001, at KOMU-TV, the NBC affiliate TV station based at the University of Missouri School of Journalism, news director Stacey Woelfel e-mailed his news staff: "Our news broadcasts are not the place for personal statements of support for any cause—no matter how deserving the cause seems to be. This includes the little red, white, and blue ribbons that a lot of people are sporting these days. Our job is to deliver the news as free from outside influences as possible." Missouri legislator Matt Bartle heard about the policy and declared, "I am going to be evaluating far more carefully state funding that goes to the School of Journalism. If this is what you are teaching the next generation of journalists, I question whether the taxpayers of this state will support it." Bartle called the ribbon ban (but not his threat to cut off funding) "censorship of journalists." Chancellor Richard Wallace declared: "MU deeply regrets that this policy has caused offense to KOMU viewers and other citizens. This was an action taken in the TV newsroom to assure editorial independence that did not in any way reflect a policy of the University." Despite this abject apology, in April 2002 the Missouri House of Representatives voted to cut $500,000 from the University of Missouri budget because of the pin decision.[71]

Intolerance toward Teaching Tolerance

After 9/11, dissent from American foreign policy became grounds for denunciations of academics. The website Campus Watch (www.campuswatch. org) urged students to spy on Middle East studies professors and publicly denounce their views, leading to death threats and harassment of professors. Founder Daniel Pipes called for "adult supervision of the faculty and administrators."[72] "Adult supervision," of course, means censorship by administrators, trustees, and legislators. Those who dare to dissent are unruly children, and conservatives like Pipes are the adults who will tell them how to act.

Pipes was also involved in the efforts to restrict academic freedom for Middle East studies departments.[73] On October 21, 2003, the U.S. House of Representatives passed the "International Studies in Higher Education Act," known as HR 3077. Among the bill's provisions was a requirement for an "International Advisory Board" to monitor Middle Eastern programs that receive Title VI grants and compel them to provide "diverse perspectives" in the eyes of the government.[74] An article in the *American Conservative* observed, "If passed into law, the bill would mandate the withdrawal of federal funding from international studies departments that fail to display sufficient support for U.S. foreign policy positions, do not contribute to homeland security, or fall short of federally mandated standards for 'diversity' of political perspectives."[75] Stanley Kurtz, who testified before Congress to denounce university area studies programs, defended the bill's attack on academic freedom by proclaiming, "The postmodern professorate has already destroyed free speech and academic freedom by killing off the marketplace of ideas."[76] The American Council on Education strongly opposed the attack on academic freedom, but ended up supporting the final bill because it increased funding for international studies and added language to prohibit the advisory board from interfering with curricula.[77] However, efforts continue to restrict academic freedom in area studies programs, and Kurtz reported in 2007 that the U.S. Senate is planning to force colleges to adopt "grievance procedures" for students who object to the content of Middle East studies programs.[78]

Even efforts to teach tolerance and understanding of Muslims and Arabs were sometimes denounced as appeasing terrorists. When the University of North Carolina asked incoming students in 2002 to read the book *Approaching the Qur'an: The Early Revelations* translated by Michael A. Sells, it even prompted lawsuits. The Family Policy Network, a conservative Christian group, sued the university, arguing that it is unconstitutional for a public university to require students to study about a specific religion. After a flood of angry calls and e-mails, the university agreed to allow those students who chose not to read the book to write a one-page paper about why they didn't want to read it. However, the lawsuit continued because the assignment of the book was "religious bigotry enforced with intimidation" according to the Family Policy Network.[79] A federal district court ruled in favor of the university, noting that "enhancing the intellectual atmosphere of a school for incoming students" is legitimate.[80]

A majority of the North Carolina House of Representatives voted to prevent UNC from using state funds on the assignment in a budget resolution: "No state funds or overhead receipts may be expended by a constituent institution of the University of North Carolina to offer for entering freshman students prior to their first semester for credit or otherwise any course or summer reading program in any religion unless all other known religions are offered in an equal or incremental way. This section is not intended to interfere with academic freedom but to ensure that all religions are taught in a nondiscriminatory fashion."[81] Of course, this resolution was intended to interfere with academic freedom, and it is also impossible to follow. There has never been a book written that teaches about all known religions equally. If the University of North Carolina ever tried to teach about pagan religions on an equal basis with Christianity, it would have outraged these fundamentalist Christian groups even more. The real problem to these conservatives was the idea of learning more about Islam; Republican state representative Sam Ellis declared that students should not be "required to study this evil."[82]

Clearly, the scholarly reading of religious texts is not an establishment of religion. For a university to submit to this intimidation by encouraging students to avoid doing any reading is unfortunate. Students should learn that part of a college education is reading books with new ideas, not avoiding different beliefs and reading only what confirms what they already think. At the University of North Carolina, no students were actually compelled to read the book; no student would be punished for failing to complete the assignment. Yet this voluntary intellectual activity was loudly denounced.

This was not the end of litigation by the religious right. The American Family Association even filed a lawsuit trying to stop the University of North Carolina from holding seminars and roundtable discussions during Islamic Awareness Week in 2002. Fortunately, courts refused to issue an injunction banning discussions about Islam.[83]

The University of North Carolina's summer reading program sparked controversy again in 2003 when Barbara Ehrenreich's book *Nickel and Dimed* was chosen for incoming students to read and discuss. Conservative pundits and legislators sought to have the book banned from the program. North Carolina state senator Ham Horton declared Ehrenreich's book was "not worthy of a university. It's hardly an appropriate introduction to the community of scholars that is a university. It makes you wonder if it's an indoctrination to particular views, rather than a balanced and scholarly

approach to issues." Senior Michael McKnight, chair of the state Federation of College Republicans, declared: "The book is made out as fact rather
than this lady's opinion about what's wrong with America. Some would say
there's nothing wrong with America." One Republican state legislator called
Ehrenreich's book "intellectual pornography," proving that some conservatives get sexually excited at the thought of multinational corporations
exploiting impoverished workers.[84]

Campus Censorship and the 2004 Election

Shortly before the 2004 election, the conservative civil liberties group FIRE
(Foundation for Individual Rights in Education) reported, "In recent weeks,
FIRE has seen a sharp increase in the number of inquiries regarding so-
called 'partisan' speech on campus. These inquiries have corresponded
with reports of speakers being 'uninvited' because college and university
administrations feared that their speech would be 'too partisan.'"[85]

On October 20, 2004, University of South Florida arts and sciences dean
V. Mark Durand sent an e-mail to faculty declaring, "We have received a
number of complaints by students about instructors interjecting their political views in class. This is occurring in classes that have no political theme or
content. While I am acutely aware of the polarized nature of this election
season and the fodder for humor, etc., this creates, please be aware that
students may not share your views and that such discussions or even asides
can cause genuine distress. Unless the content of your curriculum covers
this material it would be wise to monitor your statements, even if they may
seem to you to be flippant and inconsequential. Politics and religion are
particularly sensitive topics—especially in Florida."[86]

The University of Wisconsin at Stevens Point ordered faculty and staff not
to talk about politics. Provost Virginia Helm declared, "State statutes are
making it very clear that state employees in general cannot express opinions
that are advocating for or against a political candidate. We figured that a
lot of faculty weren't aware of the state law. We just wanted to make them
aware of those and provide some guidance."[87]

The University of Illinois at Urbana-Champaign disciplined graduate
student Tom Mackaman, a socialist candidate for the state legislature in
2004, because he sent an e-mail press release about his candidacy via his
university account. The University of Illinois created a new policy to prohibit similar political advocacy on campus, and university spokesperson Lex
Tate even contended that faculty would not be allowed to invite a political
candidate to campus.[88]

Florida Gulf Coast University cancelled a speech by author and natural-
ist Terry Tempest Williams because of fear that Williams might criticize
President Bush's environmental policies.[89] As FIRE noted, "The concern

of college administrators should not be the maintenance of an artificially imposed 'balance' but instead the protection of open discussion, expression, and candor."[90]

The goal of limiting political speech by professors does not serve the academic freedom of students. To the contrary, it denies students their right to hear what their professor thinks about important political issues of the day. More important, a ban on faculty political speech sends the message to students that they, too, are not allowed to discuss political ideas.

Michael Moore's movie *Fahrenheit 9/11* attracted particular controversy by opponents who felt that it should be banned from college campuses. McHenry County College in Illinois prevented students from showing *Fahrenheit 9/11* on campus before the election because some local residents complained.[91]

At Rowan-Cabarrus Community College in North Carolina, instructor Davis March was suspended for four days because he showed Moore's movie in his film class. That's right: He was suspended for showing a documentary in a film class. The college prohibits faculty from using "the classroom or college environment as a platform to promote their own personal, religious, or political views," and Ann Hovey, executive vice president of the college, explained: "He was insistent about wanting to show it before the election, which implied some possible political intent." March argued that he did not disobey any orders to ban the film, although the college had prohibited flyers promoting the showing of the movie (in yet another violation of the First Amendment).[92]

But the strongest efforts at censorship occurred when Michael Moore went on a campus speaking tour. George Mason University in Virginia cancelled Moore's appearance on campus a few days after conservative state legislators objected to it. Daniel Walsch, executive director of university relations, explained: "We didn't think it was appropriate to use public monies to pay for his fee."[93] Banning speakers because of their political views is unconstitutional at any time, but it's particularly wrong before an election, when students should be hearing discussions about politics more than ever.

At Utah Valley State College, public outcry over an October 20, 2004, speech on campus by Moore led President William Sederburg (a former Republican state senator) to order student leaders to find a conservative speaker to "balance" Moore. Student Sean Vreeland led a petition drive to have Moore banned from campus and the student government leaders fired.[94] Even though conservative talk show host Sean Hannity was brought in to speak, Utah state legislators found their own way to punish the university for allowing free speech: In January 2005 they cut $37 million in funding for construction on campus in retaliation for Moore's speech.[95]

California State University at San Marcos president Karen Haynes even claimed that having Michael Moore speak on her campus was illegal. Haynes wrote, "As a public university, we are prohibited from spending state funds on partisan political activity or direct political advocacy."[96] In reality, the reverse is true: Public universities are prohibited from withdrawing state funds merely because a speaker might discuss controversial political issues. State funds cannot be used to directly finance a candidate's campaign, but the First Amendment bans any such regulation of political advocacy.

The Balance of Free Speech

As in the case of Michael Moore's speeches, the cry for balance is often a cover for censorship. It is an appealing concept in theory, but when it is used to silence views, rather than adding to them, then it infringes on freedom of expression. Sometimes balancing is a bad idea: A biology class should not be balanced with creationism; a class about Nazi Germany should not be balanced with one taught by Holocaust deniers; and an astronomy class should not be balanced with astrology, even if popular opinion supports it. Balance is such a vague concept that its enforcement could overturn any speaker or class.

Even David French, then the head of FIRE, wrongly contended that in funding Moore's speeches, student fee "money was paid to him illegally" because it was "viewpoint discrimination" on campus.[97] David Horowitz wondered, "How is it possible to give a partisan political speech and get paid from taxpayer funds to do it?"—a particularly odd comment by a Republican Party activist who regularly gets paid by public universities to give his partisan attacks on Democrats.[98]

Of course, no college ever proposes that probusiness classes must be balanced with prolabor classes, or that corporate sponsors must be balanced with their critics, or that the wealthy businessmen who dominate every college's board of trustees should be balanced by appointing impoverished workers to the board. Balance is used only as a tool by conservative forces to silence liberal ideas.

At Arizona State University, administrators ordered removal of anti-Bush artwork for the "Democracy in America" exhibit in order to maintain balance. Stacey Shaw, the College of Fine Arts director of communications, declared that if the show was not balanced, "Democracy in America" would not be allowed: "We clearly understand our responsibility as a state-funded institution to have an exhibition to reflect balance and a variety of differing points of view."[99]

Bob Wills, dean of the College of Fine Arts, demanded a "balance" between "anti-Bush" art and "anti-Kerry" art. President Michael Crow told Wills, "I don't like surprises that seem to be potentially negative to the overall image of fairness and impartiality that we must take as [an] institution." Wills e-mailed museum staff, "I can assure you—from concerned legislators to university administrative folks—there is the highest level of interest and concern that I have ever seen—in forty years of dealing with controversy. We should have avoided this situation entirely, and the processes which have brought it to life. And we need to devise plans ... and agreements for how and why it will never happen again." Eventually, the art museum agreed to ban some of the anti-Bush artwork in order to make the exhibition more "balanced."[100]

Even producing artwork questioning U.S. wars could lead to investigative committees and the threat of dismissal for professors. John Leaños, an artist at Arizona State University, created a work called "Friendly Fire" about Pat Tillman, the Arizona football player who volunteered for the military and was accidentally killed by friendly fire in Afghanistan. The artwork showed Tillman and the text read, "Remember me?/I was killed by my own Army/Ranger Platoon in Afghanistan/on April 22, 2004/I am a hero to many of you/my death was tragic/my glory was short-lived/flawed perceptions/of myself/my country/and/the War on Terror/resulted in the disastrous/end to my life." Leaños put up the posters on October 1, 2004, and the artwork soon became national news. Leaños received denunciations and death threats. The Arizona Board of Regents called it an "ill-advised poster ... and an unforgivable affront to an American hero." President Crow attacked it as "offensive and insensitive." Arizona State received hundreds of e-mails calling for Leaños's firing, and the board of regents launched an investigation into Leaños's classroom teachings and copyright issues surrounding the artwork.[101]

Buffalo State College in New York banned an antiwar exhibit from campus in August 2005. The American Friends Service Committee exhibit, "Eyes Wide Open," consisted of 263 pairs of combat boots, each with the name of a National Guard soldier killed in Iraq. The exhibit was going to be sponsored by Buffalo State College Students for Peace, but Buffalo State officials demanded "upfront compensation for all expenses incurred and a certificate of liability insurance in the amount of $1 million." These demands came after top administrators rejected the proposed exhibit and wrote, "The college is unable to take a political stance on such issues."[102]

Some of the artwork in a 2004 exhibit on "The Art of War: The Effects of War on Art Making" at Ohio University was removed and kept behind a library desk because it was deemed "unpatriotic" for criticizing the Bush administration and the war on Iraq.[103]

Federal prosecutors went after Professor Steve Kurtz of the University of Buffalo because he obtained two harmless strains of natural bacteria commonly used in high school science labs for his artistic work on biotechnology. After Kurtz's wife died from unrelated causes in 2004, paramedics noticed lab equipment in the house, and agents from the Joint Terrorism Task Force searched it. The FBI confiscated artwork made by Kurtz and other members of the Critical Art Ensemble that was going to be displayed at the Massachusetts Museum of Contemporary Art.[104] Because the bacteria were harmless and absolutely no possible terrorist use or intent was ever found, the FBI instead tried to pin Kurtz on a technicality, indicting him and Robert Ferrell of the University of Pittsburgh on federal charges of mail fraud and wire fraud because Kurtz asked Ferrell for help in ordering the bacteria samples. Kurtz faces a possible twenty-year prison sentence if he is convicted in 2008 for the crime of producing art critical of biotechnology.[105]

Silencing Dissent on Campus

At too many colleges after 9/11, the war on terror became part of a war on academic freedom, with dramatic restrictions imposed on scientific research and Arab or Muslim students and scholars.

The "Uniting and Strengthening America by Providing Appropriate Tools Required to Intercept and Obstruct Terrorism Act," better known as the PATRIOT Act, was passed by the U.S. Senate on October 11, 2001, by a 99–1 vote and then approved overwhelmingly by the House of Representatives. The PATRIOT Act and similar restrictions of civil liberties have had a dramatic impact on college campuses. In March 2003 the American Studies Association released a statement entitled "Intellectual Freedom in a Time of War" that declared: "Free and frank intellectual inquiry is under assault by overt legislative acts and by a chilling effect of secrecy and intimidation in the government, media and on college campuses. This atmosphere hinders our ability to fulfill our role as educators: to promote public debate, conduct scholarly research, and most importantly, teach our students to think freely and critically and to explore diverse perspectives."[106] The AAUP created a Special Committee on Academic Freedom and National Security in Times of Crisis to examine how the war on terror has affected academic freedom.[107]

The PATRIOT Act weakened student protections under the Family Educational Rights and Privacy Act (FERPA). Colleges can be required not to record requests for private information and banned from informing students or anyone else about investigations. On November 4, 2002, the FBI sent a letter to colleges asking for information about all foreign students, including "names, addresses, telephone numbers, citizenship information, places of birth, dates of birth, and any foreign contact information" for the previous two years. The letter declared that the USA PATRIOT Act "has further granted educational institutions authority to release information to the federal government for use in combating terrorism." The Association of American College Registrars and Admissions Officers argued that the FBI request violated federal privacy laws. Becky Timmons, director of government relations for the American Council on Education, declared,

"The FBI is trying to do what the USA PATRIOT Act prevents and FERPA has long prevented."[108]

The impact of the PATRIOT Act, and plans for a second PATRIOT Act that is even more restrictive, has alarmed many in academia, but not just liberals. Tom Campbell, dean of the School of Business at Berkeley and a former Republican congressman, called the PATRIOT Act a "serious breach" of the Fourth Amendment protections against unreasonable search and seizure. Campbell noted: "Did you know that under the USA PATRIOT Act, the Department of Justice can obtain a warrant to read the e-mail or library or academic records of university students, staff or faculty? And that all the agency has to do to get the warrant is say that the information is related to an investigation involving espionage or terrorism?"[109] A survey by the University of Illinois Library Research Center found that more than 200 out of 1,500 libraries in the survey had given information to law enforcement about patrons.[110]

Immigration and research restrictions on thousands of foreign-born students and faculty, exacerbated by the PATRIOT Act, have also had a negative impact on academia, making international travel by scholars more difficult. At the Latin American Studies Association International Congress March 27–28, 2003, almost all of the 103 Cuban scholars were absent due to enhanced security checks. Many of the scholars had previously spoken at American universities, even after 9/11, but the increasing restrictions have caused thousands of scholars and students to be banned from American campuses.[111] In March 2004 the U.S. government banned American scholars from attending a conference in Cuba on brain injury. In June 2004 the government severely restricted all educational travel to Cuba and in September 2004 denied visas to all sixty-one Cuban scholars coming to Las Vegas for the Latin American Studies Association conference, forcing the cancellation of forty-five sessions. The Bush administration declared, "We will not have business as usual with the regime that so outrageously violates the human rights of the peaceful opposition," although no objection is made to scholars from other totalitarian countries such as China.[112]

Bolivian scholar Waskar Ari, who studies political activism among indigenous people, was finally granted a visa to teach at the University of Nebraska in 2007, two years after he applied. He was never told why the Department of Homeland Security had ordered him banned from the country, and only litigation forced the reversal.[113] Iraqi epidemiologist and medical professor Riyadh Lafta was denied a visa to speak at the University of Washington in 2007 about the public health effects of the Iraq War. Lafta was the coauthor of an article in the *Lancet* that estimated massive numbers of civilian deaths in Iraq.[114]

Panamanian citizen Marixa Lasso, an assistant professor of Latin American history at Case Western Reserve University, was denied her visa renewal and banned from the United States in the summer of 2007 without any explanation until her visa was finally renewed in October 2007.[115] Musicologist Nalini Ghuman, a British citizen and assistant professor at Mills College who had been working in the United States for ten years, had her visa suddenly revoked and was banned from the United States for no reason after arriving in August 2006.[116]

In March 2005, the U.S. government refused to grant a visa to historian Dora María Téllez, a former Sandinista leader and Nicaraguan minister of health, who was therefore banned from teaching at Harvard Divinity School.[117] In November 2005, Cuban scientist Vicente Verez-Bencomo was banned from entering the United States to accept an award from the Technological Museum of Innovation for developing a low-cost vaccine for meningitis and pneumonia; the U.S. Department of State claimed it would be "detrimental to the interests of the United States."[118]

Even when visas are approved, it often takes too long for scholars to teach or speak at a conference. It took nineteen months for immigration officials to approve a visa for Indonesian land reform activist Noer Fauzi, who was invited by the Institute of International Studies to spend a semester in residence at the University of California at Berkeley.[119]

Mohamed Hassan Mohamed, a Canadian born in Sudan, was going to teach a class at State University of New York at Fredonia in September 2002. When he reached the U.S.-Canadian border, Mohamed was detained for nine hours and banned from entering the United States, even after he agreed to be fingerprinted and registered. It took two weeks of protests by faculty on both sides of the border before Mohamed was allowed to teach in America.[120]

Greek economist John Milios had a valid visa, but he was still banned by border guards from returning to the United States in 2006 after he was questioned about his political views.[121] Adam Habib, executive director of the South Africa Human Science Research Council Program on Democracy and Governance, was banned from entering the United States to speak at the American Sociological Association annual meeting in New York City in August 2007 despite holding a valid visa.[122]

Canadian citizen Karim Meziane, a physicist at the University of New Brunswick (who spent several years in the United States as a graduate student), was stopped at the border in 2004 and banned from attending a conference in the United States. Meziane was interrogated for six hours about his views on religion, Israel, and the Iraq War. Later, the Department of Homeland Security claimed that he was banned because of "unlawful activities committed in Canada," and even though the Canadian government has certified that Meziane has never committed a crime, he continues to be banned from the United States.[123] In August 2006, Vancouver psychotherapist Andrew Feldmar was stopped at the border, interrogated for four hours, and banned from the United States because a search engine revealed that he had written a 2001 journal article mentioning his use of LSD in the

1960s, even though he's never been convicted of any crime. According to a U.S. Customs and Border Protection spokesperson, "If you are or have been a drug user, that's one of the many things that can make you inadmissible to the United States."[124]

In August 2002 the State Department expanded its Technology Alert List to include architecture, community development, environmental planning, geography, housing, landscape architecture, and urban design; this requires more foreign students to receive security clearances before being allowed to study.[125] The new restrictions on visas are having a dramatic impact. When the University of Connecticut's graduate program in physics recruited nine students from China in 2002, all were denied student visas.[126] America isn't made safe from terrorism by excluding foreign students and professors. There is no balance between academic freedom and national security. America is not endangered by allowing free expression on college campuses.

Banning Tariq Ramadan

The PATRIOT Act isn't merely a theoretical danger to civil liberties. Just ask Muslim scholar Tariq Ramadan, who was hired by Notre Dame University's Joan B. Kroc Institute for International Peace Studies to teach in fall 2004. After receiving his visa in May 2004 to teach at Notre Dame, Ramadan had quit his job in Europe and was preparing to leave in August 2004 when the Department of Homeland Security suddenly revoked his visa without explanation.[127]

Ramadan, a Swiss citizen, was the victim of a coordinated campaign to keep him out of the country. Daniel Pipes, director of the pro-Israel advocacy group Middle East Forum, helped some French groups lobby the United States to keep Ramadan out of America due to his criticism of Israel. Pipes declared that the groups "attempted to bring to the attention of the U.S. government who he really is."[128] In 2003 Ramadan had sparked a controversy by claiming that some French intellectuals supported Israel because they are Jewish.[129]

The State Department interviewed Ramadan at the American Embassy in Switzerland after he reapplied for a visa. Ramadan reported being asked "really strange" questions, including "who was financing my travels" to the United States, "what was your position on Palestinian resistance?" and "what was your position on the war on Iraq?"[130] The Bush administration's State Department later admitted that Ramadan had no connections to terrorism, but denied his request for a visa because he gave $770 to a French Committee for Charity and Aid to Palestinians, which has been linked to the Palestinian group Hamas. But at the time Ramadan made his donations in 1998–2002, the United States had not banned the group as terrorist linked, and it continues to be legal in France. There is no evidence that any part of Ramadan's donation was ever used for any terrorist activity, and no way Ramadan could have known that the organization would later be accused of any terrorist links.[131] As Ramadan noted, "It was a political decision," based upon his ideology rather than any plausible link to terrorism.[132]

Far from supporting terrorism, Ramadan has been one of the leading voices for peace in the Muslim world. He sharply denounced the 9/11 attacks and made a controversial call for a total moratorium in the Muslim world on the death penalty, stoning, and corporal punishment. As one profile noted, "Ramadan is in fact one of the few Muslim intellectuals to speak out against anti-Semitism."[133] Ramadan is banned from Egypt and Saudi Arabia because of his opposition to government repression.[134] As Ramadan wrote, "Anyone who has read any of my 20 books, 700 articles or listened to any of my 170 audiotaped lectures will discern a consistent message: The very moment Muslims and their fellow citizens realize that being a Muslim and being American or European are not mutually exclusive, they will enrich their societies."[135] The international Network for Education and Academic Rights issued an academic freedom alert for the United States because of the Ramadan ban, the fifth time the U.S. government had been cited by NEAR for violating academic freedom since January 2002.[136] Ramadan has not been silenced, and he continues to speak out against the U.S. government. But as Ramadan observed, "I have no job, and the message that was sent to Muslim scholars is, 'don't be critical.'"[137]

Rather than worrying about scholars who are banned by the government from teaching anywhere in the country, conservative activists celebrate this attack on academic freedom. David Horowitz claimed that Ramadan was excluded "because of his connections with al-Qaeda," a charge no one has ever made.[138] According to Horowitz, "As for Tariq Ramadan, why do you think with all the conservative academics who have been persecuted of late, the AAUP should pick as its poster boy someone whom our intelligence agencies have linked to terrorists?"[139] Of course, the AAUP does defend conservative scholars, but not one conservative professor is banned by the government from teaching in America.[140]

The precedent of revoking a visa for criticizing the U.S. government is an extraordinary threat to academic freedom. Every foreign professor or student in the United States can potentially have a visa revoked, without any reason given or any opportunity for a hearing, if he or she dares to criticize the Bush administration.

Spying on Protesters

Spying on students who oppose Bush administration policies also occurred to an alarming degree on college campuses. During the late 1960s, the FBI's COINTELPRO program included a substantial amount of spying on radical campus groups and planting agent provocateurs who would try to convince these groups to commit acts of violence. After the spying on protesters under J. Edgar Hoover was revealed, the rules were changed to limit surveillance of political groups.[141]

But after 9/11, these rules were ignored. University of Colorado campus police provided data to the FBI on animal rights activists and also gave information for years to the Denver Police Department's "spy files" on peaceful protesters. Regent Jim Martin declared that the police "clearly crossed the lines of infringing civil liberties."[142]

In Iowa, a November 15, 2003, Drake University forum on "Stop the Occupation! Bring the Iowa Guard Home!" sponsored by the Drake chapter of the National Lawyers Guild included nonviolence training for activists. The next day, twelve protesters were arrested at an antiwar rally at Iowa National Guard headquarters in Johnston. Because of this, Drake University was ordered in a February 4, 2004, subpoena from an FBI joint terrorism task force to give up "all documents indicating the purpose and intended participants in the meeting, and all documents or recordings which would identify persons that actually attended the meeting" and any campus security records "reflecting any observations made of the Nov. 15, 2003, meeting, including any records of persons in charge or control of the meeting, and any records of attendees of the meeting." Drake University was also ordered not to tell anyone about the subpoena. Federal prosecutors eventually withdrew the subpoenas. The AAUP Special Committee on Academic Freedom and National Security in a Time of Crisis declared, "To demand the naming of all persons who attended a lawfully registered campus conference will undoubtedly chill protected expression, and deter participation at similar events in the future." According to documents released in the case, two Polk County sheriff's deputies had infiltrated the Drake conference to spy on the workshop about civil disobedience.[143]

Other government agencies are also involved in spying on campus groups. Army intelligence officers sought information about a February 4, 2004, University of Texas at Austin conference about "Islam and the Law: The Question of Sexism?" Two agents from the army's Intelligence and Security Commission secretly attended the conference, and a few days later visited university offices to try to obtain the names of three "Middle Eastern–looking" men who had asked questions at the conference.[144]

Miguel Tinker-Salas, a professor of Latin American history at Pomona College in California, was questioned in 2006 about Venezuelan connections by members of a federal terrorism task force, who also asked students about the content of his classes.[145] FBI antiterrorism task forces are reportedly monitoring Muslim groups at the University of California at Irvine.[146] And FBI agents obtained a contact list for people attending the Third National Organizing Conference on Iraq in 2002 at Stanford University.[147]

In 2005 it was revealed that the federal government kept a list monitoring peaceful antirecruitment protests at Berkeley and other colleges. A peaceful protest at NYU's law school featuring antirecruiter signs and stickers was also listed.[148] The FBI watched peaceful groups like the Vegan Community Project and worried about the "semicommunistic ideology" of the Catholic Workers.[149]

The Department of Defense maintained surveillance reports on student protests against recruiters at State University of New York at Albany, Southern Connecticut State University, the University of California at Berkeley, and William Paterson University of New Jersey that were considered security threats.[150] The University of California at Santa Cruz's Students Against the War were included on a government terrorism database in 2003 for holding a peaceful protest against military recruiters on campus that was deemed a "threat."[151]

At Forest Park Community College in Missouri, speakers and participants at the May 2003 Biodevastation 7 conference were harassed and arrested by police who feared that they might disrupt the World Agricultural Forum in St. Louis. Police detained a dozen people for riding bicycles without a license. A van going to the conference was stopped by police for a seatbelt violation, and the driver was arrested (for an unmarked container with Vitamin C pills). Everyone in the van was interrogated by three groups of investigators. Police raided the Bolozone housing collective without a warrant, claiming that nails and stones used in remodeling were evidence of weapons. One police officer found a beer bottle and put a rag in it, pretending to have found a Molotov cocktail. Another police officer admitted that police vandalized bikes and slashed tires of the activists.[152]

In the summer of 2004, the *New York Times* reported that "the FBI has been questioning political protesters across the country" about events planned at the political conventions.[153] In Missouri the FBI trailed and then interrogated three students and alumni of Truman State University about their protest plans. The three men were subpoenaed to appear before a grand jury to prevent them from leaving to attend the Democratic National Convention.[154]

Sometimes conservative students do the spying. When President George W. Bush spoke at Kalamazoo, Michigan, in 2004, Kalamazoo College Republicans identified students they deemed critical of Bush and had them banned from the event for posing a potential threat of protesting.[155] Conservatives are also urging a much greater surveillance of college campuses. A 2006 House Intelligence Committee Report (condemned by Democrats for its partisan motives) asserted that in America, "universities continue to be used as potential recruitment centers for Islamist extremists," but provided no evidence to support this assertion.[156] Candace de Russy, a trustee at the State University of New York (who also has served on boards of the U.S.

Air Force Academy, the National Association of Scholars, the American Council of Trustees and Alumni, the Independent Women's Forum, and the Foundation for Individual Rights in Education), denounced academia as "self-indulgent and permissive." Warning of "the very real prospect of the metastasis of Islamist terror cells" at American colleges, de Russy declared in 2006 that authorities must "review courses seeming to exalt violent activities or revolution," and "lists of all student organizations should be established, along with procedures for monitoring." According to de Russy, the war on terror justifies imposing external control over faculty hiring, and "if faculties fail in such ways to foster a higher education 'culture of security,' then campus governing boards must lead the way toward this cultural change."[157]

Criticizing the War on Iraq

Critics of the invasion of Iraq and other conflicts found themselves (and their freedom to speak without retaliation) under attack on campus. Wisconsin state representative Scott Suder denounced the University of Wisconsin at Madison for allowing antiwar member of the British Parliament George Galloway to speak on campus.[158] At the University of California at Berkeley, Candace Falk, the director of the Emma Goldman Papers Project, used antiwar quotes from Goldman in a fund-raising letter. University officials halted the mailing, claiming that the quotes could be interpreted as a political statement. After public criticism, administrators relented and allowed the mailing.[159]

At Columbia University, after professor Nicholas DeGenova called for an Iraqi victory over the United States and said during a panel discussion that he would like to see "a million Mogadishus," colleagues and the public denounced him. A letter from 104 Republican members of the U.S. House of Representatives demanded: "We are writing to urge you to fire assistant professor Nicholas DeGenova for remarks he recently made at a 'teach-in' on the Columbia campus at which he called for the defeat of U.S. forces in Iraq." President Lee Bollinger defended DeGenova's academic freedom while condemning what he said.[160]

At Irvine Valley College in California, vice president of instruction Dennis White wrote in a March 27, 2003, memo: "It has come to my attention that several faculty members have been discussing the current war within the context of their classrooms. We need to be sure that faculty do not explore this activity within the context of their classroom unless it can be demonstrated, to the satisfaction of this office, that such discussions are directly related to the approved instructional requirements and materials associated with those classes." The memo was in response to three students, including one with a fiancé in the military, who reportedly became distraught after instructors expressed antiwar opinions in classes. Administrators promised to investigate each case.[161]

Sensitivity to the feelings of prowar students could even lead to the dismissal of faculty who dared to mention the war in class. At Forsyth Technical Community College in North Carolina, writing teacher Elizabeth Ito was fired for spending ten minutes in a class criticizing the war in Iraq in spring 2003. Although Ito apologized to the class and gave them opportunity to express their own views on the war, she refused to obey the administration's demand to promise never to mention the war in class again.[162]

Alan Temes, an assistant professor of health and physical education at Indiana University of Pennsylvania, was denied tenure after being warned by his department chair not to engage in antiwar activism by listing on a bulletin board the deaths in Iraq. Temes's chair wrote to him, "Hanging a body count is not an issue of freedom of speech, but one of using poor judgment and showing lack of sensitivity for students, faculty and staff in our office who have immediate family members who are themselves at risk of dying in Iraq every day." Temes reported that he was told in a meeting that continuing his antiwar activism would hurt his bid for tenure and shortly afterward was denied tenure.[163] Conservative writer Cathy Young noted about the Temes case, "This is one of several recent incidents in which colleges penalized faculty and students for expressing antiwar views."[164]

In an anonymous evaluation form for University of Arizona professor David Gibbs's spring 2004 class on politics, one student wrote: "I believe that the university should check into David Gibbs. He is an anti-American communist who hates America and is trying to brainwash young people into thinking America sucks. He needs to go and live in a Third World country to appreciate what he has here. Have him investigated by the FBI. FBI has been contacted." Gibbs reported that a student blog urged other students to attend the class and attempt to disrupt it.[165]

Colorado State University sociology professor Steven Helmericks had to leave his job as a part-time teacher after receiving death threats in 2004. The reason? On June 14, 2004, while introducing himself in his general sociology class, Helmericks discussed his opposition to the war in Iraq, reportedly saying that Bush "is sending boys and girls out to die for no god-damn reason."[166] A student whose husband was in Iraq spoke up to criticize his views, and Helmericks said he appreciated her views and didn't mean to offend anyone. After the class this student confronted Helmericks again, and he suggested that if she had trouble with lecture that day, she might prefer to take a different class. The student complained to the chair of the department, who talked to Helmericks. One student in the class noted about Helmericks after the first class, "He was very guarded in what he said, and I thought that took away from his teaching." But Chuck Fogland, president of the CSU College Republicans, condemned Helmericks as a "totalitarian" professor who "harassed" Republican students; he accused Helmericks of being "narrow-minded, abusive and unfair." But Bruce Tracy, a Republican student in Helmericks's class, criticized the College Republicans' crusade: "To say there was political bias in that class is a completely personal bias of the situation. He did not at any time bully or slam down our throats a political agenda." When the attacks on Helmericks were publicized in the press, he began receiving e-mail and phone threats. Helmericks declared, "The university and I came to the consensual agreement that I was in danger, as were other students and other professors," and he agreed not to teach.[167] Although Helmericks agreed to be banned from the classroom, a part-time professor has little power to resist the will of the administration. By allowing death threats to affect what gets taught, a university runs the risk of encouraging further threats.

Critics of the military were often subjected to harassment and arrest. In 2004 Boston College student Joe Previtera decided to protest torture at Abu Ghraib by American soldiers. Previtera went outside a Boston armed forces recruitment center, stood on a milk crate, put on a black cape with a hood, and dangled a couple of stereo wires from his fingers, in clear imitation of one of the photos of Iraqis threatened with electrocution at Abu Ghraib. Previtera was not only banned from protesting, he was also arrested and charged with two felonies for possession of a hoax device and making a false bomb threat (even though Previtera never said anything) because police thought that the stereo wires looked like part of a bomb.[168]

At the University of Massachusetts at Boston on April 3, 2003, a sergeant recruiting for the National Guard confronted a student wearing a "military recruiters off my campus" t-shirt who was passing out fliers for an event on the anniversary of Martin Luther King Jr.'s assassination. The sergeant called the student a "fucking Communist" and called the campus police to try to prevent him from handing out fliers. The sergeant also asked him, "Are you organizing the program for Dr. King?" and then told the student, "You should be shot in the head, too."[169] Professor Tony Van Der Meer stepped in, and the sergeant made a similar threat to him. Several witnesses saw the sergeant poke Van Der Meer in the shoulder and get in his face, with no physical response by Van Der Meer. As the recruiter left, Van Der Meer continued to yell at the recruiters, and three police officers tackled Van Der Meer, tore his jacket, and arrested him. Van Der Meer was charged with assault and battery of a police officer and resisting arrest. Several students who yelled at the police were also threatened with arrest. The police officer, when asked why the recruiter had not been arrested for making a death threat, declared: "I'm not arresting anyone in the military because I choose not to."[170] Deanna Brunetti, who was selling class rings to students in the lobby, reported about the military recruiter: "The guy in the uniform said to the black man, 'You should be shot in the head, you and all you peacemaker people.'" Brunetti then saw an "extremely angry" police officer who "poked the black man. I saw the cop grab the black man by the lapel and push him to the ground. He almost pushed the black man into my table. I didn't see the black man raise a finger to the officer. Not once."[171] Eventually, the charges against Van Der Meer were dropped.[172]

During the 2005–2006 school year, suppression of peaceful campus protests reached its highest levels at American colleges since the Vietnam War. In just two days in September 2005, college officials at three different campuses illegally banned protests and violently attacked students who tried to protest military recruiters.

On September 28, 2005, University of Wisconsin at Madison students were banned from attending an open career fair in the student center because they had signs critical of military recruiters.[173]

A peaceful protest of an army recruiting table at Holyoke Community College's cafeteria on September 29, 2005, was interrupted by violence from campus police. Peter Mascaro, head of campus security, grabbed a sign away from a student that read "Cops are hypocrites" because he considered it "inappropriate." Then Officer Scott Landry (the advisor to the College Republicans, who had gathered to urge the police to attack the students) grabbed the student and, with the help of three other officers, lifted the student off the ground and assaulted him. When another student, Charles Peterson, peaceably came to the student's defense, the police put him in a headlock, and then sprayed mace in his face. The next day, Peterson was banned from campus, preventing him from working at his campus job and prohibiting him from attending classes, without any due process.[174]

Also on September 29, 2005, George Mason University student Tariq Khan, an air force veteran, stood near a recruiting table for the U.S. Marines while wearing signs that said "Recruiters tell lies. Don't be fooled" and "U.S. out of Iraq, Israel out of Palestine, U.S. out of North America." Khan was surrounded by three conservative students who yelled at him and ripped off one of his signs. Instead of defending Khan's rights, a campus police officer attacked Khan without reason, throwing him on the ground and putting him in a chokehold. Khan was handcuffed, dragged to a police car, denied medical treatment, and threatened with being pepper-sprayed and hung by his feet from the ceiling.[175]

Three students and a staff member at City College of New York were attacked by campus security, arrested, and banned from campus because of a peaceful protest against military recruiters at a career fair; all charges were dropped after the community protested.[176]

At San Francisco State University, ten students were physically removed from a career fair on April 14, 2006, for protesting military recruiters and banned from campus for two weeks without any hearing, even though some lived and worked as well as studied on campus. The students had handed out leaflets, talked to recruiters and potential recruits, and chanted, "Killing Iraqis is no career! Recruiters are not welcome here!" One of the students, Lacy MacAuley, reported: "I was talking to a student in line waiting to speak to military recruits, and then I just felt two people grab my arms from behind and they just dragged me out."[177]

At several colleges merely handing out pieces of paper critical of war was prohibited. At Hampton University in Virginia in 2005, students were punished for the crimes of "cajoling" and "proselytizing" because they were observed handing out unauthorized antiwar flyers and involved in an unapproved protest.[178] Six Hampton students were found guilty by the administration and punished by being forced to do community service work.[179]

At the University of Nevada at Reno, campus officials tried to invoke free speech zones in order to ban protestors from handing out antiwar literature and to prevent the Queer Student Union from holding a "kiss-in for justice" against military recruiters at a career fair. The campus College Republicans even filed suit against the protesters seeking a permanent restraining order against their protests at career fairs.[180]

The new wave of patriotic correctness has also brought a revival of McCarthy era loyalty oaths. The Ohio Patriot Act requires all public employees, including university professors, to sign a loyalty oath expressing opposition to terrorism or lose their jobs.[181] An 1864 loyalty oath for professors in Nevada was recently revived, and a campus theater director was removed from teaching in 2006 for refusing to sign it.[182]

Academic Freedom after 9/11

Has the state of academic freedom improved since the days following 9/11? Although it is always difficult to measure the overall status of academic freedom, the startling conclusion from the limited evidence available is that academic freedom has actually declined further as time passes. One reason is that 9/11 united Americans. There was no massive wave of repression in America after 9/11 because there was rarely anything to suppress: American professors (and, indeed, almost the entire world) universally agreed that the 9/11 attacks were evil. But after 9/11 that consensus has faded as the Bush administration pursued a controversial war in Iraq and the 2004 election approached. As political division within the country grew, so too did the impulse to silence dissent on college campuses, especially the desire to suppress left-wing political views.

For years, Ward Churchill was a radical professor at the University of Colorado who wrote in relative obscurity his critiques of the U.S. government. He was so obscure, in fact, that an essay written immediately after 9/11 calling some of the victims in the World Trade Center "little Eichmanns" didn't get noticed until more than three years later. Churchill never defended or supported the 9/11 attacks, but called them the "natural and unavoidable consequence of unlawful U.S. policy." Churchill later explained what he meant by the most controversial line in his 2001 essay: "I have never characterized all the September 11 victims as Nazis. What I said was that the 'technocrats of empire' working in the World Trade Center were the equivalent of 'little Eichmanns.' Thus, it was obviously not directed to the children, janitors, food service workers, fire[fighters] and random passers-by killed in the 9/11 attack."[183] Churchill's comments were both obnoxious and stupid. To blame investment bankers and international traders for insane attacks by religious fundamentalists (who had no discernible interest in global poverty or its causes) is dumb, and a comparison to the architect of Nazi genocide is morally bizarre. But people should be free to express bizarre ideas without being banned by college campuses.

The controversy over Ward Churchill began in 2004, when the Kirkland Project at Hamilton College in New York invited Susan Rosenberg to campus. Rosenberg was a member of the Weather Underground who had been sentenced to fifty-eight years in prison for weapons possession (but had her sentence commuted after fifteen years by Bill Clinton), and who had also been accused of involvement in a 1981 armed robbery where three people were murdered. Under pressure, Rosenberg backed out. But the Kirkland Project had already invited Ward Churchill to speak on February 3, 2005, and a conservative government professor, Theodore Eismeier, decided to investigate the speakers invited by the Kirkland Project and exposed Churchill's views.[184]

In the firestorm of controversy that followed, Hamilton College president Joan Stewart cancelled the "Limits of Dissent?" panel with Churchill, citing "safety and security."[185] Nancy Rabinowitz, director of the Kirkland Project, resigned under duress as a result of the controversy.[186] The program's budget was cut for the 2005–2006 school year, and it was ordered to review its mission and programs (and eventually shut down). And any speakers invited by the Kirkland Project were required to receive prior approval by a dean.[187] Rather than defending free speech, conservatives like David Horowitz denounced Rabinowitz for refusing to ban Churchill on her own.[188]

Churchill quickly became the most banned speaker in America. Wheaton College, in Massachusetts, cancelled Churchill's speech in 2005 after the controversy over his views.[189] The University of Oregon cancelled Churchill's appearance at an April 2005 conference on race and immigration.[190] At Eastern Washington University, Churchill's speech scheduled for April 5, 2005, was also cancelled out of safety concerns. Eastern Washington University president Stephen Jordan declared, "Mr. Churchill still has multiple venues for the outlet of his ideas. Neither this university, nor the state's taxpayers, are under any obligation to provide an appearance venue for Mr. Churchill, if his presence threatens the safety and security of this campus."[191]

Churchill himself received more than 100 death threats.[192] But by obeying these "heckler's vetoes," colleges put all faculty and students in far greater danger: Now anyone who wants to cancel a speech or a class can merely phone in a vague threat and hope that the college will prohibit the event from happening. By giving in to terrorist threats, the university encourages further threats. What we need is not the cancellation of controversial speakers, but aggressive enforcement of the law against anyone making a death threat and support of free speech for the victims of death threats.

Politicians immediately stepped up to condemn Churchill. The Wisconsin Assembly voted 67–31 to condemn Churchill for "anti-American hate speech" and told the University of Wisconsin at Whitewater to ban him from speaking on campus. Representative Steve Nass (R-Whitewater) threatened to retaliate against the university if they allowed Churchill to speak: "It's unfortunate the university is so dug in on this that they want to go on regardless of the consequences." Whitewater chancellor Jack Miller said he would allow the speech to occur only if safety could be guaranteed and all costs were covered by donations and student fees (banning any departments from cosponsoring the event).[193]

A Denver radio talk show host suggested executing Churchill for treason, and critics launched a crusade to recall any regent who refused to fire Churchill.[194] Dan Feder wrote, "Churchill is typical of the hate-America academic left—a fifth column every bit as much a threat to our survival as Osama bin Laden and al-Qaeda."[195]

MSNBC talk show host (and former Republican congressman) Joe Scarborough hoped that firing Churchill would just be the beginning of a massive purge of the left: "It is time to call your governor and demand a full investigation into the political bias that is infecting the state colleges that you keep open with your tax dollars. It is time to take your college classrooms back. And if our elected officials won't do it, we will run them out of office and find someone who will. This is not about free speech. It is about how your tax dollars are being spent to promote agendas that the overwhelming majority of Americans would find deeply offensive."[196]

Colorado governor Bill Owens proclaimed, "No one wants to infringe on Mr. Churchill's right to express himself. But we are not compelled to accept his proterrorist views at state taxpayer subsidy nor under the banner of the University of Colorado."[197] Newt Gingrich demanded Churchill's firing, declaring that "taxpayers don't have to pay for lunatic professors to have a salary to miseducate their children."[198] Actually, they do, whether the lunatic is named Churchill or Gingrich. Academic freedom means that those in academia have the right to speak without losing their jobs.

The University of Colorado appointed a committee to investigate Churchill's entire record, desperately searching for an excuse to fire him. The faculty committee claimed that Churchill's historical errors amounted to misconduct and his ghostwriting and misuse of collectively written articles was plagiarism, so they recommended a suspension as punishment. But even this committee was troubled by the political witch-hunt that sparked the investigation.[199] As FIRE observed, "An 'investigation' of protected speech is itself improper and has a chilling effect on the free exchange of ideas. It is also improper to use clearly protected—though controversial—expression as a pretext to begin scouring the public record in hopes of finding examples of public statements that do not enjoy full First Amendment protection."[200]

Colorado state house minority leader Joe Stengel proclaimed that because of Churchill, he would demand monitoring of the University of Colorado: "If we can't get accountability from the regents and president, we may need to consider oversight."[201] When "accountability" means firing professors for their views, and "oversight" means politicians destroying academic freedom, it needs to be resisted.

The Case of Lawrence Summers

If Ward Churchill became the right's most wanted professor, the poster child for their cries about political correctness was Harvard president Lawrence Summers. Conservative columnist Jack Kelly proclaimed, "Churchill is lionized for saying vile and untrue things about his country and countrymen. Summers is hounded for saying something nonpejorative that is demonstrably true. This is the status of free speech on campuses today."[202] But no one has "lionized" Churchill for his idiotic comments; to the contrary, the only debate is whether he should be fired and banned from campuses, or whether his freedom to be wrong should be protected. Summers, by contrast, has been lionized by the right for his (demonstrably false) comments about the mental inferiority of women, and his job was never in jeopardy because of his sexism.

At a Harvard conference on "Diversifying the Science and Engineering Work Force," Summers addressed the reason why so few women work in science and engineering. Citing a discredited theory posited nearly a half-century ago by economist Gary Becker, Summers claimed that discrimination against women in academia couldn't exist because it is economically irrational. Instead, Summers concluded that the low levels of women in math and science could be attributed to two factors: Women fail to work hard because of their family obligations, and women have genetically inferior brains that cause their skills at math and logic to be worse than men (or "different availability of aptitude at the high end," as Summers put it).[203] Summers proved that girls think differently from boys by citing his daughter, who named her toy trucks "Daddy Truck" and "Baby Truck."[204]

Summers's obnoxious, uneducated comments were particularly offensive because they were a rationalization for his own administration's failure to assure equal protection for women. In 2004 Harvard offered only four out of thirty-two tenured jobs in the arts and sciences to women, a decline from previous years.[205] While Harvard's president was advocating a backward theory of women's inferiority, Harvard was moving back away from gender equity.

Should Summers be fired for his sexist comments? No, and it is troubling if his comments motivated the professors who voted against him, because we need college presidents who are willing to speak their minds, even if they say idiotic things. But Summers had already apologized for his comments, and Harvard's governing board stood firmly behind him. Summers had also insulted Harvard professor Cornel West and told him to stay away from involvement in political campaigns.[206]

The events that actually led to Summers's downfall came in 2006, when he fired Faculty of Arts and Sciences dean William Kirby in an effort to consolidate his power and remove critics of his administration. An outraged faculty planned another vote of no confidence, and Summers's supporters began to abandon him, alienated by his obnoxious personality and his lack of integrity (and, in part, because Summers exercised his free speech and apologized for his sexist comments).[207] Even his supporters considered him dishonest because of his evasive answers about his close friend, economist Andrei Shleifer, who cost Harvard a $26.5 million fine to settle fraud charges brought by the U.S. government.[208] Conservative Harvard professor and Summers supporter Stephan Thernstrom admitted that Summers is in the "top tenth of one percent of any scale measuring abrasiveness, arrogance, and overbearingness."[209] Former Harvard College dean Harry Lewis, who is well liked by conservatives, noted about Summers, "His misfortune arose from the impatience, harshness, thoughtlessness, and lack of candor."[210] Summers announced that he would voluntarily leave the presidency (in exchange for more than a million dollars in a golden parachute, a yearlong paid sabbatical, and appointment as a prestigious university professor).[211]

Harvard law professor Alan Dershowitz compared the criticism of Summers to the "trial of Galileo."[212] But presidents, unlike professors, do not have tenure. No one has suggested that Summers should be fired from the tenured post he holds in economics. However, no one is entitled to a lifetime position as president of a university. In 2002 Summers defended his bizarre description of people supporting divestment from Israel as "anti-Semitic" by proclaiming: "Academic freedom does not include freedom from criticism, and I see it as part of my responsibility to resist what I see as intolerance."[213] Summers himself shouldn't be entitled to freedom from criticism for his views.

The treatment of Summers stands in sharp contrast with what happened to University of Colorado president Elizabeth Hoffman. On March 3, 2005,

Hoffman (a lifelong Republican) warned faculty about a "new McCarthyism."[214] Representative Joe Stengel, the top Republican in the Colorado House of Representatives who demanded legislative "oversight" of professors, denounced Hoffman and called for her immediate resignation. On March 7, 2005, Hoffman announced she was resigning.[215] Hoffman reported that she resigned because of "the mounting pressure on the university" due to her refusal to immediately fire Churchill (despite approving an investigation into his work and searching for any excuse to get rid of him).[216] Under the strange double standard of conservatives, an incompetent president criticized for making sexist remarks was the victim of leftist repression, while a Republican president forced out of her job for halfheartedly defending academic freedom got what she deserved.

Fighting Patriotic Correctness

After 9/11 the enemies of academic freedom too often succeeded in their aim of silencing dissent. Both the ideal and the practice of academic freedom have been under attack, as America became a place where, in the words of former Bush press secretary Ari Fleisher, you had to "watch what you say."[217]

In the wake of 9/11 academic freedom suffered under a wave of patriotic correctness in America, as professors were fired, free speech was silenced, and politicians demanded flag waving instead of political debate. An institution of higher learning should never fear controversy. All colleges should actively seek to have commencement speakers who will address controversial views. All colleges should institute policies that prohibit banning speakers, even if they dissent from a particular orthodoxy. The response to the terrible acts of terrorism on September 11, 2001, did not require an exception to the rules of academic freedom. To the contrary, after 9/11 was a moment when intellectual scrutiny of American government policies (and the academic freedom required to utilize it) was more important than ever.

CHAPTER TWO
Censorship on Campus of Criticism of Israel

⮹

One of the most notable developments in the war on terror has been the extension of college censorship to supporters of Palestinian rights. Most of the attempts to cancel campus speakers have been aimed at critics of the Israeli government.

At the State University of New York at New Paltz, for the first time in fifteen years, the administration in 2002 refused to fund a women's studies conference, "Women and War, Peace and Revolution." University officials considered it unbalanced because one panelist was Ruchama Marton, an Israeli psychiatrist scheduled to speak about peace negotiations between Palestine and Israel, and human rights abuses against Palestinians. The administration complained that the pro-Israeli government view would not be presented.[1] No one should miss the irony that a conference with no Palestinian speakers was deemed "unbalanced" because the Israeli speaker was critical of Israeli government policies. No college can or should enforce demands for "equal time" for every view at every event, but it has become a common excuse for censorship.

The Middle Eastern Studies Summer Institute for Teachers, held at Central Connecticut State University in July 2002, was condemned for being pro-Palestinian. The *Jewish Ledger* demanded equal time for a speaker approved by the Anti-Defamation League or the cancellation of the workshop. The Connecticut Humanities Council, which funded the event, promised to monitor it. U.S. Representative Nancy Johnson (R-CT) attacked the seminar: "My concern is that the presentation of issues in the Middle East is not balanced. Intellectual honesty requires that there be a presentation of both sides."[2] Threatening e-mails and phone calls were delivered to CCSU president Richard Judd and the professors teaching the seminar.[3]

At Bucks County Community College in Pennsylvania, the Israeli consulate protested a panel discussion on the Middle East in 2001 because it focused too much on Palestinian issues. College spokesperson Marta Kaufmann told faculty, "Since emotions are running so high, everyone should tilt toward balance."[4]

In 2006, Brandeis University administrators banned a campus art exhibit of work by Palestinian youth, declaring that "it was completely from one side in the Israeli-Palestinian conflict" and therefore lacked balance.[5] On the other side, at Penn State University, a 2006 student art exhibit "Portraits of Terror," depicting Palestinian attacks on Israelis, was banned because it "did not promote cultural diversity or opportunities for democratic dialogue."[6]

At Loyola University in Louisiana, the Jewish Federation of Greater New Orleans denounced an April 23, 2003, speech by Francis Boyle of the University of Illinois Law School on "Iraq and Israel: A Legal Double Standard" and called upon Loyola to require that speakers critical of Israel be "balanced" with opposing points of view at the same event. The administration withdrew law school support for Boyle's lecture, claiming that it was too controversial.[7]

Sometimes, the demand was not for balance, but for the abolition of the pro-Palestinian viewpoint. Right-wing columnist and attorney Debbie Schlussel filed a lawsuit October 8, 2002, on behalf of the Michigan Student Zionists in an attempt to stop the Second National Student Conference on the Palestine Solidarity Movement, which was held in October 2002 at the University of Michigan. The lawsuit alleged that speakers such as Sami Al-Arian would spread hate and might provoke violent acts on campus. According to Schlussel, "This is the equivalent of adding a match to a powder keg.... It's about preventing violence and terrorism against students." Schlussel argued that the university "must ban from UM any conference speakers and organizers who have records of inciteful, violent speech" because the event "jeopardizes the safety of thousands of students." Schlussel claimed, "I respect speech rights of everyone, no matter how odious their positions may be. But free speech does not include incitement to violence." A judge refused to issue an injunction banning the conference, which did not cause any violent acts.[8]

In 2003 Rutgers University banned the same conference from its campus after initially approving the event and receiving political pressure to cancel it. Rutgers claimed that the students had failed to submit information about the conference, but Rutgers had no legal right to demand material on the conference as a condition of allowing it to be held. Attempts to hold the same conference at Duke University in 2004 resulted in similar calls for it to be banned, which the university resisted.[9]

At Ohio University, activist Art Gish, who has been involved with the Christian Peacemaking Team and nonviolent protests in Palestine, was disinvited from a May 6, 2002, public seminar about the Middle East. Gish attended the event anyway wearing a gag.[10]

At the College of the Holy Cross in Massachusetts, a November 1, 2002, speech by Reverend Michael Prior, author of *Zionism and the State of Israel*, was cancelled after David O'Brien, director of the Center for Religion, Ethics and Culture, withdrew the invitation. Political science professor David Schaefer, who protested the invitation to Prior, argued: "Colleges should not invite Nazi speakers in to extol the virtues of Hitler, or David Duke to speak about certain religious groups that are inferior. Prior falls in that category."[11]

Harvard University rescinded an invitation for a poetry reading to poet Tom Paulin because he was quoted saying about Jewish settlers on the West Bank: "They should be shot dead. I think they are Nazis, racists. I feel nothing but hatred for them."[12] In a 2001 poem, Paulin referred to the Israeli army as "the Zionist SS." He also said, "I never believed that Israel had the right to exist at all." Paulin declared, "My quoted remarks completely misrepresent my real views. For that, I apologize." After consulting with Harvard president Lawrence Summers (who on September 17, 2002, had denounced anyone urging divestment from Israel as "anti-Semitic in their effect if not their intent"), the English department and Paulin mutually agreed to cancel the December 14, 2002, lecture, to which Summers proclaimed, "I believe the department has come to the appropriate decision."[13] Harvard Law School professors Charles Fried, Alan Dershowitz, and Laurence Tribe wrote a letter declaring, "What is truly dangerous is the precedent of withdrawing an invitation because a speaker would cause, in the words of English department chair Lawrence Buell, 'consternation and divisiveness.'"[14] Harvard's English department voted on November 19, 2002, to reinstate the poetry reading.[15] The University of Vermont English Department also cancelled an appearance by Paulin.[16]

Rutgers evolutionary biologist Robert Trivers, winner of the Crafoord Prize in Biosciences, had a speech at Harvard University cancelled in 2007 because Trivers had criticized Alan Dershowitz's views on Israel and wrote to him that "Nazis—and Nazi-like apologists such as yourself—need to be confronted directly."[17]

Pro-Israeli speakers are also sometimes denied an opportunity to speak. Daniel Pipes was disinvited in October 2002 from a speech sponsored by a consortium of Baltimore-area colleges because of the controversy over his website www.CampusWatch.org, since it "might cause unseemly reactions among both the participants and the audience."[18] In December 2002 the Stanford Israel Alliance rescinded an invitation to Pipes because "there has already been a great deal of controversy over Campus Watch," and the organization feared that students might not "realize that Campus Watch in no way infringes on Freedom of Speech but is simply a resource for Jewish students."[19] In 2004 protestors at the University of California at Berkeley were thrown out of a speech by Pipes after they tried to shout him down and heckle him.[20]

When the Stanford College Republicans invited Walid Shoebat, a self-described former Palestinian terrorist, to speak on campus in 2007, Stanford administrators banned the public or the press from attending. A Stanford spokesperson claimed, "This is a controversial speaker, and we want to make sure that our students have a constructive dialogue."[21] However, the overwhelming number of efforts to ban controversial speakers at American college campuses is aimed at supporters of Palestinians.

Silencing Student Protest against Israel

Student groups involved in anti-Israeli protests have also been subjected to sanctions. University of California at Berkeley administrators banned Students for Justice in Palestine (SJP) from campus for a month after its members led an occupation of a building on April 9, 2002, where seventy-nine people were arrested (all criminal charges were dropped, but one student was denied his degree while being investigated for violating the campus code of conduct).[22]

At San Francisco State University, in response to a May 7, 2002, rally on campus where some pro-Israeli and pro-Palestinian protesters yelled hateful remarks at one another, the administration issued a warning to the campus Hillel group but banned the General Union of Palestinian Students (GUPS) for a year, cutting off their access to campus facilities and funding.[23] Administrators also banned the website of GUPS because it had texts deemed anti-Semitic and links to websites that had Holocaust denial content.[24]

The pro-Palestinian demonstrators reported that they were called "terrorists," "sand niggers," "camel jockeys," "sharmoota" (whore), "Arab losers," and were told, "Go fuck your camels," "Go back to your caves," and "Racist terrorists off our campus now."[25] Pro-Palestinian demonstrators also reported "a woman hitting the pro-Palestinian students (who were already barricaded off) with the flagpole of an Israeli flag." One pro-Israeli protester challenged several pro-Palestinian students to a fight, raising his fists and screaming "Fuck you!" and spitting at them. One man was writing messages on a large pad of paper with a magic marker: "All Muslims are terrorists" and "We will one day turn the Jordan River into a river of flowing Arab blood."[26]

Pro-Israeli demonstrators also reported numerous epithets and threats, including "Die Jews," "Go back to Russia," "All you Jews should die," "I'd kill you if I could," and, "Hitler didn't do a good enough job, he should [have] exterminated you all when he had the chance." A pro-Palestinian activist took an Israeli flag off a podium during the event, stomped on the flag, and then kicked it off a stage.[27] But penalizing student organizations for the actions committed at protests by individuals is an illegitimate form of group punishment. To eliminate funding for a group and the opportunity to meet on campus is particularly disturbing, and shutting down a website for linking to offensive views is a clear violation of free speech rights.

Defenders of Israel also have faced false charges. In March 2007, San Francisco State University dismissed harassment charges fired against College Republicans after an October 17, 2006, "antiterrorism" rally in which they stepped on drawings of the Hamas and Hezbollah flags that included the name of "Allah" in Arabic script.[28] The levels of anger and hatred at some campuses over the Israel/Palestine issue should alarm campus officials. But the solution is not censorship and punishment of groups engaged in nonviolent protest. Colleges need to find mechanisms for thoughtful and respectful debate of controversial issues. Discipline and censorship is not only a violation of students' rights, but it reflects a university's failure to use education and reason.

The repression of dissenting views in academia creates an atmosphere where critics of Israeli policies fear to speak openly. When John Mearsheimer of the University of Chicago and Stephen Walt of Harvard University issued a working paper titled "The Israel Lobby and U.S. Foreign Policy" that criticized the American government's policies toward Israel, they were met with denunciations and threats of retaliation.[29] Although academic supporters of the Israeli government certainly encounter criticism, it rarely reaches the level of punishment faced by supporters of the Palestinian cause. According to Donna Halper, who teaches at the University of Massachusetts at Amherst, "I'm an instructor at one of the colleges Mr. Horowitz criticizes, and I can tell you nobody has ever given me a hard time about being pro-Israel or disagreeing with Karl Marx."[30]

The Attack on Faculty

Faculty, especially those without tenure, are vulnerable to being fired for expressing controversial views about Israel and Palestine. At American University in Washington, D.C., after adjunct professor Laura Drake had an e-mail falsely sent in her name denouncing Israel, the university responded by distancing itself from her and declaring that her contract had expired, indicating that it would fire a nontenured professor who sharply criticized Israel. Only after it was revealed that her identity had been stolen for the e-mail did the university support her.[31]

When Juan Cole, a well-known scholar of the Middle East who writes a blog critical of Israeli and U.S. policies, was considered for a job at Yale, conservatives launched an unprecedented crusade against Yale that succeeded in stopping his hiring.[32] Frances Rosenbluth, a member of the search committee that rejected Juan Cole, noted that the smear campaigns against Cole were "hard to ignore."[33]

A graduate student teaching a literature course at the University of California at Berkeley in fall 2002 on "The Politics and Poetics of Palestinian Resistance" included in the course description, "Conservative thinkers are encouraged to seek other sections." The instructor apologized and changed the description. The Berkeley administration assigned a professor to monitor the course.[34] Although nothing was found wrong with the course, many critics demanded the class itself should be outlawed.[35] Governor Gray Davis sent a letter to UC president Richard Atkinson and CSU chancellor Charles Reed, demanding a stop to anti-Semitic "violence, harassment, and abuse," and calling for a review of all course descriptions.[36]

Harvard law professor Alan Dershowitz, who often is regarded as a defender of free speech, launched a crusade against criticism from DePaul professor Norman Finkelstein in 2005. When the University of California Press announced plans to publish Finkelstein's book *Beyond Chutzpah: On the Misuse of Anti-Semitism and the Abuse of History,* Dershowitz struck back even before the book was published. Dershowitz had his attorney, Rory Millson, threaten legal action against the University of California regents, the provost, plus the seventeen directors of the University of California Press and its nineteen-member faculty editorial committee. Dershowitz accused the press of being "part of a conspiracy to defame" him, and his attorney threatened, "The only way to extricate yourself is immediately to terminate all professional contact with this full-time malicious defamer."[37]

Dershowitz warned the University of California Press that he would "own the company" if Finkelstein's book accused him of plagiarism.[38] Finkelstein showed that Dershowitz used quotations from another author's book, but had cited the original citations for the quotes rather than the book where he found them.[39] Dershowitz's attack worked. Finkelstein's book was originally going to be published by the New Press, but Finkelstein changed publishers after Dershowitz's legal threats delayed the book. The University of California Press hired four lawyers to screen the book and forced Finkelstein to make changes to his manuscript and tone down some of his accusations.[40]

Dershowitz wasn't satisfied with his legal threats against the University of California Press. He wrote California governor Arnold Schwarzenegger asking to have the book banned and then lied to conceal this fact. Dershowitz even publicly claimed that a scholar "defamed me by saying that I had tried to prevent the publication of Norman Finkelstein's latest anti-Zionist screed, *Beyond Chutzpah.*"[41] In reality, Dershowitz personally wrote Schwarzenegger in 2004 asking him to stop the publication of the book: "I know that you will be interested in trying to prevent an impending scandal involving the decision by the University of California Press to publish a viciously anti-Semitic book by an author whose main audience consists of neo-Nazis in Germany and Austria."[42] "You have asked for the Governor's assistance in preventing the publication of this book," Schwarzenegger's office responded to Dershowitz in a February 8, 2005, letter, but "he is not inclined to otherwise exert influence in this case because of the clear, academic freedom issue it presents."[43] Unable to get Finkelstein's book banned, Dershowitz declared that he would work to get him fired by DePaul University: "I will document the case against Finkelstein. I'll demonstrate that he doesn't meet the academic standards of the Association of American Universities."[44]

Dershowitz's campaign succeeded. In May 2007, DePaul University announced Finkelstein would be denied tenure. Because Finkelstein's five books and top-notch ratings as a teacher far exceeded those of his colleagues, the "incivility" of Finkelstein's critiques of Dershowitz became the basis of his dismissal. Despite being approved by his department, Finkelstein's tenure bid was opposed by his dean, Chuck Suchar, because "the personal attacks in many of Dr. Finkelstein's published books border on character assassination."[45] DePaul's promotion and tenure committee, supported by the president of the university, followed a similar logic, denouncing Finkelstein for his "inflammatory style" and "personal attacks" in his writings. That committee declared Finkelstein's rudeness "relevant" because "an academic's reputation is intrinsically tied to the institution of which he or she is affiliated."[46] As the Illinois AAUP noted, "It is entirely illegitimate for a university to deny tenure to a professor out of fear that his published research, including those that appear under the University of California Press, might hurt a college's reputation."[47]

The decision also violated DePaul's own rules. The June 2006 report of the DePaul University Promotion and Tenure Policy Committee noted, "The Faculty Handbook does not incorporate collegiality as a criterion in promotion and tenure reviews." It recommended that "collegiality should not be a factor in a candidate's promotion and tenure review or report."[48] In academia, scholars denied tenure are always given a "terminal year" teaching at their institution. Instead, DePaul banned Finkelstein from his office and cancelled his classes. Even though DePaul paid Finkelstein, it violated his academic freedom (and the freedom of its students) by refusing to let him teach and effectively silencing his voice in its classrooms.[49] DePaul's promotion and tenure committee also rejected the unanimous view of a political science department and Dean Suchar, and denied tenure to Mehrene Larudee, who had defended Finkelstein.[50]

The Finkelstein case gave conservatives a new way to attack left-wing professors, by waging high-profile campaigns to deny tenure. Horowitz's magazine promptly targeted another DePaul assistant professor, Matthew Abraham, claiming that he should be fired for being "a very active apologist on behalf of Norman Finkelstein" and "predictable political screeds."[51]

Abraham reported: "I've been subtly and not too subtly told to back off on writing critically about the Israel-Palestine conflict."[52]

Conservative critics have openly sought to deny controversial leftists jobs and tenure. Daniel Pipes proclaimed that "robust public criticism can keep them in line" and "the more pre-tenure scrutiny, the better."[53] Horowitz's magazine and the pro-Israel group Stand with Us lobbied Wayne State University in 2006 to stop the hiring of law professor Wadie Said because he is a supporter of Palestinian rights and the son of controversial scholar Edward Said (ultimately, Wadie Said was hired by the University of South Carolina).[54]

These coordinated public attempts to deny jobs and tenure to Palestinians and their supporters are unprecedented in the history of U.S. higher education. Nadia Abu El-Haj, an anthropologist at Barnard College of Columbia University, was targeted by the far right because she wrote a book published by the University of Chicago Press criticizing Israeli archaeologists (but she ultimately won tenure).[55] Barnard alumnae have signed petitions, boycotted reunions, and threatened to stop giving donations.[56] Donald Wagner, director of the Center of Middle Eastern Studies at North Park University in Chicago, reported that he had his promotion to tenure blocked because of his "controversial advocacy of justice for Palestinians, my opposition to the war in Iraq, and my theology."[57]

Even tenure is not always a strong protection for controversial faculty. At the University of South Florida, computer science professor Sami Al-Arian was suspended from his job in 2001 after he appeared on Bill O'Reilly's television show and was condemned for having shouted "Death to Israel" at a pro-Palestinian rally in 1988.[58] Al-Arian was ostensibly suspended indefinitely for "security" reasons because the campus had received one false bomb threat that was quickly retracted. The true reason for Al-Arian's suspension was his suspected link to Palestinian terrorist groups such as Islamic Jihad, a link that turned out to be real when he was later indicted (although it is not clear that his fund-raising was illegal, and a jury refused to convict him).[59]

According to Candace de Russy, Al-Arian "violated his contract" because he made "extremist public statements" and failed to note that "they were his own views and not representative of the University."[60] Of course, since almost no professor ever makes such a statement, this means anyone accused of "extremist" statements could be fired. David Horowitz demanded that the AAUP and other groups "who defended al-Arian and collaborated [sic] his organized campaigns to attack the PATRIOT Act and other national security measures, now apologize for aiding and abetting his homicidal war against Jews and his Fifth Column efforts in behalf of radical Islam's war against the United States."[61] However, the original punishment of Al-Arian on "heckler's veto" grounds was rightly condemned by numerous groups, such as FIRE, which declared that the university "must reverse its lawless decision."[62] The University of South Florida was asserting the right to permanently suspend a professor and ban him from campus because he had been publicly denounced and threatened. A principled defense of academic freedom should not be condemned merely because the target is no saint.

A Tale of Two Adjuncts

Not every professor fired without due process is a supporter of Palestinian rights. Thomas Klocek, an adjunct instructor at DePaul University, got into an argument on September 15, 2004, with DePaul Students for Justice in Palestine at an information table. According to Klocek, "I reminded them that there were multiple perspectives involved here, including Christian ones. I also said that using the term 'Palestinian' is problematic because it was once a generic term referring to Jews, Muslims, and Christians who lived in the area rather than to a single ethnicity."[63] According to Salma Nassar, president of the student group, Klocek talked "about how Christians have more of a right to Palestine than Muslims or Jews" and quoted the claim that "not all Muslims are terrorists but all terrorists are Muslims."[64] Nassar reported that Klocek referred to Palestinians as a "made-up word," and said, "there is no such thing as a moderate Muslim, you are all fanatics."[65] Klocek ended the argument by throwing some pamphlets back on their table and flicking his thumb from his chin in a dismissive (and, the students believed, obscene) gesture. After the students complained, Klocek was suspended with pay. DePaul offered to let him teach another class, but only if it was monitored; Klocek rejected this, and he was never rehired to teach at DePaul.[66]

President Holtschneider, sounding like many of the right-wingers who urged more restrictions on left-wing faculty, declared about the Klocek case, "But freedom of speech for students requires they have a professor who treats them with respect."[67] Dean Suzanne Dumbleton explained, "The students' perspective was dishonored and their freedom demeaned. Individuals were deeply insulted.... Our college acted immediately by removing the instructor from the classroom."[68]

In an age when students are viewed as customers and the customer is always right, adjunct instructors who insult and offend students (even outside of class) put their jobs at risk. DePaul violated Klocek's academic freedom by punishing him for legitimate (albeit rude and prejudiced) extramural speech and failed to follow its own procedures on dismissing faculty.[69] Although there is no evidence that Klocek was fired because of his ideology, conservative groups launched a crusade against DePaul on his behalf, turning him into a poster child for victims of political correctness.[70]

While the right wing was pointing to Klocek as conclusive evidence of the oppression of campus conservatives, two blocks away from DePaul's downtown Chicago campus, another controversy was brewing about Palestine involving an adjunct instructor at Roosevelt University. This time, however, the instructor was being fired for allowing criticism of Israel to be heard.

Douglas Giles, an instructor at Roosevelt University, was asked a question that ended up costing him his job by a student in his spring 2005 world religions class: "I hear some people say Zionism is racism, how do I respond to that?"[71] Giles reported that in response to the Zionism question, "I explained the religious dimensions of the belief of many Jews that God has promised the land of Israel to them and will eventually lead them back to the land. I explained that both Jews and Muslims consider Jerusalem a holy city and thus religious belief is a huge factor in the current conflict over Israel. I also explained that the charge that Zionism is racism was anti-Israeli political speech and that there is nothing in Zionism itself that is racist. The class responded very positively and there was discussion about the beliefs about the land of both Jews and Muslims."[72] Jonathan Lowe, a student in the class, reported that Giles "was very careful to remain neutral and diffuse any hot comments."[73]

On the final exam, Giles included an optional question on the topic: "What was the history of Zionism and how does it affect the current conflict between Israelis and Palestinians?"[74] One student who answered the question didn't like the grade he received. A formal grade appeal went to Susan Weininger, the chair of Giles's department. On September 21, 2005, Weininger rejected the complaint, writing to the student that Giles "persuaded me that his political opinions did not figure in his assessment of your work."[75] However, Weininger added, "I did have a discussion with Prof. Giles about the political content that was introduced into the course, and I believe that he is aware that it was inappropriate and will not be covering this material in the future."[76]

Weininger told Giles not to allow any discussions in his class critical of Judaism that might be "disrespectful to any Jews in the class." According to Giles, Weininger said: "I hear you even allowed a Muslim to speak in class."[77] Giles says he responded, "Yes, of course, I allowed all students to speak, regardless of their religion." And Weininger reportedly replied: "You shouldn't! What disturbs me is that you act like the Palestinians have a side in this. They don't have a side! They are ANIMALS! They strap bombs to their bodies and blow up women and children! They are NOT CIVILIZED!"[78]

Roosevelt's associate provost, Louise Love, defended Weininger by proclaiming that "it is within the University's province to determine its curriculum," and that Weininger's demand for Giles to limit the content of the course "is not an issue of academic freedom but a pedagogical one."[79] But pedagogical issues are covered under academic freedom. Roosevelt's faculty constitution explicitly protects "the right to discuss the member's subject in the classroom with full freedom."[80]

In March 2006 Roosevelt finally announced their explanation for why they had fired Giles. Love claimed Giles's teaching in a logic class was the cause for his dismissal: "The decision not to rehire was based, in large part, on Giles's interpretation of a particular problem he submitted to his class. His interpretation of the problem was submitted for review to the full-time faculty who found his interpretation severely wanting and who, as a result, did not want him rehired."[81]

But it is difficult to believe that a college would fire an instructor because of one student's complaint about a single response to a logical fallacy without ever bothering to hear the instructor's side of the story (Giles later denied that the student's account was accurate, but Roosevelt never investigated the case).[82] As the American Philosophical Association (APA) concluded in an investigation, "The case against Giles' competence as a logic teacher is, at best, insubstantial. As philosophy teachers ourselves, we know that the labeling of fallacies in informal logic is notoriously imprecise." The APA added, "the assessment of Giles' logic teaching was anything but thorough or systematic."[83]

Even if Giles was deemed incompetent to teach logic, why would he be banned from teaching the world religions class? For Weininger (an art history professor), the logic dispute must have seemed like a convenient excuse to get rid of a politically troublesome instructor who had offended her and a student by allowing free discussion in class.

Unlike most adjuncts (such as Klocek) who are fired and can do nothing about it, Giles had a union on his side and a grievance procedure where the reasons for his dismissal had to be explained. The Roosevelt Adjunct Faculty Organization strongly defended Giles: "We continue to believe that the questioning of the instructor's competence is a diversionary tactic to shift the argument away from the academic freedom violation. We believe the so-called evidence does not in fact indict the adjunct but rather shows that the university has no commitment to collegiality toward its adjunct instructors and it demonstrates a callous disregard for the evaluation of teaching."[84]

In November 2006 Giles and Roosevelt reached a settlement that created a new Academic Freedom committee, but it may not repair the chilling effect on faculty who fear offending students by allowing discussions on controversial issues. Unlike Giles, most faculty seem to take it for granted that academic freedom is limited for adjunct instructors. Giles noted, "I have been amazed and upset that so many people hear about this case and say 'how typical' and aren't surprised that a university has acted this way. That is truly tragic."[85]

The Witch-Hunt at Columbia

Throughout the history of academic freedom, censorship most often prevails when two conditions are met: First, politically powerful enemies of academic freedom from outside the academy demand it; and second, powerful administrators, faculty, and advocacy groups within academia fail to defend academic freedom. The witch-hunt against Middle East professors at Columbia University in 2004 and 2005 was a perfect example of how this happens.

The witch-hunt began with the David Project, a right-wing think tank that produced a documentary of students denouncing Columbia's Middle East studies professors for criticizing Israel.[86] Among the various claims in the documentary, three assertions were eventually investigated by a Columbia ad hoc committee:

Student Lindsay Shrier claimed that professor George Saliba told her outside of class in a discussion, "You have no claim to the land of Israel. You have no voice in this debate. You have green eyes. You're not a Semite. I have brown eyes. I'm a Semite."[87]

Tomy Schoenfeld, a student who had served in the Israeli army, said that when he asked a question of professor Joseph Massad at an off-campus speech, the professor first asked him, "How many Palestinians have you killed?" However, even Schoenfeld opposed the idea of firing Massad and did not view the department as unbalanced.[88]

And Deena Shanker, when she asked Massad in his class if Israel gives warnings to residents before bombing buildings, reported: "Instead of answering my question, Massad exploded. He told me if I was going to 'deny the atrocities' committed against the Palestinians, I could get out of his class."[89]

Congressman Anthony Weiner of New York City and many other politicians called for Columbia to fire Massad.[90] The *New York Daily News* editorialized against Massad, "Fire this professor, Columbia."[91] Some of the opponents of academic freedom regarded dissent as a disease. The *New York Sun* editorialized that "Columbia has been infected" by faculty who hate Israel, and the *New York Daily News* declared that "Columbia University classrooms are infected by a culture of anti-Semitism and anti-Israel bigotry."[92]

The Columbia case even prompted the Foundation for Individual Rights in Education under David French to abandon its civil libertarian principles and call for an investigation of the ideology of Columbia professors: "FIRE cannot agree that professors have the right to 'suffer no recriminations, from outside the academy, for the content of their scholarship.' Nor can FIRE agree that 'critics outside the academy must avoid seeking to support their substantive arguments with threats and sanctions.'"[93] FIRE's position that scholars should suffer threats and sanctions and recriminations for their views seems to be precisely the opposite of what academic freedom means. French also argued, "A professor has an obligation to teach rather than to indoctrinate. It is obvious that the line between education and indoctrination can sometimes be vague, but in many cases it is quite clear.

There are some allegations in this case that, if proven true, would indicate that the line has clearly been crossed at Columbia."[94] FIRE even supported investigative committees to examine the ideology of Columbia professors, declaring that "it is incumbent upon the university to take steps to investigate if this ideological dominance is the case."[95] The call for investigation is particularly remarkable because Greg Lukianoff of FIRE noted about the accusations of the David Project, "Nothing described in the film constitutes either harassment or intimidation in any formal sense ... not even the worst allegations in *Columbia Unbecoming* fit the textbook definition of intimidation."[96] For FIRE to urge ideological investigations where they knew no legitimate charges of harassment existed was an extraordinary betrayal of academic freedom.

FIRE was not the only one to abandon a commitment to civil liberties. Nat Hentoff, the famous advocate for freedom of expression, turned against academic freedom at Columbia and condemned the investigation as a "whitewashing." Hentoff denounced President Lee Bollinger for refusing to investigate the political views of professors, because Hentoff concludes that "curricula reflect the views and interpretations of the professors, and the evident biases of some of them." Hentoff only weakly applauded a "permanent committee" to investigate faculty bias, astonishingly because he believes it would not go far enough to control "biased professors." The solution Hentoff demanded is to hire "scholars who teach—not inculcate" (seeming to say that any faculty member who discusses politics in class should be banned from academia).[97]

The scope of the witch-hunt soon expanded. The New York City school system decided to ban professor Rashid Khalidi from training teachers because of his "past statements" in public criticizing Israel's government.[98] Khalidi was never accused of bias in his training class for teachers on Middle East geography. A high school teacher in the class reported, "His session was completely apolitical. It was basically geographic information."[99] Khalidi has been praised even by pro-Israel students who are critical of his colleagues. But Hentoff asserted that "the school board should have brought in a team teacher for the course so that it wouldn't be one-sided indoctrination."[100] Hentoff seemed to think that anyone critical of Israel's government could be banned from teaching unless there was another teacher to "balance" the "one-sided" views.

Student academic freedom is not threatened by students hearing ideas from professors whom they don't like. It is threatened by calls for the firing of professors and official investigative committees to threaten disciplinary action against them for their political ideas. If Hentoff believes that academic freedom is not threatened when professors face official investigations because they criticize a government, he needs to think back to the McCarthy era. Columbia University held a witch-hunt. What else can you call an investigative panel asking students to squeal on a targeted group of professors about their "offensive" ideas?

Columbia president Lee Bollinger, under extraordinary pressure to suppress speech, expressed support for sharp limits on academic freedom in a March 2005 speech he gave to the Association of the Bar of the City of New York: "We should not say that academic freedom means that there is no review within the university, no accountability, for the 'content' of our classes or our scholarship. There is a review, it does have consequences, and it does consider content." Bollinger promised that courses would be scrutinized to determine if they "explore the full range of the complexity of the subject."[101] Since no courses achieve that ideal, this standard would leave all Columbia faculty vulnerable to politically motivated attacks if the administration failed to support them. And Bollinger seemed to promise such scrutiny: "When there are lines to be drawn, we must and will be the ones to do it. Not outside actors. Not politicians, not pressure groups, not the media. Ours is and must remain a system of self-government."[102]

It is true that Bollinger strongly defended the right of academics to extramural speech: "We will not punish professors—or students—for the speech or ideas they express as part of public debate and public issues."[103] However, Bollinger has a far narrower conception of academic freedom in the classroom: "We should not accept the argument that we as teachers can do what we want because students are of sufficient good sense to know bias and indoctrination when they see it. This ignores the enormous differential in power between the professor and the student in a classroom setting."[104] According to Bollinger, faculty must step carefully around delicate student egos: "Given the deep emotions that people—students and professors both—bring to these highly charged discussions, faculty must show an extraordinary sensitivity to unlocking the fears and the emotional barriers that can cause a discussion to turn needlessly painful and substantively partial."[105]

Bollinger, by adopting the rhetoric of student victimization and powerlessness, endorsed the concept of restricting what professors can say in the classroom and supported banning them from expressing any idea that might be regarded as "bias" or "indoctrination," terms he has never defined. Bollinger's efforts were aimed at appeasing Columbia's critics, and they were happy to hear his attack on academic freedom in the classroom. Charles Jacobs, president of the David Project, said that Bollinger's comments about professors "were exactly what he should say."[106] The *New York Sun*, one of the leading voices advocating the firing of anti-Israel professors, editorialized that Bollinger's speech was "decidedly encouraging."[107]

The ad hoc grievance committee, established by Bollinger after an earlier committee did not uncover any wrongdoing, found no evidence of anti-Semitism among Columbia faculty, nor was there any evidence that students had been punished by receiving lower grades.[108] Under intense pressure to denounce someone, the ad hoc committee found only one issue "credible" of poor behavior by a professor: Deena Shanker's claim that Massad threatened to throw her out of his class. Two students in the class corroborated that this incident happened; three students said it didn't happen. Massad denied the incident, declaring, "I would never ask a student to leave my class."[109] It might be tempting to claim, given these disparate accounts, that someone is lying. But in fact there is a plausible scenario that explains all of the different memories.

According to one student quoted by the committee, Massad declared: "I will not stand by and let you sit in my classroom and deny atrocities."[110] But contrary to the ad hoc committee's claim that this student "corroborated" the allegation, the student's account actually refutes the committee's assertions and gives us a glimpse at what probably happened. There is a vast difference between saying "I will not stand by" and saying, as Shanker claimed, "If you're going to deny the atrocities being committed against Palestinians, then you can get out of my classroom!" It is perfectly legitimate for a professor to say that he will not stand by silently while a student says something that is false. In fact, it would be unethical for a professor not to respond to a student who denies atrocities. The "corroborating" account suggests that Massad never threatened to make a student leave his class, although it is understandable why Shanker misunderstood him.

The ad hoc committee concluded, "While we have no reason to believe that Professor Massad intended to expel Ms. Shanker from the classroom (she did not, in fact, leave the class), his rhetorical response to her query exceeded commonly accepted bounds by conveying that her question merited harsh public criticism."[111] Columbia's committee was completely wrong: To propose that professors should be banned from any "harsh public criticism" of students is a clear infringement of academic freedom. It may be rude, and it may be poor pedagogy, but no student should be exempt from criticism, and no committee should impose vague standards of decorum on intellectual debate.

Unfortunately, the campaign of misinformation that surrounded the Columbia witch-hunt greeted the ad hoc report. Instead of being seen for what it was—an illegitimate committee that falsely accused a professor of a minor error—the right denounced the process as a "whitewash." Even the *New York Times* editors joined the crusade against Columbia. To make up for their foolish decision to allow Columbia officials to dictate the terms of leaking a report to the *New York Times,* the editors decided to sacrifice the principles of academic freedom and praised the investigation at Columbia in an editorial ironically titled "Intimidation at Columbia."[112] The *New York Times* even demanded "more determination" and a much wider witch-hunt, where investigative committees would "proceed" to examine whether professors had any "bias" on the Palestinian/Israel conflict.[113]

One conservative student, Alexandra Polsky, denounced the ad hoc report: "It's a whitewash and it's offensive. There's a feeling on campus that there is a status quo of opinions, and if you dare challenge it, you have to be overly prepared to defend yourself."[114] One can just imagine the conservative Columbia students marching on the administration building, chanting, "We demand the right not to be overly prepared!"

Politicians attacked Columbia for failing to immediately fire Massad on the false charges against him. Congressman Anthony Weiner declared, "If someone feels intimidated, then intimidation has taken place," totally abandoning any sense of due process or logic.[115]

The ad hoc committee reported that "a member of the Columbia faculty was monitoring [Massad's] teaching and approaching his students, requesting them to provide information on his statements in class as part of a campaign against him."[116] Asking students to spy on a colleague in order to gather comments to smear him with is by far the worst conduct of any Columbia professor in the ad hoc committee report (albeit still not grounds for punishment), yet the committee refused to even name the professor.

The most abusive comment made by a Columbia professor throughout this controversy came from a pro-Israeli teacher. Moshe Rubin, a faculty member in Columbia's medical school, wrote in an e-mail to Mossad: "Go back to Arab land where Jew hating is condoned. Get the hell out of America. You are a disgrace and a pathetic typical Arab liar."[117] Rubin's vile comments should be protected speech, even though they are far worse than anything stated by the Columbia professors who were subjected to this witch-hunt. Imagine how Massad would have been treated if he had called someone a "typical Jew liar." Yet no politicians demanded Rubin's firing or sought investigative committees to examine his views.

As Arthur Hertzberg, who has taught at Columbia, noted: "My Arab students never tried to shut me up when I was teaching Zionism at Columbia. We ought to be ready to brook disagreements."[118] Columbia biology professor Robert Pollack said, "Many professors have offensive opinions. If the answer to whether you can have those opinions is no, then we're cooked as an institution."[119]

Students expressed their concern about the witch-hunt and its silencing effect on campus. Leeam Azulay-Yagev, an Israeli citizen and former soldier who took a class with Massad, declared: "According to my experience at this University with those professors, these accusations are not true."[120] Eric Posner, a Columbia student who is a former Israeli soldier, worried that the investigations would silence professors: "I'm concerned that my educational opportunities are being hurt. And they already have."[121] Massad decided not to teach his class on Palestinian and Israeli politics and societies out of fear that it would affect his tenure decision.[122]

Columbia put the Middle East Asian Languages and Cultures Department in receivership to exert greater administrative control over it.[123] A new committee will review complaints at Columbia, giving students a second system for complaining about their professors' views. Bollinger praised the new system because past student complaints "didn't get too far."[124] Vincent Blasi, chair of the committee, declared that the committee wanted students to "have an appropriate opportunity to register complaints when their classes are being taught in a politically charged way they think is inappropriate."[125] When students think a professor is politically "inappropriate," they already have plenty of ways to respond: They can speak out in class, they can tell the professor privately, they can even appear in a documentary denouncing a professor. But what violates academic freedom is to have committees conduct investigations of professors for "inappropriate" politics.

Columbia's rules allow for grievances in cases of "misuse of faculty authority to promote a political or social cause within an instructional setting."[126] By this rule, a professor teaching a class about China or Cuba could never criticize these totalitarian governments because this would promote a "political cause." A professor could not express almost any idea about politics or society. In fact, the Columbia rule makes it one of the worst speech codes in the country restricting the academic freedom of faculty and the right of students to hear political viewpoints. Yet the American Council of Trustees and Alumni specifically praised Columbia's speech code as a way to stop "political bias" by faculty.[127]

Students must have academic freedom. But academic freedom doesn't mean the right to shut up professors because their opinions offend someone. What the advocates of witch-hunts demand is a radically new concept of academic freedom. Under the guise of protecting students, the conservative movement is seeking to silence liberal views on campus.

CHAPTER THREE
David Horowitz's Crusade
for the "Academic Bill of Rights"

⊸

In the latest installment of the culture wars, right-wing activist David Horowitz has written his own declaration of war against political correctness: the "Academic Bill of Rights." Introduced as legislation in Congress on October 21, 2003, and proposed in many state legislatures, Horowitz's manifesto is part of a carefully planned assault on academia. The American Association of University Professors called it "a grave threat to fundamental principles of academic freedom."[1]

Horowitz's Center for the Study of Popular Culture (now modestly renamed the "David Horowitz Freedom Center") received more than $14.5 million (through 2004) from right-wing foundations to propel its war against the left on campus.[2] In 2002 Horowitz launched his "Campaign for Fairness and Inclusion in Higher Education" with the slogan, "You Can't Get a Good Education If They're Only Telling You Half the Story."[3] Horowitz demanded that administrators "conduct an inquiry into political bias in the hiring process for faculty and administrators" and the selection of commencement speakers and allocation of student fees. Horowitz also demanded that universities "adopt a code of conduct for faculty that ensures that classrooms will welcome diverse viewpoints and not be used for political indoctrination, which is a violation of students' academic freedom."[4] While much of Horowitz's crusade against American colleges has been ignored, the "Academic Bill of Rights" has proved popular with Horowitz's allies in the Republican Party.

On October 29, 2003, the Senate Health, Education, Labor, and Pensions Committee held a hearing on the alleged lack of "intellectual diversity" in

American colleges. Senator Lamar Alexander (R-TN), secretary of education for George Bush Sr., worried that "we've created in our country these wonderful colleges and universities with enormous freedom, yet on those campuses, too often all the discussion and thought goes one way. You're not honored and celebrated for having a different point of view."[5] Senator Judd Gregg (R-NH) chaired the hearing, and echoing Horowitz's famous phrase, Gregg proclaimed, "How can students be liberally educated if they are only receiving part of the story?"[6]

Horowitz has made even greater inroads in the House of Representatives. In June 2003 Horowitz met with Jack Kingston (R-GA), the vice chair of the House Republican Conference, and then House majority leader Tom DeLay (R-TX), who had given a copy of Horowitz's book *The Art of Political War: How Republicans Can Fight to Win* to every Republican in Congress. At an October 21, 2003, press conference, Horowitz's employees and student supporters stood with Republican leaders in Congress to introduce his "Academic Bill of Rights" as legislation, and in 2005 Horowitz met with the new House majority leader, John Boehner (R-OH), who publicly praised the Academic Bill of Rights and promised to make it part of the Higher Education Authorization Act.[7]

But most accounts of the Academic Bill of Rights have told the public only "half the story." Behind Horowitz's campaign is a politically motivated assault on academic freedom, misuse of statistics, and a fundamental misunderstanding of the academic freedom principles that Horowitz invokes to promote his cause.

Horowitz's National Crusade

Horowitz's Academic Bill of Rights is one of the most widespread efforts ever made to legislate changes at American colleges. In addition to Congress, Horowitz's legislation has been proposed in twenty-seven states, including Arizona, California, Colorado, Florida, Georgia, Indiana, Kansas, Kentucky, Maine, Massachusetts, Michigan, Minnesota, Missouri, Montana, New York, North Carolina, Oklahoma, Ohio, Oregon, Pennsylvania, South Dakota, Tennessee, Texas, Utah, Virginia, Washington, and West Virginia.[8]

An Academic Bill of Rights resolution passed the Georgia Senate on March 24, 2004, by a 41–5 vote.[9] In 2004 the American Legislative Exchange Council (ALEC), a right-wing advocacy group, adopted a model statute based on the Academic Bill of Rights and promised to help Horowitz enact it as the law in every state. Senator Jeff Sessions (R-AL) agreed to sponsor an Academic Bill of Rights resolution in the U.S. Senate.

In Washington, the state legislature considered House Bill 3185, which would impose the Academic Bill of Rights on private as well as public colleges unless they explicitly reject a commitment to academic freedom.[10] In

California, Senate Bill 1335 was introduced by State Senator Bill Morrow who declared, "We're sliding into a medieval 'Dark Age' mentality that is actively hostile toward truth, learning and free speech."[11]

Horowitz is also encouraging individual campuses to enact the bill. Utah State University, Princeton University, and Occidental College in California have passed versions of the Academic Bill of Rights, and there have been efforts to do the same at Cornell University, the University of North Florida, University of Montana, Northwestern University, Roger Williams University in Rhode Island, and many more institutions.[12]

However, many of these institutions that passed the Academic Bill of Rights had no formal complaints at all about political bias. Lizzie Miller, head of the Republican students at Middle Tennessee State University, cosponsored a resolution endorsing the Academic Bill of Rights that was approved by the student government in March 2005. Miller argued that the Academic Bill of Rights is necessary because of the harm caused by professors expressing political opinions: "Not only do you feel that you're wasting your time and money, but you're feeling discriminated against or uncomfortable." But Middle Tennessee State University officials reported that despite having a grade appeal procedure, no student had ever complained about receiving a lower grade because of political or religious beliefs.[13]

Horowitz realized that the traditional protections of academic freedom would prevent his goal of banning political expression in the classroom. Horowitz made a brilliant innovation: Use the concept of student academic freedom to undermine faculty academic freedom. A *Wall Street Journal* editorial praising Horowitz noted, "Academic freedom has long been a battle cry on campus, but what makes this push distinctive is the student angle—a reflection, no doubt, of the increasing discomfort of conservative students, many of whom believe that they suffer in the classroom for their views."[14] By asserting that students have equal claim to academic freedom with their professors, Horowitz would give students a powerful stick to wield over faculty. Any bias alleged by a student could result in professors being hauled before an ideological tribunal to evaluate their teaching techniques. Although this poses a severe threat to faculty academic freedom, Horowitz justifies it by appealing to a new concept of student academic freedom.

Horowitz created a front group called Students for Academic Freedom (SAF), which claims to have established chapters on more than 150 campuses around the country in order to "appeal to governors, state legislators, boards of trustees and other appropriate officials and bodies to write the Academic Bill of Rights into educational policy and law."[15]

While Horowitz is using student academic freedom to attack faculty academic freedom, his approach threatens the academic freedom of all. For example, Horowitz has declared that universities should be banned from asking incoming students to read Barbara Ehrenreich's highly regarded book, *Nickel and Dimed*. According to Horowitz, "At thirteen universities a single book, which happened to be a socialist attack on American society, was required of all incoming freshmen. This is not education; it is indoctrination. And it is expressly forbidden under the principles of academic freedom first articulated by the American Association of University Professors in 1915 and to which all universities ostensibly subscribe."[16] The idea that the AAUP would demand the banning of a book is perhaps Horowitz's most amazing distortion of reality. Horowitz frequently uses AAUP principles to justify his crusade, distinguishing him from earlier attacks on academic freedom that were more honestly opposed to the concept. But Horowitz fundamentally misrepresents AAUP principles.

Horowitz's Misunderstanding of the AAUP

Horowitz has denounced the AAUP in the harshest terms, declaring that it is a "Stalinist organization."[17] Horowitz's national field director for SAF, Bradley Shipp, declared: "The AAUP is out to destroy education as we know it, and in its place will be a monolithic totalitarian university system that ends all debate on campuses."[18]

Horowitz denounces the AAUP because, he claims, "The AAUP was entirely absent from the battle against speech codes in the 1990s—the most dramatic infringement of free speech rights on college campuses since the McCarthy era" and a time "when university administrations in the 1980s and 1990s instituted 'speech codes' to punish students for politically incorrect remarks. These codes imposed penalties on students for using words like 'handicapped' instead of 'challenged.'"[19] But the AAUP issued a policy statement against speech codes in 1992, declaring that "no idea can be banned or forbidden," and that "rules that ban or punish speech based upon its content cannot be justified."[20] As for Horowitz's ludicrous claim that students were punished by campus speech codes for using the word "handicapped," he does not cite a single instance when this has ever happened on a college campus.

Despite his attacks on the AAUP, Horowitz claims: "I lifted my entire agenda in this matter word for word from the AAUP's own statements on Academic Tenure and Academic Freedom. Word for word."[21] In reality, much of the language in the Academic Bill of Rights is invented by Horowitz himself. But what Horowitz doesn't point out is that he selectively lifted parts of his Academic Bill of Rights from outdated statements that were replaced decades ago because the older statements had been misused to undermine academic freedom.

Horowitz admits that he was "going back to its General Report of 1915 in which it warned that there was a difference between 'indoctrination' and 'education.'"[22] Horowitz turns this into an absolute ban on indoctrination, a term so vague that the AAUP abandoned it completely in adopting the canonical 1940 Statement of Principles.

Horowitz argues that "if a teacher lectures for five minutes or 50 minutes on the Iraq war or the policies of President Bush in a class whose subject matter is not the Iraq war, or international relations, or presidential politics, that teacher is abusing students' academic rights."[23] If, as Horowitz argues, classrooms must be politics-free zones, then professors would be obligated to silence students as well as themselves in order to prevent political discussions. Even if we ignore the terrible impact on faculty academic freedom, the Academic Bill of Rights would violate student academic freedom.

Horowitz regards "academic freedom" as a useful rhetorical tool, not a principle he believes in. Horowitz is fully aware of how to manipulate language for propaganda purposes: "I encourage them to use the language that the left has deployed so effectively in behalf of its own agendas. Radical professors have created a 'hostile learning environment' for conservative students. There is a lack of 'intellectual diversity' on college faculties and in academic classrooms. The conservative viewpoint is 'under-represented' in the curriculum and on its reading lists. The university should be an 'inclusive' and intellectually 'diverse' community."[24] For Horowitz, "academic freedom" is just another liberal term to be manipulated in the war against the left.

Horowitz's Academic Bill of Rights does not profess a moral value about what teachers "should" and "should not" do; instead, it declares what faculty "shall" and "shall not" do, and establishes it as a right enforced with a grievance procedure imposed by legislative order. Horowitz wrote that his goal is "to end political advocacy by professors in their classrooms."[25]

Because the AAUP's 1940 statement was misinterpreted so often to justify punishment for political comments by professors, the AAUP and the American Association of Colleges and Universities issued Interpretive Comments in 1970 that clarified this point: "The intent of this statement is not to discourage what is 'controversial.' Controversy is at the heart of the free academic inquiry, which the entire statement is designed to foster. The passage serves to underscore the need for teachers to avoid persistently intruding material which has no relation to their subject."[26] Yet Students for Academic Freedom falsely claims that the AAUP bans "introducing controversial material that has no relation to the subject of the course (ex: making remarks on political issues in a math or science class; lecturing on the war in a class that is not about the war or about international relations)."[27] By removing the crucial "persistently" requirement and making the rule enforceable, Horowitz makes it possible for any statement, consuming a trivial amount of time, to be punished. As Horowitz puts it, "no rants against the Iraq war in English class anymore."[28] An AAUP principle that was specifically modified in order to defend "controversy" in the classroom is distorted by Horowitz as a ban on controversial comments, and then the AAUP is condemned by him for "bad faith" in objecting to his Orwellian distortion of the AAUP's policies.

In misinterpreting the AAUP's guidelines for professors, the SAF Handbook declares that "violations" of the controversy rule include "assigning required readings or texts covering only one side of controversial issues (e.g., texts that are only pro- or anti-affirmative action)."[29] Considering that nearly every article or book has a one-sided view, any professor could face discipline for any reading. Ironically, Horowitz's own writings could not be taught in a class by this narrow standard he espouses.

The Flaws of the Academic Bill of Rights

Horowitz often complains that the opponents of his Academic Bill of Rights have never criticized the actual text of his proposal. But there are many problems with the wording of the Academic Bill of Rights. Its vague language and potential for abuse make it the greatest current threat to academic freedom in America. When grievance procedures are attached to each part of the Academic Bill of Rights (as occurs in several legislative proposals supported by Horowitz), the language is extraordinarily dangerous, as an analysis of each provision shows: "1. All faculty shall be hired, fired, promoted and granted tenure on the basis of their competence and appropriate knowledge in the field of their expertise and, in the humanities, the social sciences, and the arts, with a view toward fostering a plurality of methodologies and perspectives. No faculty shall be hired or fired or denied promotion or tenure on the basis of his or her political or religious beliefs."[30]

Horowitz has repeatedly denied that the Academic Bill of Rights suggests any kind of affirmative action for conservatives, pointing to the last line of this provision against discrimination: "There is not a word in the Academic Bill of Rights that suggests the imposition of political standards on the university."[31] But Horowitz is wrong. Compelling faculty to be hired based on competence AND plurality of perspectives indicates that this provision could be used to push affirmative action for conservatives rather than merit alone. Why should there only be a plurality of views in humanities, social sciences, and the arts? Since these are regarded as the most liberal fields, it seems obvious that Horowitz is trying to give preference to conservatives in hiring. If this provision was imposed upon universities, then trustees, judges, or legislators could punish colleges for failing to give preferences to conservative scholars.

"2. No faculty member will be excluded from tenure, search and hiring committees on the basis of their political or religious beliefs."[32] This provision is contradictory to other policies of the Academic Bill of Rights. What if some professor thinks that conservatives (or liberals) should never be hired? Should such a faculty member automatically be given a place on a committee, even if doing so would violate the nondiscrimination rules professed by Horowitz?

"3. Students will be graded solely on the basis of their reasoned answers and appropriate knowledge of the subjects and disciplines they study, not on the basis of their political or religious beliefs."[33] This provision fails to make it clear that political and religious beliefs are not all equally true. A student may have a religious belief that God created the world, and it is only 4,000 years old. A student may have a political belief that the Holocaust is a myth. Such students might know their subject and give reasons for their answers while still asserting plainly wrong facts, and then think that this provision protects them from getting a bad grade for espousing their beliefs as the truth on a test.

"4. Curricula and reading lists in the humanities and social sciences should reflect the uncertainty and unsettled character of all human knowledge in these areas by providing students with dissenting sources and viewpoints where appropriate. While teachers are and should be free to pursue their own findings and perspectives in presenting their views, they should consider and make their students aware of other viewpoints. Academic disciplines should welcome a diversity of approaches to unsettled questions."[34] Once again, Horowitz limits his Academic Bill of Rights only to the social sciences and humanities, apparently because he doesn't want to encourage dissent in more conservative fields. All of this language is very vague and potentially dangerous to academic freedom if it was ever imposed and enforced (although this provision, unlike some others, uses the word "should"). However, some legislative versions of this provision restrict academic freedom by converting the "should" to a much more repressive "will."

"5. Exposing students to the spectrum of significant scholarly viewpoints on the subjects examined in their courses is a major responsibility of faculty. Faculty will not use their courses for the purpose of political, ideological, religious or antireligious indoctrination."[35] Because "indoctrination" is never defined by Horowitz, this is one of the most dangerous parts of the Academic Bill of Rights, and could easily infringe upon academic freedom. California state senator Bill Morrow declared that in order to define "indoctrination" in the Academic Bill of Rights, "It's up to common sense and Webster's."[36] So how does Webster's define "indoctrination"? "1: to instruct esp. in fundamentals or rudiments: TEACH; 2: to teach the beliefs and doctrines of a particular group."[37] Horowitz believes that any expression of political views by a professor amounts to a kind of indoctrination. This could put an extreme limit on the freedom of both teachers and students. Troy Hyde, state chairman of the Arizona Federation of College Republicans, called it "indoctrination" because an Arizona State University (ASU) professor in his sociology 101 class in spring 2006 expressed the opinion that Karl Marx was "grossly misunderstood." According to Hyde, "The office of a professor isn't a license to preach on a message. ASU has government funds and it is not a position of a government employee to favor one side or the other. It's a way of indoctrination."[38]

"6. Selection of speakers, allocation of funds for speakers' programs and other student activities will observe the principles of academic freedom and promote intellectual pluralism."[39] Again, there is no definition of this claim or discussion of the enforcement mechanism. Intellectual pluralism is a good thing, but no one knows what it means. If one-fourth of the students are creationists, should 25 percent of the funding for speakers on biology be devoted to antiscientific views? This provision is also antidemocratic, since it could empower administrators (and perhaps judges) to overrule student decisions in the false name of pluralism. At some colleges, administrators have banned speakers on the grounds that a speaker with a similar point of view has already been heard on campus, and therefore "intellectual pluralism" requires censorship by the administration.[40]

"7. An environment conducive to the civil exchange of ideas being an essential component of a free university, the obstruction of invited campus speakers, destruction of campus literature or other effort to obstruct this exchange will not be tolerated."[41] Horowitz's proposal is too vague and broad, particularly the reference to "other effort to obstruct this exchange." If any "effort to obstruct" will not be tolerated, then someone who asks a question without permission or boos a speaker during a lecture could potentially be punished, even if there is no infringement on the right of others to hear a speaker. Horowitz himself could be banned from campuses on the grounds that his intemperate views obstruct "civil" exchange.

"8. Knowledge advances when individual scholars are left free to reach their own conclusions about which methods, facts, and theories have been validated by research. Academic institutions and professional societies formed to advance knowledge within an area of research, maintain the integrity of the research process, and organize the professional lives of related researchers serve as indispensable venues within which scholars circulate research findings and debate their interpretation. To perform these functions adequately, academic institutions and professional societies should maintain a posture of organizational neutrality with respect to the substantive disagreements that divide researchers on questions within, or outside, their fields of inquiry."[42] This section particularly violates the academic freedom of faculty and associations to collectively speak out on any issue. Ironically, if the Academic Bill of Rights was adopted by a campus, then this provision would ban a university from endorsing the Academic Bill of Rights itself, since it divides researchers. Universities could also be banned from lobbying, since some scholars might disagree with increased government funding of higher education. Nor is it clear how an Academic

Bill of Rights can ban an international scholarly society from taking a political stand. Would universities be required to ban professional societies from their campuses if the group ever violated this rule of neutrality? A collective statement does not infringe upon the right of individuals to dissent from it, and it is a violation of academic freedom to prohibit universities or the participants in them from making collective judgments, even if one agreed with Horowitz's sentiments.

Of course, any analysis of Horowitz's Academic Bill of Rights is highly speculative, because no one knows what it means or how it would be enforced. That is precisely the problem: A vague document could allow virtually any kind of faculty expression to be punished, and no due process mechanisms are specified to address these controversies.

Horowitz writes, "This bad faith of the academic community explains the need for legislative redress. If the universities will not enforce their own academic freedom guidelines, but are willing to let professors abuse the academic freedom of their students, then legislators have a fiduciary responsibility to step in and see that this situation is remedied."[43] Here Horowitz finally admits what he has denied for so long. The Academic Bill of Rights is meant to impose these guidelines and grievance procedures on professors at the peril of their jobs, and Horowitz also believes that legislators should intervene to force colleges to punish the professors who dare to criticize the government.

Horowitz's Legislative Crusade

Horowitz first proposed an Academic Bill of Rights at a July 2003 conference of the American Legislative Exchange Council, a conservative policy organization for Republican state legislators. Horowitz claims, "I never intended to take my Bill of Rights to legislatures, but did so after I found when I approached university administrators their response was universally to blow me off."[44] According to Horowitz, "The sequence of these submissions is important. The Bill of Rights was submitted in the first place to universities rather than legislatures. When it encountered a stone wall in the academic world, and only then, did I take it to the legislatures."[45] This is not true. Horowitz admits that at the time he had approached only one group with his plan: the New York Board of Regents. He had never approached any group of academics to ask for a university to adopt the idea before asking legislators to impose it.[46]

Yet Horowitz declared, "I have turned to legislatures as a last resort."[47] According to Horowitz, "It took a lot of patience for me to go through these motions with university officials because I had already guessed that administrators would not act in the face of determined faculty opposition, and I already knew that that this opposition was inevitable."[48] Horowitz knew from the start that he was going "through these motions"; he knew from the very beginning that he wanted to put the Academic Bill of Rights into law, and he spoke to a few trustees in order to claim that "this left me with only one option, which was to turn to the court of last resort: legislatures."[49] There are literally thousands of colleges Horowitz never contacted to urge them to adopt an Academic Bill of Rights before he sought legislation.

Far from lobbying politicians as a last resort, the "mission and strategy" for Students for Academic Freedom declares, "Students for Academic Freedom clubs at public universities will appeal to governors, state legislators, boards of trustees and other appropriate officials and bodies to write the Academic Bill of Rights into educational policy and law."[50]

The Battle for Colorado

The Academic Bill of Rights is the story of how David Horowitz, pretending to stand up for "student rights" and moral conduct by professors, led a crusade to have legislators force every college in the country to adopt the most coercive system of grievance procedures and investigations of liberal professors ever proposed in America.

Horowitz's bill (or variations of it) has been introduced in more than half of the states as well as the U.S. Congress, including California Senate Bill 5, Massachusetts, Ohio Senate Bill 24, Washington HB 1991, Florida HB 837, Maryland HB 964, Pennsylvania, Indiana House Bill 1531, Tennessee House Bill 432 and Senate Bill 1117, Maine LD 1194, and Rhode Island Senate Bill 392. But Colorado became the first state in Horowitz's efforts to impose the "Academic Bill of Rights" on higher education. In June 2003 Horowitz came to Colorado and met with twenty-three Colorado Republicans, including Governor Bill Owens and State Senate President John Andrews. After his meeting in Colorado was revealed months later, Horowitz defended it as nothing out of the ordinary: "My office had made an appointment with the governor, and I walked in the front door of his office to spend a half hour with him, a privilege of ordinary citizens."[51] While few "ordinary citizens" from Colorado get to meet with the governor, a far-right activist from California was invited to present his plan to help Republicans exert more control over academia.

Horowitz claimed, "I have no idea what Owens or Colorado legislators are proposing in their efforts to deal with the troubles on our college campuses."[52] In reality, Horowitz knew exactly what these top Republicans wanted to do. Christopher Sanders, a Republican staffer who helped arrange the June 12, 2003, meeting between Horowitz and the Colorado Republicans about the Academic Bill of Rights, revealed: "They had the discussion ... on how to put teeth into it, to make them accountable to the legislature and the governor, how to create it in such a way that it was enforceable and that the schools had to do it, so it wasn't just a nice warm-fuzzy statement. . . . The discussion involved their funding on an annual basis, when their budget is renewed."[53]

Yet the Academic Bill of Rights that Horowitz is pushing declares, "Nor shall legislatures impose any such orthodoxy through its control of the university budget." Horowitz is vague about the enforcement of his Bill of Rights, but he has publicly declared, "Personally, I hope it's tied to funding."[54] Horowitz thinks legislators should intimidate colleges that allow faculty to express political views by cutting funding, in hypocritical opposition to the very words of his own Academic Bill of Rights.

In Colorado, four frightened college presidents agreed to a "memorandum of understanding" with the legislature in order to fend off the Academic Bill of Rights. The appeasement mostly provided Horowitz with a symbolic victory and sets the stage for future efforts at political intimidation of Colorado's public colleges. One provision declares, "Every student should be comfortable in the right to listen critically, and challenge a professor's opinions."[55] This may be the first time students have ever been given the explicit right to feel "comfortable." Considering that Horowitz believes that any public expression of liberal political views by a professor makes conservatives "uncomfortable" to speak up in class, this provision could justify a crackdown on academic freedom if it was ever enforced. That is precisely what conservatives hope will happen. Former state senate president Andrews reported in 2006 that "progress is being made on implementing the memorandum ... including grievance procedures for students who are propagandized or politically harassed by faculty."[56] Andrews has also revealed an interesting fact about the Academic Bill of Rights: Republicans in Colorado never had enough votes to get it passed by the legislature.[57] In fact, every victory heralded by Horowitz has come only when administrators and leaders of education organizations (including the AAUP) gave in and tried to appease him with vaguely worded agreements. In Georgia, after "Horowitz made himself look like a fool before a legislative committee," academics nevertheless agreed to a watered-down version of the Academic Bill of Rights approved by the Georgia Senate, the only state resolution Horowitz has ever been able to pass.[58]

In 2005, fearing that Horowitz had succeeded in twisting the public debate, the AAUP joined twenty-six other national higher education groups led by the American Council on Education (ACE) to endorse a bland statement praising "intellectual pluralism."[59] This statement didn't appease Horowitz or his allies. It was a gift to them. Horowitz called it "a victory for our campaign."[60] According to Sara Dogan, head of Horowitz's Students for Academic Freedom, "That was pretty huge for us."[61] The Association for College Trustees and Alumni is now demanding that colleges implement and enforce this statement. And worst of all, the statement was incorporated into the Higher Education Reauthorization Act, where ACE refused to oppose it (but a House committee voted it in down in 2007).

Compromising Academic Freedom in Ohio

One of the worst compromises occurred in Ohio. State senator Larry Mumper introduced the Academic Bill of Rights in Ohio so that his dream of the perfect university could be achieved: "If the system were fair, Rush Limbaugh and Sean Hannity would be tenured professors somewhere."[62] Of course, if Rush and Sean ever went to graduate school and then took a massive pay cut to teach, they might have difficulty speaking under Mumper's rules. When asked what "controversial matter" Mumper wanted to have banned from classrooms, he responded, "Religion and politics, those are the main things."[63]

The Ohio law was an example of how dangerous the Academic Bill of Rights is, since it would compel all colleges in the state not only to adopt the Academic Bill of Rights as formal policy but also to "adopt a grievance procedure by which a student, faculty member, or instructor may seek redress for an alleged violation of any of the rights specified by the institution's policy."[64]

Ohio's bill was even more dangerous at infringing upon the autonomy of private colleges. The bill would require "the board of trustees or other governing authority of each private institution of higher education" to adopt the Academic Bill of Rights and the grievance procedures to enforce each part of the bill. And one part of the Ohio bill was a ban on religious "indoctrination."[65] So Horowitz's Academic Bill of Rights in Ohio would require private religious colleges to establish a grievance procedure to allow students to stop religious indoctrination.

The Ohio bill contained other strange provisions, such as this: "Faculty and instructors shall not use their courses or their positions for the purpose of political, ideological, religious, or antireligious indoctrination."[66] Although the meaning of "indoctrination" is vague with regard to courses, the phrase "their positions" is even more mysterious. It seems to mean that faculty cannot make public comments identifying their academic positions that might be defined as indoctrination, a vast expansion of Horowitz's restrictions far beyond the classroom.

Considering that the bill decrees, "curricula and reading lists in the humanities and social studies shall respect all human knowledge in these areas and provide students with dissenting sources and viewpoints,"[67] this would mean that a history professor would be in violation of the Academic Bill of Rights for failing to provide students with Holocaust denier or pro-slavery viewpoints. Likewise, an economics professor would be obliged to offer procommunist perspectives to every subject.

In fact, the Ohio bill would compel a near-total moral relativism in the humanities and social sciences, since it requires "respect" for "all human knowledge," even the most thoroughly discredited theories.[68] Indeed, a professor who criticizes a student's beliefs or assigns any reading that denigrates another point of view (such as almost anything written by Horowitz) could conceivably be brought up on charges of failing to "respect" all "human knowledge." When a legislature starts to dictate balance in viewpoints and "respect" for all views in the reading lists of individual classes, it is going much too far toward government control of higher education.

Any student could also file a grievance against a college if it violates "organizational neutrality," an undefined term that could include any lobbying for legislation by administrators to help the university. By a strict reading of the bill, a panel at a religious college about that denomination's views would violate the Academic Bill of Rights if it did not include "a diversity of opinions," such as the atheist or Satanist point of view.[69]

Horowitz proclaimed in 2004, "There is no enforcement proposed in the Academic Bill of Rights. This would be up to the institutions that adopt it."[70] Horowitz even declared, "My Academic Bill of Rights explicitly excludes private institutions," despite the laws proposed in Ohio, Tennessee, and other states imposing it (and requiring grievance procedures) on private institutions that were enthusiastically supported by Horowitz.[71]

Rather than fighting this threat to academic freedom, Ohio's college presidents caved in for one simple reason: money. Representative Mumper warned that funding cuts for universities were "always in the back" of his mind: "Why should we, as fairly moderate to conservative legislators, continue to support universities that turn out students who rail against the very policies that their parents voted us in for?"[72]

As a compromise to momentarily dismiss the legislation, fifteen presidents at public universities agreed that "any members of the university community that believe they have been treated unfairly on academic matters must have access to an institutional process to consider their grievance."[73] In the view of Horowitz and his students, to be "treated unfairly" could include being assigned a "biased" reading list or being exposed to political opinions. By explicitly requiring "campus grievance procedures to recognize and foster respect for diversity of ideas," this means that antiharassment rules would be expanded to ban political harassment. Ohio's public colleges will open the door for Horowitz's campaign to silence political debate on campus.

Appeasing Horowitz and other enemies of academic freedom is not a wise tactic. Horowitz has trumpeted these compromises as a victory for his crusade, and these deals will allow students to file grievances against professors whose views they dislike. And if colleges fail to intimidate faculty, then it is easy enough for right-wing legislators to reintroduce the Academic Bill of Rights to enforce the "right" of students not to hear controversial ideas.

The threat of budget cuts by Horowitz's allies is not an imaginary danger. State government spending on higher education per student dropped dramatically from \$7,124 in 2001 to \$5,825 in 2005, the lowest level in twenty-five years.[74] The Academic Bill of Rights is linked to these budget cuts. Out of the fourteen states with budget cuts since 2001 larger than the national average of negative 9 percent, 50 percent of them have had the Academic Bill of Rights introduced in their state, including Georgia (which was the only state to pass Horowitz's resolution and has had the largest reductions), Pennsylvania, Florida, California, Maine, Colorado, and Ohio (the two states that agreed to compromise with Horowitz).[75] By contrast, the Academic Bill of Rights legislation is listed by Horowitz in only 22 percent of the states above the national average in funding changes since 2001.[76]

Academic Freedom in Florida

One of the best examples of the repressive aims behind the Academic Bill of Rights can be seen in Florida. Its sponsor, Representative Dennis Baxley, repeating Horowitz's distortions about academia, decried "niches of totalitarianism" on campus and contended that there are thirty liberal professors for every conservative one.[77] Baxley argued, "There is this kind of quiet prejudice that the leftist person or guest on campus gets the major auditorium and all the questions are screened and the conservative guest gets the little corner of the Fine Arts room and gets the open mike so everyone can let go on him."[78]

Baxley also complained about who was invited to speak at the University of Florida: "When they spent \$50,000 to bring in Michael Moore to vomit all over the president's record, they didn't ask you what they wanted." Never mind that the University of Florida's speakers bureau brought in Republican New York governor George Pataki to speak and tried to schedule Sean Hannity (who backed out). Baxley seemed more concerned about whether a critic of the Republicans had been allowed to talk.[79]

When the University of Florida appointed a coordinator for gay and lesbian affairs, Baxley threatened to cut the university's funding: "When I see things like UF rushing to have the first coordinator for gay and lesbian academia, it makes it difficult for me to come up here and support giving more taxpayer dollars to institutions with these kinds of values."[80]

Baxley has declared, "Some of us need to wake up and realize we're being asked to finance a culture war. And we feel like we're financing the wrong side."[81] Baxley even called upon wealthy donors to universities to require that colleges fire the "enemies of democracy and capitalism" before donating money.[82]

Baxley's support for the Academic Bill of Rights is driven by his own experience in the 1970s at Florida State University. Baxley complains that an anthropology professor "did a tirade" in class supporting evolution and opposing creationism, saying: "Evolution is a fact. There's no missing link. I don't want to hear any talk about intelligent design and if you don't like that, there's the door."[83] Baxley wants to protect students today who believe in creationism so that they will not "get blasted" like he did.[84] The *Palm Beach Post* reported, "Baxley said this bill would prevent an astronomy professor from telling students they shouldn't believe in God because the universe was created through the big bang theory, not a divine entity."[85]

Horowitz denied that the Academic Bill of Rights "would require the teaching of creationism in biology classes. It would not. It specifically requires that students be 'made aware of the spectrum of significant scholarly opinion.' The last time I checked, the Bible was neither a scientific nor a scholarly text."[86] But many of Horowitz's allies disagree with his interpretation, and some fundamentalists consider the Bible both scholarly and scientifically accurate. In 2007, the Missouri House passed HB 213, protecting the viewpoint of biblical inerrancy, even though it conflicts with scientific reality. The bill would compel colleges to "include intellectual diversity concerns in the institution's guidelines on teaching and program development, and such concerns shall include but not be limited to the protection of religious freedom including the viewpoint that the Bible is inerrant."[87] Creationism is a perfect example of why imposing "diversity" of ideas by legislative fiat is a dangerous plan. Who should decide what is scientific: Politicians and students, or science professors?

Horowitz has had nothing but praise for Baxley, "a courageous Florida legislator who ... has had firsthand experience of the intolerance and lack of professionalism of many of today's faculty who confuse their classrooms with soap boxes."[88] Horowitz, who is agnostic, might personally disagree with creationism, but he is more than willing to embrace Republican allies who want to force it upon colleges and universities.

Baxley even summoned Florida's public university presidents to a hearing, showing them a cartoon in the University of Florida's student newspaper that depicted Baxley behind a monkey on the evolutionary chain. Baxley asked the presidents to protect conservatives like him who might be ridiculed by the "liberal elite" on campus, presumably by suppressing freedom of the student press. Carolyn Roberts, chair of the Florida state board of governors, ordered university presidents to work with Baxley, reminding them that Baxley sits on a committee controlling education spending and has a lot of clout.[89]

The Florida bill passed the House Education and Innovation Committee six to two and has also been introduced in the senate, but it stalled after Governor Jeb Bush (who had called Horowitz a "fighter for freedom") withdrew his support for the bill.[90] The Florida Department of Education estimated that state colleges would need to spend $4.2 million a year in lawyers' fees just to deal with the complaints about the Academic Bill of Rights, until political pressure from Governor Jeb Bush forced the agency to rescind its findings.[91]

Enforcing the Academic Bill of Rights

The most dangerous part of the Academic Bill of Rights is the uncertainty about how it will be enforced. The Academic Bill of Rights uses the unproven claim of political discrimination to allow outside forces to enter the ivory tower, where they can exercise near-unchecked power over academic decisions and impose conservative ideas on higher education.

Horowitz has declared, "There is no enforcement proposed in the Academic Bill of Rights. This would be up to the institutions that adopt it."[92] Horowitz added, "No one is suggesting that an outside authority make these judgments."[93] Horowitz claimed, "In Ohio I proposed in my testimony that the universities step forward to provide a grievance process that would implement their own existing policy. What could be less heavy-handed than that?"[94] In reality, the Ohio bill compelled all public and private colleges in the state to adopt grievance procedures for every part of the Academic Bill of Rights. What could be more heavy-handed than that? Horowitz reported that in Ohio "the university itself has already adopted the principles of this Bill; the problem is that they will not enforce them."[95] Here Horowitz reveals that the goal of the Academic Bill of Rights all along has been enforcement, even though he omitted enforcement from it originally in order to disguise his true intentions.

Horowitz claims, "I have never sponsored legislating control of universities ... all of the legislation is resolutions."[96] He wrote, "The legislation I eventually sought was exclusively in the form of resolutions, which lacked statutory 'teeth' to enforce their provisions."[97] This is false. Maine LD 1194 required that colleges "shall adopt a grievance procedure by which a student or faculty member may seek redress of grievance for an alleged violation of a right" in the Academic Bill of Rights.[98] Minnesota Senate Bill 1988 required, "The board of trustees of each state institution of higher education shall, and the Board of Regents of the University of Minnesota is requested to, adopt a grievance procedure by which a student or faculty member may seek redress for an alleged violation of any of the rights" in the Academic Bill of Rights.[99] New York Assembly Bill A10098 required that all governing boards of an institution of higher education "shall adopt a grievance procedure by which a student or faculty member may seek redress of grievance for an alleged violation of a right specified" in the Academic Bill of Rights.[100] North Carolina Senate Bill 1139 required the University of North Carolina campus to "adopt a policy recognizing that the students, faculty, and instructors of the institution have the following rights" taken from the Academic Bill of Rights.[101] Tennessee House Bill 432 and Senate Bill 1117 not only would impose the Academic Bill of Rights on all private and public colleges, but it would take away the authority of colleges to enforce it. The Tennessee higher education commission is given the power to "develop, monitor, and enforce a statewide institutional grievance procedure by which a student may seek a redress of grievance for an alleged violation of any of the rights specified in this act," and the higher education commissioner is "authorized to promulgate rules and regulations to effectuate the purposes of this act."[102] This means that a politically appointed higher education commission would set and enforce all the rules related to the Academic Bill of Rights for every college in the state.

Sara Dogan, Horowitz's national campus director, wrote a letter to the *Columbus Dispatch* praising in particular the grievance procedures imposed by Senate Bill 24.[103] Dogan complained, "There are no grievance procedures available to students whose professors have failed to live up to the standards set for them. The Academic Bill of Rights would remedy this disconnect between existing policy and practice."[104] Dogan argued that "the problem with existing regulations" is that "they are not observed or enforced." She declared, "The academic community ... should support our efforts to see that these existing rights are enforced."[105] After a Florida House Committee approved Bill 837, Students for Academic Freedom celebrated the bill, on the grounds that existing rules with similar language "are seldom enforced."[106]

Horowitz specifically criticized the AAUP's ethical guidelines for professors because they "are not accompanied by grievance procedures."[107] Horowitz noted, "It is crucial that grievance machinery for problems associated with academic freedom issues be put in place and that students have clearly delineated academic freedom rights."[108] Horowitz wants professors fired for talking about politics: "A professor who violates the standards of his profession will be (or ought to be) subject to disciplinary measures, including possible termination, for breach of contract."[109]

It is dangerous for any legislature (or any university) to impose a certain pedagogical style on all professors, even if it might be a good one. A ban on talking about politics in the classrooms might stop the occasionally idiotic comment by a professor, just as a ban on lecturing might stop some professors who fail to engage students. But a ban on political speech will also silence the professors who help engage and educate students by doing a good job of raising political issues in class.

We need to encourage more discussions about politics on campus. A 2006 poll found that only 3 percent of those aged eighteen to twenty-four (the main college population) get their best information about current events from the classroom, a dramatic decline from 21 percent of those aged twelve through seventeen (the main high school age group).[110] Warning that young people "are largely disconnected from current events and issues," retired Supreme Court justice Sandra Day O'Connor and former Colorado governor Roy Romer recently called for better civics education because "a healthy democracy depends on the participation of citizens, and that participation is learned behavior."[111] Even the conservative Intercollegiate Studies Institute is concerned about the lack of civic education and knowledge of history and current affairs among college students.[112] At a time when thinkers like Harvard president Derek Bok worry about how colleges neglect "civic education," it would be bizarre to try to banish political discussions in the classroom.[113]

Academic freedom is not just about creating the ideal language of how the best professor ought to teach. An essential aspect of academic freedom is the system of shared governance, which prevents outside political authorities from controlling what professors do. The best language protecting academic freedom will be fatally flawed if the enforcement decision making is controlled by an arbitrary authority influenced by politicians.

The interpretation and enforcement of the Academic Bill of Right is critical. An analogy can be made to journalistic ethics. Journalists should be truthful and ethical and fair. But no one should want legislators to pass laws that prohibit "false, scandalous and malicious writing" (the words of the 1798 Sedition Act, one of the worst laws for civil liberties in American history)[114] or create campus investigatory committees to punish anyone accused of such writing. Ethical guides are perfectly appropriate when voluntarily adopted and implemented by professionals, and extraordinarily dangerous when imposed by the government.

Although the original language of the Academic Bill of Rights is ostensibly voluntary, Horowitz and Republican politicians intend to impose changes on higher education. Representative Jack Kingston (R-GA) declared, "This will cause the colleges and universities to have a self-examination and maybe make some changes. But if they're not willing to do that, we hope that the parents and the taxpayers of America will force it upon them."[115] Horowitz has written, "We call on state legislatures in particular to begin these inquiries at the institutions they are responsible for and to enact practical remedies as soon as possible."[116]

Horowitz has repeatedly expressed his belief that universities cannot be reformed from within, and faculty and administrators cannot be trusted: "If there is to be reform, it will have to come from other quarters."[117] His claim that the provisions of the Academic Bill of Rights will be purely voluntary, therefore, cannot be believed. Horowitz has noted, "Only the actions of legislators will begin the necessary process of reform."[118]

Plainly, enforcement of the Academic Bill of Rights is precisely what Horowitz wants, despite his claims to the contrary. But by leaving enforcement unstated in the original Academic Bill of Rights and denying that any enforcement would occur, Horowitz tried to make it easier to pass. This was a Trojan Horse: Horowitz wanted to gain support for his Academic Bill of Rights to be passed, and then later add enforcement procedures, as he is now doing.

Horowitz's Academic Bill of Rights has already had an impact on campus rules in many areas. In April 2005 the University of Texas system's Office of Academic Affairs quietly revised rules for all faculty so that they are "expected not to introduce into their teaching controversial matter that has no relation to his or her subject."[119] This vague standard omits a key component from the AAUP standards, the "persistently intruding" rule. Without it, a professor who utters a single word deemed controversial could be in violation of the rules if it is unrelated to the class subject.

Horowitz turned to the Academic Bill of Rights because he found that the existing law didn't allow him to exercise political pressure on hiring practices at universities. Horowitz's Individual Rights Foundation in 1998 sued the University of California at Berkeley because it didn't hire Michael Savage as dean of the school of journalism. Savage, a right-wing talk show host infamous for his incendiary racist remarks, was later fired from his MSNBC talk show after he told a caller, "You should only get AIDS and die, you pig."[120] According to Horowitz, because Savage didn't get a job interview, "We sued the Journalism School of the University of California for running a patronage operation in a state institution."[121] If refusing to hire an unqualified far-right talk show host could justify a lawsuit for political discrimination, imagine what Horowitz's lawyers will do if they have the explicit rules of the Academic Bill of Rights to support their litigation.

Horowitz announced that he had spoken to a lawyer about suing Lehigh University in Pennsylvania for allowing Michael Moore to speak on campus in 2004. Horowitz explained, "I don't desire to destroy Lehigh; I desire to reform it."[122] But Horowitz's idea of "reform" is using lawsuits to force campuses to censor speakers. At Bowling Green State University in Ohio, Horowitz declared that the university was breaking the law by showing movies: "On election eve 2004, the university through its official activities program put on a showing of *Fahrenheit 9/11,* Michael Moore's hate film against George Bush and the American liberation of Iraq. This was a fairly typical violation of federal codes by universities like Bowling Green, which, as state institutions, are barred from using their funds and facilities for partisan political activities. But as is generally the case with regard to universities these days, there seem to be no adults around to mind the playground."[123] Horowitz believes that colleges must ban all movies criticizing Republicans, and if they won't, the "adult" supervision of threatened litigation and the Academic Bill of Rights can help control them.

Horowitz has even called for the state to police and banish classes he disagrees with. Horowitz declared, "I attempted to get the Attorney General of the state of Indiana to investigate Indiana because they had a course" about terrorism in which "the lecturer devoted the entire curriculum to the Israel Palestinian conflict from the Hamas point of view."[124] Even without the Academic Bill of Rights in place, Horowitz thinks that the government should be investigating colleges to control the way classes are taught.

One of Horowitz's favorite stories is an attack on Miriam Golumb, a University of Missouri at Columbia professor whom Horowitz claimed "slandered" him and offered students double extra credit, but if only they attended a protest against Horowitz. Horowitz proclaimed, "It's just another example of how the liberal left is out of control on college campuses."[125] But an investigation by the university and a reporter found that this claim by two conservative students wasn't substantiated. Golumb and several students reported that a Horowitz fan in Golumb's class asked her to offer extra credit for students to attend Horowitz's speech, and she did.[126] But Horowitz's attack on Golumb wasn't limited to his misunderstanding about the extra credit. Horowitz felt that Golumb should be punished because of her criticism of him. Golumb was one of the faculty who put together a flyer opposing Horowitz, and the flyer quoted a *Time* magazine columnist who wrote that Horowitz was "a real, live bigot."[127] Horowitz declared, "As soon as I arrived in Columbia, I had the students take me to the university office of the Vice Chancellor of Administrative Affairs. I expressed my outrage at being slandered by Professor Golomb and wondered whether this treatment of a visiting speaker was appropriate to an institution that billed itself as one dedicated to the 'higher learning.'"[128] Astonishingly, Horowitz claimed that allowing professors to protest him was "harmful to the principle of academic freedom" because it would cause a "stigma" toward the students who invited him. Horowitz was disappointed that top administrators merely "listened sympathetically" to him but failed to promise that "any action would be taken."[129]

Horowitz believes that faculty should not even be allowed to speak publicly about politics, because this might intimidate students. Horowitz denounced Joan Foster, the president of the faculty senate at Metropolitan State College in Denver, for appearing at a rally criticizing him, arguing that it was a "betrayal of her professional role" for her to express her views in public.[130]

Horowitz has expressed a clear desire for administrators to discipline professors for expressing political views. Horowitz argued that professors have a duty not to talk about politics, and "if it's a professor's responsibility, it should be a student's right." According to Horowitz, "That's revolutionary, because it shifts the power.... That leaves it up to the administration to impose the discipline on the professors."[131]

Horowitz declared, "The Academic Bill of Rights is really about manners."[132] When asked about universities that are "especially troublesome," Horowitz complained that at the University of Rhode Island, "I started my speech and five minutes into my speech, 100 students marched in and they stood in the back. At the end of the speech, when everybody applauded, they all turned their backs. That's a terrible atmosphere. This is about manners."[133] If Horowitz's crusade for "manners" is enacted, then practically any student protester or professor could be punished for political reasons because of perceived impoliteness.

In Arizona, a bill sponsored by the state senate Republican majority leader was approved in 2007 by a senate committee. Under the bill, a professor cannot "endorse, support or oppose any pending, proposed, or enacted local, state, or federal legislation, regulation, or rule."[134] That means, for example, that a professor cannot say in class, "I support the abolition of slavery," because it is an endorsement of enacted legislation, the Thirteenth Amendment. Even worse, the bill punishes professors who "advocate one side of a social, political, or cultural issue that is a matter of partisan controversy."[135] This is one of the broadest attacks on academic freedom imaginable. Can a professor declare that the Holocaust happened? No, because there are some political parties (notably in Iran) that regard this event as controversial. Can a biology professor teach about evolution? No, because there are numerous Republican legislators who consider it controversial. In one fell swoop, the law not only bans all expressions of opinion by instructors but also the teaching of most facts. The punishment for this proposed law is particularly bad: the attorney general or a county attorney can file a civil claim for a $500 fine against any professor who violates the law, even if the university and all faculty colleagues oppose the punishment. In addition, any instructor may be subject to disciplinary action in addition to the fine.[136]

The Arizona bill was so bad that even David Horowitz distanced himself from it: "I oppose unconditionally and without reservation all those clauses of SB 1612 that refer to higher education." However, he added that he would "endorse those sections of SB 1612 that apply to the K–12 schools."[137]

Horowitz is quite capable of turning against student rights and autonomy when it suits his interests. In 2004, when a small number of student newspaper editors rejected one of his incendiary anti-Arab advertisements (just as mainstream news media routinely reject controversial ads), Horowitz promised to sue public universities to force administrators to take over control of student newspapers: "I'm going to sue San Francisco State, and we're negotiating with Texas A&M. If they insist on violating my First Amendment rights, I'll sue, and we'll win."[138] When the *Daily Princetonian* ran Horowitz's antireparations ad but also wrote an editorial that condemned Horowitz as a publicity hound, Horowitz retaliated: "When I read the editorial, I told my office to put a stop-payment on the check." According to Horowitz, "I was not going to pay for abuse."[139]

Horowitz does not tolerate criticism. In the fall of 2002 at the University of Illinois at Chicago, Horowitz reported that he came upon a woman with a sign denouncing him as "Racist, Sexist, Anti-Gay." Horowitz wrote: "I didn't regard this as speech so much as a gesture like kicking me in the groin. It seemed extremely perverse of her to be defending her right to slander me to my face. So then and there—in front of her and the university official—I ripped down her sign."[140] Politicians around the country are trying to force the world's leading universities to take lessons on academic freedom and manners from someone who destroys signs that criticize him and then brags about it.

The Language of Horowitz

Horowitz is a brilliant manipulator of language. In fact, he's written a guide-book for Republican Party activists on the tactics of rhetorical warfare, *The Art of Political War.* But his campaign "for" academic freedom may be his finest use of distortion to serve his political ambitions.

Horowitz often shows a propensity to deceive. In an appearance on Fox News network's *The O'Reilly Factor,* Horowitz talked about speaking at Hamilton College in New York and declared, "The conservative kids invited me. It's a little different when you're invited as a speaker paid by and invited by the faculty. It's not like the faculty brought me up there."[141] This assertion came as a surprise to Maurice Isserman, the Hamilton College professor who had brought Horowitz there in 2002. When confronted with his deceit, Horowitz explained that he had lied because "it was truer to say that I had to be invited by students" than to tell the truth and give the impression that faculty would invite him.[142] That wasn't the only lie Horowitz told about his campus speeches. Horowitz asserted that he is never paid with campus fees: "My kids have to scrounge up the money off campus."[143] One reason to doubt this claim is a report on Horowitz's own website that explained how Skidmore College in New York gave campus conservatives $4,000 for speakers (including Horowitz) during Conservative Challenge Week, how the college helped to publicize the events, and how college president Philip Glotzbach even met personally with Horowitz.[144]

For decades, Horowitz had led a crusade against academic freedom, at-tacking academics for their radical politics. But now he realizes that the best way to defeat his enemy is to use their own words against them. Horowitz has appropriated the language of academic freedom, diversity, and affirmative action in his efforts to destroy these things on college campuses. He uses "academic freedom" as his rallying cry to undermine academic freedom, and "intellectual diversity" as his justification for silencing diverse ideas he doesn't like.

Even Horowitz acknowledges that conservative students don't generally see their rights as being violated on college campuses: "These students who come to my events in suits and ties, have a scrubbed, honor scout look and it is I who have to point out to them that they have been abused and should think about protesting the abuse."[145] When the conservative students who wear suits and ties to campus lectures don't think they're being oppressed on college campuses and must be told so by Horowitz himself, perhaps the problem is nowhere near the exaggerated evil imagined by the advocates of the Academic Bill of Rights. Horowitz regards college students as infants who must be protected from dangerous ideas, even against their will. According to Horowitz, "Students don't know what their rights are. They don't know when they're being abused."[146]

Horowitz does not believe that higher education should be a place of diverse ideas and dissent. To the contrary, he sees colleges and universities as mere training grounds for the corporate world. According to Horowitz, "The university was not created—and is not funded—to compete with other institutions. It is designed to train employees, citizens and leaders of those institutions, and to endow them with appropriate knowledge and skills."[147] Horowitz has a vision of the university as a job training institution creating good workers who never dissent—a vision that, despite all of his complaints, colleges typically fulfill.

Horowitz blames faculty for everything, as he did in one visit to Bowling Green State University: "The tuition at Bowling Green—$15,000 a year—denied working class youngsters in the Toledo area the opportunity to get a shot at the American dream. 'Eighty percent of the school budget is salaries,' I said. 'You make between $60,000 and $100,000 a year. You teach on average two courses and spend six hours a week in class. You work eight months out of the year and have four months paid vacation. And every seven years you get ten months paid vacation. If you are really as concerned about the working class as you pretend, why don't you volunteer to teach four courses and twelve hours a week and lower the tuition costs for these kids?'"[148] As usual, Horowitz is wrong about almost every claim he makes. The average full-time faculty salary at Bowling Green is $62,275. If you include part-time faculty, the average teacher at Bowling Green makes less than what Horowitz claimed is the minimum salary. And what about that $15,000 tuition rate keeping out working-class students? The actual in-state tuition (and fees) at Bowling Green in 2004–2005 was $8,072, or about half of what Horowitz claimed. Teaching loads at Bowling Green are two classes per semester in departments with doctoral programs (where faculty must also serve on dissertation committees), but the teaching loads are higher in other departments. The sabbatical for professors, if approved, is not ten months paid vacation, but four months to allow full-time work on a research project (which is part of a professor's job, not a vacation).[149]

Horowitz treats faculty with utter disdain, claiming that professors "work five hours a week, they work eight months a year, they have lifetime jobs."[150] Full-time faculty at research universities work an average of fifty-five hours per week, according to a Department of Education report.[151] But Horowitz hopes to undermine public support for higher education by lying about how much effort they put into their jobs. Horowitz's complaint that faculty members are overpaid is particularly ironic because in 2005, David Horowitz paid himself $336,000, which doesn't count the numerous campus speeches at $5,000 each he makes throughout the year.[152] Horowitz gets paid far more than the professors he insults, without ever having to teach any classes or grade any papers.

Horowitz's Attack on Academic Freedom

Although the vague words of the Academic Bill of Rights by themselves threaten academic freedom, an even greater threat to academic freedom comes from how easily they could be distorted. Horowitz's interpretation of what should be banned on college campuses goes far beyond any mainstream concept of academic freedom. In a 2003 speech in Denver, Horowitz declared that he was appalled to find anti-Bush views expressed on the office doors of some faculty in town. Horowitz explained that the purpose of the Academic Bill of Rights is to ban professors from expressing political views in the classroom or their own offices. According to Horowitz, "There were hostile cartoons aimed at Republicans and conservatives. How does that make conservative students feel? We have arenas in which we can proselytize, but the classroom or the office where students come in for office hours is not one of them. That's what the Academic Bill of Rights is. That's why I drew it up."[153] Horowitz claimed that a political cartoon "creates a wall between faculty and students, which is injurious to the counseling process. How can a professor teach a student whom he regards as a partisan adversary? The answer is he cannot."[154]

At a legislative hearing, Pennsylvania state representative Gibson Armstrong showed copies of anti-Bush cartoons from a professor's office door as proof of indoctrination.[155] In a December 2003 speech at the University of Montana, Horowitz declared that professors who put political cartoons critical of Republicans on their office doors "should be disciplined and put on notice." The *Montana Missoulian* also reported, "Horowitz said campuses should screen their reading lists for bias, break up the 'Star Chamber' secrecy of hiring and tenure decisions, and monitor classrooms for imbalance of opinions or divergence from core class concepts."[156]

Horowitz's declared purpose for the Academic Bill of Rights is to prevent faculty from putting political cartoons on their office doors, and to monitor their classes and reading lists for "bias." Even Joe McCarthy might have hesitated before trying to ban cartoons from college campuses.

At times Horowitz has admitted the conservative agenda behind the Academic Bill of Rights he's pushing: "In the course of my visits to college campuses I became aware of problems that led to the drafting of this bill of rights. Among these were overt politicizing of the classroom (for example, one-sided faculty 'teach-ins' on the war on terror); faculty harassment of students—generally conservatives and Christians, but increasingly Jews; politically selective speakers' programs and faculty hiring practices, which have led to the virtual exclusion of conservatives and Republicans from the university public square."[157] The Academic Bill of Rights is intended to force colleges to provide more conservative voices, and presumably would even ban any teach-ins by faculty that Horowitz might regard as "one-sided."

Declaring War on Peace Studies

Horowitz's crusade against peace studies programs reflects how he interprets the Academic Bill of Rights to justify a widespread assault on academic freedom. Horowitz's attack on the peace studies program at Ball State University in Indiana reveals how his campaign for censorship has grown more bold and extreme.

The cover of Horowitz's pamphlet on Ball State is a remarkable piece of propaganda. In the background it shows the Twin Towers burning after being struck by terrorist pilots. In the foreground is an ominous dark figure playing a saxophone, leading (Pied Piper style) a group of students who hold signs that read "A+" and "A" up a hill. This grotesque link between mass murder and peace studies is made explicit by Horowitz's group, which calls the peace studies program at Ball State an "anti-American, terrorist support network."[158]

The pamphlet about Ball State began with a letter to legislators, asking them to intervene and pass the Academic Bill of Rights. According to Horowitz, his campaign to shut down the Ball State peace studies program "is the beginning of what will be a much longer campaign to stop the indoctrination of American students in a leftist ideology which is sympathetic to our terrorist enemies." Horowitz wrote, "We are going to follow this up with a mailing to every legislator in the state of Indiana protesting this program. And we are going to continue this campaign until we are satisfied and close one of the gaping holes in our Homeland Security defenses to the Zarqawi-bin Laden foe."[159]

The controversy at Ball State was sparked by conservative student Brett Mock, who claims he decided to minor in peace studies in order to pad his resume and was upset that his peace studies and conflict resolution class taught by George Wolfe did not include endorsements for war. Mock complained, "The only studying of conflict resolution that we did was to enforce the idea that nonviolent means were the only legitimate sources of self-defense."[160] Mock was demanding that a class on peace studies and conflict resolution must teach that violence is good, on the theory that war is a form of conflict resolution.

Mock declared, "How could I speak up with my own opinions, I thought, if I knew in advance they would invariably be shot down by the professor himself?"[161] This is the infantilization of the college student, who is deemed to be such a fragile creature that being challenged in class or even knowing what a professor thinks about a subject will oppress the student and prevent him from speaking. Mock's own description of the class belies his claim of indoctrinated students. Mock notes that students actively challenged and disagreed with their instructor's more extreme pacifist views.

Mock falsely claimed that students had received university funding and extra credit to attend a protest in Washington, D.C., when in reality they were attending a lobbying workshop.[162] Horowitz's pamphlet also claimed that students who attended the conference should not have been allowed to have it fulfill the class requirement because "the other students would be extremely uncomfortable attending an official function with the group if they did not share their views."[163] But why should one person who is "uncomfortable" with an event be able to veto all students from attending it for class? Mock himself received credit for attending a political rally where Dick Cheney spoke, which might make some students uncomfortable.[164]

Mock seems to imagine that a lot of professors are oppressing him: "I experienced similar situations in other classes where I felt like my thoughts and opinions were attacked by the professor."[165] Perhaps it is a coincidence that Ball State University has several unethical professors, and Mock happens to be a student in all of their classes and the only one who complains. The more likely explanation, given that no other student has complained or confirmed Mock's accusations, is that Mock himself is the anomaly here.

Horowitz claimed that students who oppose Wolfe's views "are punished gradewise."[166] The Ball State AAUP called the charges against Wolfe "scurrilous and dangerous. The professors and students attending their classes give ample testimony that classroom experiences provided students with a variety of opportunities to express their views. There is no evidence that student grades suffered as a result of contrasting personal or political philosophies."[167] Mock himself got a B+ in the class and considered it a fair grade.[168] Beverley Pitts, provost of Ball State University, noted: "We have a very complex system of opportunities for students to have grade appeals. No student ever came forward about this class. In fact, the students who have come forward have countered Mr. Mock's statements and said those things didn't happen in class at all."[169]

When Ball State investigated Mock's claims, Wolfe was completely exonerated.[170] Horowitz nevertheless denounced Ball State, claiming that it needs to prohibit the mention of politics in the classroom. Horowitz declared: "Professors should not be politicking in the classroom. Ball State University is not the Hannity and Colmes Show. It's an educational institution."[171] But what is politics? When does an idea become political? And who will decide and enforce these rules? Horowitz's theory is particularly appalling because he wants to limit political discussions even when they are a legitimate part of a course. In fact, Horowitz wants to ban certain courses and entire departments that he regards as too political.

Horowitz also denounced the Ball State student organization PeaceWorkers, which Wolfe advises, as "part of a coalition that includes the proterrorist Muslim Students Association and the Young Communist League."[172] What is this mysterious coalition? PeaceWorkers has a website that contains links to other organizations. One of those organizations in turn apparently links its website to the Muslim Students Association and the Young Communist League (neither of which embrace terrorism). By Horowitz's reasoning, anyone who links to a website that links to another group is thereby guilty by association of every evil ever linked to any organization linked to any website linked to it.

Horowitz also misunderstands the meaning of academic qualifications. Horowitz's pamphlet against Ball State argues that the authors of the textbook *Peace and Conflict Studies* "have academic degrees in psychology and philosophy which does not qualify them to write a text which covers most of human history, and includes commentaries on economics, anthropology, sociology and a broad range of geopolitical matters."[173] Apparently Horowitz feels that books should be banned from classes unless the authors hold Ph.D.s in all different fields covered by the text, regardless of the actual merits of the book. Finding a peace studies textbook written by an author with Ph.D.s in history and economics and anthropology and sociology and philosophy and psychology and political science will be rather difficult, since no such person exists.

Horowitz wrote, "There are two-hundred-and-fifty 'Peace Studies' programs in America like the one at Ball State. They teach students to identify with America's terrorist enemies and to identify America as a 'Great Satan' oppressing the world's poor and causing them to go hungry. There are equally many Provost Pittses, defending the fraudulent academic credentials of the political activists who conduct these indoctrinations and who are academically illiterate in the subject matter itself. The question is: how long can a nation at war with ruthless enemies like bin Laden and Zarqawi survive if its educational institutions continue to be suborned in this way?"[174] Horowitz distorts and denounces one peace studies program at Ball State University, and then concludes that 250 other peace studies programs around the country must be exactly the same. The idea that peace studies programs "teach students to identify with America's terrorist enemies" is crazy. Horowitz also denounced Wolfe's class because it "assigns preposterous tracts by Noam Chomsky pontificating on global issues and painting America as the Great Satan," indicating that Horowitz regards any writings by Chomsky, one of the foremost leftist political analysts, as completely illegitimate in college classes and deserving to be banned.[175]

Horowitz declares that teaching peace during a war is an act of treason, with "suborned" professors threatening the survival of the nation. If a nation at war cannot survive peace studies professors, then the solution desired by Horowitz is obvious: Fire the professors who oppose war, shut down all peace studies programs, and impose a new wave of McCarthyism to enact Horowitz's patriotic ideas on college campuses.

Banning Women's Studies and Social Justice

Horowitz also wants to eliminate women's studies programs. Horowitz argued before the Kansas legislature that since the University of Kansas women's studies program seeks "understanding of how and why gender inequality developed and is maintained in the United States and in our global society," it should be banished. Horowitz believes that this program is "nonacademic" and "partisan" because it does not give equal consideration to the view that there is no gender inequality in the world—an insane proposition that no scholar would ever suggest.[176] Horowitz told the Kansas legislature that women's studies programs "can in no way be justified as taxpayer-supported programs."[177] Horowitz claimed that women's studies is "totally inappropriate for an academic institution and totally inappropriate for a state institution," and wondered, "how is it that they have allowed this massive misuse of public funds and abuse of Kansas students to take place?"[178]

Horowitz attacked the University of California at Santa Cruz's program on similarly dubious grounds: "If I were a student at Santa Cruz, ... my conservative views would disqualify me for a degree in Feminist Studies. This is a violation of my academic freedom as a student."[179] What is Horowitz's evidence that conservatives are banned from receiving degrees in feminist studies? No conservatives have actually been banned from the department, and he does not examine what is actually taught. Instead, Horowitz cites a part of the department's website that observes, "Graduates' knowledge about power relationships and injustice often leads them to choose careers in government and politics, because they are determined to use their skills to change the world."[180] According to Horowitz, this statement is a violation of academic freedom because "Conservatives ... are philosophically disposed to thinking that that is precisely what you cannot do, i.e., 'change the world.'"[181] Not only is Horowitz completely wrong (conservatives also want to "change the world"), but he is also embracing a remarkable attack on academic freedom. If it is a violation of academic freedom for a department to mention that graduates want to "change the world," almost anything could be banned under Horowitz's regime.

Horowitz also attacked the Kansas State University School of Social Work because it described social workers as having "a belief in social justice." Even though there is no requirement for students to believe in social justice, and conservatives can obviously support social justice, based on this statement alone Horowitz concluded that the program is "training students to take one side of this debate" because he thinks social justice is "code" for "socialism." According to Horowitz, this program "violates the academic freedom policies of the Kansas Board of Regents," and he demanded that the legislature step in and ban this "training school for political party activists."[182]

Horowitz also has called for banning books he dislikes, declaring that "the entire Social Welfare course of the departments of Social Work and Sociology at Kansas State is, in fact, a chapter by chapter, class by class reading of Zinn's book, *A People's History of the United States*."[183] In reality, Horowitz was looking at a four-year-old syllabus in which Zinn's was not the sole text in the class, which also included a textbook called *A New History of Social Welfare*. Horowitz asked, "What is the relevance of this history—let alone this blatantly false history—to the training of Kansas State students for careers in Social Work? There is none."[184] Of course a work of history is entirely relevant to a class about "the historical evolution of the social welfare system in the U.S."[185] Horowitz cites this single class and his false claim that Zinn's book is the sole text as proof that "there are courses in universities across the country which are self-evidently courses in indoctrination for which there is no present remedy."[186] According to Horowitz, his Academic Bill of Rights is the "remedy" to this problem. And Horowitz contended that "legislatures have a fiduciary responsibility ... to step in and provide a remedy."[187] Clearly, there can only be a "remedy" if some kind of formal action is taken to ban professors from using books by Howard Zinn and other radicals.

Chickenshit Academia

Horowitz also wants to silence professors from expressing their own views in class, if these involve criticizing Republican politicians. Horowitz took aim at University of Georgia professor John Morrow, who told his military history class on the first day that George W. Bush and Dick Cheney were "chickenshit cowards" for evading military service in Vietnam despite their support for that war. Bradley Alexander, a student offended by Morrow's criticism of the president, objected in the class and argued with Morrow. Morrow noted, "Bradley Alexander attended only the introductory session of my 'World Wars' class, when I introduce the subject, talk about my teaching style, and purposely introduce controversial opinions to generate discussion. I teach by the Socratic method and students need to become accustomed to discussing issues openly."[188]

According to Horowitz, "A university has obligations to its students and their academic freedom." Horowitz objected to a professor "bringing irrelevant contemporary politics into his classroom in a controversial way that is disrespectful of his students who may have different views."[189] But the military record of the president is relevant to a military history class, particularly to show how today's wars are not being fought by the wide cross-section of men who served in World Wars I and II.

According to Horowitz, "Bullying them in the classroom by displaying politically partisan commitments and expressing these commitments in vulgar language—magnifying their emotional impact—does nothing to advance the educational process or enhance scholarly understanding of the subject."[190] In Horowitz's view, a professor who expresses any idea related to a current political issue is "bullying" students. Horowitz presents students as the ultimate oppressed victims, as infantile creatures held hostage in the classroom by their professors.

But Horowitz is wrong. Students are not prevented from learning by professors who express controversial ideas. The opposite is true: Students learn more when they are engaged by interesting and controversial subjects. One former student wrote to Morrow, "I do not think we would ever agree on politics but wanted to let you know that I am willing to come testify at your court-martial or whatever the academic thought-police attempt to do."[191] Another conservative student declared, "I took Morrow's course last year. I didn't agree with seventy-five percent of the things he said, but I still got a very good grade."[192]

Students for Academic Freedom declared, "We are pleased to report that the attention brought to this issue by Students for Academic Freedom and *Frontpage Magazine* appears to have convinced the University of Georgia to take Bradley's complaint seriously. We also owe thanks to the office of Georgia Governor Sonny Perdue which contacted the University to express outrage at Morrow's behavior. An attorney from the Office of Legal Affairs has been assigned by the Provost to investigate the situation and is planning to speak with other students from the class to confirm Bradley's allegations."[193]

When raising controversial topics and asking questions is denounced as "disrespect" and "bullying" and justifies the intervention of the most powerful politicians in the state, it shows how far Horowitz's crusade has gone, and how dangerous it is to academic freedom. Not one student has ever alleged any unfair grading by Morrow. Yet Horowitz would "applaud" the university for investigating Morrow because "he needs to be taught an important lesson."[194] The main lesson faculty and students learn from facing investigative committees is to shut up and stop criticizing the government.

The Triumph of Conservative Victimhood

Horowitz claims that his website proves "the overwhelming academic presence of leftists who use their classrooms as political soapboxes."[195] But the evidence provided by the forum on studentsforacademicfreedom.org shows little evidence to support this claim, instead offering a small number of cases where conservatives complain in unverified accounts. These examples from the state of Illinois are a small sample of what is found on Horowitz's website.

At Elmhurst College, a student complained of being "ideologically stalked online by instructors," contending that the college spied on postings on message boards and "teachers were coming to class bringing up the topics to creep me out!"[196]

At the University of Illinois at Springfield, a student complained, "As part of September 11th rememberence [*sic*] Student Life is showing Fahrenheit 9/11.... This has been done without any scheduled debate or rebuttal of the movie."[197] But how many movie screenings are debated or rebutted?

At Governors State University, during a speech class, a student made a persuasive speech: "This young lady held the biblical position, and used the bible as her reference, that homosexual marriage was wrong. The professor told the student that her choice of reference material was subjective and controversial and perhaps, a better source would have been the APA Guide Book of Mental Disorders, which came to the conclusion in 1973 that homosexuality was not a mental disorder. I countered that the student's opinion and reference material was as valid as the APA book which the professor suggested she used."[198]

Another posting about Governors State University by the same individual attacked a textbook, *Intercultural Communication in Contexts* by Judith N. Martin and Thomas K. Nakayama. The student denounced the book for "an anti-American bias." The student added, "The mere fact that the authors give any credence to Cornel West (page 16) should automatically make the reader suspect. West, scholar and theologian, espouses racial division and racially motivated violence." (Of course, West has never advocated any racial violence.) The student also declared, "Equally infuriating is the class-warfare rhetoric of 'economic inequality' spewed by the authors." Yet even this student's dismissal of the text was apparently supported by the instructor: "The Professor replied and stated briefly that he agreed with my analysis, which has me puzzled since he chose the text for the class."[199]

Many of the complaints came from students who feel "uncomfortable" because they disagreed with views expressed by teachers or students in a class. At DePaul University, a student claimed: "I have been singled out and criticized for my support of the Iraq war, and everything the US has done on the War on Terror. The whole class along with the teacher jumped down my throat when i said i trusted our government." The student complained that the instructor "was supporting all of the other students, and certainly not being unbiased. When i got up to leave the class room, she said if I left, that would mean i was unwilling to hear both sides of the story." The student declared, "I am actually scared to go to class because she always finds a way to beliddle [*sic*] what i say."[200]

At Illinois State University, a U.S. history professor was condemned for criticizing George W. Bush, and the student declared, "I feel out of place since the whole class agrees with her. Then the class goes on a tangent talking about how they hate bush."[201]

A Wright College student complained about an instructor who "spent a good amount of class time telling us that Osama Bin Laden was innocent and we did not have proof that it was him." The professor "told us not to be patriotic, because only stupid people are patriotic, they follow the herd and scream kill, kill, kill. We were told not to have a love of country because the rest of the world deserves as much love as us. He praised some communist regimes."[202]

Some of the views allegedly expressed by teachers are offensive (or bizarre), but there is no verification of any kind provided, or any reason to punish professors for saying what they think. There was one complaint in the state of Illinois by a student who claimed to suffer discriminatory grading, and this accusation was far from convincing. A Northern Illinois University law student declared, "Associate Dean Lenny Mandell politicized his authority recently. I noticed a letter on his door ... from some organization for the election of John Kerry, thanking Mr. Mandell for being an elector for the Democratic primary." The student added, "As a side note I have been given failing grades in half my courses. That happened after I saw the letter, and suspect that the law school is just getting rid of me because of my incompatibility with most of the teachers' political views. All the other instructors I have spoken to who have given me failing marks have all equalaterally [*sic*] said my work was bad, without any real criticism or making comments that were unjustified and nonacademic in nature anyway."[203] Could it be the case that this law student is a victim of a vast left-wing conspiracy, where a dean arranged for half of the student's professors to give failing grades for no reason, all in retaliation because that student objected to a letter on his door? Like most of the complaints offered on Horowitz's website, it seems "equalaterally" improbable.

Perhaps the best indication of how much credibility should be given to Students for Academic Freedom is this final Illinois posting, from Augustana College in Georgia: "School used funds from Student activity fees to bring in the one-sided speaker David Hororwitz [*sic*]. Through the course of his speech we all suffered under forced indoctrinization [*sic*] of conservative view points."[204] If fake postings mocking Horowitz can be found on his own site, how seriously should we regard the other unverified postings there?

The reports about colleges in other states are similar to those in Illinois: Dubious accusations by angry conservative students that, even if they could be verified, more often than not denounce perfectly legitimate textbooks and classroom opinions. As Russell Jacoby observed, "Virtually all 'cases' reported to the Academic Freedom Abuse Center deal with leftist political comments or leftist assigned readings. To use the idiom of right-wing commentators, we see here the emergence of crybaby conservatives, who demand a judicial remedy, guaranteed safety and representation."[205]

The Myth of Political Grading

The fear of unfair grading, although often invoked to excuse intervention, has little basis in reality. Among the 107,000 students in the Pennsylvania state system of higher education, there were only fourteen formal complaints over five years. And these complaints showed no evidence of systematic grade discrimination suffered by conservatives: They involved a student who claimed that a professor denigrated her political views, a student who felt a professor was too conservative, a student who complained that a professor was anti-Islam, a student who complained that a class was graded on a curve, and a student who mistakenly thought the professor had given an excused absence.[206] At the University of Pittsburgh, provost James Maher reported that they did not have a single case "where the complaint involved a student feeling they've been mistreated because of their political opinions."[207] Florida's Office of Program Policy Analysis and Government Accountability investigated campus policies at the request of legislators and found that all Florida colleges have policies for student grievance procedures, but academic freedom complaints accounted for less than 1 percent of all student grievances (only seven statewide in the previous three years).[208]

There is no evidence that conservative students systematically suffer grading penalties in college because of their ideology. In fact, the opposite may be true. A 2005 comprehensive study of 3,800 students at a major public university found that conservative students received grades similar to liberal students in classes on American culture, African American studies, cultural anthropology, education, nursing, sociology, and women's studies. But in business and economics classes, conservative students had an advantage in grades. This suggests that conservatives are not being penalized by professors in more liberal fields, but liberals may face a small penalty in more conservative departments.[209]

Another study of political discrimination found a similar bias against left-leaning students in economics. A poll of graduate students at the University of Chicago, Columbia, Harvard, Princeton, Yale, Stanford, and the Massachusetts Institute of Technology found that only 10 percent of the first-year students called themselves politically conservative, but 23 percent were conservative in the fourth or fifth year of graduate school. The proportion of students who called themselves radical fell from 13 percent of first-year students to only 1 percent of fourth-year and higher students, the clearest evidence ever presented of ideological purging in academia.[210] Even though a majority of economics faculty are Democrats, the educational system turns students in economics more conservative and clearly drives out left-wing students. By contrast, no one has ever presented any evidence that conservative students are systematically pushed out of any field in graduate school.

The rare case of unfair grading is not what Horowitz is worried about. Horowitz's book *The Professors* compiles profiles of the "101 Most Dangerous Academics," nearly exclusively based upon their leftist public speeches and writings rather than how they teach or any allegations of violating the rights of their students.[211] Horowitz admitted that he cannot name a single college where students are unable to appeal unfair grades: "Grievance machinery does exist for students to appeal grades they believe are unfair. But the idea of political discrimination has not yet been introduced into the antidiscrimination policy templates of any university to my knowledge."[212] Horowitz clearly has little interest in stopping unfair grading; instead, his focus is on stopping political expression. Horowitz wrote, "The principal issues are unprofessional conduct in the classroom, unprofessional instruction (e.g., where the professor is not academically qualified to teach the subject), unprofessional courses (i.e., courses that are ideological and not academic) and bigotry. So the lack of cases of political grading is not only insignificant; it is irrelevant."[213] Horowitz's aim is to make the comments of professors subject to grievance procedures in order to silence the expression of political ideas.

Conservatives against Horowitz

Even Republicans worry that Horowitz's Academic Bill of Rights and crusade against leftists in academia goes too far. John Donley, a Republican and former state lawmaker who now teaches political science at a Colorado community college, told the press: "The far-right conservatives control the Colorado House, Senate and Governor's Mansion, but that isn't enough—they've decided they want to control our classrooms."[214]

Daniel Anderson, the conservative president of Appalachian Bible College in West Virginia, criticized plans for a congressional Academic Bill of Rights because he feared it would "suggest we present alternate religious views as equal" or "homosexuality, lesbianism, or sex outside marriage as an alternative lifestyle."[215]

One of the first higher education groups to come out and oppose the Academic Bill of Rights was the Council for Christian Colleges and Universities. Its president, Robert Andringa, noted: "It would be anathema for people in the faith community." According to Andringa, "Government is not the one to arbitrate academic freedom."[216] Reverend Charles L. Currie, president of the Association of Jesuit Colleges and Universities, attacked the Academic

Bill of Rights as insulting to religious colleges: "While we understand that it is nonbinding, including it in the Higher Education Act implies that institutions such as ours are indeed biased and promoting ideological agendas. That is not the case."[217]

Conservative voters also don't agree with Horowitz's campus crusade. Gib Armstrong, the Pennsylvania state representative who pushed for legislative hearings about campus bias and made the Academic Bill of Rights his pet issue, lost in the 2006 Republican primary. Armstrong was defeated by Bryan Cutler, a law student who challenged Armstrong's view that conservatives faced repression on campus: "I'm a very conservative student, and I myself never experienced that, and honestly I came out more appreciative of my own viewpoints."[218]

Conservative columnist John Leo rejected Horowitz's idea of legislative action, declaring that "pressure should come from protests and persuasion, not the involvement of politicians."[219] Conservative researcher Stanley Rothman noted, "I have reservations about too much intervention by politicians. After observing how various groups have used charges of discrimination by faculty, administrators and other students to create a climate and a chilling effect on academic freedom, we should be careful not to add to a climate in which teachers, administrators and students are afraid to speak up."[220]

Harvey Silverglate, the coauthor of *The Shadow University* and the co-founder of FIRE, noted about the Academic Bill of Rights legislation: "I actually think it's a very bad idea even though I am very sympathetic with the goal."[221] Former governor Lamar Alexander declared in his keynote speech at a conference created by Horowitz, "Don't try to get the Congress to pass a law about academic freedom."[222]

David Beito, Robert "KC" Johnson, and Ralph E. Luker, three libertarian critics of the campus left, warned about the Academic Bill of Rights: "Instead of being the evenhanded vehicle it claims to be, everywhere it is a function of right-wing attacks on academic communities."[223] They worried that the Academic Bill of Rights "could snuff out all controversial discussion in the classroom."[224] Even the *Wall Street Journal* editorialized against the Academic Bill of Rights as legislation.[225]

Jesse Walker, associate editor for the libertarian magazine *Reason*, wrote about the Academic Bill of Rights: "As broad principles, these are solid stuff. As enforced rules, they open the door to, say, a biology student lodging an official complaint because her professor gave short shrift to Creationism."[226] Walker concluded, "There's no such thing as a perfectly balanced debate, and a heavy-handed effort to create one is more likely to chill speech than to encourage it. The most worrisome thing about Horowitz's group is the sneaking suspicion that that's exactly what they want."[227]

Although Horowitz claims that his crusade is being launched on behalf of students, many students don't agree. Rebecca Wasserman, president of the

United States Student Association, told a hearing of the House Education Committee in May 2004, "We cannot have officials in Washington, D.C., regulating the content of our classrooms. This intrusive oversight disrupts local control and challenges the mission of educational institutions."[228]

Other conservatives criticize Horowitz's inaccurate attacks. When conservative Ball State University student Kyle Ellis submitted an article at Horowitz's request criticizing a peace studies professor, Ellis discovered that "what Horowitz published for FrontPage Magazine was 100 percent different than the story that I wrote." Horowitz not only made Ellis's article much more inflammatory but added inaccurate information without consulting Ellis, who calls Horowitz "an embarrassment" to "the Conservative movement."[229] A writer for the right-wing *Dartmouth Review* criticized "Horowitz's sloppy political punditry under the guise of a campaign for academic freedom."[230]

Although some independent conservatives criticize Horowitz, most of the leading conservative campus groups have embraced his crusade or refuse to critique him. Horowitz has strong support from the Republican Party, and Karl Rove has embraced his work. Horowitz's Restoration Weekend conferences bringing together the conservative movement for meetings have included George W. Bush, Dan Quayle, Newt Gingrich, Rudy Giuliani, Paul Wolfowitz, John Bolton, Edwin Meese, and John Ashcroft; Senators Zell Miller, Mitch McConnell, Jeff Sessions, Lindsey Graham, Kay Bailey Hutchison, John McCain, Jon Kyl, George Allen, Jim Bunning, and Fred Thompson; Representatives Asa Hutchison, Jim Rogan, Curt Weldon, Dan Burton, Lindsey Graham, Mark Sanford, Katherine Harris, John Doolittle, J. D. Hayworth, Tom Tancredo, John Shadegg, Jeff Flake, Ed Royce, Jack Kingston, Curt Weldon, J. C. Watts, Roy Blount, and former majority whip Tom DeLay; and right-wing pundits Fred Barnes, Joe Scarborough, Ann Coulter, Bill Kristol, Sean Hannity, Bill O'Reilly, and Rush Limbaugh.[231]

Conservatives and liberals alike should worry about Horowitz's vision of colleges where political opinions are viewed like cockroaches and Horowitz is the self-appointed exterminator. Far from being a defender of student rights, Horowitz's crusade is the greater threat to student liberty, since he wants to deny students the right to take classes where freedom of political discussion is upheld.

One of the key flaws of Horowitz's Academic Bill of Rights is that it's a terrible statement of student rights. It includes nothing about freedom of the student press, freedom of expression, the freedom to protest peacefully, or due process rights. By contrast, the AAUP's joint statement on student rights and freedoms (approved in 1967 by the AAUP, along with the United States Student Association, the Association of American Colleges and Universities, the National Association of Student Personnel Administrators, and the

National Association for Women in Education) is a far superior statement of student liberty without endangering academic freedom.[232]

When Temple University in Pennsylvania decided to revise its policies in 2006 in response to the pressure from Horowitz, it didn't use the language of his Student Bill of Rights. Instead, Temple copied language from the AAUP's "Joint Statement on Rights and Freedoms of Students."[233] Horowitz's Students for Academic Freedom immediately took credit for the policy, which it bizarrely contended was "the first university to adopt an academic freedom policy which specifically addresses student rights."[234] But a quick Internet search can find hundreds of colleges that use exactly the same AAUP language. The unique part of Temple's policy was its adoption of Horowitz's approach that a violation of these vague ideals for teaching could result in a student grievance. It is bizarre to imagine that Temple students could start investigations of their professors for not encouraging students "to develop the capacity for critical judgment," whatever that means, or even for discussing anything unrelated to the subject of a class.[235]

The Academic Bill of Rights sounds appealing at many campuses where the rights of students are not fully protected. The best way to head off Horowitz's crusade, and also improve protections for student academic freedom, is to create a genuine student bill of rights that follows AAUP principles. However, a student bill of rights needs to be careful to avoid the mistakes at Temple, where grievance procedures were imposed on the AAUP's statement of ideals for teaching rather being limited to areas such as fair grading where students should have enforceable rights.

Horowitz has taken advantage of the fact that student rights are too little protected on college campuses; unless this problem is addressed, it will be easy for him to disguise his political attacks on liberal faculty as a defense of students. The worst situation of all is that Horowitz's inadequate statement of student rights might take the place of important reforms to protect students from repressive administrators.

During the McCarthy era, the enemies of academic freedom were often explicit about their attack on academic integrity. Today, the enemies of academic freedom like David Horowitz are cloaking their assault on liberal professors in the guise of student academic freedom.

CHAPTER FOUR
Biased Numbers: Counting Democrats and Republicans on Campus

❧

Defenders of the "Academic Bill of Rights" justify its passage by citing a series of deeply flawed studies cited by David Horowitz and his supporters. Horowitz and other critics of academia have told a story over and over again: Ninety percent of faculty at American universities are Democrats. This statistic became the foundation of Horowitz's assaults on academia and the key justification for his Academic Bill of Rights. There was only one problem with Horowitz's statistic: It isn't true.

Horowitz's dubious statistics about academia are repeated endlessly in the mainstream media. The *Wall Street Journal* declared in an editorial about his ideas, "Democrats outnumber Republicans by a 10–1 margin in a recent study of political affiliation at 32 leading American universities."[1] A *Chronicle of Higher Education* report claimed that Horowitz "has conducted studies finding that at 32 universities he deemed 'elite,' Democratic professors and administrators outnumbered Republican colleagues by a ratio of more than 10 to 1."[2] *U.S. News & World Report* columnist John Leo praised Horowitz's "barrage of statistics" and repeated Horowitz's lie about "10 Democratic professors for every Republican one, with the disparity rising sharply at many elite universities."[3] According to Horowitz, "We've done studies that show nearly 90 percent of the faculty are Democrats. We're not talking about quotas, just timetables and goals."[4] All of these claims were false, yet they were widely accepted in the press.

The gullibility of the media in accepting Horowitz's 90 percent lie prompted conservatives to make even more unbelievable claims. According to Representative Jack Kingston (R-GA), the head of the House Republican Conference and chief sponsor of Horowitz's bill, "some of America's finest institutions of higher learning have no conservatives on staff," an astonishing assertion made without the slightest evidence.[5] Horowitz has even further inflated his dubious 10-to-1 numbers. At a November 2003 forum, Horowitz declared, "We did a survey of college campuses, which showed that the average ratio of registered Democrats to Republicans is 10:1. That's not counting Greens, Maoists, and al-Qaeda supporters—and I'm very serious about al-Qaeda supporters. So the ratio is probably 15:1."[6] Horowitz has declared, "Our faculties are 90 percent to 95 percent people of the left."[7] Here Horowitz repeated his old lie (that Democrats outnumber Republicans 10 to 1) and added new lies (that Democrats outnumber Republicans 19 to 1, and that all of these Democratic professors are "people of the left").

What Horowitz's "surveys" examined was a small proportion of faculty at elite colleges, looking only at the voter registration of professors in fields such as economics, history, English, philosophy, political science, and sociology. Horowitz has never studied the entire faculty of any college in the country, yet he repeatedly made claims about the political affiliation of these professors.

Horowitz's studies are deeply flawed by missing data and distorted interpretations. Take Harvard University as an example: Horowitz's researchers looked at 215 professors in a handful of "liberal" departments and found 77 registered Democrats, 11 registered Republicans, and 127 whose registration couldn't be determined.[8] But Harvard in the fall of 2005 had 2,497 faculty.[9] The 77 Democrats identified by Horowitz are less than 4 percent of the total. Horowitz has no idea about the party affiliation of the 127 faculty who couldn't be identified, and no clue about the 2,000 faculty members he never examined (including 226 faculty in Harvard's business school, which is hardly a center of Marxist ideology). Horowitz doesn't know how 95 percent of faculty at Harvard vote, and because of his skewed sample, he has no basis to say anything about them. Horowitz's studies only identify the political affiliation of fewer than half of the faculty in a small number of departments. Faculty who don't bother to register to vote are probably not politically active members of the thought police, so Horowitz's omission of them is a significant bias in his studies.

Horowitz routinely fools reporters and the public into thinking that his highly selective "surveys" study all faculty at a college, even though he has never conducted a scientific survey using basic random sampling techniques at any college. To assert that a study of selected departments is representative of an entire college's faculty is a serious statistical mistake. Horowitz's own writings frequently omit all of the necessary qualifications on these studies. Horowitz wrote on his website that his study "found that registered

Democrats on these college faculties outnumber Republicans by 10–1."[10] In another article about his studies of selected departments, Horowitz also pretended that he had studied the entire faculty: "A previous report by the Center showed that the average ratio of Democrats to Republicans on 32 elite colleges was 10 to 1 and in some schools was as high as 30–1."[11]

Horowitz compounded his statistical follies by claiming, "When an applicant at an average university is 10 times more likely to be hired if he's a Democrat than if he's a Republican, obviously there's something awry."[12] Obviously, a 10 to 1 ratio in numbers (even if it were real) is not the same as the likelihood of being hired. Republicans are less likely to be hired in academia due to self-selection: They are less likely to join a low-paid profession such as college teaching, not because of discrimination.

The Politics of Political Surveys

Horowitz is not the only conservative using the technique of political surveys to attack academia for being too liberal. A study released in November 2004 by Daniel Klein and Charlotta Stern drew headlines for its claims to replicate Horowitz's findings (even though it fell short of Horowitz's magical 10:1 ratio).[13]

Klein and Stern's study received uncritical praise. The *New York Times* reported in a major article that the study "shows that Democratic professors outnumber Republicans by at least seven to one in the humanities and social sciences."[14] Rush Limbaugh proclaimed, "The balance of liberal to conservative professors on most college campuses is seven or eight to one."[15]

Klein and Stern, in fact, simply created the 7 to 1 ratio out of thin air, and even used a fraudulent "average of ratios" figure of 15 to 1, which the National Association of Scholars (NAS) promoted in its press release. (Such deceptive numbers led conservative columnist Bruce Bartlett to declare incorrectly, "On average, across all departments, Democrats get 15 votes for every one going to Republicans.")[16]

Klein and Stern's deeply flawed study is far too unreliable to make any accurate conclusions. First of all, they examined only six fields (anthropology, sociology, political science, economics, philosophy, and history) rather than all of the humanities and social sciences. Instead of doing a representative sample of college faculty in a field, they surveyed only the members of disciplinary organizations, such as the American Historical Association. The members of disciplinary groups tend to be disproportionately located at elite universities in Democratic urban areas. In several fields, conservative professors actively boycott the main disciplinary groups and form their own associations. Yet Klein and Stern write, "We have no evidence on that matter, but we doubt that any such skew would be substantial."[17]

The Klein and Stern study shows a pattern of distorting the evidence to meet their goal of exposing liberal tendencies in academia. Klein and Stern excluded faculty over the age of 70 (claiming they must be retired), who are likely to be among the most Republican in academia.[18] Another flaw in the study's reporting was the omission of Libertarians in the publicized results, even though Klein is one himself. If Libertarians are included (along with all other minor parties), the left/right ratio of the total sample in the study drops from 10.2 to 1 down to 9.1 to 1.[19]

One sign of the study's statistical flaws was its failure to weight the results. The survey results included 419 respondents in sociology and anthropology (the most liberal fields), but only 96 in economics (the most conservative field, which was disproportionately undercounted).[20] At the University of California at Berkeley, for example, the number of economists (55) equals the number of anthropologists (27) and sociologists (28) combined. Using the Berkeley figures to weight the survey, it turns out that the average of the total sample drops from 9.1 to 1 to only 6.1 to 1.

In most scholarly journals, one hopes that this kind of flagrant abuse of statistics would not be tolerated. But Stern and Klein didn't submit their research to a peer-reviewed, scholarly journal. Instead, they published the study in *Academic Questions,* the journal of NAS, a right-wing advocacy group devoted to attacking liberalism in academia.

Stern and Klein also distorted the findings by asking not about party affiliation or ideology, but this awkward question instead: "To which political party have the candidates you've voted for in the past ten years mostly belonged?"[21] This question creates a bias toward answering Democratic in urban areas and college towns where most of the voters are Democrats. By asking about all candidates rather than the vote for president, the emphasis will be on the more common House and local races, which often don't have serious Republican contenders in many cities.

Consider the hypothetical example of a conservative economist at the University of Chicago, a registered Republican who voted for Bob Dole and George W. Bush for president, but who votes for local Democrats because he has little choice in heavily Democratic Hyde Park. He likes Mayor Richard Daley, who is a conservative probusiness Democrat. And he reluctantly votes for some Democrats because he doesn't like the Republican candidates (such as Alan Keyes, an anti-free-trade U.S. Senate candidate). In one Chicago congressional district, Republicans in the 2006 primary had to choose between a self-described "white racialist" and "Spanky the clown" (the clown won).[22] A conservative Republican professor, answering Klein and Stern honestly, would be a Democrat.

Even among registered Democrats, party affiliation and ideology don't always match. Democrat John Silber, former president of Boston University, is one of the most conservative academics in the country. Stern and Klein also remove a substantial number of professors who are independents by reducing the question to Republican vs. Democrat. In understanding the full spectrum of ideology on campus, it is essential to include independent voters and nonvoters as well as devotees of a particular party.

Klein also contended that the ratio of Democrats to Republicans is more than twice as lopsided as it was three decades ago, pointing to polls of presidential voting patterns.[23] In the 1972 Nixon landslide, professors in the social sciences voted 3.5 to 1 for George McGovern over Richard Nixon, and professors in the humanities voted 2.4 to 1 for McGovern. But if one looks at the 1964 election, when social scientists voted 8.9 to 1 for Lyndon Johnson over Barry Goldwater, and humanities professors voted 6.6 to 1 for Johnson, one finds an average of about 7.7 to 1, or more Democratic than Klein and Stern's survey shows about the current professoriate. Even if Klein and Stern's numbers happened by chance to be accurate (despite all of the methodological flaws), all it would show is that professors today are less likely to vote Democratic than in 1964, long before any cries about tenured radicals and political correctness were heard. These surveys suggest the importance of the job market in creating the ideological distribution of professors: A heavily Democratic academia in the early 1960s became more Republican in the early 1970s as colleges boomed and the job market improved; then, as the job market dried up by the late 1970s, Republicans tended not to seek out these low-paying academic jobs.

Most evidence indicates no radical changes in faculty views. An analysis of the 1989 and 1997 Carnegie surveys of faculty concluded that "the replacement of older, more liberal cohorts by younger, less liberal ones has helped to produce a less liberal faculty."[24]

The liberal tendencies of university faculty have a long history; William F. Buckley contended that the Yale political science faculty in 1948 supported Truman over Dewey by 23 to 0.[25] Robert Bork was called by a Yale journalist in 1964 who could find only one other Goldwater supporter on a faculty of 1,000 professors.[26] The Democratic voting patterns of humanities and social sciences faculty are nothing new, and they certainly do not represent a sudden crisis requiring political intervention to save students from being exposed to liberal ideas.

Klein's study also claims that conservatives face discrimination in academia because they are more common among the members of disciplinary associations who do not have academic jobs. Because the nonacademic members favor the Democratic Party by a ratio of only 4.2 to 1, Klein argues that they reflect "Republicans being sorted out of academia."[27] In reality, we would expect the nonacademic members of a professional association to be more conservative, because Republicans will tend to leave academia for higher-paying jobs in the corporate world.

According to Klein, the message of his studies to taxpayers, parents, and donors is "know what you pay for" and "you might decide you don't want to pay for it."[28] Since Klein studies only the political party affiliation of academics, and not the quality of education, he is urging people to defund universities because they employ too many Democrats. Klein's advocacy research, urging attacks on his own profession, is deplorable not for its conservatism but instead for its statistical errors and misleading interpretations.

The Biases in Measuring Bias

Similar errors were made in a survey by Stanley Rothman, S. Robert Lichter, and Neil Nevitte, who studied data from the 1999 North American Academic Study Survey of 1,643 faculty at 183 four-year colleges in America.[29] Rothman, Lichter, and Nevitte found far lower ratios than those cited by Horowitz and other critics. Their study identified 50 percent of the faculty as Democrats and 11 percent as Republicans, and claimed to determine that 72 percent of professors were liberal, while 15 percent were conservative, a ratio of around 4.8 to 1 in both cases.

Rothman, Lichter, and Nevitte also concluded, "A multivariate analysis finds that, even after taking into account the effects of professional accomplishment, along with many other individual characteristics, conservatives and Republicans teach at lower-quality schools than do liberals and Democrats. This suggests that complaints of ideologically based discrimination in academic advancement deserve serious consideration and further study."[30] Their study found that 44 percent of liberals teach in major research universities and elite liberal arts colleges, compared to 28 percent of conservatives; 24 percent of Christians who attend church weekly teach in top-tier schools, compared to 47 percent of those who "seldom or never" attend religious services; and only 31 percent of women teach in top-tier schools, compared to 41 percent of men.[31]

The measurement of achievement by counting journal articles and books is suspect, since it fails to account for the quality of work. Nevertheless, even if we assume that a gap in publication quantity does reflect a gap in scholarly achievement, the lower presence of Christians and conservatives at elite institutions is not surprising.

One reason is self-selection. A top-notch scholar who is liberal and wants to be around a lot of liberals can go to an elite university; a top-notch scholar who is a conservative Christian and wants to be around Christians and conservatives might choose to remain at a less prestigious college because it is conservative. Because religious colleges requiring a statement of faith discriminate against liberals in hiring, the preferences given to conservative professors may ultimately cause them to stay in less-prestigious institutions.

Another flaw in the study is that it measures the quality of a college based on *U.S. News and World Report* rankings. But these rankings are heavily based upon both reputation and student demand for a college. Secular colleges have more applicants (a factor in ratings) because they are open to everyone. Sectarian religious colleges may also suffer in the reputation rankings, because many top administrators at major universities are unfamiliar with such colleges (which typically lack top sports teams or other methods for publicity). So the gap found in achievement, if real, may actually reflect a bias against religious colleges in the ranking system, not discrimination in hiring.

Another claim made by Rothman, Lichter, and Nevitte (and one intended to bolster the claims of discrimination against conservatives) is that faculty have become dramatically more liberal in recent years. According to Rothman, Lichter, and Nevitte, "over the course of 15 years, self-described liberals grew from a slight plurality to a 5 to 1 majority on college faculties."[32] This conclusion is incorrect.

First, the 1984 data cited by Rothman, Lichter, and Nevitte are not comparable to their current surveys because the older surveys included community college faculty and used different terms. In the 1984 Carnegie survey, 5.7 percent were "left," 33.3 percent "liberal," 27.5 percent "middle of the road," 29.4 percent "moderately conservative," and 4.1 percent "strongly conservative." Because these descriptions are unbalanced ("liberal" is a much more polarized position than "moderately conservative"), the 1984 survey (and earlier surveys that used the same terms) were biased toward increasing conservative responses. Faculty who considered themselves "moderately liberal" might often respond "middle of the road," while "moderately conservative" faculty would be counted as conservatives. The year 1984 also represented an unusually conservative political year in which Ronald Reagan won reelection in a landslide, so surveys probably overstated conservative responses.

Second, the "5 to 1 majority" asserted for the Rothman data is deceptive. Most important, it omits community college faculty (who are 20 to 30 percent less likely to be liberal than the faculty at four-year colleges because only a master's degree is required to teach, and community colleges are located in more conservative areas).[33] The survey also uses a biased 1-to-10 scale as a survey instrument that tends to bring more conservative responses, because many people regard "5" as the median point (rather than the actual 5.5)

A far better survey conducted at almost the same time is the 1997 Carnegie survey of faculty, which found that 28.5 percent of faculty were "liberal," 31.4 percent "moderately liberal," 18.9 percent "middle of the road," 16.0 percent "moderately conservative," and 5.3 percent "conservative."[34] This is a liberal/conservative ratio of 2.8 to 1, not 5 to 1.

From 1989 to 1997, the proportion of self-described liberals dropped to 23.3 percent, while self-described conservatives held steady at 6.7 percent;

the biggest jump was in middle-of-the-road professors, who increased to 19.6 percent. Although there are more liberals than conservatives in the humanities and social sciences, conservatives outnumber liberals in business, technical/vocational fields, engineering, computer science, and physical education.[35]

UCLA's Higher Education Research Institute surveyed full-time college faculty and found that in 2004–05, 7.5 percent called themselves "far left," 44.6 percent "liberal," 29.4 percent "middle of the road," 17.9 percent "conservative," and 0.6 percent "far right."[36] There is no equal balance of ideology on campus, but the fact that 48 percent of college faculty describe themselves as centrist or conservative suggests serious flaws in these claims about a liberal monopoly on campus. The ratio of far-left and liberal faculty (52.1 percent) to conservative or far-right faculty (18.5 percent) is 2.8 to 1, or similar to what other surveys have found. Surveys have also found that college administrators are slightly more conservative than the faculty.[37]

Another survey in 2006 of 1,200 faculty at four-year colleges found that the ratios of liberals to conservatives (48 percent to 17 percent), Democrats to Republicans (46 percent to 16 percent), and Kerry voters to Bush voters (72 percent to 25 percent) are all just under a 3 to 1 ratio. Even in the humanities and social sciences, the ratio is only 5 to 1.[38] These ratios closely reflect the views of college students. A 2006 national survey of college students found that 46 percent plan to vote for a Democrat for Congress, compared to only 20 percent for a Republican, a ratio of 2.3 to 1.[39]

Nor are Republicans the only group underrepresented in academia. According to the Rothman study, Republicans are 11 percent of college professors at four-year universities.[40] Since 30 percent of the general population are Republicans, this indicates an underrepresentation ratio of no more than 2.72:1.[41] However, a similar underrepresentation ratio of 2.63:1 exists for blacks, who are 12.9 percent of the population but only 4.9 percent of the full-time faculty at four-year universities.[42] And Latinos are much rarer than Republicans in academia: In the 2000 census, 12.5 percent of the population was Hispanic, while only 3.0 percent of the faculty in 1998 was Hispanic, an underrepresentation ratio of 4.17:1.[43] It is strange that conservatives who claim there's no discrimination against racial minorities in academia will presume that a smaller underrepresentation of Republicans is definitive proof of political bias. We would not expect race to affect occupational choice in an ideal world, but political ideology (and the desire to make money) will always impact a decision to pursue a low-paying profession like teaching. All of the evidence available indicates that the underrepresentation of Republicans in academia is not nearly as bad as conservatives proclaim and provides no evidence that right-wingers face systematic discrimination in higher education.

Conservative Push-Polling

One effort to push the case for the oppression of conservatives on campus was made by the American Council of Trustees and Alumni (ACTA). ACTA financed a widely publicized 2004 survey of students at fifty of the top-ranked colleges in America. ACTA head Anne Neal contended, "The response was disheartening. Forty-eight percent reported campus presentations on political issues that seemed totally one-sided. Forty-six percent said professors used the classroom to present their personal political views. Forty-two percent faulted reading assignments representing only one side of a controversial issue. In short, according to those with firsthand knowledge, in the college classroom many professors are preaching rather than teaching."[44] The *Wall Street Journal* editorialized that "liberal professors routinely harass conservative students" because "nearly half said that their professors 'frequently comment on politics in class even though it has nothing to do with the course' or use the classroom to present their personal political views."[45]

In fact, these statements were entirely inaccurate. The ACTA survey only asked students if they thought there were "some classes" on their campus where professors presented political views or one-sided readings. The survey had nothing to do with firsthand knowledge, and relied on hearsay and speculation to inflate its results. Considering that every campus has classes where professors mention their political views, and almost all campus speeches are "one-sided," these responses are surprising only because they fell short of 100 percent.

Neal claimed, "One case of political intolerance is too many. But the fact that half the students are reporting abuses is simply unacceptable. If these were reports of sexual harassment in the classroom, they would get people's attention."[46] But none of the students reported being harassed for their politics. None of the students reported being abused. It is Neal's belief that professors who mention politics in class are "abusing" their students, not the students' view. Just as talking about sexual issues in class is not invariably sexual harassment, talking about political issues does not constitute "political harassment," even if such a concept existed.

ACTA falsely declared in a press release about their survey that "29 percent feel they have to agree with the professor's political views to get a good grade."[47] In reality, the students were responding to this survey item: "On my campus, there are courses in which students feel they have to agree with the professor's political or social views in order to get a good grade." If, out of the thousands of classes taught at a university every year, two students might "feel" this way (whether it's true or not), then the answer to the question is yes. After decades of conservative denunciations of academia, the only thing surprising about this survey is the fact that a mere 29 percent agreed that any students on their campuses believe political grading has happened.

Nor can we know whether conservative or liberal students were the ones who felt silenced. The Carnegie survey of faculty nationally revealed that conservative faculty consider it more important than liberals to "shape students' values" (even though conservatives more often teach in fields seen as more objective).[48] Students in many business and economics classes are forced to agree with the free-market economic theories espoused by their professors. A student who believes in socialist economics often cannot express such ideas in a test without suffering a lower grade. Neal argued, "The majority of the students surveyed majored in subjects like biology, engineering and psychology, subjects that have nothing to do with politics."[49] In fact, biology is a subject deeply involved in politics, and many of the conservative students who feel like professors force their views on them are fundamentalists who feel that evolutionary science is imposed on them in biology class. By creating a bad survey and then misrepresenting the results, ACTA promoted the false idea that students feel oppressed by their professors.

The conservative Independent Women's Forum did a similarly biased December 2003 survey of college students and concluded that professors "push their political views." But the survey actually showed a surprising absence of political bias in the classroom. According to IWF, "42 percent of students report political discussions in the classroom lean to a leftist point of view, with only 18 percent saying they hear the conservative side of an issue."[50] In reality, students were asked: "When politics are discussed during class, does the discussion tend to be about more conservative viewpoints or more liberal viewpoints?" The question doesn't distinguish between discussions by students and faculty, and because students tend to be more liberal (especially in classes where political discussion is common), it is not surprising to find more liberal views expressed in classes.[51] But the survey never found that only 18 percent ever "hear the conservative side."[52]

Only 8 percent of students reported that their professors "often" will "express their political views during class" (which is entirely legitimate for professors to do).[53]

Because the question asked students to generalize the views of "your professors" (who obviously have a range of ideologies), it was designed to get liberal responses (since a student with three liberal professors and two conservative professors would answer "liberal"). The fact that so few students perceive their professors to be liberal strongly indicates that there is no campaign of liberal indoctrination on college campuses. Only 30 percent of students considered their professors to be more liberal than themselves, compared to 19 percent who regarded their professors as more conservative.[54]

Only 16 percent of students answered "yes" to the question, "Have you ever been afraid your grade would suffer in a class for disagreeing with a professor's political point of view?" Considering that a typical college student takes at least forty classes during college, this means that less than one in six students can identify even 2.5 percent of their classes where a disagreement might reduce their grade (and no indication of whether this happens in classes taught by liberals or conservatives). The IWF never asked students if they thought disagreeing with the professor would help their grade (as it does in some classes), nor did the survey ask how many students actually suffered poorer grades. Considering the campaigns proclaiming leftist totalitarianism on campuses, it is surprising that more students do not suffer from this fear, even when it is unfounded.

Explaining Democrats in Academia

Although the numbers given by Horowitz and other conservative surveyors are often statistical deceptions, no one questions the fact that there are more Democrats than Republicans on most college faculties, particularly in the liberal arts. But this is a creation of the free market. Many more Democrats than Republicans want to enter Ph.D. programs and become part of the professoriate. The preponderance of Democrats in no way supports Horowitz's leap of logic that "everyone knows that there is an academic blacklist that has practically eliminated conservatives from university faculties."[55]

No liberal group has ever made any list of conservative faculty deemed unacceptable. By contrast, conservatives maintain many lists of liberal faculty to demonize: CampusWatch.org "dossiers" of left-leaning Middle East studies professors, David Horowitz's compilation of the "101 Most Dangerous Academics," the Texas conservatives' list of objectionable faculty in Austin, the lists of liberal faculty on NoIndoctrination.org and studentsforacademicfreedom.org, the list by the American Council on Trustees and Alumni (ACTA) of comments by liberal faculty after 9/11, and the lists of class descriptions that the Young America's Foundation and ACTA and David Horowitz think should be banished from academia. Horowitz's disciple Andrew Jones even started UCLAprofs.com and offered to pay students to spy on their UCLA professors: "Full, detailed lecture notes, all professor-distributed materials, and full tape recordings of every class session, for one class: $100." For a $10 fee, students could help the group develop a "target list" of professors.[56] Jones had worked for Horowitz until he was fired for pressuring UCLA students to file false reports of being physically attacked by leftist students.[57] If conservatives are blacklisted, where is the list? Where is the evidence?

Professors tend to follow the public's voting patterns in the communities where they live. Most academics, especially at elite universities, work in heavily Democratic urban areas, and in many of these cities you have to register as a Democrat to have a meaningful vote in local politics. Out of the top ten universities in the country and the top ten liberal arts colleges (as ranked in 2007 by *U.S. News & World Report*), only one in each category is located in a state that voted for Bush in 2004. And even red-state colleges typically are found in towns that voted heavily for Kerry (in Kansas, which voted nearly 2–1 for Bush, districts around the University of Kansas voted about 2–1 for Kerry).[58] Independents (about one-third of academics) tend to vote in the most competitive primary elections, which in heavily Democratic areas (the overwhelming majority of college communities) will be the Democratic primary. Since studies of the political party of professors examine how they vote in primaries (no party affiliation is provided by voters in general elections), these studies tend to overstate the number of Democrats.

It is only by ignoring the large number of independent professors that these surveys can create the impression that Democrats control academia. Based on another distorted Horowitz study, this time of journalism professors, *New York Times* columnist John Tierney denounced academics for "cronyism," claiming that journalism schools hired only those who agreed with their ideology. But in Horowitz's highly selective and unscientific study, a majority of the journalism professors were nonpartisan or not registered. Out of 314 journalism professors studied by Horowitz, 120 are registered Democrats, or only 38.2 percent.[59]

Some professors may also vote for Democrats out of self-interest, because Democrats typically support greater funding for higher education. Most of today's attacks on academic freedom by politicians have come from Republicans. Why is it surprising that professors often don't vote for the Republican politicians who denounce academia with wildly inaccurate charges?

Another significant reason why conservatives are pushed away from academic careers is the resistance of colleges to liberal family-friendly policies. Conservatives, both male and female, tend to be more interested in starting a family than liberals, and at a younger age.[60] But the salaries and workloads of graduate students and assistant professors make it difficult to sustain a family. As one woman noted, "I had to decide if I wanted to pursue a career as a professor, knowing it would require that strangers essentially raise my newborn daughter."[61]

But by far the biggest factor that keeps conservatives out of academia is money. Why would the smartest college graduates spend more time than it takes to earn a law degree and an MBA combined, all for a career in which a scholar must be very talented and lucky just to get a job that pays less than the starting salary for college graduates in many fields? As Republican pundit Fred Barnes noted, "The inclination of so many young conservatives I know is to go to law school or to get an MBA."[62]

Although academics earn more than the average American, they are paid substantially less than their peers. According to the National Association for Law Placement, law school graduates nine months after receiving their degree in 2004 earned on average $80,000 in private practice, $60,000 in business, $44,700 in government, and only $40,000 in academe.[63]

A *Duke Chronicle* article noted, "After four years of college, 10 years of graduate education and the investment of a small fortune in studying the larger questions of the humanities, how are the job prospects? Dismal." By some estimates, only one in five humanities Ph.D.s gets a full-time, tenure-track job, the kind that typically pays less than $50,000 per year.[64] Part-time professors earn 64 percent less per hour of teaching than their full-time counterparts, or about one-third as much.[65]

James Engell, coauthor of *Saving Higher Education in the Age of Money* (2005), worries about the impact of low salaries in the humanities that increasingly lag behind other fields: "Who then wants to study in that field, or consider it as a career when the educational institution itself is willing to let it lag farther and farther behind? ... A lack of equity that is growing larger and larger will actually destroy fields and discourage talent from entering them."[66] Between 1986 and 2005, real salaries for faculty increased only by 0.27 percent.[67] And while salaries grow in conservative fields, humanities professors have suffered salary cutbacks. In current dollars, full-time humanities professors in 1988 made $57,053, while business professors were paid $60,851; by 2004, the average salary for humanities professors had dropped to $56,313, while the salary of business professors jumped to $76,216.[68] The lagging salaries in the humanities and most social sciences are directly related to the ideological imbalance. Fields that tend to pay more, such as economics, tend to have more conservative professors.

From a rational economic perspective, getting a Ph.D. in the humanities and social sciences is a stupid idea for a bright college graduate. As Marge Simpson put it, "Bart, don't make fun of graduate students. They just made a terrible life choice."[69] And it seems clear that many more liberals than conservatives make these economically idiotic choices, preferring the lure of the life of the mind to the likelihood of wealth.

These decisions are often made before a student ever enters college. Liberal students are more likely to major in the less lucrative humanities and social sciences, which is usually essential for anyone to pursue a Ph.D. in those fields. And money is the primary motivation. Jeremy Beer, editor of a conservative guide to college, observed: "The days when a degree in English or art history will pay as well as a degree in engineering, computer programming, or business are simply not on the horizon."[70] A young liberal is much more likely than a young conservative to possess a college or graduate degree, even after correcting for other demographic factors.[71]

The rare conservative who pursues a Ph.D. can often find a better job outside of academia. John Zmirak, who works for a conservative think tank, the Intercollegiate Studies Institute, noted: "I'm an English Ph.D. who took a long look at the profession and decided not even to bother TRYING to find a job teaching; as a white heterosexual conservative Catholic man, whose interests were in Southern Literature.... Since I didn't want to teach at a Bible college or a seminary, I went into journalism."[72] Here is someone crying out about bias who never even tried to get an academic job. Of course, when conservative think tanks provide a comfortable alternative to the hard work of teaching and researching for a living, it is not surprising that they draw right-wingers away from an academic career. Conservative think tanks outspend liberal ones by nearly $100 million a year, and among Richard Posner's list of public intellectuals, 20 percent of conservative intellectuals on it worked at think tanks, compared to only 2 percent of the centrist and liberal intellectuals.[73] Think tank jobs are much more appealing than academic positions, which require intellectuals to spend an enormous amount of time doing teaching, committee work, and research aimed at a specialized scholarly audience.

An editorial in the *Rocky Mountain News* called this economic argument "fatuous" and "silly" because "if it were correct, why would it apply to history and political science, but not to the same degree in chemistry and biology?"[74] The economic argument does apply to chemistry and biology, where professors are certainly more liberal than their higher-paid counterparts in industry. The low pay in academia is a major reason why Ph.D. programs in the sciences are often dominated by foreign students (for whom the prestige and job opportunities in America offset the low economic value of a Ph.D.). Conservative students skilled in science are likely to attend medical school and have a lucrative career as a doctor rather than enter a Ph.D. program. But the "liberal bias" in chemistry and biology in academia rarely causes concern because chemical and biological research are not being targeted by Republican activists.

According to the *Rocky Mountain News*, academics are "well-compensated" and "once tenured, they enjoy a level of economic security that most of the workforce would envy."[75] Of course, academics are not well paid for the level of education they have. Almost every other profession—from engineers to accountants to lawyers to businesspeople—receives greater average compensation with far fewer years of education and a much easier time finding an entry-level job.

Academia—perhaps the least secure professional field with the worst economic payoff—is falsely perceived to provide a job for life. Tenure is, at best, a small compensation for an economically lousy career choice. Graduate students must overcome a difficult job market, low pay, and then years of hard work before facing a tenure decision—and few corporate workers in stable industries will ever have to encounter a detailed tenure evaluation after six years of employment that can easily result in their termination even if they are doing an adequate job.

The real question is not why so few conservatives want to attend graduate school and go into academia, but why so many liberals are willing to do so despite the economic disincentives. Far from being a leftist conspiracy to take over academia, the overrepresentation of liberals on many college campuses is an example of self-sacrifice. Liberals simply appear to be more willing than conservatives to sacrifice earning power for a life of the mind.

Liberals dominate teaching at all levels. Research on voting by K–12 teachers is difficult to find, but one study of five Republican-dominated Florida counties found that 44 percent of teachers in 2002 were registered Democrats and 28 percent were registered Republicans.[76] The liberal trend is slightly exacerbated in higher education because the level of education is much higher and the job prospects are much worse than for K-12 teachers. The median annual earnings of full-time college teachers in 2004 were $51,800, while public school K–12 teachers (despite rarely having a Ph.D.) made almost as much, an average of $46,597.[77] Yet even among K–12 teachers, where jobs are much easier to get, conservatives seem to avoid the teaching profession.

It is rare for any occupation to mirror precisely the national averages for party affiliation. CEOs are almost certainly jobs filled by Republicans, and few people would say that a low-paid faculty position is as desirable as a millionaire CEO's job. Yet Horowitz and his allies are silent about proposing that corporations end the blacklist against liberal executives.

There is also a "bias" in certain academic fields against conservative thinking because new forms of research are highly valued, especially in the humanities and social sciences. Whereas scientific research tends to rely upon incremental advancement, humanities research tends to value new ideas that have not been deeply explored before. A traditionalist who loves Shakespeare and thinks the best interpretations of his work were made decades ago is unlikely to be interested in doing extensive research in new directions in order to get tenure. Because of this, a "progressive thinker" may tend to be more successful in the humanities and much more likely to pursue a career there.

Of course, not all "progressive thinking" corresponds to progressive political views. The sole conservative political approach that is usually strongly represented among professors is libertarianism. That's because libertarians tend to be progressive thinkers who embrace the pursuit of new knowledge (and enjoy the freedom granted to professors), but who reach policy conclusions that match most (but not all) of the Republican Party platform. One proof that conservatives don't face discrimination in academia can be found by examining libertarians. The Klein and Stern study found that 1.27 percent of the faculty they surveyed reported voting for mostly Libertarian candidates. Since Libertarian candidates are hard to find, the number of libertarians in academia is probably much higher. But nationwide, in 2004 only 0.32 percent of Americans voted for a Libertarian presidential candidate, an overrepresentation ratio of 4:1.[78]

So if there were widespread prejudice against conservatives in higher education, how can it be that the proportion of libertarians among the humanities and social sciences faculty is four times their proportion in the general population? The reason is that self-selection, not discrimination, explains the political views of academics. Academia attracts people with a strong commitment to academic freedom and a weak commitment to making money. Conservatives often have less commitment to academic freedom and a greater desire to make money.[79] But libertarians have a strong devotion to academic freedom and individual liberty, and so libertarians are strongly overrepresented in academia. Libertarians are the only subset of conservatives willing to sacrifice higher wages for the freedom and intellectual engagement they find in academic work. The libertarian example disproves the allegation of discrimination against conservatives.

Are there conservatives who are well qualified for academic jobs, yet unable to find anyone to hire them? Absolutely, but many more liberals are in exactly the same position. The academic job crisis, especially in the humanities and the social sciences, is so enormous that any group can compile a large number of anecdotal horror stories about unfair and unjust treatment at the hands of the academic establishment.

Former AAUP general secretary Roger Bowen noted, "I've conducted more searches than I can begin to describe, and I can tell you I have never asked a candidate what his or her party identification is, and I don't know of a search committee in the country that would do that."[80] Bowen's own experience, however, is not necessarily universal. Certainly, there must be some cases where a hiring decision is affected by the candidate's political views. But there is no evidence that political bias is more common in faculty hiring than any other job, nor is there any proof that conservatives are more often the victims of bias than liberals. As Joseph Reisert observed, "In my twenty-plus years as a conservative student and teacher at three strongly left-leaning institutions (Princeton, Harvard, and Colby), I have never felt discriminated against. I have only once witnessed an overtly propagandizing classroom presentation, and I have only once heard a student complain about being graded unfairly for not hewing to the professor's party line."[81]

Because the free market of faculty in academia is heavily Democratic, changing this fact would require a vast socialist re-engineering of the faculty via ideological preferences. And some conservatives have suggested doing exactly that. Stephen Balch of NAS proposed that colleges give "property rights" to the right wing via proportional representation to conservatives on voting for curriculum and hiring. By this plan, an isolated conservative would be given, say, twenty extra votes for any decision until an equal number of liberals and conservatives were hired.[82] Of course, such an approach is completely unworkable (Who defines what a conservative is? Do they have to pass a test? Will they be hooked up to a lie detector?) and entirely undesirable because it would put ideology above academic merit. Demanding proportionality in the ideology of faculty might lead to more

Republicans or more creationists among college professors (to match the overall population's views), but it would undermine intellectual freedom and professional standards.

No one knows what are the actual job chances of conservatives in academia, because that would require a study of the ideology of newly minted Ph.D.s for comparison. It is possible that conservatives get hiring preferences more often than they face discrimination because there are many conservative (particularly religious) colleges that openly welcome right-wing views and discourage (or ban) liberal ideas such as equal rights for gays and lesbians.

According to David Horowitz, "In the present academic system, conservatives are as rare as unicorns, and have an almost impossible barrier to overcome in order to get hired."[83] Republican professors would be as rare as unicorns—if there were well over 100,000 unicorns teaching at American colleges.[84] There would be even more Republican professors, except that there are so many political independents, apathetic instructors, and foreign citizens working in higher education.

We do need more conservative professors, both to increase the variety of different views in academia and to help bring the higher standards of academic analysis to conservative policy debates. But given the free choices of conservative students and thinkers, it seems increasingly unlikely that they will want to pursue academic careers.

The most effective way to increase conservative representation without violating academic freedom would be to increase the status of academic jobs, especially in the humanities and social sciences. This means increasing salaries (the humanities and the social sciences are among the lowest-paying jobs in academia) and increasing the proportion of full-time tenure-track jobs.

It is also important to refute the false attacks on academia that have wrongly presented conservatives as the universally oppressed victims of campus thought police, waiting to destroy any Republican who dares to step out of the right-wing closet. So long as these exaggerated denunciations of higher education are endlessly repeated, few conservatives will undertake the sacrifices required for an academic career.

More family-friendly policies and more funding for higher education, if it led to tenure-track jobs and better faculty pay, would attract more Republicans into academia and cause more wealthy professors to turn Republican. But Horowitz's goal is not really to increase the number of Republicans teaching Shakespeare; instead, the aim of Horowitz and his Republican allies is to silence and intimidate what he calls "left-wing ideologues" on college campuses.

Conservative leaders don't want to have "diversity" in higher education; they want colleges to ban radical viewpoints and silence opposing views.

Stephen Moore of the Club for Growth told a group of conservative donors: "Stop funding universities. I mean, the biggest frustration is conservative donors who give money to Harvard and Yale. Hundreds of billions of dollars a year flow into these totally corrupt institutions. Stop! Because the money talks and if conservatives would stop funding these ridiculous programs that universities run, they would have to stop their activities."[85] Even more bluntly, David Keene of the American Conservative Union declared: "The good news and the bad news about the universities is that the universities are the last privileged sanctuary in America for liberal collectivism. The bad news is that they have retreated to those universities and clearing them out is a little bit like clearing out the Japanese stragglers on a Pacific island in World War II. And so it's God's work, but it's not easy, but it is certainly something we should do."[86]

In reality, left-wing activists are rare in academia. There is an overwhelming emphasis on obscure research in academia and a strong tendency to discourage political activism. For all of the complaints about conservatives facing discrimination in academia, a dirty little secret of higher education is that left-wing political activists encounter the most discrimination of anyone. In what should be an atmosphere of intense political discussion and debate on college campuses, most faculty put their heads down, teach their classes numbly, fill the journals with the meaningless productivity they need for tenure, and stay out of politics. And students likewise learn to avoid politics.

We need to encourage more faculty, liberal and conservative alike, to talk about politics in their classes, their research, and at campus discussions. Faculty members should be the role models for students to engage in their communities and express political views. We certainly need to have more intellectual diversity in academia. We should worry that so many business and economics classes rarely present the viewpoints of workers and consumers. We should worry when so many scientific fields are swayed by corporate funding. We should worry that too many departments tend to teach students job training rather than intellectual inquiry. And we should be concerned that too few conservatives teach in some low-paying fields.

The key issue should not be whether students are learning from a Democrat or a Republican, but whether or not they're learning. Horowitz's Academic Bill of Rights seeks to obliterate what little political discussion by faculty exists on college campuses. Not only is the Academic Bill of Rights a bad solution for a minor problem, but it will undermine the goal of civic engagement that every college campus should be encouraging among its faculty, staff, and students.

CHAPTER FIVE
Conservative Correctness and Free Speech on Campus

⌁

Conservative students have portrayed themselves as the most oppressed minority on college campuses. After author Barbara Ehrenreich spoke at a freshman orientation event at Miami University of Ohio in 2003, one student proclaimed: "I felt bombarded with left-wing views. Everywhere I turned, I was being scorned for holding a conservative ideology. I couldn't help but feel as though my Republican partisanship was being threatened.... I cannot recall one instance where a conservative view was presented by any university event or faculty." In reality, P. J. Rourke, Pat Buchanan, Alan Keyes, and Rudy Guiliani all appeared on Miami's campus that semester.[1]

Theodore Hertzberg, chair of the Amherst College Republicans, proposed reserving a seat on the student senate for an oppressed minority: conservatives. Hertzberg explained, "It ought to go without saying that conservative students have been silenced on this campus."[2] At Skidmore College in New York, a group of Young Republicans held a "Coming Out Day" to mock gays and lesbians and promote their own alleged oppression. But far from being censored, Skidmore administrators gave the group $4,000 for speakers and helped to publicize the event.[3] According to John Miller in *National Review,* "Campus conservatives are 'The Other,' a barely human subpopulation whose presumed inferiorities justify the dominance of an enlightened professoriate."[4]

The other side of the rhetoric of conservative victimization is the fantasy of right-wing students as rebels going up against the powerful liberal establishment. Conservative columnist and talk show host Doug Giles claimed,

"This is what today's young high school- and college-Rosa-Park-radicals [*sic*] will look like. They will be conservative, God-honoring students who will be society's new shockers."[5] Who knows, maybe these conservative "radicals" will learn enough history to spell Rosa Parks's name correctly and will realize that their privileged lives in defense of privilege might not be today's moral equivalent of the Civil Rights Movement.

According to one conservative student, "The protest spirit of free speech is alive and well on the American campus ... but unlike the hippie generation, we protest liberal academia. Campus conservatives, for lack of a better word, are cool."[6] A *New York Times Magazine* cover story profiled these new "hipublicans" on campus.[7] Irving Kristol argued that conservatives "constitute, in effect, a counterculture on campus."[8] This pseudo-rebellion is just another side of conservative victimhood.

The conservative delusion of themselves as the oppressed minority might be merely comical if not for the accompanying demand to suppress liberals. Horowitz justifies his crusade against academic freedom by proclaiming that "students are a captive and vulnerable audience."[9] Some conservatives even compare professors who mention politics to pedophiles. Jeff Jacoby wrote, "Academic freedom is not only meant to protect professors; it is also supposed to ensure students' right to learn without being molested. When instructors use their classrooms to indoctrinate and propagandize, they cheat those students and betray the academic mission they are entrusted with."[10] But are college students like innocent children? Is hearing a professor express a political idea like being "molested"? Rather than treating college students like children and imposing surveillance over professors to ensure that students are "protected" from "dangerous" ideas, we need to treat students like adults and give them freedom, including the freedom to hear offensive ideas.

On April 24, 2003, conservatives held a "town hall" meeting at California State University in Fullerton on "The Marginalization of the Conservative Voice." In the most Republican county in California, conservatives gathered to discuss their oppression. Dick Mountjoy, a former Republican state senator from Los Angeles, declared: "Your college campuses are liberal. Those of us in the business community say, 'We need to get students out of college before they can corrupt you too far.'"[11]

This drive to destroy higher education is echoed by right-wing columnist Walter Williams, who urges conservative donors to boycott colleges: "See whether it has multiculturalism, diversity or equity offices and programs. If it has, it's probably practicing some form of racism. The next step is simple: Close your pocketbook."[12] Every college has an affirmative action officer to fill out the government-required forms. Every college teaches some classes about other cultures. Multiculturalism and diversity are not code words for a vast left-wing conspiracy; they are essential components of a traditional liberal education. But as Rush Limbaugh declared, "A liberal education is indoctrination."[13]

For centuries in America (and going back to Socrates), conservatives have worried that teachers are corrupting youth with new ideas. The innovation of today's conservative movement is that it puts right-wing students in the lead of demanding the suppression of their own teachers and uses the language of the left to argue that conservatives are the oppressed victims of liberal education.

Getting Brainwashed

Perhaps the best example of a student leading the drive for suppressing the left on campus is Ben Shapiro, a UCLA graduate and Harvard law student who began writing a column for Townhall.com after he was suspended from the UCLA newspaper for denouncing his editors on a radio show. In his book *Brainwashed: How Universities Indoctrinate America's Youth* (2004), Shapiro spins a tale about how politically correct universities are ruining young minds by imposing a left-wing ideology. Astonishingly, Shapiro's claim about brainwashing in academia has little evidence to back it.

Factual accuracy is a struggle for Shapiro. The opening quote for the book misspells Berkeley chancellor Robert Berdahl's name.[14] One example of Shapiro's shoddy use of statistics is his attempt to use polls to prove that colleges brainwash students to become more liberal. Shapiro declares in his introduction, "In an informal exit poll conducted by the UCLA *Daily Bruin* during the 2000 presidential election, Gore garnered 71 percent of the UCLA student vote, with Bush receiving a mere 20 percent."[15] Noting that national polls of entering college freshmen show only a ten-point voting gap, Shapiro claims that it proves "by the time students become upperclassmen, a ten-point political gap often becomes a fifty-point canyon" due to college brainwashing.[16] Shapiro's comparison of national and campus polls makes no sense; why would anyone expect students in one of the most liberal cities in one of the most liberal states to vote the same as students around the country?

Shapiro was appalled to report that "classes on Marxism exist at major universities across the country," listing dozens of colleges that actually dare to teach a class about Marx.[17] Among the various crimes of professors, Shapiro wrote, "Professor A. Belden Fields of the University of Illinois leads the socialist group on campus in monthly discussions."[18] No, not something so horrible as a monthly discussion! When will somebody stop this terror?

Shapiro condemned Joel Blau of the State University of New York at "Stoneybrook" [*sic*] for "communism" because Blau called Bush's tax plan "a proposal that caters to the wealthiest segment of the population."[19] But that's an objective statement of Bush's tax proposal: It benefits the wealthiest more than others. Conservatives are free to argue that the wealthiest should benefit the most from tax cuts, but Blau's claim itself is a fact. To not only dispute it, but accuse anyone who utters it of "communism" indicates Shapiro's habit of red-baiting.

Shapiro claimed that to professors, "Saddam Hussein was not an enemy, but a strong and principled leader." He wrote, "Many professors felt pangs of joy as they saw three thousand Americans dying."[20] Exactly who these professors were, Shapiro didn't say. He did object to Noam Chomsky's criticism of U.S. policies and proclaimed, "Next time, Professor Chomsky should volunteer to fly the suicide missions."[21] Shapiro saw political debate in warlike terms: "What these professors want is a jihad against God, a crusade against traditional morality. And their battlefields are lecture halls full of innocent civilians."[22] Shapiro even seemed to urge the mass murder of academics: "The professors are the intellectual terrorists. May they reap what they sow."[23]

Shapiro's title, *Brainwashed,* reflects what conservatives think brainwashing is. According to Shapiro, "At Wayne State University, professors rushed to brainwash students to oppose war and President Bush." And what was this brainwashing? A call for a day of reflection on the war "to raise questions about this war drive and its potential consequences."[24] Shapiro also denounced Brian Foley of Widener University School of Law in Delaware for indoctrinating students because he proclaimed, "I will teach my class in the hope that the skills my students learn will make them better citizens, who will ask questions and demand answers before they let their country be led into war."[25] Is this brainwashing and a betrayal of academic integrity, to teach students to ask questions?

Shapiro is vague about his proposals for the solution to the problem of "brainwashing." Shapiro proclaimed it "a decent idea" for conservatives to pull money from universities he deems too liberal, but bizarrely contended that foreigners will take over, claiming that "Saudi Arabia buys up American universities like they're going out of style."[26]

Yet Shapiro admitted, "I don't believe that large numbers of conservative students are purposefully targeted for grade penalization."[27] Shapiro, who seemingly cannot write a paragraph without making a factual error, a distortion of a statistic, or a specious argument, somehow managed to get good enough grades from all of his left-wing brainwashing professors to be admitted to Harvard Law School. If *Brainwashed* is any indication, professors are bending over backwards to give fair grades to conservatives who, imitating their political talk show idols, have only a remote familiarity with accuracy and truth.

Pie Conspiracies

The Great Pie Conspiracy began when Bill Kristol, editor of the *Weekly Standard,* was hit with a pie at Earlham College in Indiana on March 30, 2005, while salad dressing was thrown on Pat Buchanan at Western Michigan University on March 31, 2005.[28] Soon David Horowitz and Ann Coulter were also the victims of pie-launching imitators.

We will never know how long it took Horowitz, as he was wiping a creamy pie off his face, to realize what a tremendous opportunity he had been given by the crazy guy who thought that dessert tossing is a form of political protest. Shortly after Horowitz was pied, he sent out a fund-raising letter. Horowitz reported, "There's a wave of leftist violence against conservative speakers on college campuses, and tonight I was a target."[29] Horowitz speculated that this pie "violence" was part of a plot against conservatives: "It is possible a radical network has decided to pursue a strategy of intimidation to prevent conservatives from appearing on college campuses."[30]

The pinheads throwing pies at right-wingers were seemingly unaware of how much they are helping the conservative movement with their idiotic actions. Horowitz was featured on *Hannity & Colmes* on April 11, 2005, because of the pies. Ann Coulter got an appearance on *The Tonight Show* with a video of her skillful pie-evasion techniques, and she was put on the cover of *Time* magazine.

Why don't conservatives ever toss pies at left-wing speakers? Perhaps they're not as stupid as the far left. They know that Noam Chomsky will never get attention from the mainstream media or influence politicians, so why would they ever help him out by throwing a pie?

Censoring Conservatives

Donald Downs has claimed, "Over the past 15 years, the targets of speech codes and similar policies on campus have almost invariably been conservatives who strongly dissented from political correctness."[31] In reality, no one has ever done a systematic study of how many students are punished under speech codes and the reasons why. The anecdotal evidence indicates that, contrary to Downs's claim, a substantial number of left-leaning students are arrested, punished, or expelled by colleges for expressing their views.

But a conservative network of well-funded advocacy groups and right-wing talk shows promoting selective cases has created a false sense of ideological oppression. In order to promote the conservative movement, the right has spent over $100 million in the past two decades on college campuses, aimed at attacking liberal ideas. The Intercollegiate Studies Institute spends $1 million a year to support nearly 100 conservative campus newspapers, a 50 percent increase from a few years ago. College Republican chapters tripled from about 400 in the late 1990s to 1,148 in 2004, with 120,000 members.[32] Over 40,000 young conservatives have been trained by the Leadership Institute, a right-wing nonprofit group with an annual budget of over $5.4 million.[33] And numerous groups like Horowitz's David Horowitz Freedom

Center receive millions of dollars every year to transmit the image of the oppressed conservative. By contrast, investment by foundations in a progressive movement on campus has been insignificant.[34] Unlike most progressives, the right-wing students who face violations of their rights have organizations and media that publicize their cases, mobilize resistance, and provide legal assistance.

Are there cases where conservative students have been censored on campus? Of course there are. Higher education in America is a vast industry with more than 1.1 million faculty and 15 million students at 4,000 colleges across the country. Anybody can find three anecdotes about universities to prove anything.

Cases of censorship on campus that a few years ago might have disappeared without a trace can now become a cause celebre of political correctness. And this is a good thing. The problem is that liberal groups have not had a similar well-financed movement to spread the word about threats to intellectual freedom against progressive views.

Some conservatives are indeed punished because of the hyperactive paternalism that prevails at many colleges. At San Francisco State University, officials rescinded the expulsion of Tatiana Menaker, a student who had used an expletive and argued with Palestinians on campus. Menaker was falsely accused of making death threats because she told a Jewish professor who was critical of Israel that Palestinians would kill the professor if they ever gained control. Campus police sought (unsuccessfully) to have felony charges brought against Menaker.[35]

But a far worse punishment faced a student at another San Francisco college. At the Academy of Art University, a freshman student in a creative writing class who wrote a story "full of sex and violence" was expelled in fall 2003 and investigated by the San Francisco Police Department's homicide division at the request of college officials. Jan Richman, the course instructor, was blamed by administrators for assigning David Foster Wallace's story "The Girl with Curious Hair" (which features a character called Sick Puppy who puts out matches on women) and then Richman was fired.[36] When Alan Kaufman, another instructor, tried to hold a forum in his class about free expression, the university banned guest speaker Daniel Handler (also known as Lemony Snicket). One of Kaufman's students was also forced to leave the university because she wrote a short story joking about suicide threats.[37]

Most campus repression has nothing to do with ideology, but instead reflects the power of authoritarian administrators. Syracuse University removed four students from a writing class, put them on disciplinary reprimand, and forced them to create informational posters about the dangers of Facebook because they created a Facebook group expressing their hatred for their TA instructor. They were accused of "threaten[ing] the emotional and mental health" of the TA.[38] At the University of Central

Florida, administrators charged a student with "personal abuse" (but eventually dropped the case) for creating a Facebook group that referred to a student government candidate as "a jerk and a fool."[39]

Sometimes conservatives are the victims of what were originally conservative policies on campus. Bucknell University refused to allow Republican congressman Pat Toomey to give an April 8, 2004, speech on campus about "civic engagement" because of a policy banning political speakers.[40] Bans on political speeches were traditionally used by conservative campus officials to restrict controversy on campus, but these speaking bans end up affecting both Democrats and Republicans.

Some of the attacks on left-wing political correctness are actually an example of conservative repression. Charles Mitchell of FIRE denounced Indian River Community College in Florida for "the most blatant double standard of the year" because it banned a showing of Mel Gibson's *The Passion of the Christ* while allowing a theater group on campus to stage a skit entitled "F**king for Jesus" about a character simulating sex with and masturbating to an image of Jesus.[41] In fact, the incident was a clear case of conservative correctness, banning R-rated movies for fear that high school students on campus might "wander into R-rated movies that they would not normally be able to see."[42] However, since theatrical productions aren't rated, the administration couldn't pass a rule against them. Administrators indicated that they would have banned the play if they had known about it, before bowing to public pressure and reversing the entire censorship policy.[43]

Archaic policies against "disruption" can also be used against conservatives as well as liberals. Steve Hinkle of the College Republicans at Cal Poly San Luis Obispo tried to post fliers advertising a campus talk by Mason Weaver, conservative black activist and author of *It's OK to Leave the Plantation* (1996), in the campus multicultural center on November 12, 2002, during a Bible study meeting where some black students were eating pizza. The students called campus police about "a suspicious white male passing out literature of an offensive racial nature." Cal Poly tried to charge Hinkle with "disrupting" a "campus event," but eventually settled Hinkle's lawsuit and ended its ban on posting flyers.[44]

Rejecting Censorship

Although top administrators often abuse academic freedom by stepping in to impose orthodoxies or punish dissenters, some presidents and trustees deserve praise for defending free expression. University of Alaska at Anchorage president Mark Hamilton refused to allow an investigation of Professor Linda McCarriston, who had been criticized by some Native American activists about her poem "Indian Girls," which dealt with the sexual abuse of children.[45] University of Nevada at Las Vegas president Carol Harter reversed a small punishment imposed against economics professor Hans-Herman Hoppe after the ACLU intervened. Hoppe was reprimanded and lost a pay raise because a student complained that Hoppe in his money and banking class argued that homosexuals spend more and save less than heterosexuals because they are less likely to have children and more likely to take risks.[46]

The City University of New York board of trustees overruled Brooklyn College officials and gave tenure to history professor K. C. Johnson in 2003. Johnson was denied tenure for being "uncollegial" after he criticized sexist colleagues during a job search, including the chair who wrote that he wanted to interview "some women we can live with, who are not whiners from the word go or who need therapy as much as they need a job."[47] James Miller, associate professor of economics at Smith College, was initially rejected for tenure by his colleagues, in part because he had written an article for *National Review* denouncing college faculty for lack of patriotism. The tenure and promotion committee, however, recommended tenure for Miller, and Smith's board of trustees granted it.[48]

Liberals also are defended by trustees at some colleges. At College of the Mainland in Texas, the college board unanimously voted to grant tenure to David Michael Smith in 2002 despite efforts to have him dismissed for his Marxist and antiwar views. Retired professor Howard Katz led the crusade against Smith: "I can judge David Smith by his writings and the writings of his students." Katz claimed that Smith should be fired because some of his students expressed antiwar views: "They didn't get that at high school. They didn't get that at home, I don't think. There's only one place they could have gotten that, and that's in David Smith's class."[49]

But not all left-leaning faculty are so fortunate. Yale anthropology faculty voted to fire David Graeber in May 2005 after he became known as an anarchist, was active in the protest movement against globalization, and defended one of his graduate students (a union activist who was threatened with dismissal). Graeber objected to Yale's efforts to "kick out a promising graduate student you've been working with—a union organizer—for obviously concocted reasons."[50] In 2004 Yale renewed Graeber's contract for only two years instead of the normal four years, claiming that he was accused (falsely, he says) of "showing up late to class, and not doing enough service work."[51] Graeber reported, "No one had any questions about my scholarship or my teaching. So they complained about 'service' and 'collegiality' like last time—but now I'd done the service. They just fired me anyway." As nine prominent University of Chicago anthropologists noted in a letter of concern, "Dr. Graeber's contributions to anthropology have earned him a formidable reputation as a scholar, teacher, and public intellectual."[52] It is laughable to imagine that Yale would dismiss a top-notch scholar for lack of "service" (which is ignored even at low-prestige universities), unless it was being used as an excuse to get rid of a highly qualified academic whose only crime is being disliked by his colleagues.

Tyranny on Campus

Although both conservative and liberal faculty have had their academic freedom violated on college campuses, the most common attacks on the rights of professors have come from tyrannical administrators seeking to silence faculty dissenters regardless of ideology.

At Medaille College in New York in February 2002, acting president John Donahue fired tenured professors Therese Warden and Uhuru Watson "for turpitude and for active and voluntary participation in activities deliberately and specifically designed to bring discredit to the College." The faculty were fired for possessing typed notes from a meeting of the Tenure and Promotions Committee where Donahue tried to gain support for the removal of the business department chair. Warden had anonymously received the document and then distributed it to two other faculty, who received reprimands for possessing the letter even though they returned it to the administration.[53] Giving committee meeting notes to one's colleagues is not a crime at all, let alone an act that justifies firing a tenured professor.

At Riverside Community College in California, Frank Stearns, a tenured accounting professor, was removed from campus, allegedly for poor performance. He was suspended days after he conducted an audit for the teachers union and accused the administration of violating a California law that requires at least 50 percent of school funds to be spent in the classroom and on teacher salaries.[54]

In May 2003 Boston University chancellor John Silber forced the resignation of Dean Brent Baker after Baker quoted from Silber's own book at a May 18 graduation ceremony ("Deans may lose their jobs and be undone precisely because they have done their jobs exceedingly well"). When Bill Lawson, chair of the film and television department, called Silber and his allies a "cabal of misfits" at a faculty meeting, Lawson was also stripped of his position on orders from provost Dennis Berkey.[55]

In South Carolina, the Benedict College administration ordered all faculty to base freshmen grades mostly on effort, not performance. When some faculty refused to obey, they were fired. The AAUP, which already censured Benedict on a past violation of academic freedom, issued another criticism of the college's violation of faculty rights. In retaliation for the AAUP's condemnation, Benedict College demoted two faculty chairs from their positions because they were leaders of the campus chapter of the AAUP.[56]

Perhaps the most egregious firing of faculty in recent years occurred at the University of Southern Mississippi (USM). Sociology professor Frank Glamser and English professor Gary Stringer, leaders in the campus AAUP and the faculty senate, were fired by President Shelby Thames because they conducted an "unauthorized" investigation of the credentials of an administrator. Thames charged Glamser and Stringer with misuse of university resources, misrepresentation, and "contumacious" behavior. Thames claimed, "If you're selling cookies out of your office, using university equipment, university computers, that's misuse of university resources. Unless it has function that relates to instruction, research and service, it's inappropriate."[57] Thames also revealed that he had monitored the e-mail of professors. Fearing for their careers, Glamser and Stringer felt forced to agree to a settlement allowing them to remain at the university for two years (but banning them from teaching) before being fired.[58]

All of these faculty firings run counter to the dominant rhetoric about "political correctness" on college campuses, but little media attention is given to the threat to academic freedom in these cases. Faculty are far more likely to be fired for criticizing their university president than for expressing an opinion (pro or con) about the president of the United States.

Speech Codes under FIRE

Critics of American campuses often point to one campus policy as the greatest threat to free speech: the speech code. Former FIRE director David French noted, "We surveyed the speech policies of the 200 leading universities and found freedom-squelching speech codes at 70 percent of those schools."[59] French is wrong. One hundred percent of colleges regulate speech in ways that can squelch freedom. Every college, every institution, every society limits free speech with a code. The question is not whether a speech code exists, but whether it is well designed to maximize liberty. The problem in academia is not that there are too many speech codes, but too many poorly written and misinterpreted speech codes. The solution is not to repeal all speech codes, but to write better speech codes that delineate specific protections for free speech. When speech codes are abolished, speech is simply redefined as conduct and ends up being punished by far vaguer harassment-based codes or behavior codes.

FIRE's online spotlight on campus speech codes examines 365 colleges and gives 276 of them a "red light" rating for unconstitutional limitations on free expression, 80 a "yellow light" rating for serious limits, and only 9 colleges a "green light" rating indicating no important restrictions.[60] Several volumes could be filled with foolish and disturbing examples of badly designed campus speech codes. Every single college on FIRE's "green light" list (Duke University, Elizabeth City State University, University of Nebraska, Dartmouth College, Cleveland State University, Bucks County Community College, Carnegie Mellon University, University of Pennsylvania, University of Tennessee) has a rule described in detail below that could easily endanger free speech on campus, and these examples illuminate some of the common problem with campus speech codes. Some of these nine colleges have among the worst speech codes ever written, threatening to punish an amazing variety of protected expression.

Banning Sexual Harassment

Perhaps the most common restriction on free speech at college campuses is a ban on sexual harassment, because it is not protected expression and federal law requires campuses to prevent it. However, many universities define sexual harassment in overly vague or broad terms that threaten academic freedom and go far beyond the legal definition of the phrase.

Duke University defines harassment as "verbal or physical conduct—which may or may not be sexual in nature—that, because of its severity and/or persistence, interferes significantly with an individual's work or education, or adversely affects an individual's living conditions."[61] Of course, almost anything could "affect" a person's "living conditions."

The University of Pennsylvania policy includes the following as possible examples of sexual harassment: "Offensive and persistent risqué jokes or kidding about sex or gender-specific traits," "leering or ogling with suggestive overtones," and "displaying sexually suggestive pictures, calendars, or posters."[62] Although it is possible in theory for these activities to be part of a broader sexual harassment complaint under unusual circumstances, jokes and leering and posters on a college campus are not in themselves harassment, and lists such as this convey the false impression that these actions must be prohibited. The University of Pennsylvania does have a strong statement on free expression and one rule that deserves high praise and imitation: "In case of conflict between the principles of the Guidelines on Open Expression and other University policies, the principles of the Guidelines shall take precedence."[63] Unfortunately, the poor wording of other policies may lead to the restriction of free expression despite this supremacy clause.

Disorderly Rules

Another common category of vague restrictions on student rights are bans on "disorderly" or "disruptive" conduct or expression that could cover almost anything. These rules often reflect archaic restrictions that have never been updated to reflect new understandings of free speech.

Dartmouth College "requires orderly conduct of all students" and adds, "In general, any conduct which interferes with the College's responsibility to protect the health and safety of its members or visitors, to protect College property or the property of others, to carry out its functions, or to provide its members and others with services would also be in violation of this standard."[64]

Bucks County Community College in Pennsylvania has an undefined rule prohibiting "disruptive behavior or conduct" as well as some rather strange rules like "unauthorized possession of animals on College premises."[65] Duke University bans "any behavior that disrupts the peace or interferes with the normal operation of the university or university-sponsored activities."[66] Carnegie Mellon University bans "the use of abusive or obscene language or gestures" and "behavior which inconveniences or impedes other members of the campus community" as disorderly conduct.[67] Even the University of Tennessee, which otherwise has an excellent statement of student rights, prohibits "disorderly conduct or lewd, indecent, or obscene conduct" without defining the terms.[68] Such vague terminology allows for virtually any kind of censorship unless a campus makes clear that it must rise to the level of criminal conduct to be punished.

Banning Politics on Campus

Restrictions on political speech are also common on college campuses. Dartmouth College bans any publicity off campus for a political speaker and gives the administration the power to ban any political candidate: "The College reserves the right to cancel any appearance by a political candidate."[69]

The University of Pennsylvania restricts student organizations by declaring that "a student activity or program that is designed to support or oppose a particular party or candidate or to influence legislation will not be funded." This not only includes a total ban on funding for "College Democrats, College Republicans, or other groups designed to support a political party" but also any group involved in "an activity designed to influence legislation."[70]

The Vagueness of Campus Codes

Nearly every college has vague rules enforced against students that can restrict free expression. Washington and Lee University in Virginia imposes a civility rule under which "every member of the community is entitled to expect civil behavior from all other members" and "instances of uncivil behavior involving students may be reported to the Dean of Students."[71]

Cleveland State University's policies prohibit "unauthorized posting or distribution of materials on University property" rather than encouraging freedom to hand out information.[72] The University of Nebraska's "Guidelines for the Student Press" declare that "tastefulness is a part of the trust a journalist holds" and limits "the use of pictures, words, or descriptions that a significant portion of the readership finds offensive." The policy also orders that "all sides of any significant issue must be covered faithfully."[73]

But by far the worst campus speech code in the country is that of Elizabeth City State University in North Carolina, one of FIRE's "green light" institutions. The campus rules include some downright silly provisions, prohibiting "making a loud noise," "playing musical instruments without authorization," and "repeated failure to keep residence hall room clean."[74] More alarmingly, the speech code punishes students merely for "association with others who are openly engaging in a prohibited activity." Students must immediately squeal on their friends or face the same penalty.[75] Worst of all, the rules impose automatic suspension without a hearing for any student accused of "hate crimes that show evidence of prejudicial treatment or speech based on one's race, religion, sexual orientation or ethnicity" or even "any behavior or disorder that impedes, hinders or prevents the attainment of educational, research, or other goals of the University related to the mutual process of teaching and learning."[76] Just imagine being summarily suspended for "hindering" the "attainment" of "goals."

Bashing Antioch

By contrast to these "green light" colleges, FIRE gives a "red light" to many colleges that have fairly good speech codes, and even gave a "speech code of the month" denunciation of Antioch College in Ohio because "its speech code punished behavior that 'emphasizes the gender or sexual identity of persons in a manner which prevents or impairs their emotional well-being.' It also defined 'forms of personal attention which are inappropriate to the academic, employment, or residential setting ... and which may reasonably be perceived as sexual overtures or denigration' as harassment. With such vague and overbroad rules, it is a wonder anyone ever dates anyone, or discusses sex or sexuality, or even looks at another student at Antioch College."[77]

One suspects that Antioch students somehow do manage to look at one another and perhaps even discuss sexuality. In reality, Antioch's speech code is misreported by FIRE. The line about "impairs their emotional well-being" is part of the explanation of Antioch's sexual harassment policy and is not the specific definition of harassment. The restriction on "personal attention," while questionable, applies only to "unwelcome and irrelevant" actions.[78] Compared to many of FIRE's "green light" institutions, Antioch's harassment policy is quite specific and limited. In addition, Antioch's "Civil Liberties Code" is among the best in the country at protecting student rights, declaring that students are "free to state and discuss their opinions openly," have "the right to free association," and have "the right to take lawful social or political action to express or further their beliefs."[79] Far from being among the worst speech codes in the country, Antioch's code should serve a model for all colleges to protect intellectual freedom.

Enforcing Speech Codes

Of course, the fact that colleges often have poorly written rules does not mean that students are actually punished for exercising legitimate free speech. Most colleges are run by reasonable people who don't abuse the liberty of students. This does not mean, however, that campus conduct codes are meaningless. Well-written, clearly defined speech codes can help to protect freedom of expression on campus (for example, by specifically banning the theft of newspapers or shouting down speakers). Even when codes include vague proscriptions on harassment or disorderly conduct, these speech codes should include a statement on academic freedom that supersedes these restrictions. Perhaps most important, a campuswide discussion about what belongs in the college speech code can help students and administrators understand why free expression is essential to academia.

FIRE has launched a campaign to sue public colleges across the country over their campus codes. But many of their targets seem curious. At SUNY at Brockport, two students sued over its "better community standard," which declared, "We affirm that the dignity of our Brockport community is protected when free speech, academic freedom and individual rights are expressed only with responsible and careful regard for the feelings and sensitivities of others." Greg Lukianoff of FIRE declared, "As soon as universities say, 'While we adore free speech, anything that hurts someone else's feelings is bad,' it chills free speech and tells students to keep their mouths shut and that eliminates dialogue and candor."[80] SUNY at Brockport's vague statement urging students to have "responsible and careful regard" for others is better than provisions in the "green light" universities approved by FIRE. Brockport officials settled the lawsuit by removing examples of harassment and declaring that its "better community standard" is not enforceable.[81]

Some efforts to force changes in speech codes through lawsuits can make them worse. When conservative students at Georgia Tech reached an agreement with the university to change some of its policies, David French of the Alliance Defense Fund, and the attorney for the plaintiffs, declared: "It's a big win for free speech. It really does give all Georgia Tech students more rights to free speech."[82] Students for Academic Freedom proclaimed that the agreement "demolished Georgia Tech's speech code."[83] Yet the agreement actually reduced the rights of students. Georgia Tech originally had a vague residence hall policy banning "harassing" or "injurious" signs on campus property. Their new policy bans "posting, painting, engraving or otherwise displaying any sign, slogan or symbol on state property," and only exempts official information distributed by the university.[84] This policy literally bans students from putting up posters inside their own dorm rooms (or anywhere on campus), because that would qualify as a sign on state property. In the past, Georgia Tech could arbitrarily censor students if they were deemed to be expressing an "injurious" view; now, the administration can arbitrarily censor students for no reason at all.

Unfortunately, courts are reluctant to stop censorship at public universities. In 2007, a judge upheld the firing of Dena Bowers, a University of Virginia employee dismissed in 2005 because she used her campus e-mail account to send a message to a colleague about an NAACP meeting that criticized the university's policies. After the e-mail was forwarded to hundreds of people, the administration fired Bowers, claiming she "knowingly used her university title" to express a view that did not "represent a university position statement on the issues addressed."[85]

Banning Antidiscrimination Rules

Some conservatives would like to see all harassment and antidiscrimination rules eliminated. Stuart Taylor Jr. wrote, "Campus censorship lives on, often justified under the guise of enforcing vague rules against racial or sexual 'harassment.'"[86] Conservatives celebrated when the Bush administration Office of Civil Rights issued a clarification explaining that "the statutes that it enforces are intended to protect students from invidious discrimination, not to regulate the content of speech."[87] But sometimes invidious discrimination is accomplished by the bigoted content of speech. A sign that says "no blacks allowed" is speech expressing content. To claim that it isn't speech, and regulating it isn't a speech code, is to play a game of semantics.

Those who are opposed to antidiscrimination laws put universities in a quandary. If colleges provide some guidance to actions that might violate antidiscrimination rules, then they're guilty of censoring all expression; if they don't provide any explanations, then they're guilty of vague, overbroad policies. Federal law compels all employers (including colleges) to have antidiscrimination rules. The problem is not the existence of harassment policies, but the fact that many colleges go beyond what is necessary to stop discrimination, and the lack of understanding that at a university, academic freedom must also be weighed in harassment cases.

In fact, antiharassment rules are often invoked to dismiss liberal academics, not conservative ones. Part-time human sexuality professor Michael Schaffer was fired in July 2005 after seventeen years at George Washington University. When Schaffer asked why he was being fired, he was told to "check your student evaluations." In a spring 2005 course evaluation, a student threatened to file sexual harassment charges against Schaffer (but apparently did not), claiming that his teaching methods about sexuality were "disgusting and demeaning to women."[88] Firing professors without due process because of allegations that are never formally filed, let alone proven, is a serious danger to academic freedom.[89]

Obviously, harassment charges can be abused to suppress free speech. In 2007, the affirmative action officer at the University of North Dakota wrote a memo warning campus programs not to criticize the "Fighting Sioux" nickname and logo because students who disagree could file "a discrimination or a hostile environment claim based on race."[90] In 2006 at the State University of New York at New Paltz, the president and vice president of the student government (who had been highly critical of the administration) were suspended for a year and expelled for having an argument with the director of residence life, who then filed "harassment" charges against them. Even though a video of the encounter backed the students' account, a university spokesperson declared that the administration had "a responsibility to maintain civility on campus."[91] A university can encourage civility, but its ultimate responsibility is to maintain free speech on campus. Throwing your critics off campus isn't civility, it's censorship.

Puritanical tendencies have also led to the dismissal of faculty. At Harrisburg Area Community College in Pennsylvania, tenure-track history professor Stephen E. Williams was suspended and then fired because he used the word "fuck" in a class.[92] At the University of Arkansas, music teacher Kabin Thomas was suspended from his classes because a student objected to his foul language and adult humor (which he warned students about).[93]

The new sensitivity toward conservatives has even led to bizarre legislative proposals for book banning. Arizona Senate Bill 1331 would have required that every public college "shall adopt procedures by which students who object to any course, coursework, learning material or activity on the basis that it is personally offensive shall be provided without financial or academic penalty an alternative course, alternative coursework, alternative learning materials or alternative activity."[94] The bill, which was defeated, was proposed by Arizona senator Thayer Verschoor after he got complaints about literature professor Bill Mullaney at Chandler-Gilbert Community College who taught a class entitled "Currents of American Life" that included Rick Moody's novel *The Ice Storm*. A student in the class who ignored the warnings in class and on the syllabus about "adult themes" objected to the book (which includes a famous wife-swapping car keys scene) and demanded a different work. Senator Verschoor declared at a hearing, "There's no defense of this book. I can't believe that anyone would come up here and try to defend that kind of material."[95]

Conservatives like David Horowitz have argued that we should expand the parameters of harassment regulations and allow conservative students to complain about liberal professors in the same way that students can complain about racist or sexist professors. The same conservative groups who lament antiharassment rules based on race or gender oddly promote far broader antiharassment rules for politics. State senator Bill Morrow, who introduced the Academic Bill of Rights in California, wrote: "We create laws to protect workers from hostile work environments, yet we don't protect our college students from hostile learning environments. We protect them from sexual harassment, but not from intellectual harassment.... Schools, colleges and universities should be safe houses where students can feel comfortable opening their minds, ears and mouths in pursuit of a full education."[96] Republican state senator Andrew Brock, who introduced a bill in the North Carolina legislature to compel adoption of the Academic Bill of Rights, declared: "We don't want our professors to discriminate on the basis of race, sex or religious beliefs. Why should we then allow discrimination on political beliefs?"[97]

But antiharassment codes can be, and have been, abused to suppress legitimate free speech. Adding "politics" to the list of prohibited categories is especially dangerous for two reasons. First, "politics" is a vague term that—unlike race or sex—can apply to almost anything; dismissing the Nazi point of view is a form of political discrimination. Second, "political harassment" is a term with no legal meaning or precedents. We have many court decisions determining in the workplace what "sexual harassment" or "racial harassment" means. But "political harassment" is a novel term that no other workplace is obliged to follow. With no legal guidance to its meaning, colleges could punish practically any kind of political criticism. Unfortunately, this is the goal of David Horowitz's crusade to add "politics" to protected categories at universities. Once a university adds "political discrimination" to its list of prohibited criteria, then it must also stop "political harassment" (just as sexual harassment must be stopped as a form of sex discrimination). And political harassment, for Horowitz, can cover any kind of political comment inside and outside of class.

Defending Freedom for Idiots

The real test of freedom of expression is whether we're willing to defend people whose ideas we think are worthless or positively evil, because when we do that, we are defending a principle everyone should endorse, not the particular content being expressed.

The temptation for many people to urge censorship can be understandable. At a forum at Illinois State University (ISU) about the website started by an ISU student called ISUskanks.com, numerous people offended by the offensive content of the website asked, "Why can't we shut down this website?" They said the website was horrible and even encouraged rape: "Force is necessary once you have lured tonight's fuck into the bathroom" proclaimed one article on "The Art of Bathroom Fucking." ISU officials did threaten legal action because the website included the initials "ISU," but refused to punish anyone.[98] Obviously, "humorous" articles about raping women are probably not what the Founders imagined the First Amendment would protect. But we need to protect "worthless" speech because of the danger of allowing anyone to define what ideas are worth defending.

In the 1980s and 1990s, many progressives made the mistake of imagining that speech codes could be used to stop hate speech and promote a more open-minded campus. That experiment failed. Campus climates often have improved, but speech codes (which were generally declared unconstitutional) shouldn't get the credit. It was social pressure and education, not the threat of sanctions, that helped change values on campus.

Restrictions on free speech typically harm progressives more than conservatives because leftists are more likely to engage in protests than right-wingers. In March 2002 two dozen Florida State students tried to hold a protest on the grass in front of Westcott Hall, the main administrative building. The students, members of United Students Against Sweatshops, were protesting Florida State's $3 million annual endorsement deal with Nike, a notorious sweatshop abuser. Police arrested twelve students for waving American flags and singing "We Shall Overcome." Florida State, like dozens of other public colleges, had an unconstitutional speech "zone" policy that banned any protests in open, public spaces outside of two designated areas.[99] When students moved their tents to the designated free speech zone and began a 114-day protest, Florida State officials banned all tents on campus.[100] Although a few colleges have also banned antiabortion protests using speech zones, the Florida State case marked one of the largest arrests on a college campus for constitutionally protected protest. Six months later, the students were finally tried and acquitted, while Florida State quietly abandoned its speech zone policy.[101] Speech zones, whether used to suppress conservative or liberal views, violate the First Amendment along with the common understanding of college campuses as centers of free expression. By misinterpreting acceptable regulations on "time, place, and manner," administrators imagine they can declare vast swaths of open space off-limits to any protest. Equally unacceptable is the practice of demanding advance notice for any protest; in reality, no reservation or permit is ever needed for a protest unless it involves some extraordinary action (preventing others from using the same space, walking down the middle of a street, ignoring traffic signals).

University of North Carolina–Greensboro (UNCG) student Laura Steigerwald was arrested and punished by the university in March 2007. Her crime? Dancing. Yes, dancing. Her punishment was decided by an administrator who refused to listen to any witnesses on her behalf. She was put on "probation through the spring of 2008, required to perform 25 hours of community service, required to attend a 'making good choices' workshop, and required to write a five-page paper reflecting on what she has learned from her experience."[102] Steigerwald's illicit dancing occurred during a "Morals Week" event held by the UNCG College Republicans, the "People for the Eating of Tasty Animals" barbeque. Steigerwald and other members of Food Not Bombs protested the protest, and the administration claims (incorrectly) that it can compel forty-eight hours' notice from anyone holding any kind of protest on campus. A drumming group showed up, and Steigerwald was dancing nearby when police approached her, asking her to stop the protest. She told the police that unless they planned to arrest her, she would resume dancing, which she did. One week later, the police arrested her on the grounds that she violated a law that a police officer "may issue a command to disperse ... if he believes that a riot, or disorderly conduct by an assemblage of three or more persons, is occurring."[103]

Affirmative Action Bake Sales

A surprising amount of the controversy over the suppression of conservative views on campuses comes down to the danger posed by bakery products. Beginning in 2003, College Republican groups held "affirmative action bake sales" on campuses across the country. The conservative bake sales were an idea stolen from campus feminist groups that occasionally hold pay inequity bake sales, selling baked goods and basing the price on wage gap statistics—white men pay $1.00, African American men 78 cents, white women 76 cents, African American women 65 cents, Hispanic men 63 cents, and Hispanic women 54 cents.

The conservatives often sell cookies at similar prices, but with a different spin. The higher prices for white males are supposed to represent the "difficulty" white men have getting into college, or the discrimination imposed on them by affirmative action. In some cases Republicans charged whites as much as forty times the amount charged to certain minority groups to reflect the extent of the oppression of Caucasians on campus.[104] While feminist bake sales were universally ignored, the Republican bake sales attracted enormous attention, particularly after being shut down as discriminatory at the University of California at Irvine, Northwestern University, the College of William and Mary in Virginia, and Southern Methodist University in Texas.[105]

According to Charles Mitchell, "University administrators apparently being unaware of their own laughability, these bake sales—intended to showcase the discrimination the students see as inherent in affirmative action—are often shut down for being 'discriminatory.' Yet other extremely offensive expression, such as Eve Ensler's play *The Vagina Monologues,* which depicts such things as a 24-year-old woman seducing a 16-year-old girl, are permitted. The obvious conclusion is that only some sensibilities are sacrosanct—the politically correct ones."[106] This "obvious conclusion" is wrong. While performances of the *Vagina Monologues* are perfectly legal (despite being banned at more campuses than these bake sales), affirmative action bake sales technically are illegal.

State public accommodation laws prohibit discrimination by anyone (whether a licensed business or not) who is offering products for sale to the public, and differential pricing based on race is a classic type of unlawful discrimination. These laws allow an exemption only for private clubs, which clearly do not apply to student groups selling cookies to anyone in the middle of the quad.[107]

If administrators banned affirmative action bake sales because they are offensive (which appears to have happened at a few campuses), then their reasoning is wrong. Offensive ideas cannot be prohibited. But it is difficult to blame administrators for stopping illegal activity by students. It is unfortunate for any protest to be shut down by administrators, yet hardly surprising when a law is being broken. Someone who illegally smokes marijuana on campus to protest drug laws will be stopped and arrested. (Even perfectly legal protests against the drug war sometimes are banned at colleges, as when Ohio State University administrators cancelled Hempfest in June 2004 and Macalester College in Minnesota in 2006 banned a student festival promoting marijuana legalization.)[108]

Opponents of affirmative action have an alternative to violating the law. For example, the University of North Carolina at Charlotte College Republicans regularly stage a mock bake sale with a list of discriminatory prices (charging $5 for white men and $1.25 for black women), but they do not actually sell anything.[109] This protest against affirmative action may be untrue, offensive, and ridiculous, but it is perfectly legal. Selling cookies based on racial pricing, however, is not legal.

The law should be changed to allow small-scale discriminatory sales as political protests (whether against affirmative action or pay inequity). And colleges and universities should ignore the law and allow these illegal protests to occur anyway. But it is strange for law-and-order conservatives to denounce colleges for "political correctness" simply because they are enforcing the law.[110]

Commencement Speakers and "Liberal" Bias

Many conservative complaints against colleges stem from the belief that too many liberals are allowed to speak. Conservative groups have launched pressure campaigns attacking graduation speakers deemed too "liberal." In 2004 the Young America's Foundation cited Yale as the worst example of colleges with "an outrageous track record of hosting liberal commencement speakers."[111] Since 1996 Yale had invited one actor (Henry Winkler), four moderate writer/journalists (David McCullough, Tom Brokaw, Bob Woodward, Thomas Friedman), one Democrat (Hillary Clinton), and two Republicans (David Gergen, George Pataki).[112] Nothing is "outrageous" about these speakers.

Left-wing commencement speakers supposedly outnumber conservatives by more than a 15–1 margin according to David Horowitz. Horowitz looked at the list of commencement speakers from 32 elite colleges, nearly all of them located in Democratic-dominated states. Horowitz concluded that there were 226 speakers on the left and only 15 speakers on the right. But Horowitz achieves these remarkable figures only by counting all of the following speakers as "left-wingers": Ted Koppel, Jim Lehrer, Cokie Roberts, Bob Woodward, Thomas Friedman, Judy Woodruff, Dan Rather, Tom Brokaw, Peter Jennings, Claire Shipman, Charlie Rose, Bill Cosby, Scott Turow, David McCullough, Stephen Carter, Kofi Annan, Doris Goodwin, Steven Bochco, Henry Winkler, Steve Wozniak, and former Republican governor Lowell Weicker. Meanwhile, Horowitz deemed Republicans like Alan Greenspan and David Gergen to be "neutral" speakers.[113]

One Horowitz fund-raising letter even declared, "A CSPC survey found that 99 percent of graduation day speakers called themselves liberals, Democrats, or Green Party Members. This is unacceptable. Please endorse our Academic Bill of Rights and make as generous a contribution as you can afford to CSPC today."[114] Of course, 99 percent of graduation speakers don't call themselves liberals, Democrats, and Greens, but the idea that the Academic Bill of Rights could be used to force more Republican speakers on colleges is alarming.

Horowitz claims, "The totalitarian bent of what is absurdly called the liberal mind was never so clear as in its relentless cleansing of conservatives from Commencement rostrums."[115] Yet no one has ever done a systematic study of the political affiliation of commencement speakers. To remedy this, I examined the 2005 commencement speakers at ninety-two colleges promoted by the PR Newswire.[116] These colleges represent a diverse sample of the nation's higher education institutions, with colleges ranging from elite universities to community colleges, and covering much of the country. It is difficult to measure political bias, so I tried to use two objective measures: the party membership of political speakers, and the partisan trend of campaign donations by nonpoliticians.

Out of 112 speakers (some colleges had multiple commencement speakers), I found 11 current and former Democratic politicians, and 10 current and former Republican politicians. In most cases, it was not possible to identify any federal campaign donations by these commencement speakers. But among those who could be clearly identified, there were 16 donors to Democrats and 14 donors to Republicans (and one donor to both parties) among the commencement speakers who were not politicians. A majority of the commencement speakers were not politicians and could not be identified as campaign donors, so we have no clear-cut way of knowing their political views. But among the commencement speakers with an identifiable party affiliation, Democrats and Republicans were split almost equally.

To confirm these data, I examined the larger dataset of the *Chronicle of Higher Education* list of commencement speakers, looking for current elected officials. In 2006, out of 775 speakers, there were 38 Democrats and 29 Republicans.[117] This pattern matched the slight Democratic edge found in 2003 (44 Democrats and 31 Republicans) and 2002 (26 Democrats and 17 Republicans). However, the reverse was true in 2005 (35 Democrats and 37 Republicans) and 2004 (29 Democrats and 39 Republicans). Since it was possible that former politicians distorted the data, I looked at the 2006 data for former public officials: There were 17 former Democratic officials and 19 former Republican officials as commencement speakers. Altogether, the evidence of political bias is slight. Of course, the large number of speakers who are not politicians may represent a particular viewpoint. Artists, writers, and celebrities tend to be popular selections for commencement speakers, and the members of these professions are overwhelmingly liberal. Still, it's not clear why the politics of commencement speakers would matter. Commencement addresses tend to be short, pointless, apolitical, and full of pleasant clichés.

Instead of falsely claiming that all commencement speakers are liberals and seeking to ban political comments, conservatives should seek to promote freedom of expression on campus. Unfortunately, conservative pundits have often celebrated censorship of liberal commencement speakers.

At California State University at Sacramento during a December 15, 2001, commencement speech, when Janis Besler Heaphy, president and publisher of the *Sacramento Bee*, urged that citizens safeguard their rights to free speech and a fair trial, the audience booed her. The crowd cheered the idea of racial profiling, and then when Heaphy argued that "the Constitution makes it our right to challenge government policies," the crowd started clapping, stomping their feet, and heckling her. When the interruption went on for five minutes, and university president Don Gerth unsuccessfully tried to quiet the audience, Heaphy gave up speaking.[118]

At Harvard University, 4,000 faculty, staff, and students signed a petition objecting to allowing Harvard senior Zayed Yasin to give his 2002 commencement address, "Of Faith and Citizenship: My American Jihad." Yasin argued that "jihad" referred to a personal struggle for faith and had been misinterpreted by Muslims and non-Muslims. Yasin was allowed to give his address in June 2002, but gave in to demands to keep "My American Jihad" out of the printed title.[119]

Phil Donahue's commencement speech at North Carolina State University in 2003 was repeatedly interrupted by boos and jeers after he criticized the war against Iraq. North Carolina State University officials seemed to indicate that the university would oppose future commencement speakers who might say controversial words. Chancellor Marye Anne Fox wrote about Donahue's speech, "I share your disappointment in Phil Donahue's address to our graduates."[120]

When E. L. Doctorow gave a 2004 commencement address at Hofstra University that criticized George W. Bush, students and parents booed so loudly in interrupting the lecture that the president of the college had to intervene and ask them to allow the speech to continue. Far from criticizing this effort to silence a political speech, Peggy Noonan in the *Wall Street Journal* praised the booing and denounced faculty for cheering the university president's call for free speech. A Hofstra official criticized Doctorow for supposedly violating an unwritten rule that commencement speakers should say nothing controversial.[121]

At Rockford College in Illinois in 2003, *New York Times* reporter Chris Hedges had to cut his commencement speech short after being heckled and booed by some in the audience for being critical of the war against Iraq. Hedges faced boos, people walking out, turned backs, catcalls, foghorns blaring, people singing "God Bless America," chants of "USA! USA!," audience members trying to climb onto the stage, and people shouting, "Go home!" and "Send him to France" during his eighteen-minute speech. Hedges's microphone was unplugged twice during the speech.[122] As Oliver North put it, approvingly, "An enraged audience of graduating seniors and their families finally forced Hedges from the stage, bringing his diatribe to an abrupt end."[123] Conservative talk show host Sean Hannity responded to the Hedges speech by declaring, "This man should be fired."[124] Hedges noted, "I have certainly spoken at events where people disagreed—that is to be expected. But to be silenced and to have people clamber onto the platform with the threat of physical violence was something new, and frightening."[125] Pribbenow received death threats and changed his home telephone number. As libertarian columnist Cathy Young observed, "The hecklers didn't just express their distaste for Hedges's speech; they actively, and successfully, tried to silence him."[126]

While conservatives have tried to shout down liberal speakers (a tactic sometimes also used against conservative speakers by left-wing opponents), they typically face little criticism or punishment. But at the University of Maryland, three liberal students faced disciplinary action for "disorderly or disruptive conduct" for merely shouting a question (and, in one case, allegedly speaking an obscenity) at Lynne Cheney during a February 29, 2004, appearance (where only written questions were allowed). University of Maryland policy specifically permits heckling that is not a major disruption. Susan Goering, executive director of the ACLU of Maryland, noted: "What the university officials appear to have done appears not only to be in violation of their own speech code, but also of the First Amendment."[127]

Banning Speakers

Although commencement addresses attract the greatest attention, other speakers on college campuses are also censored. While conservative religious colleges impose the greatest restrictions on campus speakers, a variety of public and private institutions have tried to ban or "disinvite" speakers whose words might offend someone.

At Bucknell University in Pennsylvania, the dean of students office withdrew funding for a Conservatives Club speech by Thor Halvorssen, then executive director of the Foundation for Individual Rights in Education (FIRE). The University claimed FIRE had threatened to sue Bucknell, and therefore they would not fund any speakers from the organization. General Counsel Wayne Bromfield declared, "Our refusal to allow funding of his speech was based on the principle that we do not suppress speech, but we also do not subsidize antagonistic suits. It would be foolish to contribute legal fees to an organization whose avowed intention is to use their legal resources against us."[128] Halvorssen waived his honorarium and spoke at Bucknell anyway on October 24, 2002, to a standing-room-only crowd. Bucknell University's claim that speaking fees are the equivalent of "legal fees" is absurd. By the logic of Bucknell administrators, anyone affiliated with an organization who assisted anyone in a suit against the university could be banned from receiving speaking fees. Restricting free speech only to those who support the administration is a clear violation of academic freedom.

But administrators attack liberal groups for controversial speakers, too. When Malik Shabazz, who is often denounced for racist and anti-Semitic views, spoke at Carnegie Mellon University in Pennsylvania, university officials tried to convince the campus group sponsoring his speech to ban him, and Michael Murphy, dean of student affairs, denounced Shabazz's "hurtfulness and hatefulness."[129]

At Yeshiva University in New York, the Israel Club disinvited Israeli Defense Forces refusnik Guy Grossman after the other speaker in a planned debate withdrew. Reportedly, the group was "under pressure from those who feared the consequences of giving an 'open forum' to a left-wing speaker."[130] At the University of Southern Indiana, animal rights activist Gary Yourofsky was disinvited in 2007 from giving a speech on "Ethical Veganism."[131]

Even Archbishop Desmond Tutu, winner of the Nobel Peace Prize and one of the most admired figures in the world today, was temporarily barred in 2007 from speaking at the University of St. Thomas in Minnesota because the administration declared, "We had heard some things he said that some people judged to be anti-Semitic and against Israeli policy."[132] (In a 2002 Boston speech, Tutu had declared, "We don't criticize Jewish people. We criticize, we will criticize, when they need to be criticized, the government of Israel.")[133] Even worse, Cris Toffolo, the chair of the Justice and Peace Studies Program at St. Thomas that had invited Tutu, was demoted for informing Tutu about the reason for the university's decision.[134]

College of Southern Idaho administrators disinvited Jeremy Rifkin, who was scheduled to speak on biotechnology at the October 3, 2001, Success

Breakfast sponsored by the college after farm groups threatened to boycott the event because Rifkin had criticized the meat industry. College President Jerry Meyerhoeffer declared, "We are an agriculture community.... I think us bringing him in would be a violation" of the college's partnership with agriculture groups.[135] The administration at the University of Akron in 2007 banned poet Jimmy Santiago Baca from being selected to speak on campus because of his criminal background before he turned his life around and became a writer.[136]

Some conservatives, upset that Cornel West was invited to speak at a 2002 conference at City University of New York on the legacy of Sidney Hook, threatened a boycott in an effort to have him disinvited. Hilton Kramer, John Patrick Diggins, Gertrude Himmelfarb, and Irving Kristol all promised to boycott the event and sought to convince the Olin Foundation to withdraw $5,000 in funding for the conference because they disliked the liberal West, who examined Hook's work in his 1989 book, *The American Evasion of Philosophy: A Genealogy of Pragmatism.*[137]

In 2006 Columbia University president Lee Bollinger withdrew a dean's invitation to Iranian president Mahmoud Ahmadinejad to speak because it would not "reflect the academic values that are the hallmark of a University event."[138] Bollinger was widely attacked for allowing Ahmadinejad to speak in 2007 (U.S. Representative Duncan Hunter called for a ban on all federal funding for Columbia), but he's been guilty of failing to protect free speech on both the far left and the far right.[139] When campus leftists disrupted a speech by Jim Gilchrist, leader of the anti-immigration Minutemen, Bollinger failed to invite Gilchrist back, although the students involved were disciplined.[140]

What kind of "free speech" do conservative groups want on campus? One indication is the Intercollegiate Studies Institute (ISI), which sponsors right-wing newspapers on campuses. Each April Fool's Day, ISI gives out its "Polly Awards" for campus outrages. But rather than consistently opposing all censorship, the Polly Awards have frequently opposed free speech for liberals on campus campuses. In 2006 ISI complained that the University of Iowa allowed student groups to hold a "Peacefest" on September 11.[141] In 2005 ISI rebuked Duke University for failing to ban a pro-Palestinian conference.[142] Among the 2004 award winners, ISI objected to Yale allowing its students to sponsor a "Sex Week at Yale" and attacked the University of California at Santa Barbara for allowing a student to write a thesis on "Gay Men of Color in Porn."[143] For its 2003 award winners, ISI opposed allowing two speakers on college campuses, Laura Whitehorn at Duke University and famed scholar Gayatri Spivak at Columbia University (because she gave an academic description of suicide bombings).[144] In 2002 ISI complained that an antiwar teach-in was allowed at the University of North Carolina at Chapel Hill.[145] In 2001 the Polly Awards urged Princeton to summarily fire philosopher Peter Singer because of his controversial ideas.[146] Although the Polly Awards do point out ridiculous cases where conservatives have been wrongly censored on college campuses, these right-wingers refuse to defend free speech for liberals.

Defunding Student Groups

The right-wing attack on campus speakers is matched by a similar campaign against liberal student organizations. In the 1990s, conservative groups took the University of Wisconsin all the way to the U.S. Supreme Court, hoping to abolish all student fees at public colleges that might be used to fund controversial student groups offensive to conservatives. The Supreme Court unanimously defended the use of student fees in the *Southworth* case, but the right wing continues to seek defunding of left-leaning groups.[147]

Academic Bill of Rights cosponsor Representative Walter B. Jones (R-NC) issued a press release that declared, "Statistics have shown that while campus funds are available for distribution to all on-campus organizations, funding is doled out to organizations with leftist agendas by a ratio of 50:1. Such biased financing results in a deluge of liberal speakers being invited to step up to their soapboxes far more often than those with a conservative bent."[148] This claim, like others made by Horowitz and his political allies, is completely imaginary. There has been no accurate study of funding for campus speakers, and the notion that groups with "leftist agendas" receive fifty times as much funding as all other organizations is absurd.

According to Representative Jack Kingston (R-GA), the head of the House Republican Conference and chief House sponsor of Horowitz's bill, "At almost every American university, ... the number of liberal guest speakers outnumbers the number of conservative guest speakers by a margin greater than 10–1, limiting the opportunities for conservatives or anyone else who does not sing from the same liberal songbook."[149] An editorial in *Investor's Business Daily* proclaimed, "A study of bias in the selection of college speakers by David Horowitz and Students for Academic Freedom found that over a 10-year period at 32 elite colleges and universities the ratio of speakers on the left to speakers on the right was more than 15 to 1."[150]

No one knows about the ideological leanings of speakers on campuses, because no systematic study has ever been done on even one campus, and certainly not a statistically valid sample of colleges in America. Because the most common student organizations are Christian-based, and these groups frequently have guest speakers, it is quite possible that there are more conservative speakers on college campuses than liberal ones.

But if conservative speakers are rarer than liberal ones on college campuses, one reason is that it is financially more difficult to bring conservatives.

Dinesh D'Souza has noted, "I lecture to college groups and to business groups. The business groups pay me better and treat me better."[151] When conservatives like D'Souza have business groups to offer huge fees, they are much less likely to take the relatively small amounts of money offered by universities.

Sean Hannity's standard $100,000 lecture fee, for example, would almost never be paid by any university, and only corporations and trade groups typically can afford him. But liberal speakers are rarely hired by corporations, which means they are more likely to speak at colleges that can afford their cheaper rates. David Horowitz estimates it costs about $1,750 to bring a "nationally renowned scholar in the humanities or social sciences to campus," a sum that is about one-third of Horowitz's own $5,000 fee.[152] Most speakers on college campuses receive very little or no money. They are faculty who speak for academic reasons (because it is part of their scholarly activities) or activists committed to a political cause.

The most common conservative student group at universities is the College Republicans, who tend to be most interested in bringing in politicians (who are typically not allowed to receive funding from colleges). By contrast, a wide range of liberal groups beyond the College Democrats can be found on most campuses, each of them interested in bringing speakers to campus. Until more conservatives are willing to speak for free on college campuses and more conservative students are willing to organize activities, it is impossible to demand an equal balance of views to be heard on campus.

The largest share of student fee money subsidizes athletic teams and recreation activities. Only a tiny portion of the money is allocated for student organizations to use, and left-wing groups are a tiny part of this group. It may be true that left-wing groups receive much more money than right-wing groups (if you don't count the numerous Christian groups as conservative). But that's because leftists on campus are far more active than conservatives, starting many more groups and organizing many more events. Even the Young America's Foundation advises conservative students, "If they award funding on a per-group basis, form front groups that will increase your chances of funding."[153]

The idea that conservatives deserve to be affirmative action recipients of equal funding, even if they don't request it and even if they do almost nothing on campus, shows how the right-wing movement wants their notion of "balance" to replace merit. Ironically, while David French of FIRE denounced the payment of fees to Moore as illegal, he ignored several colleges where administrators sought (illegally) to ban Moore from speaking on campus.

French claimed that student fees are "hijacked by political activists who use the millions of dollars of student fee money to provide massive subsidies to leftist political causes." French urged students to investigate student fee funding because "if those guidelines are vague or provide the student fee funding board (whether elected or appointed) with broad discretion to grant funding requests with little or no guidance, than those guidelines are most likely unconstitutional."[154]

The idea that it is unconstitutional for students to have "broad discretion" to disperse their own student fees is astonishing. Students, rather than administrators, should have the discretion to decide on funding. Yet French declared that if "funding guidelines are vague" (as all of them are), "contact FIRE or Students for Academic Freedom," and "FIRE or SAF will make universities comply with the law."[155] What FIRE and Horowitz's SAF hope is that conservative groups, by threatening expensive lawsuits, will be offered free money by administrators who will overrule legitimate funding decisions by students. Far from protecting student rights, their aim is to undermine student power.

The notion that conservatives should receive extra funding because they're too lazy to start up organizations is not only wrong, it's unconstitutional. The Supreme Court prohibits public universities from engaging in viewpoint discrimination, and giving extra funding to a conservative group is a type of funding based on viewpoint. Even if ideological balance in funding for student groups was a workable and desirable idea (and it isn't), it is illegal.

Politics and Student Fees

One reason for the alleged disparity in campus funding is that conservative groups often don't want to be bothered with getting funding from student fees. The Young America's Foundation regularly subsidizes conservative campus speakers. Conservative students can raise such large amounts of money that it sometimes leads to abuses. The College Republican National Committee (CRNC) was recently embroiled in a fund-raising scandal. In the 2004 election cycle, the CRNC hired professional direct mail firms to raise $6.3 million by misleading elderly donors into thinking that they were aiding the Republican Party. One fund-raising letter asked donors for $1,000 so that an American flag lapel pin could be given to President Bush at the Republican National Convention.[156]

It is understandable why conservative groups (accustomed to getting large sums of money from rich Republicans and conservative foundations) are less likely to utilize campus funding systems, which require students to navigate an extensive bureaucracy to obtain small amounts of money. But at many campuses, Republicans get preferential treatment. At Middle Tennessee State University, for example, the College Democrats in 2005 received $820 out of a $4,710 request (17 percent), while the Republicans got more than three times as much, $2,696 for a $6,175 request (44 percent). This disparity occurred even though the Democrats' request (for an AIDS forum) was far more educational to the campus than the Republican request for funding to attend George W. Bush's second inauguration.[157]

Conservatives have also used student funding systems to defund liberals and promote right-wing causes. At the University of Wisconsin at Madison in 2002, conservatives took over the Student Services Finance Committee and denied funding to MEChA (a Latino activist group) and diversity education.[158] Jason Mattera, a conservative at Roger Williams University in Rhode Island, described how he "ran for a student senate seat with the prime objective of working my way up to control the flow of money on my campus. Within a year, I became chairman of the finance committee."[159] Mattera bragged about how effective he was: "Sure enough, our club had one of the largest budgets for two years in a row.... Moreover, the amount of funding that went to homosexual and multicultural student organizations decreased considerably."[160] Mattera urged defunding of liberal student groups: "This is an intellectual war, and in wars the goal is to win! If not, your enemy will wipe you out without any hesitation."[161] While Mattera's declaration of war against liberals is not an isolated view, his plan to defund the left is the opening essay in a guide for conservative student activists published by the Young America's Foundation. Other conservative groups have sued campuses, trying to prevent students from providing student fees to student-run organizations. By contrast, no liberal student groups have called for activists to eliminate funding for conservatives on campuses. The threat to funding diverse speakers on college campuses comes from the right, not the left.

The attack on student fees is typical of many conservative assaults on academia: The unproven cry of bias is used as a weapon to call for silencing liberal viewpoints, defunding the left, and seeking to narrow the broad range of ideas that are heard on college campuses. Instead of attacking the freedom available in higher education, we need to expand civil liberties on campus and increase the amount of reasoned debate in the halls of academe.

CHAPTER SIX
What Would Jesus Censor?

⊸

While right-wing advocates cry out about slights against conservatives on campus, they ignore a far worse threat to free expression in academia: religious colleges. Conservative religious institutions are unquestionably the worst violators of academic freedom in America. In the name of God, campus officials at religious colleges impose the worst repression in higher education.

Gay and lesbian students are often banned from religious colleges. Brigham Young University (BYU) student Matthew Grierson was expelled because he held hands with a man in an Orem, Utah, shopping mall in January 2001. He was recognized and reported to BYU's honor code office. Because Grierson was on probation for kissing a man on campus (which Grierson denies), he was threatened with suspension and forced to withdraw from the school. Although the Mormon Church has recently accepted gays and lesbians so long as they remain celibate, BYU bans "homosexual conduct." Grierson said, "I didn't think you could be kicked out just for being gay. I thought [the prohibition] had to do with sexual acts."[1]

BYU student Ricky Escoto was also suspended in 2001 after his roommates accused him of kissing a man on their couch, receiving flowers from men, talking about dates with men, and spending time in gay Internet chat rooms. Escoto denied the allegations, but he was expelled after BYU officials believed the accusations were "more probable than not." According to Escoto, thirteen other BYU students were kicked off campus in 2000 because they were caught watching Showtime's TV series *Queer as Folk*.[2]

Grierson and Escoto were given letters detailing nine steps they must take to be readmitted to BYU. They must convince ecclesiastical leaders and counselors that they are abiding by the honor code and are no longer gay. And they must "totally refrain from inappropriate same-sex behavior, including but not limited to dating, holding hands, kissing, romantic touching, showering, clubbing, etc., as well as regular association with homosexual men."[3]

BYU not only wants to suppress student sexual conduct, but also the right to speak and protest. BYU's letter told Escoto it is "inappropriate for a BYU student to advocate for the [homosexual] lifestyle, speak or write papers for public consumption, demonstrate in a public forum, or advertise your same-sex preference in any other public way." BYU's letter to Grierson declared that "it is inappropriate to demonstrate intimate affection for a person of the same gender."[4] Although the conduct of heterosexuals at BYU is regulated, it is nowhere near as stringent, since heterosexuals are allowed to kiss and hold hands. In the late 1990s, BYU added "homosexual conduct" to a list of sexual conduct prohibitions in the BYU Honor Code, which must be signed by students to enter the university. BYU's code proclaims, "Advocacy of a homosexual lifestyle (whether implied or explicit) or any behaviors that indicate homosexual conduct, including those not sexual in nature, are inappropriate and violate the Honor Code."[5]

At BYU, merely supporting the legal recognition of equal rights for gays and lesbians is prohibited. Adjunct philosophy instructor Jeffrey Nielsen was fired in 2006 by BYU a few days after publishing an op-ed supporting legalization of gay marriage. A BYU spokesperson proclaimed that Nielsen was dismissed "because of the opinion piece that had been written, and based on the fact that Mr. Nielsen publicly contradicted and opposed an official statement by top church leaders."[6] The repressive atmosphere at BYU extends beyond homosexuality. In 2006 BYU fired Todd Hendricks, an adviser in the BYU Student Association, for a "disloyal act": writing a letter to the campus newspaper expressing concern about the student election process.[7] And repression of Mormon history scholars extends even to secular universities. D. Michael Quinn, a leading expert on Mormon history, has been blacklisted from academic jobs because he was excommunicated by the Mormon church. Brigham Young University threatened to withdraw all funding for a conference cosponsored with Yale University if Quinn was allowed to speak at the event. At the University of Utah, Quinn was the only finalist for a job but was not hired because of fear of angering Mormons in the state legislature. In 2004 Arizona State University administrators vetoed the hiring of Quinn after the chair of religious studies "thought that it is probably not wise to undertake such risks."[8]

Faculty at many religious colleges put their jobs at risk by coming out of the closet. Albertus Magnus College in Connecticut removed Michael Hartwig from teaching duties and then fired him because it was publicly revealed that Hartwig was an ex-priest and a gay man.[9] At Chestnut Hill College in Philadelphia, part-time teacher Meghan Sullivan attended a lecture on gay rights at the University of Pennsylvania in 2003, and was quoted in its student newspaper identifying herself as a lesbian. Sister Carol Jean Vale, president of Chestnut Hill College, gave Sullivan a choice between identifying herself publicly as a Chestnut Hill professor or as a lesbian, but not both. Sullivan decided to resign.[10] Barbara Kelly, a part-time psychology teacher at North Park University in Illinois, filed a discrimination complaint in 2003 contending that she was not hired for a tenure-track job because she is a lesbian, which made her "too controversial."[11] North Park president David Horner quoted from the Evangelical Covenant Church's 1996 resolution on human sexuality: "Heterosexual marriage, faithfulness within marriage, abstinence outside of marriage—these constitute the Christian standard."[12]

Students at religious colleges face expulsion if they come out of the closet. A University of the Cumberlands student, Jason Johnson, was expelled in April 2006, three weeks before the end of the semester, because his home page on MySpace.com revealed that he is gay.[13] John Brown University, a Christian college in Arkansas, expelled a student in January 2006 because his Facebook page revealed that he is gay.[14] Baylor University in Texas banned a prominent alum and donor from an advisory committee for the business school because he is gay.[15]

The New York Medical College disbanded a student group, Gay, Lesbian, Bisexual, Transgender People in Medicine, because its goal of advocating better health care for the GLBT population was deemed by administrators to be "inconsistent with the values" of the college and its "Catholic tradition."[16] Hampton University in Virginia refused to grant recognition to a gay and lesbian student organization in 2007.[17] When gay and lesbian student groups are permitted at religious colleges, they often face severe restrictions on expression. In 2005 Duquesne University finally lifted a ban on a gay student group, but prohibited it from protesting any university or Catholic Church policies.[18] Boston College banned a dance in 2005 because it was sponsored by a gay and lesbian student group.[19]

When the gay rights group Soulforce held an "Equality Ride" at conservative colleges in 2006, they were regularly met by police: Twenty-four members of the group were arrested for trespassing because they dared to set foot on the campus of Jerry Falwell's Liberty University in Virginia. Falwell proclaimed that he would not allow the group on campus: "Neither will we permit them to espouse opinions or otherwise suggest beliefs or lifestyles that are in opposition to the morals and values that this institution promotes."[20] One of the riders, David Coleman, had been kicked out of North Central University (which also banned the Equality Ride) because he revealed that he was gay while seeking protection from a student who threatened him.[21] When the newspaper at North Central University in Minneapolis reported about the Equality Ride, administrators called the printer and stopped the presses. Later, they fired the student editors because they refused to let administrators review the newspaper before it was published.[22]

The University of the Cumberlands in Kentucky not only expelled a student for being gay, but it censored the campus newspaper to prevent news of this incident from being reported.[23] In 2003, when professor Robert Day created a website criticizing the administration, he was fired and banned from setting foot on campus. According to a 2005 AAUP report, "an atmosphere of intimidation that effectively forestalls the exercise of academic freedom" exists at the college.[24] A play called *Noises Off* was banned from campus, and one professor (who was later fired) was warned in the 1990s not to read passages in class from John Steinbeck's *The Grapes of Wrath* because it was objectionable.[25]

Even secular colleges run by conservatives attack the equal rights of gay students. At Boston University in 2002, then-chancellor John Silber banned a gay-straight alliance from the university-controlled Boston University Academy, claiming that the group was "forcing young people to define themselves in terms of sexual orientation."[26]

Politicians appealing to homophobic views have suggested amazing restrictions on free speech. In Alabama, state representative Gerald Allen proposed a law banning public funds for activities (including books taught by professors at public colleges) that "sanction, recognize, foster or promote a lifestyle or actions prohibited by the sodomy and sexual misconduct laws of the state."[27] Allen declared that gay-themed novels and college textbooks suggesting that homosexuality is natural would be banned: "I guess we dig a big hole and dump them in and bury them." Allen added that the law would prohibit university theater groups from performing plays such as *Cat on a Hot Tin Roof*, by Tennessee Williams.[28] Allen declared that any professor who teaches one of these banned books should be tried in court for committing a misdemeanor crime.[29]

Religious groups have even sought to prevent public colleges from promoting tolerance. Stephen Crampton, chief counsel for the American Family Association, complained that having University of Maryland students read *The Laramie Project* (a play about the murder of Matthew Shepard) "raises the specter of the imposition of the orthodoxy of belief." According to Crampton, "Here, the University of Maryland is singling out one religion for criticism, Christianity, that holds homosexuality as immoral. That is treating academic freedom as an excuse to indoctrinate."[30] It is bizarre for anyone to contend that a college cannot ask students to read a book because it is imagined to be criticizing a religion—particularly when there is no punishment for a student who fails to read it. Joe Glover, president of the Family Policy Network, attacked the play as "heavy-handed liberal bias masquerading as open discussion and free inquiry" and threatened to sue the University of Maryland for distributing copies of the play.[31] The antigay Westboro Baptist Church in Kansas brought demonstrators to campus to oppose the distribution of the book, led by Fred Phelps, who called it "a lying piece of fag propaganda."[32]

Religious colleges that respect the rights of gay students can face severe punishment. At Mars Hill College in North Carolina, the student government voted in April 2005 to reject recognition of a group to support gay students, because Baptist groups had threatened to cut off funds to the college.[33] The Georgia Baptist Convention ended all ties with Mercer University, and eliminated its $3.5 million in annual funding, because a gay rights group was not banned from campus, even though the group disbanded after complaints and Mercer's president R. Kirby Godsey proclaimed, "Mercer University has never promoted, advocated or encouraged gay or lesbian behavior."[34] At Averett University, Virginia Baptist groups cut off all funding to the college because officials refused to ban a gay student group.[35]

The Legislative Sex Police

Public universities also are often targeted by religious groups and legislators for allowing freedom of expression to gays and lesbians. One of the most controversial plays in America is Terrence McNally's *Corpus Christi*, featuring a gay Christ character. At Florida Atlantic University, state legislators threatened to cut the university's budget in 2001 because it allowed the theater department to stage *Corpus Christi*.[36] At Grand Rapids Community College, after a state legislator on the finance committee asked if state money was being used for the Actors' Theatre production of *Corpus Christi*, the college moved the play off campus.[37] Indiana University–Purdue University at Fort Wayne was sued for an August 2001 production of the play. In *Linnemeir v. Purdue,* the U.S. Court of Appeals for the Seventh Circuit ruled that although the play was "blasphemous," it did not constitute an establishment of antireligion, and outsiders could not force the cancellation of the play.[38] However, even when litigation aimed at censorship is dismissed, the publicity surrounding it can have a chilling effect. Tulane University dropped plans in 2007 to perform the play *The Pope and The Witch,* written by Dario Fo, winner of the 1997 Nobel Prize for Literature, after angry complaints from Catholics.[39]

Because a class titled "How to Be Gay: Male Homosexuality and Initiation" was taught at the University of Michigan, Gary Glenn, president of the Michigan American Family Association, asked the governor, the state legislature, and the board of trustees to "stop letting homosexual activists use our tax dollars to subsidize this militant political agenda."[40] Michigan state representative Jack Hoogendyk proposed amending the state constitution to give legislators control over what courses are taught because he objected to classes such as "The Individual, Marriage and the Family" and "Language and Sexuality."[41]

Antigay views can also occasionally cause calls for censorship. At Indiana University, business professor Eric Rasmusen's website, which includes stridently antigay comments opposing homosexual teachers, doctors, and politicians, was voluntarily moved by Rasmusen from the university website. After university lawyers determined that his postings were protected free speech, Rasmusen returned them to the university website the next day. Chancellor Sharon Brehm criticized Rasmusen's comments as "deeply offensive, hurtful, and very harmful stereotyping," but defended his right to express them.[42]

Repression against sexual content in academia is much more severe. After legislators objected to University of Kansas professor Dennis Dailey showing "obscene" videos in his "Human Sexuality in Everyday Life" class, the Kansas Board of Regents passed a policy on sexually explicit material ordered by the state legislature, declaring that "academic freedom must be balanced with academic responsibility." State senator Susan Wagle declared, "I think the Legislature would prefer not to micromanage human sexuality classes, but on the other side, we do recognize that these are tax-funded institutions, and there needs to be some sort of respect within these institutions for the taxpayers." According to Wagle (who learned about the class from one of her interns who had taken it), "We're living in a time and age when we need to set standards." Earlier, Wagle had introduced an amendment cutting $3.1 million from the University of Kansas budget in retaliation for Dailey's class (a move vetoed by the governor), and Wagle filed a formal complaint with the university, accusing Dailey of using "street" language and suggestive remarks in his class.[43]

When Penn State University in spring 2000 put on the Safer Sex Cabaret as part of Pride Week, state lawmakers, led by Representative John Lawless, attacked the university for allowing the student-run event and cut $9,520 from the state's appropriation for the university. During a Pennsylvania house appropriations committee hearing, Penn State president Graham Spanier was interrogated for almost four hours about the Safer Sex Cabaret. However, in March 2001, Terrell Jones, vice provost of educational equity, told the student group making plans for a second Safer Sex Cabaret, "It's not going to happen." Jones ordered them to move the event off campus, or the university would shut it down. In April 2001 the Undergraduate Student Government Senate refused to allocate $573.52 for Pride Week because of fear over the state legislature's objections.[44] Democratic state representative John Myers declared, "The issue is, 'Am I going to allow my children to go to Happy Valley and be intimidated out of their wits?'"[45] Apparently risqué bingo and gingerbread penises at purely voluntary events must be banned in order to save the poor witless students.

The fear of sex extends even to the U.S. Congress. In October 2003 Republican congressmen gave the National Institutes of Health a list from the Traditional Values Coalition of 181 researchers they opposed for "awful and pornographic" studies of prostitution, AIDS, and drug use. Johns

Hopkins researcher Chris Beyrer reported what happened at an NIH meeting with scientists after the Republican attack on the agency: "A project officer stood up and said, 'We have to tell you that there is a new policy at NIH, and the policy is that if any of the following words or terms are in your grant title or abstract, we're going to send it back to you to take them out.' Then she proceeded to list the words: sex worker, injection drug use, harm reduction, needle exchange, men who have sex with men, homosexual, bisexual, gay, prostitute. It was unbelievable."[46] Gilbert Herdt, head of the National Sexuality Resource Center, noted: "I have been in this field for 30 years, and the level of fear and intimidation is higher now than I can ever remember."[47] The Union of Concerned Scientists reported in May 2004, "The administration has picked candidates with questionable credentials for advisory positions, used political litmus tests to vet candidates for even the least political of its government review panels, and favored the candidates put forward by industry lobbyists over those recommended by its own federal agencies."[48]

Censorship at Religious Colleges

Many of the most appalling cases of censorship on college campuses occur on religious campuses. A majority of evangelical colleges ban Catholics from being faculty.[49] Joshua Hochschild, an assistant professor of philosophy at evangelical Wheaton College in Illinois, was fired after he became a Catholic in 2005.[50] Wheaton College forces all faculty not only to be Christians but also to believe in creationism and Biblical inerrancy. In addition to a statement of faith, Wheaton also requires faculty to obey a "community covenant" that bans homosexuality, adultery, and even watching "immodest, sinfully erotic, or harmfully violent" movies off campus.[51] Conservatives who happen to be atheists are also victimized by this religious orthodoxy. At Ashland University in Ohio, historian John Lewis was denied tenure in 2007 because of his "objectivist views that are hostile to the University's mission."[52]

Some religious colleges engage in book banning. In 2003 Louisiana College president Rory Lee banned *The Road Less Traveled* by M. Scott Peck and *A Lesson before Dying* by Ernest Gaines from the college bookstore because a student and a trustee complained about profane words and a sex scene in these books, which were assigned in a philosophy class.[53] A December 2, 2003, policy approved by the trustees even required faculty to submit all class materials to administrators for prior approval, and all future staff are compelled to write an essay explaining their religious beliefs before being hired. After the Southern Association of Colleges and Schools put Louisiana College on probation, the trustees in 2005 unanimously voted to overturn their textbook policy.[54] Repression is common at Louisiana College. A 2004 visit by an accrediting team reported "a general climate of fear" among faculty.[55] Students have to earn "spiritual credits" through mandatory chapel and are not allowed to show R-rated movies.[56]

At Regent University in Virginia, founder and chancellor Pat Robertson imposed censorship guidelines for student-made films because he was offended by "horrible" and "inappropriate" films at a student film festival in spring 2002 and walked out. At an October 2002 forum, Robertson denounced dark satirical comedies: "If we go into this black stuff... I don't think that exactly pleases the Lord."[57]

At Christendom College in Virginia, not only are R-rated movies banned, but PG-13 movies with sexual content must be approved by a resident assistant in order for students to watch them.[58] Even television is banned in dorms at Bob Jones University in South Carolina, Christendom College, Thomas Aquinas College in California, and Magdalen College in New Hampshire (which also bans students from reading popular magazines and novels).[59] Bob Jones University bans all modern music, including Christian contemporary music.[60]

At tiny Patrick Henry College in Virginia, the nation's leading source of Bush's White House interns, two professors were fired and three other faculty resigned in protest, meaning that almost one-third of the college's sixteen professors left in 2006 because of its violations of academic freedom.[61] President Michael Farris fired government professor Erik Root because he discussed Hobbes and Locke in a class, and when a student responded by quoting the Bible, Root replied, "That's great, but it's too simplistic."[62] Farris fired professor Robert Stacey because Stacey read the college's "Biblical Worldview" and statement of faith to his class and then asked any students who thought he had betrayed these rules to leave.[63] Patrick Henry College also banned a book about the birth of Hinduism and forced theology instructors to remove a book unless another view to balance it was added to the curriculum.[64]

The Creed of Censorship

Many religious colleges are creedal, forcing faculty to sign a statement of beliefs in order to get a job. Cedarville University in Ohio requires all faculty to agree in writing with a specific set of religious beliefs. Students must sign an oath proclaiming a personal relationship with Jesus.[65] Jerry Falwell's Liberty University requires faculty to believe that the Bible is inerrant, the universe was created in six days, and Jesus will return to the earth for a thousand-year reign.[66] Job applicants at Biola University in California must have their church investigated to determine if their doctrines are sound.[67] Calvin College in Michigan requires all professors to agree with the tenets of the Christian Reformed Church (including the Heidelberg Confession, the Belgian Confession of 1561, and the Canons of Dordt), and they must send their children to Christian Reformed schools unless they receive a special exemption from the provost.[68]

Anthony Diekema, former president of Calvin College in Michigan, compared teaching at a religious college with working for Coca-Cola. A Coca-Cola worker who promotes the virtues of Pepsi would be fired, and Diekema says they should be: "Your obligation is to find a more compatible place, not to try to turn Coke into Pepsi."[69] But is a university really the same as caramel-colored carbonated sugar water? Someone who drinks Pepsi probably does not have much to learn from a devotee of Coca-Cola. But someone who believes in a religion can learn a lot from having their views challenged by a different viewpoint. And just because you have some critical things to say about Coca-Cola doesn't mean that you want to turn it into Pepsi. The faculty fired by religious colleges are genuine believers in that faith who dare to challenge the existing orthodoxy (or worse, challenge the management skills of administrators), not heretics who want to destroy the religion.

Diekema argued, "Academic freedom is a right that is given in the academic community, a right to pursue scholarship and truth. It is a special right, but not a right to violate the mission or the worldview embraced by a community or a specific institution."[70] Diekema is wrong. The fundamental mission of any university is to educate, not inculcate. A religious college that seeks doctrinal purity may be protecting its sectarian aims, but it is sacrificing its mission as a college. Even Diekema, for all his efforts to defend different standards for religious colleges, worried about these oaths: "There has been a significant 'chilling effect' operative among Christian scholars. There are simply too many 'horror stories' in the pipeline of Christian-scholar scuttlebutt to deny the reality of this chilling effect."[71]

Forbidden Speakers

Religious colleges frequently ban speakers who are deemed to be too liberal. At Gonzaga University in Washington on September 12, 2003, the board of trustees passed a new policy requiring all faculty and students to receive prior approval for speakers and events. Any speakers can be banned if "it would not constitute a legitimate educational experience or contribute to the university's mission"; if "there is substantial risk the speech or event would create a hostile learning environment"; or if "it is likely to confuse the public or students about the university's core values, or offend the university's mission by advocating positions or activity contrary to Catholic teachings." Ironically, this policy permitting censorship is actually seen as more open-minded than the arbitrary cancellations of liberal speakers and plays made in the past by the president, Reverend Robert Spitzer.[72]

In September 2004, Catholic University of America president David O'Connell banned actor/filmmaker Stanley Tucci from speaking at a forum on Italian film because of his support of Planned Parenthood.

And O'Connell banned all political speakers before the November 2 election, squelching plans to bring Republican and Democratic visitors. Two-thirds of the School of Arts and Sciences faculty signed a petition protesting this attack on academic freedom, and more than 100 students staged a sit-in on October 13, 2004.[73] Catholic University had temporarily banned a campus chapter of the NAACP (because the national group supported abortion rights) and in 2003 banned Eleanor Holmes Norton from appearing at a campus bookstore because she supports abortion rights.[74]

In 2002 College of the Holy Cross president Reverend Michael McFarland prohibited the women's studies program from bringing in Frances Kissling, president of Catholics for a Free Choice. McFarland wrote that if Kissling spoke on campus it would be "an embarrassment to the institution" and "deeply offensive to many people here." As a result, Kissling's speech about sexual exploitation was cancelled.[75]

In 2006, the Boston College administration banned a discussion organized by the Women's Health Initiative about Samuel Alito's appointment to the Supreme Court because it was deemed to be unbalanced.[76]

The conservative campaign for repression of dissent at religious colleges is so extreme that Patrick Reilly, head of the far-right Cardinal Newman Society, called upon Catholic University of America in 2006 to ban politician Bob Casey from speaking on campus. Although Casey is a Catholic who opposes abortion rights, Reilly proclaimed that "Bob Casey has no business delivering a lecture on public morality" because Casey does not want to ban contraceptives.[77]

The Monkey Trial Evolves: Creationism in Academia

More than a century after the fact of evolution became fully accepted among scientists, there are professors at American colleges today who are fired for teaching evolution to their students in biology classes and universities where teaching scientific truth is banned by the institution.

In December 2000, Wheaton College anthropologist Alex Bolyanatz was dismissed because he "failed to develop the necessary basic competence in the integration of Faith and Learning, particularly in the classroom setting." Bolyanatz received positive reviews and a unanimous recommendation from the Faculty Personnel Committee, but the administration could get rid of him in a fit of theological correctness. Bolyanatz apparently was guilty of violating Wheaton's statement of faith, which requires a belief that "God directly created Adam and Eve." The provost sat in on some of his classes and ordered Bolyanatz to treat creationism with respect.[78]

The fact of evolution has been scientifically settled. But as the Scopes Trial in 1925 over a ban on teaching evolution revealed, the political reality is very different among those who believe that science should follow the Bible. Senator Rick Santorum (R-PA) declared, "Anyone who expresses anything other than the dominant worldview is shunned and booted from the academy. My reading of the science is there's a legitimate debate. My feeling is let the debate be had."[79] George W. Bush weighed in with his opinion that creationism should be taught as a competing scientific doctrine.[80] The advocates of creationism appeal to a noble ideal ("let them debate") in order to justify a scientific fraud. We do not demand that students debate astronomy and astrology on equal terms in order to learn about the stars, or that the Flat Earth Society should be represented in geography class. We want students to learn about scientific truth.

Students should study creationism in their science classes. They should learn about all the reasons why creationism is wrong, because so many students believe the fantasies disguised as truth by the religious right. According to a recent poll, 51 percent of Americans reject the theory of evolution and endorse creationism.[81] An August 2005 poll by the Pew Research Center found that 38 percent of people want creationism to be taught instead of evolution.[82] But we must reject any idea that college teaching should reflect majority opinion rather than the truth.

The critics of creationism can face censorship on campus. Paul Mirecki, the chair of the religious studies department at the University of Kansas, withdrew a course called "Special Topics in Religion: Intelligent Design, Creationism and Other Religious Mythologies" because his comments critical of religion on a listserv were made public.[83] University of Kansas administrators had promised to make his lectures public so they could be monitored. Religious leaders in the state called for his firing and a ban on courses critical of intelligent design.[84] In 2007 at the University of Colorado in Boulder, threatening messages were put under the doors of evolutionary biology labs, apparently from a religious group that objects to research on evolution.[85]

Certain conservative religious colleges demand that science professors betray their obligation to teach scientific truth. At Jerry Falwell's Liberty University, creationism is a mandatory class, and evolution is mentioned to attack its doctrines. David DeWitt, an associate professor of biology, reported that "we cover evolution, but we bring up problems with it.... I think it's dishonest to shove evolution down these students' throats as a fact." Biology professor Terry Spohn noted, "Unlike secular institutions, we give both sides."[86]

At Biola University, officials call it "unacceptable" for science professors to teach that one species can evolve into another.[87] Palm Beach Atlantic University requires all faculty and staff to believe that "man was directly created by God," and teachings in the college "shall always be consistent with these principles."[88]

Patrick Henry College demands that its science professors "teach creationism from the understanding of Scripture that God's creative work ... was completed in six twenty-four hour days.... Evolution, 'theistic' or otherwise, will not be treated as an acceptable theory." The American Academy for Liberal Education (AALE) was founded in 1992 to provide a conservative alternative to traditional accrediting groups that right-wingers feared were too politically correct. But in 2002, AALE refused to grant accreditation to Patrick Henry College because of its ban on teaching evolution. AALE president Jeffrey Wallin noted, "You can hardly educate students if you cut off fields of inquiry. You can indoctrinate them, but you can't educate them."[89] *Christianity Today* editorialized that AALE was undermining academic freedom because "Christian colleges' efforts to delineate—and regulate—their points of view actually serve the academy as a whole by adding a distinct kind of scholarship to the marketplace of ideas."[90] Creationism is indeed a distinct kind of scholarship—the fraudulent, irrational, incompetent kind of scholarship.

The notion that we need a diverse set of institutions—those that support academic freedom and those that deny it—fails to convey what the academic enterprise is. A religious institution is not defined by the ideas it prohibits, but by the ideas it exalts. What happens to a religious university when it has academic freedom? The same thing that happens to a religion when it has free believers, instead of those compelled by force to obey: Their faith is real, not forced. Their religion is understood, not recited. Academic freedom poses no threat to religious truth. But it is a threat to religious orthodoxy. If some trustees and administrators value obedience over religious understanding, then they will object to the danger posed by allowing freedom on campus.

In Illinois, Wheaton College president Duane Litfin argued, "We in Christian higher education ... believe that a healthy academic marketplace of ideas will view academic freedom as the right not only of individuals, but also of those institutions."[91] This idea—that the absence of academic freedom at religious college is a "special" kind of academic freedom—should be rejected as sophistry. It is like saying that freedom of speech is improved if we allow one city to ban dissent, because the freedom of communities is being promoted. It is like supporting a dictatorship on the grounds that the world should have a healthy marketplace of different styles of government rather than universal democracy and freedom. If all colleges defend academic freedom, it does not mean they will all become the same or cease to be religious. Nations with freedom do not become identical because they allow liberty to their people. There is not one kind of academic freedom for secular colleges and another kind of academic freedom for religious universities. For a university to attack an individual's academic freedom in the name of "institutional" academic freedom is a contradiction in terms.

Censorship of Religion at Public Colleges

Outspoken Christians, at both secular and religious institutions, should never be punished for expressing their faith. A professor should be free to discuss religious issues with a class just as easily as discussing political beliefs. It may not be good teaching or ideal professional behavior, but it would be dangerous to forbid such comments. Cases of secular colleges punishing religious expression are rarer than repression at religious colleges, but they are still troubling.

At Lakeland Community College in Ohio, adjunct philosophy professor James Tuttle had his course load reduced and didn't get to teach the classes he wanted after a student complained that he often discussed his Catholic faith in class and that Tuttle put an explanation of his religious beliefs on his syllabus. James L. Brown, dean of the division of arts and humanities, wrote Tuttle, "I think that you would be happier in a sectarian classroom." Brown reduced Tuttle's teaching load to one ethics class and had another professor monitor the class. For spring 2004, Brown offered Tuttle three sections of logic, but Tuttle declined to teach them. As David French, president of FIRE, noted: "When an institution tries to make professors hide their personal beliefs, it has grave implications for academic freedom."[92] But Tuttle was ultimately a victim because he lacked tenure, not because he was a believer. As an adjunct, Tuttle has no formal rights and the fact that he refused an offer to teach makes it almost impossible to prove any discrimination.

Another adjunct, University of Colorado history instructor Phil Mitchell, was not rehired by an administrator because he was accused of not meeting department standards and of proselytizing students in class.[93] Another adjunct, James W. Johnson, an openly gay Roman Catholic who is a religion professor at Broward Community College in Florida, accused his department in 2007 of refusing to hire him full-time because they favored hiring evangelical Protestants.[94] There is no way to know if adjunct faculty are fired for their religious (or nonreligious) beliefs, because all adjuncts lack basic job protection and adequate grievance procedures. The trend toward hiring faculty without a tenure track, and the lack of protections for adjuncts, puts any faculty with strong beliefs at risk. The best way to protect religious faculty from discrimination is to protect the rights of all faculty by expanding protections of due process to all faculty and reducing dependence on adjunct faculty.

Religious students also can sometimes face discrimination. The freedom of students to select their course of study is a fundamental part of student academic freedom, and that must include the study of religion. Joshua Davey qualified in 1999 for a Washington state "Promise Scholarship" of $1,125. He was admitted to Northwest College, a Christian school. When he declared a double major in pastoral ministries and business administration, Davey was no longer eligible for the scholarship because state law banned funding theology studies (similar laws exist in fifteen states). Davey sued, and the district court upheld the state law. But the U.S. Court of Appeals for the Ninth Circuit reversed, ruling that the policy discriminated against religion, and the U.S. Supreme Court in *Locke v. Davey* correctly agreed that the law must be struck down and students allowed to study theology.[95] Restricting state scholarships based solely on a student's choice of majors is a violation of both student academic freedom and religious nondiscrimination.

At Washtenaw Community College in Michigan, administrators settled a lawsuit in April 2002 after the college rejected student John Luton's application to form a club called "Mission Christ" because the club's goal was to tell others about Christianity. The college paid a $10,000 settlement, rewrote its speech policy, and acknowledged Luton's right to preach, hand out Bible tracts, and display prolife posters.[96]

However, efforts to protect religious students go too far when they receive special privileges to spare their feelings. In 2005, Rhode Island College president John Nazarian ordered the removal of signs near the campus entrance placed by the Women's Studies Organization that declared "KEEP YOUR ROSARIES OFF OUR OVARIES" after a priest objected to them.[97] At the University of Utah, former drama student Christina Axson-Flynn sued because she felt forced out of the theater program for refusing to say the f-word in classroom exercises using professional scripts. Axson-Flynn claims that the school violated her religious liberty as a Mormon. Her attorney Michael Paulsen told the U.S. Court of Appeals for the Tenth Circuit, "She's not asking for much here, just to change words or scripts in classroom exercises."[98] Shockingly, the Court of Appeals agreed with Axson-Flynn, and the University of Utah agreed to a settlement.[99]

If students can rewrite plays that offend them, they might also be entitled to refuse to read books or watch films or listen to lectures that they regard as offensive. The American Family Association complained about allowing R-rated movies to be shown in a class at Grand Rapids Community College in Michigan, declaring that it created a "hostile environment that weeds out students whose religious or moral convictions lead them to object to such material." English instructor James Hayes showed students the movie *American Beauty* to teach them about writing a film analysis.[100]

Critics of religion at public colleges can also be subject to attacks on academic freedom. Captain MeLinda Morton, a chaplain at the Air Force Academy in Colorado, reported that she was fired from her job in 2005 and ordered overseas after she refused to follow her bosses' demands for her to attack a report by a Yale Divinity School team on religious intolerance at the Air Force Academy.[101]

Timothy Shortell withdrew as chair of the sociology department at Brooklyn College in 2005 after there were calls for his removal because he wrote in a 2003 article that "those who are religious are incapable of moral action" and called believers "moral retards." The *New York Sun* editorialized, "How could someone who compares Karl Rove's tactics to those of Goebbels or deems people of faith 'moral retards' possibly be fair in evaluating the tenure candidacies of an Orthodox Jew, or an observant Catholic, or a supporter of the Bush administration?"[102] But having strong personal beliefs does not mean that one is incapable of judging others fairly. David Horowitz argued that because Brooklyn College had allowed someone with these views to be hired, "This university should be put under an external audit."[103]

Christoph Kimmich, the president of Brooklyn College, started an investigation of Shortell and denounced his "offensive, antireligion opinions." Kimmich apparently even banned any criticism of religion by Brooklyn College professors in their classes: "While his right to express these views is protected, what is not protected is the injection of views like these into the classroom or into any administrative duties he might assume as chair of the sociology department." As Shortell noted, "If I can be denied the opportunity to lead a department based on presumptions about my political beliefs, so too can anyone else. Whose unpopular viewpoint will be questioned next?"[104] Suppose that a religious person believed (as many do) that atheists are morally inferior because they lack a belief in God. In fact, suppose that person phrased it to say that atheists are "moral retards." This is a perfectly reasonable, if extreme, opinion (as is Shortell's). If atheists are removed from their jobs for holding strong beliefs, then should the same happen to religious believers? Do we really want colleges to ban anyone with strong opinions about religion (or nonreligion)? Whether the victims of censorship are atheists or true believers, it's still wrong to silence them. Whether censorship is done in the name of God or for the sake of sensitivity, it is a violation of academic freedom.

Conservative politicians have limited academic freedom for religious purposes. George W. Bush used the first veto of his presidency to limit the academic freedom of scientists by banning new federal research funding of stem cell research.[105] In Missouri, Republicans proposed a bill in the state senate in 2005 that would have made it a felony to conduct most stem cell research.[106]

The Cardinal Newman Society and Academic Freedom at Catholic Colleges

A right-wing Catholic advocacy group called the Cardinal Newman Society is among the leading attackers against academic freedom. The Cardinal Newman Society demands that all Catholic colleges impose an unprecedented regime of censorship; in 2005, the society presented a list of eighteen professors at Catholic colleges that the group believed should be fired because these professors took a position on the Terri Schiavo case contrary to that of the Vatican.[107] These attacks have had a strong influence on Catholic colleges, and administrators fear being the next target of the group.

Bishop John D'Arcy denounced the Notre Dame Queer Film Festival as "an abuse of academic freedom" and called for the university to ban it.[108] D'Arcy contended, "The rights of others are violated. What about the rights of the Church to have its teachings properly presented? What about the rights of parents of those students at Notre Dame who find the contents of this seminar offensive?"[109] These so-called rights do not exist. The "right" to censor dissenting views is not a power any individual or university should have. Notre Dame president John Jenkins decided to allow the festival to continue, although it was compelled to adopt a different name.[110]

The Cardinal Newman Society opposes allowing Barack Obama, Howard Dean, Barney Frank, Al Gore, Ralph Nader, Eve Ensler, Angela Davis, Maxine Waters, Patricia Schroeder, Andrew Sullivan, and anyone else who supports abortion rights or equal rights for gays and lesbians from ever speaking at any Catholic college, even if they never mention these views.[111] In 2007, Creighton University disinvited author Anne Lamott because of her views on abortion rights and suicide, declaring that "at a featured lecture like this, the degree to which the speaker's views do not harmonize with the Catholic mission becomes more salient."[112]

The Cardinal Newman Society attacked St. Louis University for allowing columnist Bill McClellan to be commencement speaker, due to McClellan's prochoice views and support of stem cell research. In Illinois, Quincy University commencement speaker (and well-known conservative radio legend) Paul Harvey withdrew in 2003 after the group's criticism of his prochoice beliefs. Other commencement speakers denounced included Supreme Court justice Stephen Breyer, New York City mayor Michael Bloomberg, Chris Matthews, and Pete Seeger.[113]

Perhaps the most dramatic case of the Cardinal Newman Society's attack on academic freedom came at the University of St. Francis in Illinois in spring 2004. Dr. Nancy Snyderman was disinvited from giving the commencement address four days before graduation after a campaign against her by the Cardinal Newman Society. A surgeon, author, and former ABC medical correspondent, Snyderman, who is personally opposed to abortion, had mentioned in a medical report on ABC's *Good Morning America* on October 30, 1997, that some doctors recommend "selective reduction" via abortion for a woman pregnant with septuplets because of the high risk in having seven babies. A letter to her from the university read, "The university recently received information ... containing comments by you on the topic of abortion, and these comments appear to be contrary to the teachings of the Catholic Church. As a Catholic university, we have no choice but to rescind our invitation."[114] When a journalist and doctor is banned from a campus for accurate reporting on abortion issues, it indicates how far the repression of freedom at Catholic colleges has gone.

In 2005 the Cardinal Newman Society denounced nineteen Catholic colleges for their commencement speakers, including biotech researcher Leroy Hood (who supports stem cell research), California attorney general Bill Lockyer (because even though he enforced California's laws prohibiting gay marriage, he has supported the concept of gay marriage), and writer Jacquelyn Mitchard (for supporting abortion rights and disagreeing with the Vatican's position on the Terri Schiavo case).[115] The Cardinal Newman Society even objected to a drag show at the College of St. Catherine in Minnesota.[116]

In 2005 the St. Elizabeth College of Nursing in New York invited Representative Sherwood Boehert as commencement speaker. But under pressure from local bishop James Moynihan and the Cardinal Newman Society, St. Elizabeth's president, Sister Marianne Monahan, banned Boehert from speaking.[117] Cardinal Keeler of Baltimore refused to attend the 2005 commencement at Loyola College of Maryland and threatened "consequences" because Republican Rudy Giuliani (who supports abortion rights) was being honored.[118]

In Pittsburgh, Duquesne University president Charles J. Dougherty barred the law school in 2007 from considering Senator Barack Obama, Senator John McCain, or Representative John Murtha as commencement speakers because of "the likelihood that some or all of these politicians have taken public positions on issues in opposition to Catholic Church teachings."[119] In 2007, the College of St. Mary in Nebraska disinvited commencement speaker Roberta Wilhelm, executive director of Girls, Inc., in Omaha, because the organization favors abortion rights.[120]

Occasionally, a conservative commencement speaker at a religious college will also draw criticism. Cardinal Francis Arinze, speaking at Georgetown College's 2003 commencement, was asked to talk about Christian-Muslim relations, but instead he discussed the decline of the family, which he said was "mocked by homosexuality." Seventy faculty signed a letter protesting Arinze's speech as insensitive and inappropriate. Tommaso Astarita, a professor of European history, declared: "You don't go to a commencement ceremony to hear that you're a bane on the Christian family." Theresa Sanders, professor of theology, protested by leaving the stage. Some students also left the ceremony in protest.[121] But students and faculty are free to criticize commencement speakers, and there was no censorship of Arinze, who was free to give his entire speech.

Another form of retaliation used by the Cardinal Newman Society is to remove institutions from official designation as Catholic colleges, hurting their recruiting and fund-raising. In 2003 the Cardinal Newman Society was able to apply pressure to have Marist College in New York removed from the list after Eliot Spitzer was allowed to speak at its graduation. In 2005, Marymount Manhattan College was similarly derecognized after it allowed Hillary Clinton to speak.[122] This kind of intimidation forces colleges that wish to remain Catholic to censor the speakers allowed on their campuses on the orders of a right-wing splinter faction.

The Cardinal Newman Society also targets faculty. In January 2005 the group attacked Rachel Shteir at DePaul University for writing a book called, *Strippers: The Untold History of the Girlie Show.*[123] The group objects to scientific research dealing with sexuality. In 2003 at St. Louis University, the Cardinal Newman Society and the American Life League sought to ban a herpes vaccine trial because it allegedly recruited "sexually promiscuous (female) participants who are at high risk of sexually transmitted disease" and supposedly encouraged contraceptive use.[124] The Cardinal Newman Society urged Catholic colleges to ban all Amnesty International student groups because the global organization opposed imprisoning women for having abortions and supported "access to abortion for women who are victims of rape and for women whose life or health is endangered by pregnancy."[125]

But the group, although adept at getting publicity, is far outside the Catholic mainstream. The Association of Catholic Colleges and Universities denounced the Cardinal Newman Society for making accusations that are "distorted, inaccurate and in some cases simply untrue."[126]

Repression of free speech at Catholic colleges is common. According to the Associated Press, "Most Catholic schools already vet commencement speakers and honorary degree recipients for their positions on key Catholic issues."[127] At Ave Maria College, Domino's Pizza founder Tom Monaghan, and funder of this new conservative Catholic university, promised that "there will be no proabortion politicians on campus giving talks or getting honorary degrees."[128] When Monaghan decided in 2004 to move the campus from Michigan to Florida, he issued a memo threatening to fire any faculty who publicly criticized the decision.[129]

Religious officials denounced Seton Hall University in New Jersey and called the "conferral of awards to people who publicly espouse views contrary to the university's fundamental Catholic identity" to be a "serious lapse" after a judge who had struck down a ban on so-called partial-birth abortion was honored. Newark archbishop John Myers, the president of the board of trustees, called it "profoundly offensive and contrary to the Catholic mission and identity" for the university to allow Supreme Court justice Sandra Day O'Connor to present an award to Judge Maryanne Trump Barry, and promised to prevent it from happening again.[130]

On February 13, 2004, Archbishop James P. Keleher of Kansas City declared that Catholic institutions must ban politicians who support abortion rights from speaking on campus, and no proabortion rights speaker or politician should be allowed to "address, give workshops, or otherwise make any presentation" at Catholic institutions.[131]

The U.S. Conference of Catholic Bishops 2004 statement on "Catholics in Political Life" declared, "The Catholic community and Catholic institutions should not honor those who act in defiance of our fundamental moral principles. They should not be given awards, honors or platforms which would suggest support for their actions."[132] Of course, unless the individual is being specifically honored for their work supporting abortion rights, it does not violate the statement. But the Cardinal Newman Society and other conservative Catholics are trying to turn this vague statement into a total ban on any campus speakers who support abortion rights, gay rights, stem cell research, drag shows, or anything else deemed illegitimate. The idea that allowing someone to speak or even giving them an award amounts to "support" for all of their beliefs is a particularly pernicious threat to academic freedom.

The Vagina Censors

The most frequently banned play in America is Eve Ensler's *The Vagina Monologues,* a series of vignettes about women and their sexual experiences. And the place where it is banned is the religious college. With more than 650 colleges around the world organizing performances of *The Vagina Monologues* around Valentine's Day (which Ensler has renamed "V-Day"), the play is amazingly popular for its frank discussion of sexuality. The Cardinal Newman Society has called for a total ban of the play from all Catholic colleges, and it has been successful at preventing *The Vagina Monologues* from being performed at numerous campuses.

Patrick Reilly, president of the Cardinal Newman Society, declared, "The *Monologues* have no place on a Catholic campus. But it's difficult to be cheerful when one of every eight Catholic colleges in the U.S. appears ready to host this filthy play. It is evidence of the continued crisis in Catholic higher education."[133] The Cardinal Newman Society is taking credit for "a marked decline in planned performances of the *Monologues*" at Catholic colleges. According to the Cardinal Newman Society, "The number of Catholic campus performances has steadily declined," from thirty-two in 2003 to twenty-seven in 2005, and only twenty in 2006 and twenty-one in 2007.[134]

David O'Connell, president of Catholic University of America (CUA) in Washington, D.C., declared: "I find the play crude, ugly, vulgar and unworthy of staging or performing at CUA in any manner whatsoever."[135] It is perfectly fine for college presidents to become theater critics, even if they are lousy at the job. But no president should become a literary dictator deciding what plays can be performed on campus. Brian Shanley, president of Providence College in Rhode Island, explained his reasons for banning the play: "Any institution which sanctioned works of art that undermined its deepest values would be inauthentic, irresponsible and ultimately self-destructive."[136]

In recent years, the play has been banned at the University of Portland, Iona College, the College of New Rochelle, Loras College, Rivier College, Xavier University (Ohio), Catholic University of America, Providence College, Loyola University of New Orleans, Emmanuel College, St. Ambrose University, St. John's University, St. Joseph's College (Indiana), Wheeling Jesuit University, Alverno College, College of Saint Mary (Nebraska), Edgewood College, Fontbonne University, Loyola Marymount University, Marquette University, the University of St. Francis, and several other institutions.[137] Censorship has discouraged students from trying to organize performances at many other colleges.

Non-Catholic colleges are also targeted for censorship. In 2003 the head of the American Family Association in Missouri denounced William Jewell College for allowing *The Vagina Monologues* to be performed and permitting progay speakers on campus, and the Missouri Baptist Convention cut off about $1 million a year in funding for the college because of the play.[138] Resistance to the play can also be found at some public universities; in 2004 campus police contacted the play's organizers at Illinois State University because a woman had made a complaint about a "pornographic" poster promoting the play, which showed a flower painting by Georgia O'Keefe.[139]

The Cardinal Newman Society has been protesting the play since 2002, and in 2005 it ran a full-page ad in *USA Today* denouncing *The Vagina Monologues*. The ad (which refused to use the word *vagina* because of its offensiveness, and instead wrote "V*****") condemned the "X-rated 'play'" for committing a "psychosexual assault" on students. According to the society, the play's "nonstop sex talk uses vile descriptions, sleazy details and obscenities to trash Judeo-Christian sexual morality and to entice impressionable college students to commit sexual acts." The ad declared that *The Vagina Monologues* "does more violence to the consciences and modesty of women and girls than any play ever has," and warned of the threat to student health if they tried to act out some of the scenarios in the play.[140] (Of course, the same is true of many dangerous scenarios in the Bible, but nobody proposes banning passion plays or Bible readings.)

Although the Cardinal Newman Society is a fringe group with no official backing from the Catholic Church, it has numerous influential allies. Reverend John D'Arcy, the bishop of Fort Wayne–South Bend Indiana, made a February 2004 pronouncement that "*The Vagina Monologues* is offensive to women; it is antithetical to Catholic teaching on the beautiful gift of human sexuality and also to the teachings of the church on the human body relative to its purpose and to its status as a temple of the Holy Spirit." According to D'Arcy, allowing this play on campus "is in opposition to the highest understanding of academic freedom. A Catholic university seeks truth. It is never afraid of truth, but it seeks it with respect for both reason and faith."[141] But how does censorship respect students' reason and faith? Are college students so fragile that watching a play will turn them into sex-crazed atheists?

Notre Dame President John Jenkins refused to entirely ban *The Vagina Monologues*, provoking anger from conservatives. But students were not allowed to sell tickets and raise money for abused women, and Jenkins did not endorse academic freedom: "An event which has the implicit or explicit sponsorship of the university as a whole, one of its units, or a university recognized organization, and which either is or appears to be in name or content clearly and egregiously contrary to or inconsistent with the fundamental values of a Catholic university, should not be allowed at Notre Dame."[142] In 2007, the play had to be moved off campus because no Notre Dame department would sponsor it.[143] Reilly has praised the campuses that banned *The Vagina Monologues*: "These leaders stood against political correctness in defense of their students' spiritual and mental health."[144] But far from resisting political correctness, the censorship of *The Vagina Monologues* imposes a conservative political correctness on college campuses.

Conservative Views of Christian Colleges

Conservative organizations seem particularly unwilling to confront the crisis of censorship at religious colleges. For example, in 2003, Baylor University faculty expressed concern over the campus climate: "This climate is marked by fear—fear of losing one's job, one's hope for tenure, a promotion, a pay raise, or a friend, over an opinion or activity that might be labeled 'disloyal' or 'not mission-friendly' by a representative of the administration."[145] Matt Bass, a student at Baylor's George W. Truett Theological Seminary, lost his scholarship in December 2003 because he expressed support for gay rights and gay marriage. Bass had to drop out because he could not afford the tuition. In the Baylor student handbook, the school mentions "homosexual acts" along with incest, adultery, and fornication as part of the sexual misconduct policy.

Yet a *National Review* article praised Baylor president Robert Sloan: "Thanks to Sloan, Baylor, perhaps like no other major institution, has sponsored the growth of ecumenical orthodoxy."[146] For conservatives at the *National Review*, violations of academic freedom at Baylor are perfectly acceptable in pursuit of orthodoxy.

The repression of student and faculty rights at religious colleges is so common and accepted that no one pays much attention to it. The right-wing group Intercollegiate Studies Institute produces a guide to conservative colleges called *Choosing the Right College*, which endorses elite religious colleges despite (or perhaps because of) the lack of free expression. The guide reported that Baylor University's administration has not been "lax in monitoring the campus political atmosphere," noting that all student groups must have goals "consistent with the mission of Baylor University."[147] Brigham Young University bans "premarital sex, cross-dressing, and homosexual conduct"; an MTV *Real World* cast member from BYU was even expelled for living in a home with men in it.[148]

At Catholic University of America, "the university bans prochoice speakers if they intend to present their views on abortion." One student reported, "Nobody publicly advocates legalized abortion. The real debate is whether people who are known to be prochoice should even be allowed to speak on unrelated subjects on campus." The guide adds with seeming approval, "Some college guides advocating condom use were removed from the bookstore recently."[149]

At Georgetown University, a Women's Center staff member reported: "We'd be kicked off campus if we suggested abortion to a student."[150] At right-wing Grove City College in Michigan (praised for its "real diversity"), a professor bragged, "There are no pockets of opposition." According to the guide, "Another professor reports that one of the primary consequences of the lack of tenure is that faculty members tend to avoid voicing strong criticisms of administration policy." Another added, "Sometimes the students complain that all the speakers are Republican or free market economists." Grove City students must attend chapel sixteen times per semester, and drugs, alcohol, premarital sex, and homosexuality or "any other conduct which violates historic Christian standards" are grounds for disciplinary action.[151]

In some cases, the faith imposed at Christian colleges is free-market economics. Colorado Christian University's president, former U.S. senator William Armstrong, fired Andrew Paquin as a professor of global studies in 2007 because the assignments in his classes included critics of free-market capitalism. Even though Paquin founded a charity to help Africans start up businesses, Armstrong decreed, "What the university stands for, among other things, is free markets."[152]

We should stand up equally for everyone's rights: the right to praise religion, the right to criticize religion, the right to pray in school, and the right to freedom from a religious establishment created by official prayers at public events. Sometimes these rights stand in conflict, but most of the time it's easy to support freedom of expression for everyone. Secular colleges should ensure that the individual rights of religious (and nonreligious) students and faculty are fully protected. All religious colleges should protect the right of students and faculty to dissent and follow their own consciences. Unfortunately, in American higher education, a double standard persists where censorship at religious colleges is praised, while secular colleges are expected to offer special privileges to religious groups that refuse to follow the same valid rules as everyone else.

Too Gay for God

The latest battleground of the culture wars can be found in college lecture halls on Thursday or Friday nights across the country. That's where the praying and singing members of InterVarsity Christian Fellowship hold their large group meetings. With approximately 34,000 students on 560 campuses, no other organization—religious or secular—can claim the allegiance of more college students.[153] Nor is any group on campus today as controversial as InterVarsity, which has fought battles on several campuses over violating nondiscrimination rules. To most of its members, InterVarsity is just a fun and welcoming atmosphere for Christian songs, worship, and fellowship. But to the national organization, InterVarsity chapters are seen as an effective way to spread its particular brand of evangelical Christianity—a brand that sharply opposes homosexuality.

InterVarsity has increasingly moved to the far right, adopting fundamentalist ideas about the literal interpretation of the Bible and the evils of homosexuality. In 2000 the InterVarsity group Tufts Christian Fellowship (TCF) sparked a national controversy after InterVarsity denied a senior leadership position to Julie Catalano because of her sexual orientation. Catalano had been a member of the group for three years. But when she informed them that she was a lesbian, she was told by an InterVarsity staffer that she was unfit to become one of the group's leaders. Catalano had asked Jesus to make her heterosexual and contemplated suicide, but she eventually decided that she could not change and her orientation was not sinful. Catalano filed a complaint with the Tufts Community Union Judiciary, and TCF was derecognized until they agreed to submit a revised constitution with a democratic process for electing leaders without a religious test.[154]

The Foundation for Individual Rights in Education (FIRE), a conservative civil liberties group, made the Tufts debate its first major fight. FIRE takes credit for successfully defending antigay religious groups in similar cases at Ball State University, Williams College, Middlebury College, Rutgers University, and the University of North Carolina at Chapel Hill. Alan Charles Kors, cofounder of FIRE, argued: "How could a religious student group possibly fulfill its religious mission if it is prevented from selecting its religious leadership on the basis of religion? These universities—public institutions bound by the U.S. Constitution and the Bill of Rights to protect both the free exercise of religion and legal equality—seem to think they have the power to demand allegiance to the values and beliefs of current academic administrators."[155] However, public institutions not only have the power but also the obligation to ensure open access to student organizations, including religious groups. Free exercise of religion requires public universities to allow members of any religious faith to participate in all student organizations.

David French, at the time the president of FIRE, claimed that the non-discrimination cases amount to "an outpouring of censorship" in higher education: "In four years, FIRE has fought for religious liberty at almost 50 colleges and universities—from the highest levels of academia (Ivy League schools and Ivy equivalents) to the community college level. At each one of these schools, Christian student groups were either expelled from campus or threatened with expulsion. Imagine the public outcry if almost 50 schools sought to exclude African American or gay rights groups from campus."[156] In reality, far more than fifty colleges ban gay rights groups on campus (and FIRE has never criticized a single college that expels students for being gay), while absolutely no college in the country excludes Christian student groups.

Although critics cite the fear of atheists taking over Christian groups, homosexuality is the true underlying issue in these disputes. While disputes at Harvard, Rutgers, and the University of North Carolina involved InterVarsity's refusal to obey antidiscrimination rules based on religious belief, several other cases addressed actual bans on gay students.

Middlebury Christian Fellowship faced a challenge for banning gays and lesbians. The senior leaders of the group refused to put a gay student's name on the ballot when electing leaders in 2000, claiming that all candidates must uphold InterVarsity's teachings, including a belief in biblical infallibility, and must therefore denounce homosexuality.[157]

Brad Clark, a leader in InterVarsity Christian Fellowship at Central College in Pella, Iowa, did the unforgivable in fall 2002: He came out of the closet. Clark, who was the president of the student body, was forced to resign as an InterVarsity leader. Although the college has a nondiscrimination clause regarding sexual orientation, student senators at Central College voted 22–12 to continue recognizing InterVarsity as a student organization.[158]

InterVarsity tries to evade its discriminatory policies by claiming that they are based upon beliefs, not sexual orientation. Betsy Loomans, an InterVarsity staffer, told the Associated Press about Clark: "He was basically asked to step down because he didn't agree with our statement of beliefs."[159] Yet InterVarsity's formal statement of beliefs is silent about homosexuality, and it never announces itself as antigay when the group is recruiting members. As Clark pointed out, InterVarsity is not an openly antigay group: "I am a Christian, and this really was the only Christian organization on campus. I wanted a place to worship and fulfill my spirit, and there was not really an alternative. It wasn't until this year that I knew they had a stance on homosexuality."[160]

Clark's experience, in addition to showing that InterVarsity's paid staffers often control the student groups, indicates that InterVarsity has shifted its tactics from banning gay leaders to compelling belief in heterosexual marriage. InterVarsity's position also reveals why the group fights so hard to oppose antidiscrimination rules based on religion. Technically, the InterVarsity rules demanding antigay beliefs do avoid discriminating based on sexual orientation. But they discriminate based on religious belief about sexuality. Therefore, in order to impose its antigay stance on student chapters, InterVarsity needs to be allowed to discriminate against dissenting Christians on the basis of religion.

God in Court

On December 30, 2002, InterVarsity filed its first lawsuit ever in federal court to defend its selection of leaders in a student chapter at Rutgers University. The University of North Carolina narrowly escaped a similar lawsuit by caving in to InterVarsity a few days earlier. InterVarsity has often butted heads with university rules, but the conflicts have escalated as religious groups openly challenged the routine nondiscrimination codes that everyone took for granted in the past.

Rutgers vice president for student affairs Emmet Dennis noted the basis for the dispute: "The national religious organization is claiming that it should be able to veto the leadership elected by the student group."[161] Paid InterVarsity staff members on nearly every campus keep a careful eye on the selection and decisions of leaders. And in most of the cases where gay leaders have been excluded from InterVarsity, it seems to have come directly from the orders of these staffers, not student leaders. In April 2003, InterVarsity agreed to eliminate the faith requirement in the student group's constitution, while Rutgers reassured them that students could select the leaders they wanted. While InterVarsity treated this as a victory for freedom of religion, in fact it was InterVarsity that gave in to accept the nondiscrimination requirements.[162]

The First Amendment requires Rutgers to reject a provision in a student group's constitution that compels leaders to be "committed to the basis of faith," and the prohibition against an establishment of religion forces any public university to ban such religious tests. No public university should decide what defines a religion. And for that reason, no public university can allow discriminatory religious tests, even for the leadership of religious student organizations. Because the university must supervise and enforce the constitutional requirements of student groups, it will be forced to resolve any disputes involving this rule, and thus would have to evaluate the "faith" of students.

A public university is obligated to protect the freedom of expression of all students. To prohibit certain students from serving as leaders of a group based on their beliefs, even if they are the legitimate choice of their peers, is a violation of their First Amendment rights. No college has ever forced an InterVarsity chapter to accept a leader who was not selected by the members of that student group. The fear that atheists and satanists will be imposed upon InterVarsity student chapters is absurd. The real danger, which has repeatedly occurred, is that staffers for InterVarsity will overrule the choices of students and force out student leaders for their religious views or homosexuality.

The Legal Debate over InterVarsity

InterVarsity's lawyer, David French, defended the antigay policies by pointing to the case of *Boy Scouts v. Dale* (2000), in which the Supreme Court upheld a ban on gay leaders.[163] But there is a fundamental difference between a private organization's rights and those of a group chartered by a public university for all students. The *Boy Scouts* case has no relevance to a public institution. Instead, the guiding legal authority is the Supreme Court's *Southworth* case, in which the justices unanimously upheld the right of public colleges to collect and allocate student fees even when students disagreed with the groups receiving the money. The Court ruled that because these student groups were open to anyone, and because a viewpoint-neutral system was used to allocate funds, they were legal. Antidiscrimination requirements are plainly legitimate and viewpoint neutral (because they apply to all groups). Some courts have upheld this view. A federal judge in 2006 upheld the right of the University of California's Hastings College of Law to require the Christian Legal Society to obey the antidiscrimination rules applied to all student groups. The student organization had previously been approved, but when it affiliated with the national organization, it was forced to adopt the national group's antigay policies, which violated the rules.[164]

However, other courts have ruled against universities. Southern Illinois University, facing a judge determined to overturn a ban on discriminatory student groups, reached a settlement with the Christian Legal Society to recognize the student organization, pay legal expenses, and set up a $10,000 scholarship controlled by the group. Michael Mattox, a lawyer for the Christian Legal Society, declared "This sends a message to public universities that you cannot require a religious student organization to give away its ability to make sure its members and officers agree with the organization's beliefs in order to be recognized."[165] Originally, the national Christian organizations claimed they only wanted to control the leadership of student groups but allow any students to participate in them. But this case showed that the ultimate goal is to create exclusionary student groups where all members must obey the orthodoxy.

These court rulings have pushed campuses to cave in. In 2007, the University of Wisconsin at Superior agreed to reinstate the InterVarsity Christian

Fellowship (allowing it to ban leaders who do not sign a statement of religious belief), give it $1,564 in student fees, and pay $20,000 in legal fees.[166] But the Supreme Court rulings reject the idea that colleges must offer a special right to discriminate to religious groups.

InterVarsity supporters point to the 1995 *Rosenberger* case, in which the Supreme Court ruled that a public university cannot deny funding to a student newspaper simply because it is religious.[167] But the *Rosenberger* case stood for the principle that religious groups cannot be treated differently from other organizations. InterVarsity is demanding the opposite "right"—to refuse to follow viewpoint-neutral campus rules.

The key reason why the Supreme Court in *Rosenberger* rejected a ban on religious funding is that it would force a public institution to determine what content is and is not religious. InterVarsity's approach would compel public universities to determine whether a student group is religious in nature, and then grant only those groups a special exemption from nondiscrimination rules. And InterVarsity's constitution would require the university to judge the religious faith of students in any dispute over the student group's leadership, since the university must adjudicate the interpretation of any student group constitution.

Kors declared, "Everyone on campus would immediately see the absurdity of such a requirement if an evangelical Christian who believed homosexuality to be a sin tried to become president of a university's 'Bisexual, Gay, and Lesbian Alliance.' The administration would have led candlelight vigils on behalf of diversity and free association.... There is an unspeakable double standard toward believing Christians. It must end now."[168] However, no gay/lesbian student group has a constitution that prohibits evangelical Christians from serving as leaders, since they would violate the same campus rules prohibiting religious discrimination. The only double standard is what InterVarsity and FIRE are demanding, for religious groups to be given a special exemption from antidiscrimination rules.

No one is targeting Christian groups for special enforcement of nondiscrimination rules. At the University of North Carolina at Chapel Hill, campus officials looked at student organization charters and sent letters to seventeen student groups that had exclusionary rules, including the Native American Law Student Association, Phi Beta Kappa, and eleven religious groups. Only InterVarsity refused to change its student group charter. In 2005 a federal district judge ruled that UNC's nondiscrimination policy "raises significant constitutional concerns and could be violative of the First Amendment of the United States Constitution."[169]

While InterVarsity has often sought to avoid conflict and allow its discriminatory religious tests for leaders to fly under the radar of campus rules, some advocacy groups are beginning to mount direct legal challenges against antidiscrimination rules at colleges and universities.

Jordan Lorence, legal counsel for the Alliance Defense Fund, declared: "It is absurd for the university to require this Christian group to allow people with other religious beliefs to lead it. Will the university require the campus animal rights group to allow hunters as members, and the campus Socialists to have free market libertarians leading them? I thought the University was supposed to be a marketplace of ideas."[170] Actually, animal rights groups do allow hunters to be members, and campus socialists must permit a free market libertarian to be their leader if the legitimate members elect one. To require students to take any kind of religious oath or ideological test in order to run for a leadership position is a violation of their academic freedom and religious freedom. The leadership of a student organization cannot be closed off from sincere students who happen to have a different interpretation of the Bible.

Imagine, for example, if the Catholic Church decreed that any Catholic student group at a public university must have leaders who subscribe to Catholic doctrine. That sounds reasonable—until you consider that it excludes any Catholic who believes that women should be priests, or that priests should be allowed to marry. By such a rule, a devout Catholic freely selected by her Catholic peers in the student organization could be banned—with the public university enforcing religious doctrine by taking orders from the Catholic Church.

Religious groups do have the freedom to express a certain point of view, even if it's a repulsive one like homophobia. But when InterVarsity and other fundamentalist groups demand that universities violate their own antidiscrimination policies—and the First Amendment rights of their students—to accommodate this bigotry, they go too far. No university should enforce bias against gays and lesbians in the name of freedom of religion.

The Christian Legal Society requires all of its chapters to adopt detailed bylaws compelling all members to obey a statement of faith and "live their lives in a manner consistent" with it.[171] Under pressure from the Christian Legal Society, Ohio State University exempted its sixty-seven religious organizations from the university's antidiscrimination policy.[172] By giving an exception solely to organizations with "sincerely held religious beliefs" and allowing them to discriminate, Ohio State confers certain advantages on religious groups while imposing stricter regulation of nonreligious groups. A gay and lesbian student group, OutLaws, is banned from restricting membership, while the Christian Legal Society can now openly discriminate.[173] The exemption of religious groups is dangerous to the separation of church and state because it requires government employees to determine whether students have "sincerely held religious beliefs" in order to qualify.

Other colleges have given in to the threat of lawsuits. Arizona State reached a settlement with the Christian Legal Society allowing them to ban gays and anyone who dissents from their ideology.[174] The Milwaukee School of Engineering (MSOE) granted recognition to ReJOYce in Jesus Campus Fellowship on April 18, 2005, after initially denying approval because the student group required voting members to obey its "Standards of Personal Conduct," which prohibit actions "expressly forbidden in Scripture," including "homosexual behavior" and "idolatry, premarital or extramarital sex ..., drunkenness, coveting, theft, profanity, occult practices and dishonesty."[175] Compelling voting members of a student group to refrain from "homosexual behavior" raises many questions. Is reading a gay newspaper or a book by a gay author "homosexual behavior"? Will universities hold hearings to determine whether a student has ever engaged in homosexual behavior? What kinds of behavior will count? How recent does the behavior have to be in order to disqualify someone for the organization? When you add on the vagueness of thought crimes such as "coveting," almost anyone could be expelled from the group for any reason.

Investigating the religious beliefs, moral values, and sexual activities of students is not something that any university should be doing. But when student groups are allowed to impose ideological oaths and tests for membership or leadership, universities may be placed in these impossible dilemmas.

Instead of imposing unconstitutional religious tests, InterVarsity and other conservative religious groups should have faith that students in their organizations will select the best people to serve as leaders. If InterVarsity refuses to trust its students, then a university has no choice but to refuse to enforce any oaths that violate the rights of students. Students who want to form private discriminatory groups are still free to do so, but they are not entitled to use the resources of the university in order to discriminate.

Instead of submitting to these false cries of freedom of religion, colleges need to protect the religious liberty of individual students by allowing them to participate in all student organizations and letting the students choose their own leaders without any ideological or religious tests.

The drive to impose religious orthodoxy on student groups at public colleges is simply an expansion of the crusade for censorship at conservative religious colleges. The apologists for censorship at religious colleges are empowering petty dictators to violate academic freedom and betraying the true potential for these institutions to be distinctive while also being free. The fact that an administrator might be holding up a Bible while infringing academic freedom doesn't justify any kind of suppression.

Chapter Seven
Dangerous Words:
Freedom of the Press on Campus

⊷

I know what censorship looks like. I've seen its face. In Normal, Illinois, it looks like a normal-looking white guy with a crew cut and a fondness for throwing my newspapers in the trash.

It was April 8, 2003, at Illinois State University's Bone Student Center, where I was distributing some copies of the *Indy*, the progressive campus newspaper I cofounded. A student saw me with the papers and politely asked to see them. Great! I thought. A potential fan. I handed him the copies of the *Indy*—and he prompted deposited them in the nearest trash receptacle.

I've read many reports of those cowardly newspaper thieves who sneak around on college campuses trashing papers if they feel offended. But I've never met anyone who brazenly did it in front of my face. Our censor was so confident that he was doing something not only legal, but also good and moral, that he proudly tossed out our newspaper (or, "that crap," as he called it). In fact, he told me his name and spelled it out for me: Brad Walle. W-A-L-L-E.

Walle reported that he, and a few friends, threw out the *Indy* whenever they saw it: "I've been throwing them away for quite a while," he said, and promised that he would continue to do so in the future. In fact, he said he would come back ten minutes later and if any copies of the *Indy* were in our rack, he would trash them. Walle told me, "I find it offensive," and he said it is "my right to throw it away."[1]

He seemed especially upset by the April Fool's issue of the *Indy* mocking George W. Bush. But we'd found many issues trashed; in one particularly ironic example, I found copies of an issue about academic freedom torn in half and placed neatly back on the newspaper rack.

I sent an e-mail about the problem to the president and other top administrators, with a copy to Walle, and wrote about the incident in the next issue of our newspaper. I never received any response from the administration, and there is no explicit campus rule banning newspaper trashings. Many free newspapers have been stolen at campuses across the country where police and administrators sometimes declared that free newspapers could be freely stolen.

That April Fool's issue wasn't the only one that offended would-be censors. When we published a parody of the College Republican newspaper, the *ISU Patriot*, on the back page of the April Fool's edition of the *Indy*, a member of the College Republicans actually filed a complaint against us with the administration for our crime of mockery.[2] This wasn't the first time that humor got us in trouble with the authorities. When we ran a parody of the Walt Disney World College Program, the student Disney group on campus (yes, there is such a thing) got upset and cried copyright infringement. They tried to have parody posters banned from campus, and an administrator told us to remove them; fortunately, we knew enough about the First Amendment to understand that parodies are protected expression.

The trashings and attempts to censor our progressive newspaper stand in sharp contrast to the right-wing rhetoric about political correctness. Conservative critics of higher education often point to newspaper trashings by leftist students as a sign of the liberal intolerance that supposedly dominates college campuses. *Investor's Business Daily* declared, "Conservative college newspapers are routinely seized and destroyed by college brownshirts before they can be read."[3] However, the most common campus thieves are members of the groups typically regarded as conservative: fraternity and sorority members, followed by athletes. Other common campus thieves include student government candidates, university employees, people accused of criminal activity, progressive students, and conservative students like Brad.

A list of campus newspaper thefts reported by the Student Press Law Center during the 2006–2007 school year refutes the idea that liberal censorship of conservatives is the primary threat to a free press on campus. The subjects covered that led to thefts included the arrest of fraternity members at Texas A&M University at Commerce,[4] possible sexual misconduct by a professor at Weber State University in Utah,[5] satirical photos criticizing student government at Arizona State University,[6] a car accident at Bryant University in Rhode Island,[7] drunk students who died in accidents at the University of Kentucky,[8] fraternity hazing violations at the University of North Carolina at Chapel Hill,[9] students arrested on drug charges at Rowan University in New Jersey,[10] a student charged with rape at Truman State University in Missouri,[11] the omission of a candidate for student elections at the University of North Carolina at Charlotte,[12] a front-page photo of women at Framingham State University in Massachusetts they thought made them look fat,[13] an article about a campus rape cut out of newspapers at Notre Dame de Namur University in California,[14] and papers taken for use in a fraternity party at Tulane University in New Orleans.[15]

Are there left-leaning censors who steal newspapers? Sure. The University of Georgia conservative paper, GuardDawg, had 1,200 copies stolen in 2006 and distribution bins vandalized.[16] However, progressive papers are also stolen. In 2006, 550 copies of *Third Rail,* a progressive magazine at the College of Staten Island in New York, were taken for having a nude man and woman on the cover.[17] Half of the press run of the University of Southern Mississippi *Student Printz* was trashed by unknown thieves in November 2006, a few weeks after religious groups and the president of the university denounced a sex column in the paper.[18]

Although the *Indy* newspaper continues to struggle against the censors who throw out our newspaper on a regular basis, newspaper trashings are declining nationally. After reaching a record high of forty during the 1990s, the Student Press Law Center reported twenty-nine thefts in both 2000–2001 and 2001–2002, twenty-eight in 2002–2003, eighteen in 2003–2004, twenty-five in 2004–2005, twenty in 2005–2006, and twenty-one in 2006–2007.[19] Unlike in past years, more thieves have faced punishment.[20]

Censorship by Administration

Although most of the attention about freedom of the college press focuses on the problem of newspaper trashings, administrative censorship poses a far greater threat to campus publications. A stolen newspaper is usually a temporary problem. But administrative censorship imposes an enormous chilling effect on the student press, and a recent federal court decision has given colleges nearly unchecked power to censor most campus newspapers.

Administrators sometimes seek to censor conservative papers. At Delta College in Michigan, the administration tried to stop the editors of *Vox Veritas,* a conservative Christian newspaper, from handing out copies in 2006.[21] But it happens to leftists, too. Administrators at the Art Institute of California at San Francisco in 2006 temporarily confiscated 500 copies of a student magazine that included corporate logos and criticized the college owner, Goldman Sachs.[22]

But the vast majority of administrative censorship is directed at newspapers that simply make mistakes or, worst of all, criticize administrators. During the 2006–2007 school year, Grambling State University administrators in Louisiana suspended publication of the *Gramblinite* and required a faculty advisor to edit the newspaper.[23] In 2006, 3,000 copies of the Boston College *Heights* orientation guide were trashed by administrators because a student described orientation as "miserable."[24] In 2006, the Flagler College (Florida) newspaper, the *Gargoyle,* had an issue pulled by the administration because of an inaccurate headline about a tuition hike.[25] In 2007, the Flagler administration demanded the power of prior review and edited an article for the paper about a Gay-Straight Alliance on campus, which administrators had banned.[26] The Central Connecticut State University president launched a review in 2007 of the student newspaper after a satirical article on the benefits of rape was published.[27]

Administrators at Craven Community College in North Carolina banned the release of any copies of the *Campus Communicator* because it printed the name and address of a student charged with an assault on campus. On October 1, 2004, newspaper staffers were forced to blank out the student's name with correction fluid on all 1,100 copies of the newspaper before they were allowed to distribute the newspaper, even though newspapers routinely report such information from police incident reports.[28] In 2005, administrators proposed outsourcing control of the paper to a local commercial newspaper, but campus newspaper staffers protested and the company backed out. In March 2005, after the newspaper printed a sex column, the administration proposed that the faculty advisor engage in prior review of the paper and a committee decide on censoring anything the advisor felt should not be printed. Under pressure, the editor in chief banned the sex column and apologized, and agreed to allow the faculty advisor to see articles in advance.[29]

At Manatee Community College in Florida in spring 2004, the administration cancelled a journalism course used to produce the *Lance* newspaper, and cut off all funding for the newspaper after a controversy in which the faculty advisor demanded prior review of the paper. In fall 2004, the administration announced plans to create a new student newspaper, *Veritas,* and transferred all the money allocated to the *Lance* to this new paper.[30]

Hampton University administrators prevented publication of the September. 29, 2004, issue of the student newspaper, the *Script,* for two weeks because the paper lacked a faculty advisor. In October 2003, acting university president JoAnn Haysbert banned an issue of the paper because it printed her letter responding to complaints about the school cafeteria inside the paper rather than on the front page as she demanded.[31]

At Essex County College in New Jersey in June 2005, Dean of Student Affairs Susan Mulligan ordered the printer not to publish the student newspaper, the *Observer,* because it did not have an advisor. In fact, the student editors had selected an advisor, but Mulligan had vetoed the choice. The printer alerted the students to the censorship, and the student editors paid to have the paper published themselves.[32]

At Spokane Falls Community College in Washington, campus rules allow administrators to fire or punish student journalists and require advance permission for publishing any "controversial material." Two student editors who printed a small photo of a couple having sex (covered with black bars) were not fired only because the previous policy protected freedom of the press.[33]

Student governments can also join administrators in punishing papers. In June 2005 at SUNY Rockland Community College, the student government locked newspaper staff out of its own office because the newspaper decided not to accept any student fee funding due to the restrictions being imposed. The newspaper staff was finally allowed back into their office a week later.[34]

After the University of Northern Colorado's student newspaper, the *Mirror,* wrote articles critical of the student representative council and the board of trustees, the paper had its funding cut by 40 percent.[35] In 2006, the student legislature voted to cut about $10,000 from the *Missouri Miner*'s budget at the University of Missouri at Rolla due to biased content and grammatical errors.[36]

And even state legislators seek to silence campus papers. The 2006–2007 Arizona state budget included a requirement that "appropriated monies shall not be used to support any student newspaper."[37] Legislators imposed the rule because Arizona State University's weekly *State Press* student magazine showed a pierced nipple, and a column about oral sex appeared in Northern Arizona University's *Lumberjack* newspaper.[38] Russell Pearce, cochair of the Arizona House Appropriations Committee, declared: "If you want to be a free press, be a free press, but we're not going to subsidize articles that are over the top."[39] Americans for Decency listed the ASU *State Press* as the second biggest threat to decency in Arizona.[40] Criticism of the newspaper from real estate mogul Ira Fulton, who has given $58 million to Arizona State University, prompted ASU president Michael Crow to threaten to cut funding off or dictate content to the student newspaper because of the body piercing cover. Crow declared, "I think as an investor in the business, we want some say in how it's run."[41] Arizona State University also threatened to sue to stop a student-run newspaper, the *ASU Underground,* from using its acronym. The paper had to change its name to *ASYou Underground.*[42]

Conservative Newspapers under Fire

Like other campus newspapers, conservative publications can face censorship when they challenge the status quo. After the *Hawk's Right Eye,* a conservative student paper at Roger Williams University in Rhode Island, published articles denouncing two campus speakers (Judy Shepard, mother of slain homosexual Matthew Shepard, and James Dale, a gay man excluded from the Boy Scouts), President Roy Nirschel responded by sending an e-mail to the entire campus stating that paper had "crossed seriously over the lines of propriety and respect" and accusing the editors of having "flirted with racist and anti-Islamic rhetoric." Despite claiming to support the free speech rights of campus groups, the administration in 2003 froze $2,700 in funding granted to the *Hawk's Right Eye*, effectively silencing them temporarily.[43]

At the State University of New York at Albany, Scott Barea, publisher of the *College Standard*, sued in 2003 because the student government allocation council denied funding because they believed the conservative newspaper had misquoted people and printed lies.[44] At the University of Oregon, the conservative *Oregon Commentator* was derecognized in 2004 by the student government and denied funding because the newspaper mocked a transgendered student; the student government reversed its decision three months later.[45]

Sometimes administrators take action against mainstream papers for accusations of insensitivity. At Southwest Missouri State University, officials investigated the faculty advisor and student editor of *The Standard* for publishing an editorial cartoon (drawn by an American Indian student) on November. 21, 2003, that a Native American group found "offensive." It showed two Native Americans meeting a Pilgrim woman with a gift of canned corn, and the Pilgrim responds, "Gladys, the Indians are here and it looks like they brought corn. Again." Editor in chief Mandy Phillips was ordered to attend "mediation" and told that reporting on the administration's investigation could violate university policy.[46]

Censorship of Progressive Newspapers

Because conservative foundations heavily subsidize right-wing student newspapers, there are about twice as many of them as progressive campus newspapers. Perhaps most important, these conservative newspapers are well trained to complain loudly when they encounter censorship, so incidents are more likely to be reported than the progressive papers, which do not have wealthy organizations defending them. Nevertheless, progressive papers do report occasional acts of censorship.

At the University of Southern California, copies of the January 27, 2004, issue of the left-wing alternative newspaper *The Trojan Horse* were stolen, probably because the issue focused on the Israeli/Palestinian conflict.[47]

In 2002 a student went into the offices of the College of Staten Island's progressive newspaper, the *College Voice*, tore a flag off the wall, denounced an editor as a "fucking communist bitch," and threatened to hit one of the editors. Editors also received several threatening phone calls for their antiwar stands.[48]

Administrators also punish progressive student papers. On February 23, 2001, Portland State University officials padlocked the door of *The Rearguard*, an alternative student publication, after discovering the paper had decided to investigate a story involving a box of six-year-old university confidential files labeled "to be destroyed" that an unknown individual had left in front of the publication's office. Campus police followed the editor around campus for two hours and threatened to arrest him until he agreed to turn over the box.[49]

Sex is another common theme that incites censorship. When Harvard students Katharina Cieplak-von Baldegg and Camilla Alexandra Hrdy created a magazine about sex called *H Bomb,* Harvard officials imposed prior review on the magazine, which the *Boston Globe* described as "a glossy mix of essays, fiction, and poetry, along with artsy photographs." The editors were forced to show images planned for the magazine to two deans and were warned that the group's status as a student organization would be removed if any "pornographic" material was printed.[50]

At the University of North Florida, the student government sharply cut funding for the student-run radio station and required Osprey Radio to survey students every other week about what music it should play. One student senator complained that the station was playing "the filthiest, most vulgar, disgusting, unbelievable stuff."[51]

Progressive or leftist political views are a common reason why campus papers are targeted. My Dixie Forever, a "Southern heritage" group, called for East Carolina University administrators and trustees to punish the *East Carolinian* student newspaper for running an opinion column that criticized "the racial implications" of the Confederate flag. My Dixie Forever started a petition drive calling for the university to revoke funding for the newspaper and evict it from its offices because of this "hate speech" criticizing the Confederate flag.[52]

University of Massachusetts at Amherst student Rene Gonzalez wrote an opinion column in *The Daily Collegian* in April 2004 declaring that "Pat Tillman is not a hero. He got what was coming to him," one week after the former football player turned Army Ranger had been killed in a friendly fire incident in Afghanistan. Gonzalez was denounced by the university president and soon left the country for Puerto Rico because of numerous death threats against him.[53]

The Godly Press

Many examples of conservative administrators censoring liberal ideas occur at religious colleges. There are rare cases where religious publications have faced censorship at secular colleges, despite the Supreme Court ruling in the *Rosenberger* case prohibiting it. At the University of Oklahoma, the *Beacon OU,* a Christian student newspaper, received only $150 of the $2,300 requested for funding; the students sued, claiming that a policy banning student fees for "religious services" had been the reason for lack of funding by student government. An April 2, 2004, settlement eliminated the funding policy and paid the students $2,500.[54] But the greatest threat to the freedom of religious students comes from Christian colleges that regularly restrict student newspapers and prevent dissenting views from being heard. The worst restrictions on student papers are typically found at religious colleges.

At the University of Scranton, the 2004 April Fool's edition of the *Aquinas* led officials to shut down the newspaper for more than a month, fire the editor, and remove all remaining copies of the newspaper. The edition of the *Aquinas* included a "fictitious reference to a priest caught fooling around with a woman during the screening of *The Passion of the Christ*," and a celebrity death match between the former and current university president.[55] In a special full-page "statement of ethics" in the May 13, 2004, issue of the *Aquinas* compelled by the university before the newspaper was allowed to publish again, the staff and editorial board of the newspaper promised: "It is important that we strive for the same goals as our University," and added, "Though our mission is to serve as a paper of record and voice of the student community, we cannot appropriately foster the overall mission without respect for the ideals of Jesuit pedagogy."[56]

An editorial in the same issue of the *Aquinas* proclaimed, "Through errors of omission and commission the newspaper developed a forked tongue. This will be no more." The editorial promised, "The *Aquinas* has not been reborn but rather returned to its traditional unadulterated standards that it has attempted to maintain since its inception in 1916."[57] A new editorial policy ironically announced, "The University adheres to the principle of responsible freedom of expression for its student editors."[58]

At Baylor University, the *Lariat* staff was threatened with disciplinary action for writing a February 27, 2004, editorial supporting gay marriage. Baylor president Robert B. Sloan Jr. denounced the editorial: "Espousing in a Baylor publication a view that is so out of touch with traditional Christian teachings is not only unwelcome, it comes dangerously close to violating university policy, as published in the student handbook, prohibiting the advocacy of any understandings of sexuality that are contrary to biblical teaching."[59] The student publications board also denounced the editorial as a violation of the policy prohibiting student publications that "attack the basic tenets of Christian theology or of Christian morality." The board reported, "The guidelines have been reviewed with the *Lariat* staff, so that they will be able to avoid this error in the future."[60] Rather than defending the right of a free press, many Baylor faculty endorsed censorship. Doug Ferdon, chairman of the Baylor journalism school and one of the faculty advisors to the newspaper, noted: "The kids certainly have a right to free speech. But Baylor has certain rules. They shouldn't advocate things that would be against the basic tenets of Baylor and Baptists."[61]

At Brigham Young University, advisors for the *Universe* student newspaper made the paper eliminate the weekly insert for *Sports Illustrated* on Campus because even though the magazine followed BYU's ban on all alcohol and tobacco ads, it included an ad for its swimsuit issue and ran a photograph showing naked butts. The *Universe* is so scared of controversy that it banned an ad for a T-shirt that says, "I Can't.... I'm Mormon."[62]

At Jerry Falwell's Lynchburg College, administrators threatened to confiscate the alternative newspaper *Lynchburg Current* because it refused to get official recognition from the student government.[63] College Media Advisers censured Oklahoma Baptist University after it dismissed the student newspaper adviser in 2005 because he refused to engage in prior review.[64]

In February 2005 Catholic University of America announced that it would eliminate scholarships for its *Tower* student newspaper editors. A few months earlier, university president David O'Connell and university spokesman Victor Nakas declared that they would refuse to speak to any *Tower* reporters after the newspaper reported on the administration banning actor Stanley Tucci from a campus film festival because he is prochoice. Then the *Tower* reported how O'Connell, after banning all political speakers from campus before the election, give the benediction at a political rally for George W. Bush.[65]

The solution to the problem of censorship of campus journalists is not to blindly blame "conservatives" or "liberals," but to directly oppose all censors and to develop clear policies that protect freedom of the press at every college.

Targeting Faculty Advisors

Perhaps the most vulnerable faculty job in academia is the faculty adviser to a student publication. Non-tenure-track faculty who advise college newspapers frequently bear the brunt of administrative anger, even though advisers at public colleges cannot constitutionally demand prior review, and legal precedents establish that a university becomes liable for defamation in a student newspaper only if it seeks to control the publication.

In 2004, Kansas State University fired faculty newspaper advisor Ron Johnson. Kansas State's *Collegian* newspaper had come under fire from some African American students who objected to the lack of diversity in the newspaper's coverage. The School of Journalism and Mass Communications director Todd Simon ordered a "content review," compared the paper's stories with those on the websites of other student newspapers, and claimed that the *Collegian* had fewer stories with diverse viewpoints. Simon also proposed a new policy allowing the editor in chief to be fired for failing to meet diversity goals in hiring. The Student Press Law Center called Kansas State's arguments "unprecedented, bizarre and offensive to the First Amendment."[66] The Society of Professional Journalists condemned

Johnson's firing as a "clear violation of the principles of free speech and a free press."[67]

Many other faculty advisors have been fired for offending administrators. In Kansas, the Barton County Community College board of trustees fired Jennifer Schartz, a part-time professor and adviser of the *Interrobang*, on April 20, 2004. The *Interrobang* had published a letter to the editor, written by a former basketball player, critical of the coach, despite being asked by the administration to censor it. University lawyers wrote to Schartz, "Since Barton County Community College is ultimately responsible for the content of this publication, it is the Administration's position that letters of this type will not be printed as letters to the editor."[68]

At Long Island University, faculty adviser Mike Bush was fired and editor Justin Grant was suspended from the newspaper for a month because an article appeared in the January 21, 2004, *Seawanhaka* about the grades of the student government president who resigned. Administrators took control of the newspaper and changed the office locks. In a story about the resignation of the student government president, a reporter had discovered the president was flunking classes and confirmed this with several students. Although no university records were released, the university claimed that the student newspaper was violating federal privacy laws that prohibit the administration from releasing personal records of students.[69]

At Tennessee State University in 2002, Maurice Odine, chair of the communications department, ordered the student newspaper's faculty advisor, Pamela Foster, to "perform mandatory prior review" of *The Meter*. After Foster refused, Odine denounced her and then in 2004 ordered her to read every article before publication and meet with the student who wrote it.[70]

Michael Mullen, chair of the journalism department at Vincennes University in Indiana and faculty advisor to the *Trailblazer*, was demoted by the administration, which had denounced a 2003 April Fool's issue. The university threatened to cancel the paper and refused to give Mullen a pay increase. After students published another April Fool's issue in 2004 against the explicit orders of a dean, on May 11, 2004, Mullen was removed as faculty advisor and transferred to the English department.[71]

Marquette University fired journalism instructor and faculty advisor to the student newspaper Tom Mueller in 2005. Although the *Marquette Tribune* won nine awards from the Wisconsin Newspaper Association, administrators claimed the quality of the paper had declined. Administrators criticized the newspaper for printing the address where a sexual assault occurred and for publishing the name of a teacher with tuberculosis. As journalism professor Lawrence Soley noted, "The students will not act as public relations agents for the administration. That's been a recurring problem at Marquette, because the students have done reporting the administration doesn't want to see."[72]

At Florida Atlantic University in fall 2004, the student government tried to have *University Press* adviser Michael Koretzky fined $6,000 and fired because of a controversy over the selection of a new editor. The paper had reported on the retroactive raises student government officials gave themselves. Then the student government threatened to lock the editors out of their offices before backing down.[73]

At California State University at Long Beach, *Daily Forty-Niner* publisher William Mulligan was removed from his job in 2004 after printing a full-page ad criticizing journalism department chair William Babcock for his "chilling censorship warning" to the staff. Babcock discouraged the newspaper from reporting the dispute within the journalism department, declaring, "It's not a news story."[74]

Druann Durbin, faculty advisor to the *Peru State Times* at Peru State College in Nebraska, was fired in 2005 because she "wasn't a team player" and didn't "support the policies of the college."[75] Durbin reported that the president "does not like professors who speak out or challenge his ideas or criticize the college in any way. I allowed the students to cover what was going on campus, and he simply wanted to terminate me before I got tenure."[76] President Ben Johnson had fired a previous faculty adviser in April 2000 after the administration objected to a story about sexual assault on campus.[77]

The flood of fired campus media advisors is astonishing. At Arapahoe Community College in Colorado, Chris Ransick was dismissed as newspaper adviser after battles over content of the paper.[78] In 2007, Western Oregon University punished a student journalist (and fired the newspaper's faculty advisor) for discovering (and reporting) that the administration had posted a file of former students' Social Security numbers on a public server. The administration forced the student to write a newspaper editorial about "acceptable computer use" because the reporter had downloaded a copy of the file, even though he or she immediately informed the university about the security breach.[79]

The very small field of college media advisors probably has more faculty dismissals infringing on academic freedom than any other discipline. The lack of respect for student rights, and for faculty who defend student rights, leads to campus newspapers where students and their advisors are always wary of offending the administration rather than constantly looking for important news.

Student Journalists under Arrest

Administrators are not the only threat to student journalists. Several campus reporters have been arrested for trying to report the news at colleges across the country. At BYU, broadcast journalism student Cliff Kelly was arrested and charged with trespassing and obstructing a peace officer because he videotaped a campus police officer giving a jaywalking ticket to a student. Although Kelly identified himself as a journalist, the police officer grabbed him, handcuffed him, took his camera, and then took him to police head-quarters and searched him. The charges were eventually dismissed.[80]

Omar Vega, a San Francisco State University student journalist, was arrested in 2005 for burglary and evicted from his dormitory for taking photographs (and posting them on a website) of students who found a set of car keys and took CDs and money from the car, even though Vega never participated in the crime.[81]

The arrests of student reporters also happens off campus. At the Repub-lican National Convention in August 2004, several reporters (including stu-dent journalists) were arrested and detained for more than twenty hours for the crime of covering a legal protest despite having press identification.[82]

In addition, public colleges and other institutions routinely deny infor-mation requested by student journalists under the Freedom of Information Act.[83] Administrators see campus newspapers as vulnerable to censorship because many student journalists are not aware of their rights or lack the resources to put up a fight for freedom of the press.

Censoring the Web with Lawsuits

Censorship also comes from the threat of litigation. Swarthmore College officials declared that any campus website linking to the site www.why-war. com to provide information about Diebold voting machines would result in terminating the student's Internet connection. A whistleblower had leaked 15,000 internal e-mails from within Diebold about flaws in its voting system, which embarrassed the company. Diebold filed cease-and-desist orders against anyone making the memos public, including Swarthmore students. Tom Krattenmaker, Swarthmore's director of news and information, re-ported: "The administration explained that we are obliged, according to the law, to advise them to take the memos off the network, and to pursue the legal recourse that is available to them."[84]

Some students have even been threatened with criminal charges for expressing their views publicly. In 2003, University of Northern Colorado student Thomas Mink's web newsletter, *The Howling Pig*, showed a photo of finance professor Junius Peake altered to look like KISS guitarist Gene Simmons and the caption "Mr. Junius Puke" with the note that Puke and Peake should not be confused. Peake complained to Greeley police, who seized Mink's computer and threatened to arrest him for violating Colorado's criminal libel law unless he stopped publishing his newsletter. An ACLU lawsuit led to an injunction preventing Mink from being charged. The law criminalizes anyone who "blackens the memory" of a dead person or impeaches the honesty, integrity, virtue, reputation, or exposes the natural defects of someone.[85]

In 2005, St. Lawrence University in New York sued to demand the names of anonymous bloggers criticizing the administration and conservatives on campus, and promised to take action against them if they insulted students. The blog *Take Back Our Campus!* posted parodies of photos used on the university website and also posted the match.com ad of a professor who didn't want to date black or Asian women. Campus officials defended the litigation because they fear a "chilling effect" on faculty. Of course, this is a gross distortion of a "chilling effect." Just because criticism may make some people reluctant to speak up is no reason to silence free speech. Parody and fair use laws clearly protect the blog's use of the photographs for noncommercial purposes.[86]

Full Sail Inc., a for-profit technical college, filed a defamation lawsuit on February 18, 2004, against the anonymous authors of critical comments about the college that appeared on the website fullsailsucks.com. In June 2003, Full Sail unsuccessfully asked the World Intellectual Property Organization to rule that the protest website's name violated its trademark and then filed a suit against the website's creators, which was dismissed by a federal court.[87]

Colleges even jealously guard their initials to prevent criticism. The University of California at Santa Barbara threatened legal action against the owner of the website thedarksideofucsb.com, trying to force the removal of the initials "UCSB" from the site. Although UCSB officials eventually capitulated, attempts to ban criticism of a university cause a chilling effect across a campus.[88] Arizona State University successfully forced the independent, student-run newspaper and website *ASU Underground* to remove "ASU" from its name.[89]

Hazelwood Revived and *Hosty v. Carter*

Perhaps the greatest threat to student rights in recent years has come from efforts to suppress freedom of the press. Campus administrators justify censorship with the Supreme Court's 1988 *Hazelwood* case, which gave high school principals limited authority to control newspapers created in the classroom. Citing the *Hazelwood* case, in spring 2005 a dean at Long Beach City College imposed prior review over a student-run television show and began censoring content for the news show.[90]

In what may be the worst decision for college student rights in the history of the federal judiciary, the U.S. Court of Appeals for the Seventh Circuit in 2005 turned back the clock a half-century with *Hosty v. Carter* and reinstated the old discredited doctrines of *in loco parentis* and administrative authoritarianism.

The *Innovator* newspaper at Governors State University (GSU) in suburban Chicago was banished by the administration's demands for prior approval of its content. The facts of the *Hosty* case are particularly appalling. When *Innovator* editor in chief Jeni Porche and managing editor Margaret Hosty were first appointed in May 2000, GSU dean of student affairs Patricia Carter told them to print only "sunshine news."[91] When they began to investigate the GSU administration, Carter had them detained by campus police and then took away their keys to the *Innovator* office. Hosty and Porche still managed to put out an issue on October 31, 2000, which included an article about a grievance filed by *Innovator*'s faculty advisor who had been dismissed (and later won a settlement). On November 1, 2000, Carter called the *Innovator*'s printer, attempting to stop the publication of the newspaper. When she discovered that she was too late, she ordered the printer to give her the newspaper in the future before it was printed so that she could approve its content.[92] Two days later, GSU president Stuart Fagan wrote a campuswide memo in which he declared that the editors "failed to meet basic journalistic standards."[93] Porche and Hosty fought back, refusing to accept the administration's demands for censorship. Prior restraint is a classic violation of freedom of the press, and they sued the university and prevailed in an April 20, 2003, ruling by the U.S. Court of Appeals for the Seventh Circuit. But the Illinois attorney general appealed the ruling to the entire Seventh Circuit, and more than two years later they sided with the GSU administration. After the June 20, 2005, decision by the Seventh Circuit, the *Innovator* may never be seen again—and many other campus newspapers may soon join it on the list of publications censored or eliminated for questioning the status quo. Society of Professional Journalists (SPJ) president Irwin Gratz noted, "It is a sad day for journalism in the United States."[94] The majority opinion, written by conservative judge Frank Easterbrook and supported by other conservatives on the court such as Richard Posner, is a classic example of judicial activism.[95] Easterbrook's convoluted opinion abandons well-established precedents supporting the free expression rights of college students and gives college administrators near-absolute authority to control the content of student newspapers. The *Hosty* decision not only applies *Hazelwood* to college students, but greatly expands the scope of censorship to cover any newspaper or, potentially, any activity subsidized with student fees. The judges eliminated *Hazelwood*'s limitation to curricular-based newspapers and then eviscerated any constitutional protections for a "limited public forum" such as a newspaper.

Easterbrook's opinion also annihilated the common understanding of "limited public forum," a term created by the Supreme Court to provide a middle ground between the unregulated public forum (such as standing on a soapbox on the quad) and a nonpublic forum (such as a university-controlled alumni magazine). "If the paper operated in a public forum, the university could not vet its contents," Easterbrook wrote.[96] He then asked, "Was the reporter a speaker in a public forum (no censorship allowed?) or did the University either create a nonpublic forum or publish the paper itself (a closed forum where content may be supervised)?"[97] Of course, a newspaper isn't a public forum like a soapbox. It's limited to the students who run the newspaper. By declaring that only a pure public forum is entitled to constitutional protection, Easterbrook eliminates the First Amendment on college campuses for any limited public forum, including any student-funded activities.

"What, then, was the status of the *Innovator*?" Easterbrook continued. "Did the University establish a public forum? Or did it hedge the funding with controls that left the University itself as the newspaper's publisher?"[98] By his logic, the only speakers or newspapers on a public college campus that fall under public forum protection would be those that receive no funding from student fees or university funds (a rare commodity indeed). Any funding "controls" can be directly tied to ideological controls.

Easterbrook concluded, "Freedom of speech does not imply that someone else must pay," a philosophy that the Supreme Court has rejected over and over again at public colleges.[99] In *Rosenberger v. University of Virginia,* the Court ruled that a public university cannot ban funding for a newspaper based on its religious content.[100] Now the Seventh Circuit has declared that a public university may be obliged to fund a newspaper, but it could impose any control over its contents. In *Board of Regents v. Southworth,* the Supreme Court ruled that public colleges must ban all viewpoint discrimination in funding student groups.[101] It would be bizarre if college administrators were granted the direct power to control the viewpoints expressed in student newspapers while expressly banned from making funding decisions based on viewpoint. Yet this is what Easterbrook's opinion permits.

In essence, Easterbrook argued that there is only one kind of censorship that is impermissible on a public college campus: banning someone from speaking for free on a soapbox on the quad. In all other cases, under the *Hosty v. Carter* ruling, college administrators across the country now have a green light to ban anything they want, from controversial campus speakers to critical student newspapers.

The *Hosty* decision could also threaten faculty academic freedom. If college students have no more constitutional protections than first graders, then college professors may have no more rights than elementary school teachers. Easterbrook also hauled out the dubious concept of institutional academic freedom: "Let us not forget that academic freedom includes the authority of the university to manage an academic community and evaluate teaching and scholarship free from interference by other units of government, including the courts."[102] If "academic freedom" means only the power of administrators to "manage an academic community," then students and professors alike will be subject to censorship by the administration.

Other conservatives worry about the threat this case poses to the First Amendment. Charles Mitchell, a program officer at the right-leaning civil liberties group Foundation for Individual Rights in Education, noted: "*Hosty* will give college administrators yet another excuse to indulge their taste for squelching speech—and that's never a good thing for liberty."[103]

Although the Seventh Circuit Court of Appeals covers only Illinois, Wisconsin, and Indiana, this case will enable administrators across the country to censor papers without penalty. Under the "qualified immunity" standard, state officials are only liable for violating constitutional rights when the law is clear, and the *Hosty v. Carter* decision raises serious doubts across the country about whether college students have any legal rights.

Because the U.S. Supreme Court refused to hear the appeal of the Seventh Circuit's 2005 ruling, the *Innovator* may only be the first among many newspapers and student organizations silenced by administrators at public colleges, with the blessing of the courts.

The *Hazelwood* case has had a disastrous impact on high school student newspapers and a ripple effect on free expression. A 2004 survey of more than 100,000 students by the Knight Foundation found that more than one in four high schools in America does not have a newspaper, with 40 percent of those missing newspapers having eliminated them since 2000. Among students who are not involved with student media, half believe that journalists should be able to report news only with prior government approval, and more than one-third agree that the First Amendment "goes too far" in guaranteeing free speech and freedom of the press. Although there are many reasons for the lack of faith in journalism and a free press among youth, we should not be surprised that students are not willing to support a principle of freedom that is not granted to them.[104]

How dangerous is *Hazelwood* if applied to college campuses? In the 2004 case of *Chiras v. Miller*, a federal district court ruled in favor of the Texas School Board of Education, which rejected an environmental science textbook after conservative opponents denounced it as anti-Christian and opposed to free enterprise. The court ruled that the *Hazelwood* precedent gave Texas authorities the power to ban anything in public schools that might offend "the traditional, conservative values of most Texans."[105] If a similar view is accepted for colleges, censorship will spread throughout the country.

Less than two weeks after the *Hosty* ruling, a memo to California State University presidents from CSU general counsel Christine Helwick included a discussion of "Student Newspaper Censorship" and the *Hosty* decision. Based on the Seventh Circuit case, Helwick informed college presidents that they are now allowed to censor newspapers produced by college students, and "the censorship may include material that is 'ungrammatical, poorly written, inadequately researched,' and 'biased or prejudiced, vulgar or profane, or unsuitable for immature audiences," as well as material that associates the school with "any position other than neutrality on matters of political controversy."[106] It is difficult to imagine any newspaper, including the *New York Times* or the *Wall Street Journal,* which could meet this standard. Every newspaper includes a news article or editorial that someone might consider "biased." Every newspaper covers disturbing news, such as crime, that someone could think is "unsuitable for immature audiences." Every newspaper expresses opinions that might vary from political "neutrality." Helwick concluded, "The case appears to signal that CSU campuses may have more latitude than previously believed to censor the content of subsidized student newspapers, provided that there is an established practice of regularized content review and approval for pedagogical purposes."[107] In response to this memo, the California legislature in 2006 passed a law restoring freedom of the student press.[108] In 2007, Oregon and Illinois enacted laws to protect freedom of campus newspapers.[109] But in the rest of the country, student press rights are in danger.

Student journalists are the canaries in our First Amendment coal mine. The willingness to silence the most prominent source of news on campus sends a message to everyone, from students to faculty to staff: Dissent will not be tolerated. That's why *Hosty v. Carter* may be the most important academic freedom case ever decided in the courts, because the ripple effects of losing freedom of the press will impact all of academia.

CHAPTER EIGHT
The Wal-Mart University

⊸

The best metaphor for higher education today is the "Wal-Mart University." The Wal-Mart University, run by cost cutters (when it comes to faculty salaries, not their own) and union busters, seeks profit as its ultimate goal. The corporate model of higher education is dangerous because it brings the free market into a nonprofit universe. Wal-Mart doesn't teach its customers. Wal-Mart doesn't grade its customers. It simply gives them what they want at the highest possible profit margin.

The corporate model of education is one of the primary causes of grade inflation in America. The student-customer must be satisfied at the Wal-Mart University. A profitable company doesn't punish its customers, or give them below-average grades. The prevalence of adjuncts, administrative control over the tenure process, post-tenure review, "accountability," and other tools allow management to have enormous power over faculty. The full-time tenured faculty are dinosaurs lumbering toward extinction, oblivious to their fate and unable to organize any resistance.

But higher education is not (yet) just another cheap plastic product manufactured for pennies in China. Lowering the quality of education comes at a serious price, even if it might not be immediately apparent to the student who is interested only in getting a discounted diploma. Perhaps the worst part of the Wal-Mart University is that exploiting workers doesn't deliver low prices to students. Tuition keeps rising at the Wal-Mart University, and the money saved by cutting tenure-track faculty is used to create a vast administrative apparatus run by executives with the fastest-growing salaries in all of academia.

Exploiting Faculty

Colleges have always used part-time faculty to supply specialized expertise and to fill in the natural ebb and flow in enrollment. But in the 1980s and 1990s, college administrators became obsessed with corporate management theories. As a result, they adopted outsourcing and temporary workers in order to cut costs. The number of part-time faculty increased 79 percent in the 1980s and 1990s, and now they represent a majority of all faculty.[1] The proportion of faculty who work part-time grew from 23 percent in 1971 to 33.8 percent in 1987–1988 to 52.3 percent by 2005–2006.[2] By 2003, the number of part-time faculty jobs increased to 543,137, growing at four times the rate of full-time jobs.

One consequence is that low salaries in academia are driving away potential professors. From 1986 through 2005, median faculty salaries adjusted for inflation increased by only 0.25 percent, or about 0.01 percent per year. By contrast, the real salaries of lawyers increased by 18 percent over the past two decades, and the salaries of doctors grew by 34 percent.[3] A 1999 survey by the Modern Language Association found that only 35.3 percent of English and foreign language instructors were tenured or tenure track, and only 42.1 percent of courses were taught by them. For adjunct instructors, pay was only $2,358 per course on average, meaning that someone teaching four courses per semester would make less than $20,000 a year teaching full-time as an adjunct.[4] The massive use of non-tenure-track faculty positions reduces the economic incentive for people to enter Ph.D. programs in fields where academic employment is the primary goal.[5] A profession where half of the jobs pay poverty wages and provide no job security cannot be sustained.

The dirty little secret about adjunct faculty is that they don't save much money for colleges. As colleges have become increasingly reliant upon part-time faculty, growing administrative costs have absorbed the savings. Whereas full-time faculty used to do much of the work of academic advising, assisting student activities, and helping run universities, now professional administrators must be hired to fill all these roles. Although part-time faculty do little to save colleges money, they are popular among administrators because they create hierarchical control. Instead of dealing with full-time faculty who have a voice in running the institution, most college employees today are part-time faculty who can easily be dismissed and low-level administrators and staffers who must follow orders. Ivy Tech Community College in Indiana refused to renew the contract of adjunct professor (and chair of the liberal arts program) Becky Meadows Wilson after she angered administrators by organizing a charity concert in 2007 to help instructors who lack health benefits.[6]

The problem is not that contingent faculty are bad teachers, but that the conditions under which they teach (overworked, underpaid, lacking adequate office space, and not having time to prepare for classes or work with students outside of class) certainly lower the quality of instruction.

Researchers have found that using non-tenure-track instructors tends to result in increased dropout rates and reduced student interest in taking further classes in a field of study.[7] The danger is that a system reliant upon huge numbers of adjunct teachers will undermine academic freedom, high standards, and the intellectual aims of higher education.

For-Profit Higher Education

One reason why the Wal-Mart University model is so appealing to public and private college administrators is due to the rise of Wal-Mart–style corporations in higher education. From 2001 to 2003, the number of faculty working at for-profit colleges increased 46 percent, or 15 times the rate of increase at public colleges.[8] For-profit colleges are the parasites of academia, surviving and growing only because the federal government provides them with subsidized student loans. These colleges turn a profit despite large marketing budgets by spending as little as possible on faculty and taking advantage of the fact that public higher education is underfunded and inadequate in many areas.

Academic freedom is often lacking at for-profit institutions. Meg Spohn, a professor at for-profit DeVry University and chair of the communications department, was summarily fired in 2005 after administrators became aware of her blog and felt that she wrote disparaging things about DeVry.[9] The Art Institute of California, a for-profit college in San Diego, fired instructor Greg Campbell in 2007 (ostensibly on sexual harassment charges for telling jokes in his classes), who was helping lead a union organizing drive at the college. Art Institute president Elizabeth Erickson had warned faculty in a memo one month earlier not to support a union: "YOU MAY BE SIGNING UP FOR MORE THAN YOU BARGAINED FOR!"[10]

One of the largest higher education institutions in America is the Career Education Corporation, a $1.7 billion company with 100,000 students. The company gets 60 percent of its tuition payments from the federal government, and it is being investigated by the Justice Department and the Securities and Exchange Commission. Vinod Kapoor, a "teacher of the year" at the company who became a whistleblower, revealed that the Career Education Corporation ordered him to register students who "had no intention of attending," created fake courses, and forced faculty to raise grades in order to increase graduation rates; 10 days after revealing these abuses to the company's board, he was fired along with another employee who complained about the corporation's unethical and illegal practices.[11]

The Trouble with Tenure

No aspect of higher education is so misunderstood as tenure. A 2005 survey of college presidents found that 53 percent want to eliminate tenure. A primary reason is that tenure allows critics of the administration to speak out without fear of losing their jobs. One president decried "the ability of a very FEW tenured faculty members to harass and harangue" the administration without being fired.[12]

Victor Davis Hanson of the right-wing Hoover Institution has called for the destruction of tenure, proposing instead "renewable five-year agreements." According to Hanson, "Tenure in our universities is simply unlike any other institution in American society.... No equivalent for chief executive officers or for dishwashers exists."[13] Hanson is right: No corporation has a system as meticulous as university tenure, where competent employees of a stable business are carefully scrutinized after working for six years and then fired if they fail to meet the highest standards.

CEOs don't have tenure because they receive large salaries (and generous golden parachutes) instead of a limited form of job security. Tenure actually saves higher education huge sums of money because professors sacrifice higher salaries for an opportunity to get job security. Far from being a problem, tenure is one of the great management innovations created by higher education. Instead of imitating corporations, higher education's tenure system ought to serve as a model for schools, businesses, and other organizations. The only reason why tenure isn't used in corporate America is because it maintains excessively high standards. Corporations would have trouble attracting employees if they knew they might be fired despite doing an adequate job after a long commitment to the company. Higher education "tenure" is far more restrictive than tenure in most fields. K–12 unionized teachers typically receive tenure automatically after only two years of teaching, without any extensive analysis of the teacher's performance and no peer review.

The primary problem with tenure is the mistaken impression that it provides lifelong employment to faculty no matter what they do. Contrary to common belief, tenure is not a job for life. After the Hurricane Katrina disaster, Tulane University alone eliminated the jobs of sixty-five tenured professors, and hundreds of professors at New Orleans colleges were summarily fired.[14] Layoffs of tenured professors are very rare because higher education is a stable, recession-proof industry where colleges almost never go out of business. Tenure merely assures that a stricter standard of due process must be followed in order to dismiss a professor. "Due process" means fair protection, not immunity from punishment.

Abolishing tenure won't improve higher education; to the contrary, it will endanger both academic freedom and intellectual quality. Abolishing tenure will also threaten academic standards. If there is no extensive peer review process like tenure to evaluate the quality of a professor's work, then there will be three possible results: (1) no professors will ever get fired, and de facto tenure of the automatic K–12 variety will prevail; (2) professors who annoy the administration will get fired, so faculty will avoid any controversial statements or criticism of their college's leadership; or (3) student evaluations will prevail as the measure of faculty quality, and professors will raise grades and lower academic standards in order to get positive reviews.

The tenure process does need to be improved. Too many decisions are made by top administrators with little knowledge of the professors (such as Ward Churchill, who received tenure from the University of Colorado administration to prevent other colleges from recruiting him, and never went through the serious scrutiny of a normal tenure process).[15] Arbitrary quantitative measures (such as a certain number of books or peer-reviewed articles) have replaced qualitative judgments in tenure decisions. Because teaching cannot be quantified easily, its importance has steadily declined in tenure decisions, especially at research universities.

To save tenure, colleges need reforms. They need to speed up the system to make it possible to fire faculty who deserve dismissal, while still protecting due process. They need to adopt a similar system of quasi-tenure for long-term non-tenure-track faculty to protect them from retaliatory firings. And they need to make evaluation of teaching by colleagues (and helping faculty improve their teaching) a vital part of the tenure process. Unfortunately, these kinds of reforms are unlikely in the Wal-Mart University because the drive to increase "accountability" usually means giving unaccountable administrators more power to control faculty and students.

Corporate Correctness

While conservatives worry about liberal thought police on campus, professors, students, and staff face a much greater threat to their free expression rights and their jobs if they challenge corporate interests.

When colleges make deals with corporations, academic freedom often gets abandoned. A University of Wisconsin contract with Reebok in 1996 decreed, "University will take all reasonable steps necessary to address any remarks by any University employee, agent or representative, including a coach, that disparages Reebok." Although the clause was removed after an outcry on campus, antidisparagement rules on campus continue. Slaughter and Rhoades's study of athletics contracts found that three out of eight universities (Adidas at Arizona State and Nike at Kentucky and Texas A&M) included antidisparagement clauses. The Arizona State clause even banned criticism of the company after the contract ends: "University shall not, during the Contract Term and for a period of two (2) years following the termination or expiration of this Agreement, disparage the Adidas brand name, Adidas Products, or Adidas."[16] Jim Keady was an assistant soccer coach at St. Johns University in New York and a theology student when he began to raise concerns about Nike's use of sweatshops and Nike's sponsorship of the top-ranked soccer team. Keady was ordered to wear the Nike apparel and stop criticizing the company, and he was pressured to resign when he refused.[17]

Even conservatives can face punishment when they question corporate interests. In 2000, University of Oklahoma geology professor David Deming wrote a bizarre letter to the campus paper attacking gun control in which he compared an unregistered handgun to an "unregistered vagina." Although Deming's conservative views outraged many people, his academic freedom was protected. But when he challenged the corporate ties of his colleagues, Deming was removed from his department, exiled to a small basement office, and unable to teach his courses without special permission from the people who punished him.[18] In 2003 the department hired Alan Huffman for an endowed professorship. He was the vice president at Fusion Geophysical, a consulting firm founded by a professor in the department. Although Deming and two other professors raised concerns about Huffman's qualifications, he was hired anyway. Deming sent an e-mail to professors at Oklahoma wondering if Huffman "came to OU to (a) be a professor or (b) use it as a base of operations to build up a private business?"[19] Dean John Snow of the College of Geosciences wrote an e-mail in June 2003 urging that Roger Slatt, director of the School of Geology and Geophysics, "needs to basically ignore and then marginalize Deming." In November 2003, Bob Stephenson, an oil executive and major donor to the university, wrote to the provost denouncing Deming for "pursuing academic and personal interests outside of and not supportive of the school's mission" and threatening to withhold donations unless Deming was punished. Slatt, who was also an associate in Fusion Geophysical, ordered Deming to "quit creating a hostile, disharmonious, uncollegial environment" and then removed him from the department.[20]

University of California at Berkeley professor Ignacio Chapela, despite winning approval for tenure from his department by a 32–1 vote in May 2002 and from a unanimous tenure committee, was not granted tenure until 2005 after top administrators sought to fire him. Chapela had criticized the Department of Plant and Microbial Biology's $25 million deal with Novartis and had also published controversial research that brought negative publicity.[21]

When a research study by Oregon State University forestry graduate student Daniel Donato challenged the view that logging is good for forests after wildfires, nine professors who supported logging (which helped fund the department) denounced his work and tried to stop the journal *Science* from publishing it.[22] The prologging U.S. Bureau of Land Management temporarily suspended funding for Donato's study in retaliation, accusing him of violating a ban on lobbying because an online summary of the article (which the authors had asked to be removed) merely mentioned legislation about logging.[23]

When John Buse, a University of North Carolina medical school professor, reported in 1999 that the diabetes drug Avandia was linked to an increased risk of heart attacks, the drugmaker (now GlaxoSmithKline) threatened to hold him liable for billions of dollars if the stock price dropped.[24]

Why don't the people crying out about "political correctness" make a similar critique of "corporate correctness"? Of course, such a term does not exist because thought policing in corporate America is taken for granted. The right to criticize one's employer and make controversial comments that reflect badly on one's institution are unique to academic employees. But for the vast majority of American workers, these rights do not exist at all. Much of what gets denounced as "politically correct" restrictions at college campuses is commonplace in corporate America.

The "speech zones" and "speech codes" attacked at college campuses are far less restrictive than the typical corporate environment, which bans free speech on the entire property, compels strict regulation of political and other speech, and even imposes dress code regulations that would be unthinkable in academia. At most shopping malls in America, for example, you will be arrested if you try to hand out copies of the Bill of Rights. University of Iowa professor Kembrew McLeod tried handing out copies of the First Amendment at a mall in Iowa and found that it took less than five minutes before a security guard (well aware of what he was passing out) warned him not to do it. Soon, the police arrived and threatened to arrest him, and confiscated the Bill of Rights from him.[25] Colleges and universities are freer than any other institution in society, with much greater protections of due process and free speech. The irony is that the journalists who wring their hands about "political correctness" on college campuses can only dream of working at a place where there are so many protections for free speech.

Many of the problems with academic freedom in American colleges stem from the adoption of corporate models for higher education.[26] Presidents who think of themselves as CEOs try to silence internal dissent by firing troublesome faculty. At Philander Smith College in Arkansas, President Trudie Kibbe Reed justified firing a tenured professor because "as a leader, just like all other CEOs, my authority cannot be challenged."[27]

Some conservatives literally want a "Wal-Mart University." Jim Abbate, president of Citizens for the Betterment of Merced County, sent a letter to the University of California at Merced and dozens of government and business officials, demanding that the administration silence two local anti–Wal-Mart activists who are married to Merced professors. Abbate declared that the administration should screen all hires and their spouses to make sure they "fit in" with the conservative area.[28]

In an age of budget cuts, corporate influence over higher education is growing. At Clemson University, candidates for the BMW endowed chairs are interviewed by the company to make sure that they're acceptable to BMW.[29]

Clemson's International Center for Automotive Research let BMW determine much of its curriculum and research, and even gave BMW approval rights over the design of the school. According to a Clemson official's notes of a meeting with BMW, "BMW is going to drive the entire campus."[30] In 2005, the North Carolina Partnership for Economic Development dropped a $50,000 study of the automotive industry by University of North Carolina at Charlotte economist John Connaughton after a top assistant of the Speaker of the North Carolina House of Representatives noted, "The Speaker is not in favor of rewarding someone who espouses these views in the newspapers and ... feeds off state monies in private." Connaughton had criticized sales and income taxes in the state as being too high and opposed a temporary tax increase being proposed.[31]

At Howard University, the Anheuser-Busch/John E. Jacobs chair in marketing was originally offered to Jerome D. Williams in 2002, but he wasn't hired because, the dean of the business school wrote, "Anheuser-Busch has requested that we seek other candidates."[32] Howard's president had requested copies of two articles Williams wrote criticizing breweries that market alcohol to particular minority groups. Although a faculty grievance committee ruled in Williams's favor and said he should receive back pay and research money, Howard University has refused to comply.[33]

Adrienne Anderson, a highly rated adjunct professor at the University of Colorado–Boulder, who taught environmental studies courses for eleven years, was fired because her research uncovered corporate polluting and the failure of Governor Bill Owens's administration to enforce environmental laws.[34] Owens is now the president of the University of Colorado. A faculty grievance committee unanimously recommended her reinstatement, but the administration refused. The campus AAUP chapter concluded, "Anderson was removed from the University's teaching ranks because of intense and protracted pressure from corporate donors and politicians hostile to the environmental research."[35]

Administrators who see students as their customers try to serve them by banning anything that might offend their tender sensibilities. Trustees who run their businesses to maximize profit find it reasonable to fire faculty whose unpopular views might cost the university money. Politicians who get donations from CEOs see universities as just another pork barrel project for corporations. The corporate model is antithetical to academic freedom, and its growing influence in higher education poses one of the greatest threats to dissent.

The Military-Industrial-Academic Complex

In today's academy, the military is one of the biggest and most powerful influences.[36] By imposing secrecy on some research and limiting foreigner participation, the Pentagon poses severe limits to academic freedom. Even worse, the Department of Defense has the power of the government behind it. When colleges and universities objected to the ban on gay and lesbian soldiers by restricting military recruiters on campus (since all recruiters are required to abide by nondiscrimination rules), Congress responded with the Solomon Amendment, which forces all colleges receiving federal funds to open their doors to military recruiters.[37]

Military control over colleges may soon increase dramatically. In 2007, the Department of Defense announced a proposed rule for implementing the Solomon amendment that would give the military extraordinary power over campuses. The rule would require all colleges, public and private, to allow the military to create ROTC programs that would be "treated on a par with other academic departments."[38] As a result, colleges would be forced to give college credit, faculty status, and office space to programs under the total control of the military, where academic standards and academic freedom are not guaranteed. In addition, the rule would force colleges to restrict student protests against military recruiters if the protests cause recruiters to "experience an inferior or unsafe recruiting climate."[39] Obviously, if military recruiters are being protested, then their recruiting climate is inferior to recruiters who are not being protested. And according to the Department of Defense, that is justification for withdrawing all federal funds.

Banning Unions on Campus

Higher education ranks among the worst union-busting industries in America. As conservative writer Victor Davis Hanson noted, "Some of the worst sorts of labor exploitation are also routine on campus."[40] Even Wal-Mart, the biggest union-busting company in the world, at least pretends that its workers have the right to choose a union. Not one of the so-called liberal universities is willing to acknowledge the right to unionize for its graduate assistants and faculty.

At Quinnipiac University in Connecticut, the administration has tried to ban the faculty union, claiming that faculty are managers (despite the fact that they do not manage any employees) and therefore it can prohibit any union.[41] The American Council on Education, the Council of Independent Colleges, and the National Association of Independent Colleges and Universities have all supported efforts by colleges to ban faculty from forming unions.[42]

In 2001, New York University became the only private university that has ever recognized a union of graduate student instructors.[43] And that was only under the legal compulsion of the National Labor Relations Board (NLRB) after years of fighting against it. NYU quickly banned the union again when the NLRB (with new appointees by George W. Bush) reversed course in 2004.[44] Not one private university in America has ever voluntarily recognized the right of graduate student instructors to decide for themselves if they want to form a union.

But the NLRB's new ruling does not in any way change the moral obligation of all universities to recognize the choices of graduate students to organize.[45] Academic freedom violations at private universities are not banned by the government, but the moral obligation to protect free expression on campus is clear, and the AAUP will censure those institutions for infringing upon the right of academic freedom.

Students and faculty do not give up their rights when they enter a college's gates, and those rights must include the right to form a union and collectively bargaining for better working conditions. Whatever the arguments pro and con for unions in academia, such a debate is possible only once the fundamental right to organize is acknowledged.

University of Pennsylvania president Judith Rodin argued: "We don't think our students are our employees. We think they're our protegees. We think we're nurturing and nourishing them, and the first time a student files a union grievance against a faculty member, it will transform that relationship forever."[46] But students file complaints against faculty all the time. Should students be unable to appeal an unfair grade, or complain about sexual harassment, simply because it might "transform" their relationship with faculty?

Universities appeal to "education" as an excuse to violate the rights of students. Alissa Kaplan Michaels, a spokeswoman for Columbia University, declared: "The university's relationship with graduate students is educational and collaborative. It is not an employer-employee relationship." Michaels proclaimed that "teaching is an integral part of the training of men and women preparing for academic careers."[47] If teaching is an "integral part" of graduate training, then how many graduate students get academic credit for their teaching? How many have their teaching evaluated by a professor and receive a grade for it? How many graduate students are required to show knowledge of teaching to get a Ph.D. (as they must show knowledge of their field through coursework and a comprehensive exam and knowledge of research skills through the dissertation)? Graduate instructors are not doing what anyone would call part of their formal education, even if they may be learning from it. If it looks like a job and pays like a job and everyone treats it like a job, we might be reasonable in concluding that teaching students is, in fact, a job.

Most universities have a shameful record of neglecting to prepare graduate students for college teaching, yet they have the audacity to ban unions in the name of "educational" needs. A TA union typically makes many demands that improve the quality of teaching: more training in how to improve teaching; more advance notice of what classes TAs will be teaching so that preparation is possible; limits on the number and size of classes so that TAs can provide high-quality instruction; adequate office space; and adequate pay so that TAs can focus on teaching and their studies without having to get another job to survive. Anyone concerned about the quality of college instruction should be the first to support a graduate student union.

The relationship between graduate students and their professors, of course, should not be an employee/employer relationship, and it isn't. But the relationship between graduate student instructors and the administrators who hire them to teach classes is undeniably an employee/employer relation- tion. This is not a collaboration, this is a job. The fact that this is academic work doesn't make it any less "work." If teaching is merely "educational," then why do graduate students always get paid to do it rather than paying tuition for the privilege?

There's nothing inherently antiacademic about a union. A union is a democratic, representative organization that exists to help a particular inter- est group pursue their aims. How is that any different from similar groups accepted as part of a university? A student government is a democratic, representative organization created to help students pursue their interests. A faculty senate is a democratic, representative organization created to help faculty pursue their interests. Should faculty senates and student govern- ments be banned from "interfering" in academic decisions?

Only administrators imagine that the unchecked power of the administra- tion is essential for the efficient functioning of a university. Everybody else understands that the best university is a product of many different interests having a voice. Considering that hierarchical corporations have accepted unions and found a way to function with them, why can't a university (which is supposed to be democratic and serving diverse interests, and which is supposed to listen to its students and its teachers) deal with a union?

John Beckman, vice president for public affairs at New York University, argued: "A union could not bring itself to embrace a new paradigm, pre- ferring instead to rely upon a traditional employer/employee labor model that has proven to be ill-suited for an academic environment."[48] Perhaps he is right that universities would function better without unions; perhaps he is right that benevolent dictatorships are better than democratic unions. Then NYU should seek to convince the students to abandon their union. But taking away their right to form a union will only educate them that the administration wants to exploit graduate students, not listen to them.

The fact that students benefit from a union is undeniable. NYU's Gradu- ate Student Organizing Committee (GSOC), working with the United Auto Workers, negotiated a contract that raised stipends 40 percent and provided full health insurance coverage.[49] NYU's Faculty Advisory Committee on Academic Priorities, assigned by the antiunion NYU administration to study the issue, declared "the process of negotiating a union contract facilitated progress" in the treatment of graduate students. Nevertheless, the faculty declared that "graduate students should be regarded, first and foremost, as students, apprentice researchers, and trainees of their faculty mentors rather than employees."[50]

NYU declared that it would ban strikers from teaching for two semesters. NYU physics professor Alan Sokal noted: "It's totally unprecedented to say, because you've been on strike for four weeks, you will therefore have the next semester—or two semesters—of your salary docked."[51] In the fall of 2006, NYU students temporarily halted the strike, which was unsuccessful because of NYU's threats and refusal to recognize student rights.[52]

It is theoretically possible that unions of graduate student instructors will have a destructive effect on higher education. Giving students the freedom to drink undoubtedly has a negative influence on the academic performance (and sometimes the lives) of students. Nevertheless, we still believe in giving students freedom to choose for themselves. Of course, unions have never been shown to inflict the kind of harm that drinking causes. At the State University of New York, unionized graduate students in 2005 won substantial pay increases and improvements in health benefits.[53] No graduate students in America have ever voted to decertify a union that represented them. No other unionized industry can claim that record of success, and it indicates that graduate students see unions as a genuine benefit to them.

Threatening Graduate Students

Faculty, students, and staff who support unions have faced sanctions in retaliation for their beliefs. Graduate students who try to organize a union on campus can put their academic careers at risk. In 1996 the NLRB filed charges against Yale faculty and administrators who retaliated against union leaders who held a strike by threatening to ban them from teaching assignments, kick them out of graduate school, and write negative recommendation letters to keep them from getting jobs.[54]

A Columbia University memo of February 16, 2005, from provost Alan Brinkley to top administrators outlined a series of retaliatory actions the university could take to "discourage" graduate students from striking. The memo declared that students could "lose their eligibility for summer stipends" and "lose their eligibility for special awards." The memo also proposed forcing students to "teach an extra semester or a year" as punishment for striking.[55] Although Columbia decided not to implement the memo, it indicates how far administrators are willing to go to retaliate against graduate students who seek to unionize.

Graduate assistants are vulnerable to punishment for expressing their ideas. Benjamin Balthaser and Scott Boehm, two graduate teaching assistants at the University of California–San Diego, were fired in 2007 for daring to criticize the efforts to make their program more appealing to conservatives. Abraham Shragge, the Dimensions of Culture Program director, admitted that "they get good ratings as teachers" but added that "they have gone all over the campus to stir up a lot of campuswide dissent that I find very damaging to the program. They've created a very hostile atmosphere; they've been very hostile to me. This is a working environment that depends on collegiality."[56]

Faculty who support the rights of graduate students to organize also suffer retaliation from university administrators. At New York University, education professor Joel Westheimer was denied tenure in July 2001 after he was the only untenured professor to testify on behalf of the Graduate Students Organizing Committee (GSOC) at an NLRB hearing. Until he testified, Westheimer received unanimously positive reviews from his department and outside reviewers, but a negative universitywide review declared that he had insufficient scholarship. Westheimer published more than a dozen articles, and his 1998 book, *Among Schoolteachers,* was widely cited and praised. Robert Cohen, a tenured education professor at NYU, called Westheimer "on par with, or ahead of everyone who went up for tenure this year" in the education school and "definitely is ahead of most people who get tenure."[57] NYU eventually agreed to expunge the tenure denial and pay a small settlement to Westheimer.[58]

At the State University of New York at Buffalo, Barbara Bono, chair of the English department, was removed from her job by the dean of the College of Arts and Sciences, Charles Stinger, because she refused to sign a May 17, 2001, letter to teaching assistants. The letter threatened that the TAs would be "subject to serious penalties" if they failed to turn in grades, including losing their jobs, and that they would be considered to be breaking the law. Stinger declared that Bono had been dismissed as chair because "she expressed considerable sympathy for the student situation and didn't see that forceful action was required. Being unwilling to take action in those circumstances made it impossible for her to fulfill her responsibilities as chair." Bono said that she refused to sign the memo because "I was not going to turn to threatening my students."[59] Signing a threatening letter to TAs (especially when serious doubt existed about the factual claim that students could be prosecuted for disobeying) is not among the necessary duties of a department chair, and it is clear that Bono was removed for expressing "sympathy" with students seeking a union.

Supporters of faculty unions are also targeted for retaliation. When 140 part-time and emeritus faculty at City Colleges of Chicago refused to cross a picket line of striking full-time faculty in fall 2004, administrators fired all of them, in violation of the contract that banned reprisals against anyone.[60]

Faculty who seek to form unions are also vulnerable to attacks on academic freedom. At Emerson College in Massachusetts, President Jacqueline

Liebergott announced in 2003 that the faculty union affiliated with the AAUP would have to be disbanded or faculty would be barred from any participation in college governance, and, she promised, "we will negotiate an agreement appropriate for a group of nonmanagerial employees." Emerson College officials explained that because it wanted to compete with top liberal arts colleges, and since none of them are unionized, it believed that the union must be eliminated.[61]

Individual faculty who serve as union leaders may have the most vulnerable jobs in academia. Teresa Knudsen, who taught English as an adjunct instructor at Spokane Community College for seventeen years, suddenly found herself out of a job after she cofounded a union for the adjuncts. Knudsen reported that after she wrote an op-ed about the low wages of adjuncts in February 2005, the dean summoned her to a meeting and told her, "There are limits and consequences to free speech. I think you should leave SCC."[62]

At Southern West Virginia Community and Technical College, George Trimble, an English professor, had an unblemished nineteen-year record. Trimble organized and became president of a faculty labor organization, and his proposals prompted the faculty's unanimous no-confidence vote against the college president Travis Kirkland. But when the president ordered all faculty to use a particular computer software program for writing course syllabi, Trimble refused on grounds of academic freedom because faculty have the authority to determine their own syllabi. After Trimble failed to attend mandatory training meetings for using the software, the college told him that his resistance to the software was a "flagrant and willful disregard for directions and/or inquiries of your employer" that constituted "insubordination." When Trimble again refused to use the software, the college terminated him, and a court upheld the firing.[63]

Administrators are also under pressure from politicians to attack unions. The *Wisconsin State Journal* reported, "state lawmakers still expect campus administrators to punish UW–Madison teaching assistants for their illegal strike about a month ago."[64] California governor Arnold Schwarzenegger sought to eliminate all funding for the University of California's Institute for Labor and Employment, which had been denounced by conservatives for being critical of business. Matt Tennis, legislative director for the Associated Builders and Contractors, declared: "This body operates like a taxpayer-funded, prounion think tank, churning out endless reports that promote a pro–labor union ideology and a labor union agenda."[65] In the 2005 California budget, Schwarzenegger proposed eliminating the $3.8 million budget for the UCLA Labor Center, even while increasing state funding for higher education. Schwarzenegger made a similar effort in 2004, only to be blocked by the state legislature, which cut the center's budget by 5 percent in a compromise. By contrast, the wealthy UCLA Anderson School of Management received $15.8 million in state funding. Kent Wong, director of the Labor Center, warned: "If funds for a university should be based on how one provides a business-friendly environment, then there are a lot of areas at the university that would be superfluous."[66]

Legislators and administrators are increasingly targeting the few labor programs in the country for budget cuts. In Wisconsin, Republican Representative Steve Nass sought to cut funding in 2007 for the University of Wisconsin Extensions School for Workers, which trains union leaders. Nass also proposed eliminating the Havens Center, which studies social change, because he felt it was "too far to the left."[67] In 2007, the University of Missouri–Kansas City eliminated the Institute for Labor Studies to save $15,000 in administrative costs.[68]

The attacks on labor studies and teacher unions are part of a larger assault on campus unions. Billy Embree, a student at Cincinnati State Technical and Community College, was escorted off campus by police in 2007 and threatened with suspension because he handed out "unauthorized" fliers on campus supporting a union campaign to get higher wages for janitors at the school.[69] By using temp labor and outsourcing, administrators quietly drive out unions on campus.

Unions undermine the carefully constructed self-image of elite colleges and universities. The myth of the "community of equals" prevails, even though it was never true and is becoming more and more implausible every day. A union implies a world of haves and have-nots, of the powerful and the exploited, which many people in academia can never accept. But to make higher education a just workplace where the rights of all workers are respected, academics must confront the serious flaws of the current system and escape from their state of denial. The right to unionize on campus is an essential component of academic freedom, and increasingly it is only union representation that can protect academic freedom from the desire of administrators for a corporatized university.

CONCLUSION
Fighting for Academic Freedom

❧

Conservatives and liberals face a common enemy on college campuses: repressive administrators who want to squelch dissent and apathetic students uninterested in political ideas. Unfortunately, many conservatives hold on to the delusion that right-leaning students are the sole victims of censorship, and so they see themselves as being at war with the left. According to columnist Don Feder, "The only people who get punished for expressing political views on the college campus are conservatives."[1] In reality, censorship in academia by conservatives is more common than censorship by the left. Progressive students usually face worse violations of their rights on most college campuses than conservatives. Because liberal groups rarely speak out to defend student rights, left-leaning students are often more vulnerable to these attacks.

But arguing about who is censoring what ideology the most on campus, although it is an interesting intellectual debate, ought to be a secondary issue for liberals and conservatives alike. We should all, regardless of our views, support the right of free expression on college campuses and their importance as the institutions in our society where liberty is prized above all others.

When conservatives and liberal unite together in opposing attacks on academic freedom, they form a powerful alliance. After Erwin Chemerinsky was hired in 2007 as dean of the law school at the University of California–Irvine, Chancellor Michael V. Drake rescinded his appointment, telling Chemerinsky he was "too politically controversial" due to his liberal views.[2] But because of widespread outrage over the dismissal, including from many conservative outlets, Drake reversed his decision and rehired Chemerinsky.[3] Unfortunately, the left and the right rarely unite to censorship.

Liberals committed to the debate of ideas should be the first to leap to the defense of conservatives. Nor is it enough merely to protect the academic freedom of right-wingers. Progressives need to actively promote the expression of conservative ideas. The leftist claim that conservatives control talk radio and corporate media and mainstream political debates is true, but it is no excuse for avoiding conservative arguments in academia. Colleges are not outposts of liberal values in a society controlled by conservative corporations and interest groups; instead, higher education is a place where an enormous range of ideas can be debated. Scrutiny of conservative and leftist values alike requires honest expression of these views.

The Battle for Higher Education

Many conservatives see colleges as a battleground for the future of politics. James Piereson, executive director of the Olin Foundation, called universities "key institutions in our country and places where we ought to wage war and combat for our ideas and principles."[4]

Conservatives often speak of higher education in absurd terms, comparing elite American colleges to Soviet prisons and proclaiming that they are "Liberating America's Intellectual Gulags."[5] Jake Stanford, a conservative student at the University of Alabama, declared in 2004: "Political correctness is the newest form of slavery, originally created by those people who are intimidated by the slightest urge of brutal language or attempts to discipline a new generation. These individuals should have had their jaws broken when they first suggested that some things are undermining and dejecting to specific people, and furthermore, they should be exiled from society."[6] According to Ann Coulter, "Your professors and instructors are, by and large, evil people whose main goal is to mislead you."[7] It may be impossible to have a rational conversation about the real problems with freedom on college campuses until the right comes to its senses and recognizes that professors are not evil people, those who urge sensitivity should not have their jaws broken, and universities are not slave camps oppressing political dissidents.

Instead of seeking more freedom of speech on campuses, many conservatives aim to take over universities and silence dissent. While some right-wing activists like David Horowitz hide their attacks on academic freedom behind the veil of student rights, others are quite blunt about the conservative movement's goal of patriotic correctness.

Former House Speaker Newt Gingrich told the American Enterprise Institute in 2005, "We ought to say to campuses, it's over. We should say to state legislatures, why are you making us pay for this? Boards of regents are artificial constructs of state law. Tenure is an artificial social construct. Tenure did not exist before the 20th century, and we had free speech before then. You could introduce a bill that says, proof that you're anti-American is grounds for dismissal."[8] Gingrich (a former college professor) expresses the Republican Party's aim for academia: to have state legislatures fire regents who defend academic freedom, and make politicians the rulers of universities in order to fire critics of the government.

Conservative pundit Cal Thomas wondered, "Why do so many conservative parents send their children to these colleges and often subsidize their tuition when so many undermine their beliefs and values? Stories are legion of young people who are sent to these schools and emerge with a far different worldview from when they entered."[9] Thomas thinks that parents own their children and are entitled to purchase a product that will hand students a degree without the danger of challenging their parents' worldview. Some students share this same mistaken view of education, believing that universities exist to pump information into their skulls without ever challenging their values.

Instead of treating college campuses as political turf to fight over and conquer, conservatives and liberals alike should see them as precious, unique institutions where serious intellectual debate takes place in a world otherwise full of angry pundits reciting the party line. Higher education is too important to be turned into a political prize for whatever group is skillful enough to capture it.

Conservative and left-wing extremists alike tend to turn to censorship when they want to avoid the hard work of organizing and teaching people. How would silencing professors increase the diversity of views on campus? How will students learn habits of civic engagement if their professors are banned from commenting on contemporary politics? Some conservatives might feel happier if the government is never criticized in their college classes. But if they are denied the opportunity to hear an important voice in political debates, they will be denied the chance to have their views disputed and be informed about other perspectives.

Conservatives and liberals should be equally concerned about protecting academic freedom. Conservatives and liberals should be equally concerned about defending student rights. Conservatives and liberals should be equally concerned about maintaining shared governance and stopping autocratic administrators. Conservatives and liberals should be equally concerned about the lack of political debate and engagement on campus. Conservatives and liberals should be equally concerned about the growing commercialization of campuses and the sacrifice of academic standards. Conservatives and liberals should be equally concerned about the shift from tenure-track to temporary faculty. Conservatives and liberals should be equally concerned about the lack of emphasis on quality teaching at many research universities.

Conservatives and liberals should be equally concerned about the danger of political intrusions by legislators into academe. Conservatives and liberals should be equally concerned about the lack of general education for students who are turning toward specialized job training.

Although there will always be arguments between the left and the right (and the center) over higher education, it should still be possible to form alliances toward these common causes. Conservatives and liberals alike need to be forthright in defending academic freedom, especially when the liberty of ideas different from our own is threatened. It may not always be pleasant for liberals to defend the free speech rights of racists, sexists, and homophobes, but it is essential. Universities are strongest when they work according to consistent principles. The denial of freedom of expression for one group endangers freedom for everyone. Liberals should be worried when conservatives are silenced, because liberals may be the next group that runs afoul of the censors. And conservatives ought to worry when administrators punish liberal thought at any college because they may be the next ones deemed to speak improperly. But there is a bigger reason other than the fear of censors that should lead us to support academic freedom. We learn the most when we understand why an opposing idea is wrong, and that is only possible when we directly grapple with other viewpoints. Conservatives and liberals need one another for the sake of genuine education.

The lack of conservative viewpoints on some college campuses should be a matter of concern for everyone, just as the lack of progressive viewpoints on talk radio (where conservatives reportedly outnumber liberals by up to 80:1) should concern anyone committed to the fierce debate of ideas.[10] But the best way to bring more leftist voices into talk radio is for progressives to organize themselves and create alternative radio. Leftists who support reimposing the "Fairness Doctrine" for broadcast media and hope that a government official can force balance upon talk radio are engaged in a dangerous plan. We should also fear the conservative hope that an Academic Bill of Rights will allow an administrator to impose balance on academia. The best way to bring more conservative voices into academia is for conservatives to organize themselves and recruit right-wingers to bring conservatives to campuses and then become academics themselves.

Uniting Left and Right

As a student and teacher, I have tried to live up to the ideal of a campus where left and right work together against repression and engage in free debates; I even assigned David Horowitz's writings for a class I was teaching. Intellectual diversity and the debate of ideas is not an abstraction to me; it represents the education I have tried to pursue for myself.

The *University of Chicago Free Press,* an alternative newspaper I helped to start in 1995, began life when the main campus newspaper decided to get rid of its left-wing and right-wing political supplements. The liberals and conservatives got together to form the *University of Chicago Free Press* as this strange alliance against the status quo. The conservatives quickly faded away, and the newspaper became more openly progressive (before dying off due to lack of funding). But it shows that conservatives and liberals can have shared interests on campus.

I also worked with conservatives at the University of Chicago in the late 1990s to protest the dumbing down of the university. Consider this description from the right-wing Intercollegiate Studies Institute: "The best illustration of the character of life at the University of Chicago comes from an incident that occurred in the spring of 1999. This was in the midst of Hugo Sonnenschein's attempts to transform the university. He and others were worried that Chicago had acquired too stern and humorless a reputation. The campus, they thought, just was not fun enough to compete with the Ivies. Students spent too much time studying, and not enough time partying: life at the University of Chicago was too much the antithesis of *Animal House.* So the administration embarked on a campaign to lighten the academic load and exhorted the students to have more fun. How did the undergraduates respond? They threw a party, all right, but it was not the kind that Sonnenschein had in mind. Some 1,700 students staged a mock 'fun-in,' complete with food, games, and live entertainment, all in the spirit of lampooning Sonnenschein, who resigned as president of the university a few months later."[11]

The University of Chicago "fun-in" was my idea, and I helped to organize it, so it amuses me to no end to see conservatives praising it. The "fun-in" was an alliance of conservative and liberal critics of the Sonnenschein regime who objected to his efforts to shift the University of Chicago toward the Ivy League model and sacrifice its uniqueness in the drive to make it more profitable.

The conservatives were mad at Sonnenschein because he was watering down the Common Core. The liberals were mad at Sonnenschein because he was corporatizing the University of Chicago: cutting back on funding for graduate education, increasing class sizes, and centralizing power. The "fun-in" combined all of these causes together. We had a big party on campus, our own "fun-in" newspaper, T-shirts (featuring Sonnenschein's face on a beer can for "U of C Lite"), free food, parody songs, and games (such as trying to fit as many students as possible inside our string-enclosed "classroom" on the quad).

Of course, Sonnenschein didn't resign because of our protests. The protests (and the change in presidencies) didn't really change any of the policies, but they helped fight off some of the worst excesses. Perhaps more important, they sparked a debate on campus about the purpose of a university.

At Illinois State University in the fall of 2004, I was the only one on campus I can recall who invited a Republican official (our state representative) to give a public speech. I also invited four other Republican candidates and conservative political activists to campus that semester. I was the only one to show a conservative documentary on campus (the dreadful *FahrenHYPE 9/11*, on election eve, along with Michael Moore's much superior *Fahrenheit 9-11*). I even proposed inviting David Horowitz to campus (unfortunately, his fee is far beyond the budget of any organization I was involved with).

As committed as I am to intellectual debate, I think conservatives need to do less whining and more organizing. With rare exceptions, no one is stopping conservative (or liberal) voices from being heard on campus. The problem is that conservative students don't seem interested in organizing events, and prominent conservative speakers, with their schedules filled and speaking fees inflated by corporate events, are often not available. Conservatives openly discourage students from seeking academic careers. And conservative donors are more interested in funding business programs that support their views than seeking to expand the public debate on campus.

While progressive groups aim to help students organize on campuses, many conservatives like David Horowitz are organizing to silence their leftist enemies rather than open up the debate. Liberals should help bring more conservatives to campus. But ultimately it is up to conservatives themselves to make sure their voices get heard.

In the battle of ideas, liberals and conservatives benefit from having each other. We need more conservative voices on college campuses. We also need more radical, and liberal, and centrist voices. The problem is not an imbalance of views favoring liberals, but the general absence of debate and discussion on most campuses. The solution is not to silence left-wingers, but to encourage everyone to speak out more.

A New Organization for Academic Freedom

We need more defenders of academic freedom on campus. One of the reasons why free speech in academia is better protected today than almost any other period in history is because advocates for campus liberties have worked to bring attention to the problems. But all of these groups have flaws. The AAUP focuses almost exclusively on faculty rights, and the AAUP's process is too slow. It often takes many years before a college is ever condemned by the AAUP, and many of the worst offenders are never punished. FIRE is much more aggressive, but although FIRE will defend both liberals and conservatives, it categorically refuses to address the most severe restrictions on freedom at religious colleges and has never condemned the most serious national threat to academic freedom, David Horowitz's Academic Bill of Rights. The ACLU, although the traditional defender of student and faculty rights for many decades, has largely abandoned higher education except for a few cases taken up by state affiliates.

We need a new organization to protect academic freedom and make a renewed effort to promote academic freedom. Call it the Institute for College Freedom, or ICF. ICF would engage in five main projects: research, education, policy advocacy, defense of individual rights, and global advocacy for academic freedom.

1. Research. We need empirical data to find out how many students are being disciplined by colleges, and why. Every college, public and private, should reveal this information voluntarily. Freedom of Information Act (FOIA) requests to all public colleges should be made to reveal their annual data about the number of official complaints made against students and faculty, the number put through the disciplinary process, the number disciplined, the level of discipline, and the reasons for the discipline. So long as student names are not revealed, there will be no danger of violating privacy rights. This information will help reveal whether there is a serious problem on college campuses, and it may also indicate which campuses are punishing students for their expression of ideas. We also need research on how many faculty are denied tenure or dismissed by universities, and how contingent faculty are treated. And we need solid survey research of graduate students and new Ph.D.s seeking faculty jobs to determine if conservative claims of discrimination have any validity.

2. Education. We need to make issues of academic freedom and free speech part of the campus debate. But we also need more intellectual debates and discussions on a wide range of topics on campuses by bringing together conservative and liberal activists. A 2004 report by Political Research Associates found that college students today, on the left and on the right, rarely experience campus debates and tend not to listen to opposing ideas.[12] Bringing conservative and liberal groups together to sponsor discussions and debates should be a top priority of national organizations as well as individual campuses.

3. Policy advocacy. We need to create model codes of conduct for universities to adopt, which protect freedom of expression rather than endangering it. These model codes, endorsed by national groups of liberals and conservatives, as well as organizations of students and faculty and administrators, can help campuses improve their codes. The AAUP has been enormously successful at changing campus policies on faculty academic freedom by presenting a widely embraced model to colleges, but no one has done the same for campus conduct codes. We need sentencing guidelines in conduct codes to prevent excessive penalties for minor violations. We also need a grand jury system

to dismiss inadequate complaints in order to prevent the chilling effect of unwarranted investigations.

4. Defense of individual rights. One of the most important needs is to defend the rights of students and faculty (whether conservative, liberal, or moderate) at all kinds of public and private universities. This includes investigating attacks on academic freedom, speaking out in defense of free expression, and helping faculty and students to obtain legal assistance and mobilize support for their cause. Although FIRE has been effective at defending many people on the left and the right, we need more than one organization to monitor the vast enterprise of higher education in America and to pressure colleges to protect freedom.

5. Global advocacy of academic freedom. Academic freedom for faculty and free expression rights for students are fairly well protected at American colleges, despite the concerns about the recent wave of attacks on them. The violation of these rights is the exception, not the rule. But around the world, the tradition of intellectual freedom is much weaker. By helping to create international standards of academic freedom and student liberty, we will not only help improve colleges globally, we will also create institutions that can help change an entire society. Students who are educated in free institutions will desire that freedom for the rest of their lives.

The Future of Academic Freedom

As a student at the University of Illinois in Urbana, the University of Chicago, and Illinois State University, I've probably taken more college courses than almost anyone else in the world. I've had at least a dozen conservative professors, ranging from Michael McConnell to Edward Shils to Richard Posner, and many more teachers whose political ideology I will never know. I wish more of my professors had openly discussed their ideological views and expressed controversial political opinions in class, since I think it makes an education more interesting. I believe that a professor who is open about politics is usually more likely to encourage political debate by others and refrain from punishing students who disagree.

We cannot scrub a university clean of political ideas, even if we accepted the bizarre belief that we should. The nonpolitical university requires massive surveillance and censorship to enforce such rules, and even then students would still learn to detect the hints of political views uttered by professors. The only alternative is to have more freedom of political expression, not less.

The enemies of academic freedom imagine that intellectual liberty in the classroom is a zero-sum game: Every political idea expressed by a professor, they seem to think, squelches a student's willingness to speak out. These critics of academic freedom want to silence any political expression by all professors based upon the objections of a few students to a handful of the most inept professors. But intellectual diversity comes from adding more ideas to the debate on campus, not by trying to subtract unpopular viewpoints.

American colleges thrive on freedom. Sometimes this freedom is abused. Sometimes professors say things that are inappropriate or idiotic. But do we want a Big Brother University watching over what professors say? Do we want an educational system government? Instead of restricting academic freedom, we must expand it. When professors fall short of the ideal of good teaching, they should be criticized, not silenced.

Academic freedom may seem like an unimportant liberty, designed to protect an obscure intellectual elite. But academic freedom belongs to all of us, and it serves everyone. When liberty is threatened at colleges and universities, the chilling effect extends throughout a society, because the loss of the ivory tower as a refuge for freedom has wider repercussions. Academia is the place in American society where dissent is most protected and the free debate of ideas is encouraged. When professors are fired and students are banned from expressing themselves, it sends a message to everyone else in America that dissent will not be permitted anywhere.

The War on Terror has inspired a new front: the war on academic freedom. As with previous crusades against liberal academics, today's campaign uses legislative hearings and public pressure on colleges to restrict the debate over controversial ideas. A study by Harvard professor Neil Gross found that one-third of social science professors surveyed in 2006 reported that their academic freedom has been threatened, a larger number than a similar study discovered a half century earlier during the McCarthy Era.[13]

College campuses host the most diverse and open debate of ideas in America today. Even while we criticize the shortcomings in higher education, we must defend academia from the forces of intolerance that seek to impose a narrow-minded vision of what a patriot is.

A free society requires free universities. And free universities require both protection from political control and a commitment to hearing dissenting ideas of all kinds. In an age of patriotic correctness, faculty, students, and administrators must not be afraid to stand up against conventional wisdom and to stand up for the free exchange of ideas.

Notes

⁓

Notes to Introduction

1. AAUP, 1940 Statement of Principles on Academic Freedom and Tenure, http://www.aaup.org/AAUP/pubsres/policydocs/1940statement.htm; AAUP, 1915 Declaration of Principles, http://www.campus-watch.org/article/id/566.

2. Statutes of Harvard, 1646, in L. F. Goodchild and H. S. Wechsler, eds., *The History of Higher Education: An ASHE Reader,* 2d ed. (Old Tappan, NJ: Pearson, 1997), 125–128.

3. Richard Hofstadter, *Academic Freedom in the Age of the College* (New York: Columbia University Press, 1955), 89.

4. Ibid., 108.

5. Emily Gordon, "Horowitz Speaks about Liberal Bias," *Cornell Sun,* April 27, 2005; there is no record of Harvard actually burning any witches.

6. John Saltmarsh, *Scott Nearing: An Intellectual Biography* (Philadelphia: Temple University Press, 1991), 84.

7. Ibid., 97.

8. Ibid.

9. Ibid., 99.

10. Ibid., 101.

11. See Walter Metzger, ed., *Dimensions of Academic Freedom* (Urbana: University of Illinois Press, 1969), 13–14.

12. Ibid.

13. Saltmarsh, *Scott Nearing,* 109.

14. Ibid., 120.

15. Carol Gruber, *Mars and Minerva: World War I and the Use of the Higher Learning in America* (Baton Rouge: Louisiana State University Press, 1975), 170.

16. AAUP, "Report of Committee on Academic Freedom in Wartime," *Bulletin of the American Association of University Professors* (February–March 1918): 41.

17. Gruber, *Mars and Minerva,* 199.

18. Ibid., 256.

19. Peggie Hollingsworth, ed., *Unfettered Expression: Freedom in American Intellectual Life* (Ann Arbor: University of Michigan Press, 2000), 10.

20. Richard Allen Swanson, "Edmund J. James, 1855–1925" (Ph.D. diss., University of Illinois at Urbana, 1966), 316.

21. Ibid.; see *Daily Illini* (Urbana, IL), November 3, 1917.

22. *Los Angeles Daily News*, April 10, 1953, quoted in Dwight Bolinger, "Who Is Intellectually Free?" *Journal of Higher Education* (December 1954): 464.

23. Sigmund Diamond, *Compromised Campus: The Collaboration of Universities with the Intelligence Community, 1945–1955* (New York: Oxford University Press, 1992), 243–244.

24. David Horowitz, *The Campaign for Academic Freedom* (Los Angeles: Center for the Study of Popular Culture, 2005), 41.

25. Lionel Lewis, *Cold War on Campus* (New Brunswick, NJ: Transaction, 1988), 49.

26. Sidney Hook, *Heresy, Yes, Conspiracy, No* (New York: John Day, 1953), 61.

27. Paul Lazarsfield and Wagner Thielens, *The Academic Mind* (Glencoe, IL: Free Press, 1958), 69.

28. Lewis, *Cold War on Campus*, 5.

29. Ibid., 61.

30. Venuri Siriwardane, "David Horowitz Interview Transcript," *Temple News* (Philadelphia, PA), January 19, 2006.

31. Scott Jaschik, "Murderers, Video and Academic Freedom," InsideHigherEd.com, March 23, 2006, http://insidehighered.com/news/2006/03/23/academic; see also http://www.crooksandliars.com/2006/03/21.html#a7604.

32. Ann Coulter, 2005 Conservative Political Action Conference, http://ace.mu.nu/archives/068066.php.

33. *Sean Hannity* radio show, November 22, 2005.

34. "Campus Watch Stifles Freedom of Expression," *Stanford Daily*, October 9, 2002, http://www.campus-watch.org/article/id/257.

35. David Horowitz speech, "Center for the Study of Popular Culture," Restoration Weekend, February 2006, http://rightalk.listenz.com/!ARCHIVES/9.DavidHorowitz.mp3.

36. David Horowitz, "Dangerous Academics at Duke," FrontPageMagazine.com, April 27, 2006, http://frontpagemag.com/Articles/ReadArticle.asp?ID=22183.

37. Bill Steigerwald, "Invasion of the Mind-Snatchers," *Pittsburgh Tribune Review*, March 18, 2006.

38. See John K. Wilson, *The Myth of Political Correctness: The Conservative Attack on Higher Education* (Durham, NC: Duke University Press, 1995).

39. Matthew Streb, "The Reemergence of the Academic Freedom Debate," in Evan Gerstmann and Matthew Streb, eds., *Academic Freedom at the Dawn of a New Century* (Palo Alto, CA: Stanford University Press, 2006), 3–18.

40. Robert O'Neil, "Academic Freedom in the Post-September 11 Era: An Old Game with New Rules," in Gerstmann and Streb, *Academic Freedom at the Dawn of a New Century*, 43–60.

41. Ibid., 49–50.

Notes to Chapter One

1. Andrea Billups, "Campus Hawks and Doves Find Speech Is Not So Free," *Washington Times*, October 1, 2001.

2. ACTA, "Defending Civilization," 2001, www.goacta.org/Reports/defciv.pdf; the original version is at www.eecs.harvard.edu/~aaron/defciv.pdf.

3. Stuart Eskenazi, "Is Report a Blueprint for a New Blacklist?" *Seattle Times*, December 16, 2001.

4. Michael Fletcher, "Dissenters Find Colleges Less Tolerant of Discord Following Attacks," *Washington Post*, October 30, 2001, A6, http://www.thefire.org/index.php/article/4626.html.

5. "Berthold to Remain Off Campus Following Threats," *Daily Lobo* online, October 2, 2001, http://www.dailylobo.com/media/paper344/news/2001/10/02/News/WebExclusiveberthold.To.Remain.Off.Campus.Following.Threats-109590.shtml?norewrite2006 03190217&sourcedomain=www.dailylobo.com.

6. Jennifer Sanchez, "Professor: Pentagon Deserved to Be Blown Up," *Albuquerque Tribune,* September 26, 2001, http://www.knoxstudio.com/shns/story.cfm?pk=SIEGE-PROFESSOR-09-26-01&cat=AN.

7. John Doggett, "Academic Freedom, Yes—Treason, No," *WorldNetDaily.com,* October 12, 2001, http://www.worldnetdaily.com/news/article.asp?ARTICLE_ID=24898.

8. Sanchez, "Professor: Pentagon Deserved to Be Blown Up."

9. Fletcher, "Dissenters Find Colleges Less Tolerant of Discord Following Attacks."

10. Associated Press, "University Punishes Professor for Sept. 11 Remark," *Freedom Forum,* December 11, 2001, http://www.freedomforum.org/templates/document.asp?documentID=15515.

11. David Glenn, "The War on Campus," *Nation,* December 3, 2001, http://www.thenation.com/doc/20011203/glenn; Fletcher, "Dissenters Find Colleges Less Tolerant of Discord Following Attacks."

12. ACTA Press Release, "Controversial Comment on Terrorist Attack Is Not Grounds for Punishment," November 14, 2001, http://www.goacta.org/press/Press%20Releases/11-14-01PR.htm.

13. Stephen Balch, "NAS Sends Letter to UNM President," October 1, 2001, http://www.nas.org/print/pressreleases/hqnas/releas_01oct01.htm.

14. Gail Epstein Nieves, "UM Employee Fired over Sept. 11 Remarks," *Miami Herald,* November 16, 2001.

15. Ibid.

16. Ibid.

17. Glenn, "The War on Campus."

18. Ibid.

19. Diana Jean Schemo, "New Battles in Old War over Freedom of Speech," *New York Times,* November 25, 2001, B6; Tom Mashberg, "Pro or Con, War Talk's Risky on Campus," *Boston Herald,* December 16, 2001, 1; Stephanie Armour, "War of Words: Free Speech Vexes Employers," *USA Today,* December 7, 2001, 1B; Andrea Foster, "Union Objects to Suspension of Librarian," *Chronicle of Higher Education,* October 26, 2001, http://chronicle.com/weekly/v48/i09/09a03702.htm.

20. Michael Gerber and Jonathan Schwarz, "What Falwell Really Meant," *Village Voice,* September 19, 2001, http://www.villagevoice.com/news/0138,schwarz,28430,1.html.

21. Robin Wilson and Ana Marie Cox, "Terrorist Attacks Put Academic Freedom to the Test," *Chronicle of Higher Education,* October 5, 2001, http://chronicle.com/weekly/v48/i06/06a01201.htm.

22. Mary Jane Smetanka, "Subject of Terrorism Is Tricky for Colleges," *Minneapolis Star Tribune,* September 24, 2001, 4A.

23. Associated Press, "University Trustees Echo Condemnation of 'Un-American' Forum," October 8, 2001, http://www.freedomforum.org/templates/document.asp?documentID=15094.

24. Tom Mashberg, "War on Terrorism," *Boston Herald,* December 16, 2001, http://www.thefire.org/pdfs/4385_2623.pdf.

25. Maria Fisher, "The Big Chill," *Community College Week,* December 24, 2001.

26. Michael Fletcher, "Trust, and Interest, in Government Soar on College Campuses," *Washington Post,* November 23, 2001, A3.

27. Casey Krautkramer, "'Patriots' Use Home-Made Bombs against Peace Activists," Gannett Wisconsin Newspapers, October 11, 2001, http://www.overthrow.com/lsn/news.asp?articleID=943.

28. Fletcher, "Trust, and Interest, in Government Soar on College Campuses."

29. Susan Thomson, "Washington University Closes Campus during Peace Rally," *St. Louis Post-Dispatch,* September 21, 2001.

30. Glenn, "The War on Campus."

31. Ibid.

32. Barbara Kantrowitz and Keith Naughton, "Generation 9-11," *Newsweek,* November 12, 2001, 53.

33. For a detailed list of reports, see the *Indy* (Normal, IL), September 19, 2001.

34. Virginia Pelley, "Campus Spies," Alternet.org, October 16, 2001, http://www.alternet.org/story/11725.

35. Ibid.

36. Jacques Steinberg, "U.S. Has Covered 200 Campuses to Check Up on Mideast Students," *New York Times*, November 12, 2001.

37. Lois Romano and David Fallis, "Questions Swirl around Men Held in Terror Probe," *Washington Post*, October 15, 2001.

38. Richard Schlesinger, "Is Fear Crushing Freedom?" *CBS News*, October 31, 2001, http://www.cbsnews.com/stories/2001/10/31/archive/main316565.shtml.

39. Richard Serrano, "Abuse of Rights for Detainees Reported," *Los Angeles Times*, October 15, 2001, http://www.webcom.com/hrin/magazine/detainees.html.

40. Sara Russo, "Professor Suspended for Remarks against Terrorism," *Campus Report*, December 2001, www.academia.org/campus_reports/2001/dec_2001_2.html.

41. Jonathan Last, "The Faculty's Fight against Freedom," *Weekly Standard*, December 21, 2001.

42. Michael A. Fletcher, "Dissenters Find Colleges Less Tolerant of Discord Following Attacks," *Washington Post*, October 30, 2001.

43. Jonathan Last, "Liar, Liar," *Weekly Standard*, November 29, 2001; Wilson and Cox, "Terrorist Attacks Put Academic Freedom to the Test."

44. Peter Beinart, "Talk Show," *New Republic*, October 22, 2001, 6.

45. Associated Press, "Critic of Koran Temporarily Barred from Speaking at Ohio College," October 11, 2001, http://www.freedomforum.org/templates/document.asp?documentID=15125.

46. Lou Marano, "School Warns Man Who Rebuked Saudis," United Press International, October 25, 2001, http://www.thefire.org/pdfs/99_3252.pdf.

47. Gregg Krupa, "MSU Prof Says E-mail Biased," *Detroit News*, April 25, 2006, http://www.detnews.com/apps/pbcs.dll/article?AID=/20060425/SCHOOLS/604250334/1026/rss06.

48. Ibid.

49. Eric Scigliano, "Naming—and Un-naming—Names," *Nation*, December 31, 2001, http://www.thenation.com/doc/20011231/scigliano.

50. Arlene Levinson, "College Faculty, Staff, Find Chilling New Climate for Free Speech on Campus," Associated Press, October 13, 2001, http://www.thefire.org/pdfs/67_3156.pdf.

51. Mashberg, "Pro or Con War Talk's Risky on Campus."

52. Mark Schreiner, "UNCW Action Called 'Absurd,'" *Wilmington Star*, November 3, 2001, http://www.thefire.org/index.php/article/4138.html.

53. Student Press Law Center, "UC San Diego OK's Web Site Link to Revolutionary Armed Forces of Colombia," October 8, 2002, http://www.splc.org/newsflash.asp?id=487&year=.

54. Betsy Z. Russell, "Deportation Ordered for Saudi Student," *Spokesman Review*, April 26, 2003, http://www.spokesmanreview.com/pf.asp?date=042603&ID=s1341984; see also http://fl1.findlaw.com/news.findlaw.com/hdocs/docs/ins/usalhussayen21303ind.pdf.

55. Paul Barrett, "Idaho Arrest Puts Muslim Students under U.S. Scrutiny, Examination," *Wall Street Journal*, May 28, 2003, http://www.msa-natl.org/articles/WSJ_com%20-%20Idaho%20Arrest%20Puts%20Muslim%20Students%20Under%20U_S_%20Scrutiny,%20Examination.htm.

56. Dahlia Lithwick, "Tyranny in the Name of Freedom," *New York Times*, August 12, 2004.

57. Scott Jaschik, "Furor over an E-Mail," InsideHigherEd.com, November 21, 2005, http://insidehighered.com/news/2005/11/21/warren; "Pre-emptive Strike," WorldNetDaily, November 23, 2005, http://www.worldnetdaily.com/news/article.asp?ARTICLE_ID=47562.

58. Michael Tremoglie, "Academics at War, with the Military," *Campus Report*, January 12, 2004, http://www.campusreportonline.net/main/printer_friendly.php?id=54.

59. Richard Morgan, "Saint Xavier U. Suspends Professor for E-Mail Message," *Chronicle of Higher Education*, December 6, 2002, http://chronicle.com/weekly/v49/i15/15a01402.htm; Editorial, "The Professor and the Cadet," *Wall Street Journal*, November 12, 2002, A20; see also www.collegefreedom.org/kirstein.htm.

60. AAUP, "Committee Statement on Extramural Utterances," 1964, in AAUP, *Policy Documents and Reports* (Baltimore, MD: Johns Hopkins University Press, 1995), 32.

61. Morgan, "Saint Xavier U. Suspends Professor for E-Mail Message."

62. Lou Marano, "University President Backs Speech Rights," United Press International, November 7, 2002, http://www.thefire.org/pdfs/94_3240.pdf.

63. "Students, Teachers Face Free Speech Limitations after Terrorist Attacks," Student Press Law Center, September 21, 2001, http://www.splc.org/newsflash.asp?id=304.

64. Christopher Chow, "American Flag Banned on Campuses across the Nation," *Campus Report*, November 2001, http://www.academia.org/campus_reports/2001/nov_2001_1.html.

65. AAUP, "Academic Freedom and National Security in a Time of Crisis," http://www.aaup.org/statements/REPORTS/911report.htm; City Journal, Autumn 2001.

66. John Leo, "Talk about Getting Religion!" *U.S. News and World Report*, August 9, 2004, 59.

67. Kristin Lombardi, "Climate of Fear," *Boston Phoenix*, July 25–August 1, 2003, http://www.bostonphoenix.com/boston/news_features/top/features/documents/03044184.asp.

68. Marlon Castillo, "Student Alleges Anti-Muslim Hate Speech," *Yale Daily News*, April 9, 2003, http://www.yaledailynews.com/articlefunctions/Printerfriendly.asp?AID=22491.

69. ACLU, "Freedom under Fire," May 8, 2003, http://www.aclu.org/safefree/general/17259pub20030508.html.

70. Florida Statute 1000.06, "Display of Flags," http://www.flsenate.gov/statutes/index.cfm?App_mode=Display_Statute&URL=Ch1000/ch1000.htm.

71. Michael Miner, "Proper Display of the Flag," *Chicago Reader*, October 12, 2001, http://www.chicagoreader.com/hottype/2001/011012_2.html; Deborah Potter, "Flagging the Problem," *American Journalism Review*, June 2002, http://www.ajr.org/article_printable.asp?id=2541.

72. Daniel Pipes, "Profs Who Hate America," *New York Post*, November 12, 2002, http://www.danielpipes.org/article/923.

73. Daniel Pipes, "The Future of Academia," FrontPageMagazine.com, December 30, 2003, http://www.danielpipes.org/article/1386.

74. Joel Beinin, "Thought Control for Middle East Studies," *Foreign Policy in Focus*, March 31, 2004, http://www.alternet.org/print.html?StoryID=18296.

75. Anders Strindberg, "The New Commissars: Congress Threatens to Cut Off Funding to Collegiate Mideast Studies Departments That Refuse to Toe the Neocon Line," *American Conservative*, February 2, 2004.

76. Stanley Kurtz, "Reforming the Campus: Congress Targets Title VI," *National Review*, October 14, 2003, http://www.nationalreview.com/script/printpage.asp?ref=/kurtz/kurtz200310140905.asp.

77. Alisa Solomon, "The Ideology Police," *Village Voice*, February 25, 2004.

78. Stanley Kurtz, "Title Bout," *National Review* on-line, April 2, 2007, http://article.nationalreview.com/?q=NTlkYmJlNTk5MDYyZDdkYmU2YWM4YWI2NTRlYjM1OWE=.

79. William Saleton, "Save the Bigots," *Slate*, August 9, 2002, http://www.slate.com/id/2069249.

80. AAUP, "Academic Freedom and National Security in a Time of Crisis," *Academe*, November–December 2003, http://www.aaup.org/statements/REPORTS/911report.htm; *Yacovelli v. Moeser*, 2004 U.S. Dist. LEXIS 9152 (M.D.N.C. May 20, 2004), *aff'd* 324 F. Supp. 2d 760 (2004).

81. Richard Veit, "For the Record: Twenty-first Alexander Meiklejohn Award," *Academe*, September–October 2003, http://www.aaup.org/AAUP/about/awards/meiklejohn.htm.

Notes

82. Kate Zernike, "Talk, and Debate, on Koran as Chapel Hill Classes Open," *New York Times,* August 20, 2002, A1; Jonathan Yardley, "Inquisition at Chapel Hill," *Washington Post,* August 12, 2002, C2; Mary Beth Marklein, "Assigned Reading of Book on the Koran Spurs Rights Lawsuit against UNC," *USA Today,* August 5, 2002, 6D; *Yacovelli v. Moeser,* No. 02 CV 596, 2004 U.S. Dist. LEXIS 9152 (M.D.N.C. May 20, 2004), *aff'd* 324 F. Supp. 2d 760 (2004); Donna Euben, "Curriculum Matters," *Academe,* November–December 2002.

83. Rusty Pugh and Jody Brown, "UNC's Islam 'Indoctrination' Program Re-Enters Spotlight," *AgapePress,* October 9, 2002, http://headlines.agapepress.org/archive/10/afa/92002a.asp.

84. Patrick Reardon, "Valuable Lesson," *Chicago Tribune,* September 29, 2004.

85. FIRE Press Release, "FIRE Issues Statement Regarding Censorship of 'Partisan' Speech on Campus," October 21, 2004, http://www.thefire.org/index.php/article/4983.html.

86. Lynn Stratton, "USF: University of Silence in Florida," *St. Petersburg Times,* November 1, 2004; FIRE Press Release, "FIRE Issues Statement Regarding Censorship of 'Partisan' Speech on Campus."

87. "UW Profs Reminded Politicking against Law," *Wausau Daily Herald* (Wausau, WI), October 23, 2004.

88. Kate Clements, "UI Prohibits E-mail Politics," *Champaign News-Gazette,* September 17, 2004.

89. "Censored: Public Fla. School Cancels Campus Speaker Fearing She Would Criticize Bush," *Democracy Now,* October 8, 2004, http://www.democracynow.org/article.pl?sid=04/10/08/1531203.

90. FIRE Press Release, "FIRE Issues Statement Regarding Censorship of 'Partisan' Speech on Campus."

91. Brian Slupski, "MCC Film Spat Was Avoidable," *Northwest Herald* (Crystal Lake, IL), October 20, 2004, http://www.nwherald.com/CommunitySection/slupski/287162888438547.php.

92. Paul Nowell, "Heated Dispute on *Fahrenheit,*" *Boston Globe,* November 20, 2004, http://www.boston.com/news/nation/articles/2004/11/20/heated_dispute_on_fahrenheit/?rss_id=Boston%20Globe%20—%20National%20News.

93. Aaron Bals, "Campuses Rethink, Balance Moore Invitation," *Daily Nebraskan* (Lincoln, NE), October 25, 2004, http://www.dailynebraskan.com/media/storage/paper857/news/2004/10/25/News/Campuses.Rethink.Balance.Moore.Invitation-1743383.shtml?norewrite200608231355&sourcedomain=www.dailynebraskan.com.

94. Mike Cronin, "UVSC Seeks to 'Balance' Moore," *Salt Lake Tribune,* September 18, 2004, http://www.sltrib.com/portlet/article/html/fragments/print_article.jsp?article=2416752; see also the documentary, *This Divided State,* http://www.thisdividedstate.com.

95. Jeff Chu, "Fighting Words 101," *TIME,* March 9, 2005, http://www.time.com/time/magazine/article/0,9171,1034711,00.html; see also Joseph Vogel, *Free Speech 101: Do Conservatives Fear Free Speech?* (Silverton, ID: WindRiver, 2006).

96. Lisa Petrillo, "CSU San Marcos President: Moore Visit Illegal," *San Diego Union-Tribune,* September 22, 2004, B3.

97. David French, "Michael Moore and the Scandal of Student Fees," FrontPageMagazine.com, November 11, 2004, http://frontpagemag.com/Articles/Read.aspx?GUID={37FD91A4-F473-4FA0-812C-55332072DD3B}.

98. David Horowitz Blog, "Hitchens for Bush; Moore against Bush; Taxpayers Screwed," FrontPageMag.com, October 30, 2004, http://www.frontpagemag.com/Blog/Read.aspx?guid=1e310272-38a1-496c-8e6c-814bbd8b9841.

99. Joe Watson, "Heil to the Chief," *Phoenix New Times,* July 1, 2004, http://www.phoenixnewtimes.com/issues/2004-07-01/news/feature.html.

100. Joe Watson, "Bush League," *Phoenix New Times,* August 19, 2004, http://www.phoenixnewtimes.com/issues/2004-08-19/news/news.html.

101. John Leaños, "Intellectual Freedom and Pat Tillman," *Bad Subjects,* May 26, 2005, http://bad.eserver.org/reviews/2005/leanosstatement.html.

Notes

102. Mark Sommer, "Buffalo State Draws Fire with Refusal of Peace Exhibit," *Buffalo News*, August 23, 2005.

103. "Alden's Missing Pieces," *Ohio University Post*, September 23, 2004.

104. Martin D. Snyder, "State of the Profession: Dangerous Art," *Academe*, January–February 2005, http://www.aaup.org/AAUP/pubsres/academe/2005/JF/Col/sotp.htm; see also the documentary *Strange Culture*, http://www.strangeculture.net.

105. Robin McKie, "Professor Faces Jail in Bio-terror Scare," *London Observer*, February 27, 2005; Robin Wilson, "U.S. Grand Jury Indicts 2 Professors over Getting Bacteria for Artwork," *Chronicle of Higher Education*, July 9, 2004, http://chronicle.com/weekly/v50/i44/44a00901.htm; AAUP Action Alert, July 12, 2004, http://www.aaup.org/kurtzact.htm; Randy Kennedy, "The Artists in the Hazmat Suits," *New York Times*, July 3, 2005; Critical Art Ensemble Defense Fund, http://www.caedefensefund.org.

106. Amber Hussung, "Academic Freedom under Fire," *OAH Newsletter*, May 2003, http://www.oah.org/pubs/nl/2003may/hussung.html.

107. AAUP, "Academic Freedom and National Security in a Time of Crisis," October 2003, http://www.aaup.org/AAUP/comm/rep/crisistime.htm.

108. Audrey Hudson, "Librarians Dispute Justice's Claim on Use of Patriot Act," *Washington Times*, September 18, 2003, http://washtimes.com/national/20030918-103507-3583r.htm.

109. Tom Campbell, "Government Snoops May Find Door Barred at Berkeley," *Los Angeles Times*, May 20, 2004.

110. Leigh Estabrook, "Public Libraries and Civil Liberties: A Profession Divided," University of Illinois Library Research Center, 2003, http://lrc.lis.uiuc.edu/web/PLCL.html; Leigh Estabrook, "Public Libraries' Response to the Events of September 11, 2001," University of Illinois Library Research Center, 2002, http://lrc.lis.uiuc.edu/web/911.html.

111. Burton Bollag, "A Cuban Scholar Shut Out," *Chronicle of Higher Education*, April 11, 2003.

112. Letter from Roger F. Noriega to the AAUP, October 14, 2004, http://www.aaup.org/Issues/international/country/Cuba/LASATravel2.htm.

113. Rachel B. Levinson, "Legal Watch: Ideology in the Academy," *Academe*, July–August 2007, http://www.aaup.org/AAUP/pubsres/academe/2007/JA/Col/lw.htm; Scott Jaschik, "A Visa at Last," *InsideHigherEd.com*, July 23, 2007, http://www.insidehighered.com/news/2007/07/23/ari.

114. Brad Wong, "Iraqi Doctor Who Disputes Official Death Tolls Is Denied Visa to Visit UW," *Seattle Post-Intelligencer*, April 20, 2007, http://seattlepi.nwsource.com/local/312411_iraqvisa20.html.

115. Scott Jaschik, "Another Professor Denied Entry," *InsideHigherEd.com*, September 25, 2007, http://www.insidehighered.com/news/2007/09/25/lasso.

116. Nina Bernstein, "Music Scholar Barred from U.S., but No One Will Tell Her Why," *New York Times*, September 17, 2007.

117. Burton Bollag, "Scholars Kept Out," *Chronicle of Higher Education*, June 15, 2007, http://chronicle.com/free/v53/i41/41a04101.htm.

118. Ibid.

119. Cathy Cockrell, "Post-9/11 Laws Source of Campus Delays, Unease," *Berkeleyan*, May 7, 2003, http://www.berkeley.edu/news/berkeleyan/2003/05/07_patriot.shtml.

120. AAUP, "Academic Freedom and National Security in a Time of Crisis," http://www.aaup.org/statements/REPORTS/911report.htm.

121. Levinson, "Legal Watch: Ideology in the Academy."

122. Scott Jaschik, "Sociologists and ACLU Blast Visa Denial," *InsideHigherEd.com*, August 13, 2007, http://www.insidehighered.com/news/2007/08/13/habib.

123. Scott Jaschik, "Kafka at the Border," *InsideHigherEd.com*, March 13, 2007, http://www.insidehighered.com/news/2007/03/13/canada.

124. Adam Liptak, "The Nation's Borders, Now Guarded by the Net," *New York Times*, May 14, 2007.

125. AAUP, "Academic Freedom and National Security in a Time of Crisis."

Notes

126. Mark Clayton, "Academia Becomes Target for New Security Laws," *Christian Science Monitor,* September 24, 2002.

127. Julia Preston, "Hearing for Muslim Barred by U.S.," *New York Times,* April 14, 2006.

128. Stephen Kinzer, "Muslim Scholar Loses U.S. Visa as Query Is Raised," *New York Times,* August 26, 2004, http://www.nytimes.com/2004/08/26/national/26scholar.html?ex=1251172800&en=290fb6c157cb0498&ei=5090&partner=rssuserland.

129. Deborah Sontag, "Mystery of the Islamic Scholar Who Was Barred by the U.S.," *New York Times,* October 6, 2004.

130. Tariq Ramadan, "Academic Freedom in a Global Society," AAUP Annual Meeting, Washington, D.C., June 11, 2005.

131. Reuters, "Muslim Scholar Barred by U.S. Denies Support for Terrorism," *New York Times,* September 26, 2006, http://www.nytimes.com/2006/09/26/world/europe/26scholar.html?_r=1&oref=slogin; Rachel Ehrenfeld and Alyssa A. Lappen, "Why Tariq Ramadan Lost," *Washington Times,* October 11, 2006; Olivier Guitta, "The State Dept. Was Right to Deny Tariq Ramadan a Visa," *Weekly Standard,* October 13, 2006, http://frontpagemag.com/Articles/ReadArticle.asp?ID=24876.

132. Ramadan, "Academic Freedom in a Global Society."

133. Ian Buruma, "Tariq Ramadan Has an Identity Issue," *New York Times,* February 4, 2007.

134. Ramadan, "Academic Freedom in a Global Society."

135. Ramadan, "Too Scary for the Classroom?" *New York Times,* September 1, 2004.

136. Jane Lampman, "Muslim Scholar Barred from U.S. Preaches Tolerance," *Christian Science Monitor,* September 21, 2004, 16; Preston, "Hearing for Muslim Barred by U.S."

137. Ramadan, "Academic Freedom in a Global Society."

138. David Horowitz, "Betraying Academic Freedom," FrontPageMagazine.com, January 20, 2006, http://www.frontpagemag.com/Articles/Read.aspx?GUID={4F2D458A-1A19-4742-A8B2-158D6977565F}.

139. John K. Wilson, "Interview with David Horowitz," *Illinois Academe* (Spring 2006), http://collegefreedom.org/horint.htm.

140. See University of Colorado AAUP, "Statement on the Termination of Phil Mitchell," September 21, 2007, http://collegefreedom.org/aaupco.html.

141. See Chip Berlet, "Attacks on Greenpeace and Other Ecology Groups," Political Research Associates, August 22, 1991, http://www.publiceye.org/liberty/greenspy.html.

142. Mike McPhee, "'Spy Files' Shared with FBI, Others," *Denver Post,* May 22, 2003, http://www.ccmep.org/2003%20Articles/052203_spy_files_shared.htm.

143. Sharon Walsh, "The Drake Affair," *Chronicle of Higher Education,* March 5, 2004, A8–A10; Monica Davey, "Subpoenas on Antiwar Protest Are Dropped," *New York Times,* February 11, 2004, A18; Statement of the AAUP Special Committee on Academic Freedom and National Security in a Time of Crisis, "Subpoenas Issued to Drake University," February 11, 2004, http://www.aaup.org/statements/SpchState/Statements/subpoenas.htm.

144. Michael Arnone, "Texas Campus Is Puzzled by Federal Agents' Inquiry into Conference on Islam," *Chronicle of Higher Education,* March 5, 2004, A10.

145. Richard Winton and J. Michael Kennedy, "Deputies' Questions Unsettle University," *Los Angeles Times,* March 11, 2006, http://www.latimes.com/news/local/la-me-prof11mar11,0,6118935.story.

146. Frank Mickadeit, "Feds Warn O. C. of Terror Lurking 'Down the Street,'" *Orange County Register,* May 25, 2006.

147. Joe Garofoli, "ACLU Asks State If It is Providing Data to FBI," *San Francisco Chronicle,* December 22, 2005.

148. *Democracy Now,* December 15, 2005, http://www.campusantiwar.net/index.php?option=content&task=view&id=136&Itemid=2.

149. Eric Lichtblau, "F.B.I. Watched Activist Groups, New Files Show," *New York Times,* December 20, 2005.

150. Samantha Henig, "Pentagon Surveillance of Student Groups as Security Threats Extended to Monitoring E-Mail, Reports Show," *Chronicle of Higher Education*, July 6, 2006, http://chronicle.com/daily/2006/07/2006070601n.htm.

151. Robert Dreyfuss, "The Pentagon's New Spies," *Rolling Stone*, April 20, 2006, 38–42.

152. ACLU FOIA request, May 18, 2005, http://www.aclu.org/spyfiles/missouri_foia_org.pdf.

153. Eric Lichtblau, "F.B.I. Goes Knocking for Political Troublemakers," *New York Times*, August 16, 2004, http://www.nytimes.com/2004/08/16/politics/campaign/16fbi.html?ex=1250308800&en=201bec967e07fb80&ei=5090&partner=rssuserland.

154. "FBI Trails and Interrogates Missouri Activists," Progressive.org, August 23, 2004, progressive.org/node/2502/print.

155. "Kalamazoo College Republicans Rat Out Fellow Students at Bush Event," Progressive.org, May 13, 2004, http://www.progressive.org/mcwatch04/mc051304.html.

156. House Permanent Select Committee on Intelligence, "Al-Qaeda: The Many Faces of an Islamist Extremist Threat," June 2006, http://www.npr.org/documents/2006/sep/alqaida.pdf, 18.

157. Candace de Russy, "Thin Red Line," *National Review*, September 28, 2006, http://article.nationalreview.com/print/?q=YjliMTkwYjlkNTYyYTIyZWRkYzE5ZTY5MmEzMzAxNzQ=.

158. Patrick Barrett, "Galloway Talk Fits UW Credo, and Taxpayers Won't Foot Bill," *Capital Times*, September 8, 2005.

159. Russell Schoch, "Q&A: A Conversation with Candace Falk," *California Monthly*, April 2003, http://www.alumni.berkeley.edu/Alumni/Cal_Monthly/April_2003/A_conversation_with_Candace_Falk.asp.

160. Thomas Bartlett, "The Most Hated Professor in America," *Chronicle of Higher Education*, April 18, 2003, http://chronicle.com/weekly/v49/i32/32a05601.htm; Thomas Bartlett, "Columbia U. Professor Tells Teach-In He Hopes Iraq Will Defeat U.S.," *Chronicle of Higher Education*, April 11, 2003, http://chronicle.com/weekly/v49/i31/31a02602.htm.

161. Scott Smallwood, "Professors at Irvine Valley College Protest Warning on War Discussions," *Chronicle of Higher Education*, April 11, 2003.

162. FIRE,"Writing Instructor Loses Job for Discussing Iraq War in Class," January 27, 2004, http://www.thefire.org/index.php/article/165.html; Gary Green, "Statement on Elizabeth Ito," October 7, 2003, http://www.forsyth.tec.nc.us/welcome/pressconf.html.

163. Scott Jaschik, "Casualty of Anti-War Activism," InsideHigherEd.com, December 2, 2005, http://www.insidehighered.com/news/2005/12/02/suit; Jason Cato, "Professor Sues IUP, Claims Anti-War Backlash," *Pittsburgh Tribune-Review*, November 18, 2005.

164. Cathy Young, "A New Wave of PC on Campus," *Boston Globe*, December 12, 2005.

165. "University of Arizona Professor Reported to FBI for 'Hating' America," *Democracy Now*, September 27, 2004, http://www.democracynow.org/article.pl?sid=04/09/27/1435222.

166. Amy Resseguie, "Colorado State U. Professor Withdraws from Teaching over Political Statements," *Rocky Mountain Collegian*, September 29, 2004.

167. Ibid.

168. Camille Dodero, "Recruitment-Office Protest," *Boston Phoenix*, June 4–10, 2004, http://www.bostonphoenix.com/boston/news_features/this_just_in/documents/03885837.asp; "Boston Protester Faces Felony Charges for Protesting Abu Ghraib Abuse," *Democracy Now*, June 3, 2004, http://www.democracynow.org/article.pl?sid=04/06/03/142254.

169. Tara Sadooghi, "U Mass Professor Speaks Out on Assault Charge," *Boston University Student Underground*, May 2003, http://www.thestudentunderground.org/old_website/print.php?ArticleID=304.

170. Nadine Hoffman, "UMass-Boston Professor Arrested While Trying to Help Students," April 3, 2003, http://www.refuseandresist.org/police_state/art.php?aid=692.

171. Kristen Lombardi, "Climate of Fear," *Boston Phoenix*, http://www.bostonphoenix.com/boston/news_features/top/features/documents/03044184.asp.

172. Bryan G. Pfeifer, "The 'Ugly Face of American Racism,'" Indymedia.org, February 23, 2006, http://www.indymedia.org/en/2006/02/833921.shtml.

173. Elizabeth Wrigley-Field, "We Will Not Be Intimidated," October 4, 2005, http://www.campusantiwar.net/index.php?option=content&task=view&id=107&Itemid=2.

174. Vijay Prashad, "Melee of the Young Republican Berserkers," *Counterpunch,* October 3, 2005, http://www.counterpunch.org/prashad10032005.html; Wrigley-Field, "We Will Not Be Intimidated."

175. Elizabeth Wrigley-Field, "A New Battleground on Campuses," CampusAntiWar.net, April 19, 2006, http://www.campusantiwar.net/index.php?option=content&task=view&id=161&Itemid=2.

176. Ibid.

177. Three days later, the ban was finally revoked. See Kimberly Turner, "SFSU Cuts Time Protesters Kept Out of Classes," *Oakland Tribune,* April 19, 2006, http://www.insidebayarea.com/oaklandtribune/localnews/ci_3726291.

178. Monique Angle, "HU Students Facing Discipline," *Daily Press,* November 23, 2005.

179. Andrew Petkofsky, "Clash of Campus Freedom, Civility," *Richmond Times Dispatch,* December 11, 2005.

180. Stewart Stout, "Nevada Students Protest Recruiters, College Republicans File Lawsuit," CampusAntiWar.net, November 14, 2005, http://campusantiwar.net/index.php?option=content&task=view&id=126.

181. Levinson, "Legal Watch: Ideology in the Academy."

182. Ibid. See also Dustin Wax, "Party Like It's 1954," Savage Minds blog, October 3, 2005, http://savageminds.org/2005/10/03/party-like-its-1954.

183. Howard Pankratz, "Prof Quits Chair over 9/11," *Denver Post,* February 1, 2005; http://www.denverpost.com/Stories/0,1413,36%257E53%257E2686093,00.html#.

184. Scott Smallwood, "Anatomy of a Free-Speech Firestorm: How a Professor's 3-Year-Old Essay Sparked a National Controversy," *Chronicle of Higher Education,* February 10, 2005.

185. Howard Pankratz, "N.Y. College Cancels Talk," *Denver Post,* February 2, 2005.

186. Patrick Healy, "Hamilton College and Lecturer in Fee Dispute," *New York Times,* February 12, 2005; Scott Jaschik, "Resignation at Hamilton," InsideHigherEd.com, February 14, 2005, http://insidehighered.com/insider/resignation_at_hamilton.

187. Scott Jaschik, "Fallout at Hamilton," InsideHigherEd.com, July 5, 2005, http://insidehighered.com/news/2005/07/05/hamilton; David French, "Hamilton Builds a Fence," Thefire.org, February 14, 2005, http://www.thefire.org/index.php/article/5293.html?PHPSESSID=.

188. David Horowitz, *The Professors* (Washington, DC: Regnery Publishing, 2006), viii, xv.

189. Scott Smallwood, "Anatomy of a Free-Speech Firestorm."

190. Associated Press, "Controversial Colorado Prof Dropped from UO Conference, *News-Review* (Roseburg, OR), February 15, 2005, http://www.newsreview.info/article/20050215/NEWS/102150007.

191. Charlie Brennan, "Controversy Fuels Interest in Churchill," *Rocky Mountain News,* February 10, 2005; Rob McDonald, "Controversial Professor's EWU Visit Back On," *Spokesman Review,* March 10, 2005, http://www.spokesmanreview.com/breaking/story.asp?submitDate=2005310131637.

192. AAUP, "AAUP Releases Statement on Professor Ward Churchill Controversy," February 4, 2005, http://www.aaup.org/AAUP/newsroom/prarchives/2005/Church.htm.

193. J. R. Ross, "College Professor Brings Controversy to UW–Whitewater," Associated Press, February 27, 2005, http://www.duluthsuperior.com/mld/duluthsuperior/11008065.htm.

194. George Joe, "Ward Churchill responds to controversy," *Indian Country,* March 18, 2005, http://www.indiancountry.com/content.cfm?feature=yes&id=1096410567.

195. Don Feder, "Ward Churchill: Useful Idiot," FrontPageMagazine.com, February 11, 2005, http://www.frontpagemag.com/Articles/Read.aspx?GUID={18D26358-C223-468B-826B-9C215089823C}.

Notes

196. Joe Scarborough, "Time Is Up for Radical Professors Like Ward Churchill," MSNBC.com, February 5, 2005, http://www.msnbc.msn.com/id/6330851.

197. "Text of Governor Owens' Letter on Churchill," *Denver Post* online, February 1, 2005, http://www.denverpost.com/Stories/0,1413,36%257E53%257E2686241,00.html#.

198. *The O'Reilly Factor,* February 1, 2005.

199. Report of the Investigative Committee of the Standing Committee on Research Misconduct at the University of Colorado at Boulder Concerning Allegations of Academic Misconduct against Professor Ward Churchill, May 16, 2006, http://www.colorado.edu/news/reports/churchill/churchillreport051606.html.

200. "FIRE Issues Analysis of Churchill Report," March 25, 2005, http://thefire.org/index.php/article/5469.html.

201. Bill Scanlon, "CU Oversight Weighed," *Rocky Mountain News,* February 24, 2005.

202. Jack Kelly, "Free Speech Failing on Campus," *Jewish World Review,* March 1, 2005, http://www.jewishworldreview.com/0305/jkelly030105.php3.

203. Lawrence H. Summers, "Remarks at NBER Conference on Diversifying the Science and Engineering Workforce," January 14, 2005, http://www.president.harvard.edu/speeches/2005/nber.html.

204. Ruth Marcus, "Summers Storm," *Washington Post,* January 22, 2005.

205. Derrick Z. Jackson, "Summers's Tortured Logic," *Boston Globe,* January 19, 2005.

206. Chanel Lee, "Black to the Future," *Village Voice,* August 2, 2005, http://villagevoice.com/arts/0531,education2,66453,12.html.

207. Richard Bradley, "The Crimson Coup," *Boston Magazine,* June 2006, http://www.bostonmagazine.com/articles/the_crimson_coup.

208. Harry Lewis, *Excellence without a Soul* (New York: Public Affairs, 2006), 260; Bradley, "The Crimson Coup."

209. Student Academic Freedom Conference, Washington, D.C., April 7, 2006.

210. Lewis, *Excellence without a Soul,* 258.

211. Bradley, "The Crimson Coup."

212. Justin Pope, "Summers's Ability to Run Harvard Debated," Associated Press, February 18, 2005, http://www.msnbc.msn.com/id/6994922.

213. Calev Ben-David, "Big Man on Campus," *Jerusalem Post,* January 5, 2005.

214. John C. Ensslin, "Hoffman Warns CU Faculty of 'New McCarthyism,'" *Rocky Mountain News,* March 4, 2005.

215. Arthur Kane, "Regents Face Dilemma over Firebrand Professor," *Denver Post,* March 6, 2005.

216. Interview by author with Elizabeth Hoffman, May 4, 2006.

217. Bill Carter and Felicity Barringer, "In Patriotic Time, Dissent Is Muted," *New York Times,* September 28, 2001, A1; see Ari Fleischer, letter, *New York Times,* March 24, 2004, A20.

Notes to Chapter Two

1. Alisa Solomon, "Plotzing in New Paltz," *Village Voice,* September 25–October 1, 2002, http://www.villagevoice.com/news/0239,solomon,38632,1.html.

2. Adam Schupack, "Update on CCSU Institute," *Jewish Ledger,* July 24, 2002, http://www.campus-watch.org/article/id/428.

3. Adam Schupack, "CCSU Middle East Institute Lacked Balance, Participants Say," *Jewish Ledger,* August 7, 2002, http://www.campus-watch.org/article/id/427.

4. Maria Fisher, "The Big Chill," *Community College Week,* December 24, 2001.

5. Michael Levenson, "Brandeis Pulls Artwork by Palestinian Youths," *Boston Globe,* May 3, 2006, http://www.boston.com/news/education/higher/articles/2006/05/03/brandeis_pulls_artwork_by_palestinian_youths/.

6. Jessica Remitz, "PSU Censors Exhibit," *Daily Collegian* (Penn State University), April 21, 2006, http://www.collegian.psu.edu/archive/2006/04/04-21-06tdc/04-21-06dnews-13.asp.

7. Lola Thelin, "Boyle Outrages JF," *Loyola Maroon*, April 25, 2003, http://www.loyola-maroon.com/home/index.cfm?event=displayArticlePrinterFriendly&uStory_id=b7bd8c29-f26b-43d7-b1f2-a810fe74ca4a.

8. Jordan Schrader, "Judge Denies Hearing in Suit Brought against U. Michigan Conference," *Michigan Daily*, October 11, 2002, http://www.michigandaily.com/media/storage/paper851/news/2002/10/11/News/Judge.Denies.Hearing.In.Suit.Brought.Against.Conference-1412971.shtml?norewrite200607180860&sourcedomain=www.michigandaily.com.

9. AAUP, "Academic Freedom and National Security in a Time of Crisis," http://www.aaup.org/statements/REPORTS/911report.htm.

10. Megan Kuhn, "Ohio U. Middle East Seminar Continues Despite Disinvitation of Speaker," *Post* (Ohio University), May 7, 2002.

11. Emilie Astell, "Second Speaker Disinvited at HC," *Massachusetts Telegram and Gazette* (Worchester, MA), December 10, 2002.

12. Max Gross, "ZOA: Shun Ivy Colleges That Host Israel-Bashing Poet," *Forward*, December 6, 2002, http://www.forward.com/issues/2002/02.12.06/news4.html.

13. Patrick Healy, "Harvard Speech Canceled," *Boston Globe*, November 13, 2002, http://www.ccmep.org/2002_articles/Israel-Palestine/111302_harvard_speech_canceled.htm; see also Andrew Peyton Thomas, *The People v. Harvard Law: How America's Oldest Law School Turned Its Back on Free Speech* (San Francisco: Encounter Books, 2005), 136.

14. Letter, *Harvard Crimson*, November 15, 2002, http://www.thecrimson.com/printer-friendly.aspx?ref=255310.

15. Alexander Blenkinsopp, "In About-Face, English Dept. Re-Invites Anti-Israeli Poet," *Harvard Crimson*, November 20, 2002, http://www.thecrimson.com/article.aspx?ref=255387.

16. Alexander Blenkinsopp, "Paulin Likely to Speak in Spring," *Harvard Crimson*, November 21, 2002, http://www.thecrimson.com/printerfriendly.aspx?ref=255425.

17. Scott Jaschik, "Name-Calling and a Canceled Lecture," InsideHigherEd.com, May 29, 2007, http://www.insidehighered.com/news/2007/05/29/lecture.

18. Stanley Kurtz, "Speech Down the Pipes," *National Review* online, January 7, 2003, http://www.nationalreview.com/kurtz/kurtz010703.asp.

19. Ibid.

20. Sara Dogan, "Academic Freedom Abuses at Duke and Berkeley," StudentsforAcademicFreedom.org, February 19, 2004, http://www.frontpagemag.com/Content/read.asp?ID=76.

21. Megan Reiss, "Op-Ed: Restricted Access to Event Is Censorship," *Stanford Daily*, April 13, 2007, http://www.stanforddaily.com/article/2007/4/13/opedRestrictedAccessToEventIsCensorship; Nanette Asimov, "Officials Bar Public from Panel Featuring 'Ex-Terrorists,'" *San Francisco Chronicle*, April 13, 2007, http://www.sfgate.com/cgi-bin/article.cgi?f=/c/a/2007/04/13/BAGASP84SF1.DTL.

22. ACLU, "In Letter to UC Berkeley Chancellor, ACLU Opposes Suppression of Pro-Palestinian Student Protest," May 7, 2002, http://www.aclu.org/studentsrights/expression/12817prs20020507.html.

23. Ron Harris, "SFSU Pro-Palestinian Group Loses Funding; Jewish Group Warned," Associated Press, June 22, 2002, www.sfsu.edu/~news/sfsuresp.htm; http://www.sfgups.org.

24. Joe Eskenazi, "SFSU Yanks Pro-Palestinian Web Site Denying the Holocaust," *Jewish Bulletin of Northern California*, June 21, 2002, http://www.jewishsf.com/content/2-0-/module/displaystory/story_id/18459/edition_id/370/format/html/displaystory.html.

25. San Francisco State University, "DA Press Release: Offensive Speech Not Deemed Hate Crime," July 16, 2002, http://www.sfsu.edu/~news/response/darelease.htm.

26. General Union of Palestine Students, "Accounts of May 7, 2002," http://www.sfgups.cjb.net (website no longer functional).

27. San Francisco State University, "DA Press Release: Offensive Speech Not Deemed Hate Crime."

28. FIRE Press Release, "Victory for Free Expression at San Francisco State University," March 20, 2007, http://www.thefire.org/index.php/article/7839.html.

29. Salim Muwakkil, "The Israel Lobby and Its Discontents," InTheseTimes.com, April 8, 2006, http://www.inthesetimes.com/site/main/article/2590; see John Mearsheimer and Stephen Walt, "The Israel Lobby," *London Review of Books*, March 23, 2006, http://www.lrb.co.uk/v28/n06/mear01_.html; John Mearsheimer and Stephen Walt, "The Israel Lobby and U.S. Foreign Policy," KSG Working Paper No. RWP06-011, March 2006, http://ssrn.com/abstract=891198.

30. Donna Halper, letter, "On Campus, a Multiplicity of 'Isms,'" *Washington Times*, March 12, 2006.

31. Evan Wagner, "American U. Professor Impersonated in Malicious E-mail," *American University Eagle*, September 16, 2002.

32. John Fund, "Cole Fire," *Wall Street Journal*, April 24, 2006, http://www.opinionjournal.com/diary/?id=110008282.

33. Elizabeth Kraushar, "An Air of Caution in the Blogosphere," *Columbia Spectator*, September 15, 2006, http://media.www.columbiaspectator.com/media/storage/paper865/news/2006/09/15/News/An.Air.Of.Caution.In.The.Blogosphere-2279814.shtml?sourcedomain=www.columbiaspectator.com&MIIHost=media.collegepublisher.com.

34. UC Berkeley press release, "Update on the Fall 2002 Course 'The Politics and Poetics of Palestinian Resistance,'" May 21, 2002, http://www.berkeley.edu/news/media/releases/2002/05/21_palest-class.html; http://www.berkeley.edu/news/mideast/syllabus.html.

35. Roger Kimball, "The Death of Objectivity," *National Review*, May 14, 2002, http://www.nationalreview.com/comment/comment-kimball051402.asp.

36. Kelly Rayburn, "Davis Addresses Anti-Semitism," *Daily Bruin*, July 29, 2002.

37. Jon Wiener, "Giving Chutzpah New Meaning," *Nation*, July 11, 2005, http://www.thenation.com/doc.mhtml?i=20050711&s=wiener; Alan Dershowitz, "Why Is the University of California Press Publishing Bigotry?" *FrontPageMag.com*, July 5, 2005, http://www.frontpagemag.com/Articles/Read.aspx?GUID={C431E949-9FAB-4EE3-8A4F-04ED86C4AD6F}.

38. Michael Kunzelman, "Dershowitz, Prof Spar over Plagiarism," *Washington Post*, July 14, 2005, http://www.normanfinkelstein.com/article.php?pg=11&ar=40.

39. Richard Posner, *The Little Book of Plagiarism* (New York: Pantheon, 2007), 15.

40. Wiener, "Giving Chutzpah New Meaning"; Scott Jaschik, "First Amendment Furor," InsideHigherEd.com, June 27, 2005, http://insidehighered.com/news/2005/06/27/dershowitz; Jeffrey Felshman, "Whose Holocaust Is It Anyway?" *Chicago Reader*, August 26, 2005.

41. Alan Dershowitz, "Neve Gordon Can't Take Criticism," *Jerusalem Post*, November 8, 2006, http://www.normanfinkelstein.com/article.php?pg=11&ar=656.

42. Letter from Alan Dershowitz to Arnold Schwarzenegger, December 22, 2004, www.collegefreedom.org/LetterToGov-ONLY.pdf.

43. Jon Wiener, "Chutzpah and Free Speech," *Los Angeles Times*, July 11, 2005; Dershowitz denies writing a letter.

44. Felshman, "Whose Holocaust Is It Anyway?"

45. Scott Jaschik, "Furor over Norm Finkelstein," InsideHigherEd.com, April 3, 2007, http://www.insidehighered.com/news/2007/04/03/finkelstein.

46. Stefanie Pervos, "Finkelstein Denied Tenure: The Jewish Community Responds," *Jewish United Fund News*, June 14, 2007, http://www.juf.org/news/local.aspx?id=23722.

47. Letter from Leo Welch, president of the Illinois AAUP, to Rev. Dennis H. Holtschneider, June 22, 2007, http://collegefreedom.blogspot.com/2007/06/illinois-aaup-on-depaul-cases-illinois.html.

48. DePaul University, "Summary Report of the Promotion and Tenure Policy Committee," June 2006, 8, http://oaa.depaul.edu/_content/what/documents/Final%20Report%20of%20the%20Promotion%20and%20Tenure%20Committee%2006.pdf.

49. Scott Jaschik, "Terminating the Terminal Year," InsideHigherEd.com, August 27, 2007, http://www.insidehighered.com/news/2007/08/27/depaul.

Notes

50. Scott Jaschik, "DePaul Rejects Finkelstein," InsideHigherEd.com, June 11, 2007, http://www.insidehighered.com/news/2007/06/11/finkelstein.

51. Steven Plaut, "The Next Piece of Housekeeping for DePaul?" FrontPageMagazine. com, September 06, 2007, http://frontpagemag.com/Articles/Read.aspx?GUID=B24F5BF9-A8CF-4951-80F5-F9E4B99F7039.

52. Jonathan McNamara, "Q&A: Abraham on Freedom," *Daily Texan* (Austin, TX), January 31, 2006, http://www.dailytexanonline.com/media/paper410/news/2006/01/31/TopStories/Qa.Abraham.On.Freedom-1545105.shtml?norewrite&sourcedomain=www.dailytexanonline.com.

53. Daniel Pipes, "Redeeming the Wayward University," *New York Sun,* November 28, 2006, http://www.danielpipes.org/article/4167.

54. Roberta Seid and Roz Rothstein, "Wayne State: The Possible Hiring of Wadie Said," *StandWithUs.com,* November 28, 2006, http://www.standwithus.com/news_post.asp?NPI=1045; Aaron Hanscom, "Jew-Hate on Campus," FrontPageMagazine.com, November 9, 2006, http://www.frontpagemag.com/Articles/Read.aspx?GUID={96859063-AE48-42AA-88EA-00373FB40A2B}; Pipes, "Redeeming the Wayward University."

55. Karen Arenson, "Fracas Erupts over Book on Mideast by a Barnard Professor Seeking Tenure," *New York Times,* September 10, 2007.

56. Scott Jaschik, "Middle East Tensions Flare Again in U.S. (Update)," InsideHigherEd. com, September 5, 2007, http://www.insidehighered.com/news/2007/09/05/middleeast.

57. Rami G. Khouri, "Christian Prophetic Voices Face Many Battles," *North Park University Daily Star,* October 12, 2005, http://campus.northpark.edu/centers/middle/don_wagner.htm.

58. Philip Fairbanks, "Academic Repression Update: 'We Shall Rise': The Persecution of Dr. Sami Al-Arian," CUNY Graduate Center *Advocate,* March 2007, http://gcadvocate.org/index.php?action=view&id=138.

59. FIRE Press Release, "FIRE and Constitutional Rights at the University of South Florida," February 25, 2003, http://www.thefire.org/index.php/article/49.html.

60. Candace de Russy, "Thin Red Line," *National Review,* September 28, 2006, http://article.nationalreview.com/print/?q=YjliMTkwYjlkNTYyYTIyZWRkYzE5ZTY5MmEzMzAxNzQ=.

61. David Horowitz blog, "Al Arian Guilty. Will the AAUP Academic Freedom Committee," FrontPageMag.com, April 15, 2006, http://www.frontpagemag.com/Blog/Profile.aspx?ba=3d9e0209-1206-4f63-94c6-99a0aa6a4456.

62. FIRE Press Release, "The University of South Florida Betrays the Rule of Law," January 29, 2002, http://www.thefire.org/index.php/article/5283.html.

63. John J. Miller, "Pariahs, Martyrs—and Fighters Back—Conservative Professors in America," *National Review,* October 24, 2005.

64. Kelsey Snell, "Loop Professor Takes Heat for Conduct," *DePaulia,* October 1, 2004, http://www.thedepaulia.com/story.asp?artid=77&sectid=1.

65. Ibid.

66. Miller, "Pariahs, Martyrs—and Fighters Back."

67. Ron Grossman, "I'm Not the Ideal Poster Boy," *Chicago Tribune,* December 20, 2005.

68. FIRE, "DePaul Professor Suspended without a Hearing after Arguing with Students on Middle East Issues," May 18, 2005, http://www.thefire.org/index.php/case/678.html; Richard Baehr, "DePaul's Jihad against Academic Freedom," *American Thinker,* April 18, 2005, http://www.americanthinker.com/articles.php?article_id=4428&search=depaul.

69. Michael McIntyre, "The Klocek Case," *Illinois Academe,* Spring 2006.

70. Miller, "Pariahs, Martyrs—and Fighters Back."

71. E-mail to author from Douglas Giles, May 9, 2006.

72. Ibid.

73. E-mail to author from Jonathan Lowe, May 14, 2006.

74. E-mail to author from Douglas Giles, May 15, 2006.

75. Susan Weininger memo, September 21, 2005.

76. Ibid.

77. E-mail to author from Douglas Giles, May 15, 2006, his transcript of September 20, 2005, conversation. Weininger and Roosevelt University officials did not respond to requests for an interview.

78. Ibid.

79. Memo from Louise Love, March 14, 2006.

80. See www.roosevelt.edu/selfstudy/chapter4.pdf.

81. Memo from Lynn Weiner, March 15, 2006.

82. E-mail to author from Douglas Giles, September 2006.

83. American Philosophical Association Committee for the Defense of Professional Rights of Philosophers, letter to Roosevelt University, September 18, 2006.

84. "More Details on Academic Freedom Grievance," www.rafo.org.

85. E-mail from Douglas Giles, May 9, 2006.

86. David Project, *Columbia Unbecoming*, http://www.davidproject.org/index.php?option=com_wrapper&Itemid=68.

87. Douglas Feiden, "Call Columbia a Poisoned Ivy," *New York Daily News*, October 28, 2004.

88. N. R. Kleinfield, "Mideast Tensions Are Getting Personal on Campus at Columbia," *New York Times*, January 18, 2005, 1.

89. Douglas Feiden, "Hate 101 at Columbia," *New York Daily News*, November 22, 2004.

90. Jacob Gershman, "'Witch-hunt' Laid to 'Pro-Israel Groups,'" *New York Sun*, November 4, 2004.

91. Editorial, "Fire This Professor, Columbia," *New York Daily News*, April 10, 2005, http://www.nydailynews.com/news/ideas_opinions/story/298243p-255375c.html.

92. Editorial, "The Bollinger Whitewash," *New York Sun*, November 19, 2004; James Romoser, "Professors Contest Charges of Anti-Semitism," *Columbia Spectator*, March 28, 2005, http://www.columbiaspectator.com/vnews/display.v/ART/2005/03/28/4247bc65ede53.

93. David French, "FIRE Letter to Columbia University President Lee Bollinger," thefire.org, January 10, 2005, http://www.thefire.org/index.php/article/5100.html?PHPSESSID=.

94. Ibid.

95. Ibid.

96. Greg Lukianoff, "Defining Free Speech," *Columbia Spectator*, February 18, 2005.

97. Nat Hentoff, "Columbia: The Awakening," *Village Voice*, May 3, 2005; Nat Hentoff, "Columbia Whitewashes Itself," *Village Voice*, April 8, 2005; Nat Hentoff, "Columbia Implodes!" *Village Voice*, February 25, 2005, http://www.villagevoice.com/news/0509,hentoff,61510,6.html; Nat Hentoff, "Intimidated Classrooms," *Village Voice*, January 25, 2005; Nat Hentoff, "Telling It Like It Is," *Village Voice*, January 4, 2005.

98. Committee on Academic Freedom on the Middle East and North Africa, "Exclusion of Rashid Khalidi from Participation in NYC Teacher Development Workshops," *Middle East Studies Association*, April 7, 2005, http://fp.arizona.edu/mesassoc/CAFMENAletters.htm#050407Bloomberg.

99. Nathaniel Popper, "N.Y. School Board Bans a Controversial Arab Professor," *Forward*, February 25, 2005, http://www.indypressny.org/article.php3?ArticleID=1945.

100. Ibid.

101. Karen Aronson, "Columbia Chief Tackles Dispute over Professors," *New York Times*, March 24, 2005, http://www.columbia.edu/cu/news/05/03/cardozo_lecture.html.

102. Ibid.

103. Ibid.

104. Ibid.

105. Ibid.

106. Scott Jaschik, "Academic Freedom Wars," *InsideHigherEd.com*, March 25, 2005, http://www.insidehighered.com/news/2005/03/25/acfreedom.

107. Editorial, "Bollinger at the Bar," *New York Sun*, March 25, 2005.

108. Ad Hoc Grievance Committee Report, Columbia University, March 28, 2005, http://www.columbia.edu/cu/news/05/03/ad_hoc_grievance_committee_report.html.

109. Ibid.
110. Ibid.
111. Ibid.
112. Editorial, "Indoctrination at Columbia," *New York Times,* April 7, 2005.
113. Ibid.
114. David Andreatta, "Columbia Jews Want Outside Probe," *New York Post,* April 1, 2005, http://www.nypost.com/news/regionalnews/43582.htm.
115. John Giuffo, "Report from the Upper West Bank," *Village Voice,* April 7, 2005.
116. Ad Hoc Grievance Committee Report, Columbia University, March 28, 2005.
117. Bari Weiss, "In the Name of Academic Freedom," *Columbia Spectator,* November 16, 2004.
118. Popper, "N.Y. School Board Bans a Controversial Arab Professor."
119. Kleinfield, "Mideast Tensions Are Getting Personal on Campus at Columbia."
120. Liz Fink, "Students Speak Up to Defend MEALAC," *Columbia Spectator,* December 8, 2004, http://www.columbiaspectator.com/vnews/display.v/ART/2004/12/08/41b6b67628920.
121. Liz Fink, "Committee Addresses, Causes Conflict," *Columbia Spectator,* December 10, 2004.
122. Kleinfield, "Mideast Tensions Are Getting Personal on Campus at Columbia."
123. Editorial, "What Columbia Must Do Now," *New York Daily News,* April 1, 2005, http://www.nydailynews.com/news/ideas_opinions/story/295210p-252746c.html.
124. Sam Dolnick, "Columbia Issues New Guidelines for Filing Complaints against Teachers," Associated Press, April 11, 2005, http://www.columbia.edu/cu/news/clips/2005/04/12/columbiaissuesNEWSDAY.pdf.
125. Jacob Gershman, "Columbia Considers Limits on Political Expression at University," *New York Sun,* April 19, 2004, http://electronicintifada.net/v2/article2677.shtml.
126. Columbia College, "Policy on Academic Concerns, Complaints, and Grievances," http://www.college.columbia.edu/students/grievances.php.
127. ACTA, "Intellectual Diversity: A Time for Action," December 2005, 14, http://www.goacta.org/publications/Reports/IntellectualDiversityFinal.pdf.

Notes to Chapter Three

1. AAUP, "Academic Bill of Rights," 2003, http://www.aaup.org/AAUP/comm/rep/A/abor.htm.
2. "David Horowitz Freedom Center," Media Transparency, http://www.mediatransparency.org/recipientgrants.php?recipientID=63.
3. David Horowitz, "The Campus Blacklist," FrontPageMagazine.com, April 18, 2003, http://www.studentsforacademicfreedom.org/essays/blacklist.html.
4. David Horowitz, "The Problem with America's Colleges and the Solution," FrontPageMagazine.com, September 3, 2002, http://studentsforacademicfreedom.org/essays/problem_solution.html.
5. Robert Bluey, "GOP Senators Condemn Campus 'Thought Control,'" CNSNews.com, October 30, 2003, http://www.cnsnews.com/ViewPrint.asp?Page=/Nation/archive/200310/NAT20031030b.html.
6. Statement of Judd Gregg, October 29, 2003, www.senate.gov/~gregg/statements/sp102903.pdf.
7. David Horowitz, "Leading the Fight for Academic Freedom,"FrontPageMagazine.com, March 28, 2006, http://www.frontpagemag.com/Articles/ReadArticle.asp?ID=21793.
8. See Free Exchange on Campus, "Legislation Tracker," 2007, http://www.freeexchangeoncampus.org/index.php?option=com_content&task=section&id=5&Itemid=61; Students for Academic Freedom, "National and State Legislation Texts," http://cms.studentsforacademicfreedom.org//index.php?option=com_content&task=view&id=1904&Itemid=43.

9. Valerie Richardson, "'Pluralism' Manifesto Lights a Furor," *Washington Times,* September 15, 2003, http://www.studentsforacademicfreedom.org/archive/2003/WashTimesPluralism091503.htm.

10. Washington HB 3185, 2004, http://apps.leg.wa.gov/billinfo/summary.aspx?bill=3185&year=2004.

11. Press Release, "Morrow Re-Opens California Front in 'Revolutionary War' for Academic Freedom in America," December 6, 2005, http://republican.sen.ca.gov/news/38/pressrelease2951.asp.

12. Sara Dogan, "The Power of Student Governments," studentsforacademicfreedom. org, http://cms.studentsforacademicfreedom.org//index.php?option=com_content&task=view&id=1969&Itemid=52.

13. Matt Anderson, "SGA Passes Student Bill of Rights," *MTSU Sidelines,* March 16, 2005, http://media.www.mtsusidelines.com/media/storage/paper202/news/2005/03/16/News/Sga-Passes.Student.Bill.Of.Rights-894892.shtml.

14. Editorial, "There He Goes Again," *Wall Street Journal,* September 19, 2003, http://www.studentsforacademicfreedom.org/archive/2003/WSJ091903.html?news_id=415.

15. Students for Academic Freedom, "Mission and Strategy," July 1, 2006, http://cms.studentsforacademicfreedom.org//index.php?option=com_content&task=view&id=1917&Itemid=43.

16. David Horowitz, "Academic Values Sullied by Partisan Professors," *Spokane Spokesman-Review,* February 1, 2004, http://www.spokesmanreview.com/allstories-news-story.asp?date=020104&ID=s1481414.

17. John T. Plecnik, "Liberal Bias against Campus Conservatives Confronted," *Truth News,* October 22, 2004, http://www.frontpagemag.com/Articles/Printable.asp?ID=15622.

18. Bradley Shipp, "Academic Freedom News," StudentsforAcademicFreedom.org, March 11, 2005, http://cms.studentsforacademicfreedom.org//index.php?option=com_content& task=view&id=1938&Itemid=50.

19. David Horowitz, "Why an Academic Bill of Rights Is Necessary: Testimony before the Education Committee of the Ohio Senate," Frontpagemag.com, March 15, 2005, http://www.studentsforacademicfreedom.org/archive/2005/March2005/DHohiotestimony031505.htm; David Horowitz, "A Campaign of Lies," FrontPageMagazine.com, February 10, 2005, http://www.frontpagemag.com/Articles/Read.aspx?GUID=5F601954-989A-481D-B4C2-0A67AF4E35D2.

20. AAUP, "On Freedom of Expression and Campus Speech Codes," 1992, http://www.aaup.org/AAUP/pubsres/policydocs/speechcodes.htm.

21. David Horowitz blog, "Re: More Urban Legend (#56886)," Frontpagemag.com, March 20, 2005, http://www.studentsforacademicfreedom.org/archive/2005/March2005/DHCliopatriablogexchange032105.htm.

22. David Horowitz, "Academic Freedom at Princeton," *Daily Princetonian,* March 24, 2005, http://www.dailyprincetonian.com/archives/2005/03/24/opinion/12413.shtml.

23. David Horowitz, "Students Deserve the Academic Bill of Rights," *Minnesota Daily,* February 9, 2004, http://www.mndaily.com/articles/2004/02/09/48197.

24. Horowitz, "The Campus Blacklist."

25. David Horowitz, *Indoctrination U.: The Left's War Against Academic Freedom* (New York: Encounter Books, 2007), 5.

26. AAUP, "1940 Statement of Principles on Academic Freedom and Tenure with 1970 Interpretive Comments," http://www.aaup.org/AAUP/pubsres/policydocs/1940statement.htm.

27. Sara Dogan, "Students for Academic Freedom Handbook," http://www.studentsforacademicfreedom.org/texts/SAF%20handbook%20FINAL%202.pdf, 21.

28. Horowitz, "A Campaign of Lies."

29. Dogan, "Students for Academic Freedom Handbook," 21.

30. Academic Bill of Rights, http://studentsforacademicfreedom.org/abor.html.

31. David Horowitz blog, "AAUP Dishonesty," January 16, 2005, http://www.studentsforacademicfreedom.org/archive/2005/January2005/DH blog AAUP dishonesty011805.htm.

32. Academic Bill of Rights.

33. Ibid.

34. Ibid.

35. Ibid.

36. Lisa Petrillo, "Faculty Members See Bill as 'Grave Threat' to Freedom," *San Diego Union-Tribune,* April 20, 2005.

37. "Indoctrinate," Merriam-Webster online, http://m-w.com/dictionary/indoctrination.

38. Sonu Munshi, "Are Professors Too Liberal?" *ASU State Press,* July 11, 2006, http://www.statepress.com/issues/2006/07/11/webextra/697086.

39. Academic Bill of Rights.

40. See AAUP, "Academic Freedom and Outside Speakers," 2007, http://www.aaup.org/AAUP/comm/rep/A/outside.htm.

41. Academic Bill of Rights.

42. Ibid.

43. David Horowitz, "The Strange and Dishonest Campaign against Academic Freedom," FrontpageMag.com, April 29, 2005, http://www.studentsforacademicfreedom.org/archive/2005/April2005/DHStrangeandDishonestCampaign042905.htm.

44. Horowitz, "Academic Freedom at Princeton."

45. Horowitz, "A Campaign of Lies."

46. John K. Wilson, "Interview with David Horowitz," *Illinois Academe* (Spring 2006), http://collegefreedom.org/horint.htm.

47. Horowitz, "The Strange and Dishonest Campaign against Academic Freedom."

48. Ibid.

49. Ibid.

50. Students for Academic Freedom, "Mission and Strategy," studentsforacademicfreedom.org.

51. David Horowitz, "The Battle for the Bill of Rights," FrontPageMagazine.com, October 15, 2003, http://frontpagemag.com/Articles/ReadArticle.asp?ID=10325.

52. David Horowitz, "Diversity, Not Quotas, for Faculties," *Rocky Mountain News,* September 12, 2003, http://www.studentsforacademicfreedom.org/archive/2003/DHRMNoped091203.htm.

53. Peggy Lowe, "Colorado GOP Officials Meet with David Horowitz to Take on Leftist Education," *Rocky Mountain News,* September 6, 2003, http://www.freerepublic.com/focus/f-news/977155/posts.

54. Erin McIntyre, "Horowitz Challenges Campus to See Both Sides of Issues," *Daily Sentinel,* October 3, 2003, http://www.studentsforacademicfreedom.org/archive/2003/GrandJunction100303.html.

55. "Memorandum of Understanding," http://www.studentsforacademicfreedom.org/reports/COmemorandumofunderstanding.htm.

56. John Andrews, "Dangerous Professors," *Denver Post,* March 5, 2006.

57. John Andrews speech, Student Academic Freedom Conference, Washington D.C., April 7, 2006.

58. Jeffrey Dubner, "College Try," *American Prospect,* April 1, 2005, http://www.prospect.org/web/page.ww?section=root&name=ViewPrint&articleId=9349.

59. Valerie Richardson, "Academic Manifesto Takes Root," *Washington Times,* July 3, 2006, http://www.washtimes.com/functions/print.php?StoryID=20060703-123445-8832r.

60. Horowitz, *Indoctrination U.,* 100.

61. Ibid.

62. Jeff Chu, "Fighting Words 101," *TIME,* March 14, 2005, http://www.thefire.org/index.php/article/5414.html.

Notes

63. David Steigerwald, "The New Repression of the Postmodern Right," InsideHigherEd. com, February 11, 2005, http://www.insidehighered.com/views/the_new_repression_of_the_ postmodern_right.

64. Ohio Senate Bill 24, 2005–2006, http://www.studentsforacademicfreedom.org/ actions(boxattop)/OhioPage/OhioSenateBill24.htm.

65. Ibid.

66. Ibid.

67. Ibid.

68. Ibid.

69. Ibid.

70. David Horowitz, "Putting Professors' Politics under the Microscope," *Chronicle of Higher Education Colloquy Live,* February 18, 2004, http://chronicle.com/colloquylive/2004/02/ politics.

71. Wilson, "Interview with David Horowitz."

72. Kevin Mattson, "A Student Bill of Fights," *The Nation,* April 4, 2005, http://www. thenation.com/doc.mhtml?i=20050404&s=mattson.

73. Inter-University Council of Ohio, "Resolution on Academic Rights and Responsibilities," October 11, 2005.

74. In constant 2005 dollars per full-time equivalent student, State Higher Education Executive Officers, "State Higher Education Finance FY 2005 Summary Report," http://www. sheeo.org/finance/shef_sv06_v2.pdf, p. 5.

75. Ibid.

76. See "National and State Legislation Texts," studentsforacademicfreedom.org, which lists the remaining eight out of thirty-six states.

77. James Vanlandingham, "LGBT Position Hurts UF in Fla. House, Legislator Says," *Florida Alligator,* February 25, 2005, http://www.alligator.org/pt2/050225freedom.php.

78. Joe Follick, "Bill Aims to Limit Debate in Class," *Gainesville Sun,* February 25, 2005.

79. Vanlandingham, "LGBT Position Hurts UF in Fla. House."

80. Ibid.

81. Bill Cotterell, "Academic Freedom Comes to Florida," *Tallahassee Democrat,* February 25, 2005.

82. Vanlandingham, "LGBT Position Hurts UF in Fla. House."

83. Joe Follick, "House OKs Student 'Free Speech' Bill," *Lakeland Ledger* (Lakeland, FL), March 23, 2005.

84. Scott Jaschik, "Academic Freedom Wars," InsideHigherEd.com, March 25, 2005, http://www.insidehighered.com/news/2005/03/25/acfreedom.

85. Kimberly Miller, "Classroom Bill Draws Fire," *Palm Beach Post,* March 8, 2005.

86. Horowitz, "Academic Freedom at Princeton."

87. Scott Jaschik, "Intellectual Diversity or Intellectual Insult?" InsideHigherEd.com, April 16, 2007, http://www.insidehighered.com/news/2007/04/16/missouri.

88. David Horowitz blog, "University Officials Attack a Young Warrior," Frontpagemag. com, April 6, 2005, http://www.studentsforacademicfreedom.org/archive/2005/April2005/ FLYoungWarriorattacked040605.htm.

89. David Karp, "Lawmaker Takes Complaints about Liberal Bias to the Top," *St. Petersburg Times,* April 22, 2005.

90. "Jeb Bush: Horowitz a 'Fighter for Freedom,'" NewsMax.com, April 7, 2005, http:// archive.newsmax.com/archives/ic/2005/4/6/233459.shtml.

91. Allison North Jones, "Bill Seeks Class Time for Other Opinions," *Tampa Tribune,* March 26, 2005.

92. Horowitz, "Putting Professors' Politics under the Microscope."

93. Ibid.

94. David Horowitz blog, "Re: More Urban Legend (#56893)," FrontPageMag.com, March 20, 2005, http://www.studentsforacademicfreedom.org/archive/2005/March2005/ DHCliopatriablogexchange032105.htm.

95. Horowitz, "Why an Academic Bill of Rights Is Necessary."

96. David Horowitz speech, Student Academic Freedom Conference, Washington, D.C., April 7, 2006.

97. Horowitz, *Indoctrination U.,* 8.

98. Maine LD 1194, http://www.studentsforacademicfreedom.org/actions(boxattop)/Mainepage/MaineLD1194.htm.

99. Minnesota Senate Bill 1988, 2005, http://www.studentsforacademicfreedom.org/actions(boxattop)/Minnesotapage/MinnesotaSenateBill1988.htm.

100. New York Assembly Bill A10098, 2006, http://www.studentsforacademicfreedom.org/actions(boxattop)/NewYorkpage/NYAssemblyBillA10098.htm.

101. North Carolina Senate Bill 1139, 2005, http://www.studentsforacademicfreedom.org/actions(boxattop)/North%20Carolina%20page/NCsenatebill1139.htm.

102. Tennessee House Bill 432 and Senate Bill 1117, 2005, http://cms.studentsforacademicfreedom.org//index.php?option=com_content&task=view&id=1481&Itemid=59.

103. Letter, "Senate Bill 24 Would Help Students," *Columbus Dispatch,* March 19, 2005.

104. Sara Dogan, "A Victory in Florida," Letter from the National Campus Director, March 31, 2005.

105. Sara Dogan, "Academic Freedom Wars," InsideHigherEd.com, March 25, 2005, http://www.insidehighered.com/news/2005/03/25/acfreedom.

106. Dogan, "A Victory in Florida."

107. Horowitz blog, "Re: More Urban Legend (#56893)."

108. David Horowitz blog, "What We Have Inspired at Georgia Tech," FrontPageMag.com, April 18, 2005, http://www.frontpagemag.com/Blog/Read.aspx?guid=7e15964e-d04b-468f-8129-bd4ccbc7fbe7.

109. Horowitz, *Indoctrination U.,* 63.

110. Times/Bloomberg poll, *Chicago Tribune,* August 13, 2006.

111. Sandra Day O'Connor and Roy Romer, "Not By Math Alone," *Washington Post,* March 25, 2006.

112. Intercollegiate Studies Institute, "The Coming Crisis in Citizenship," September 2006, http://www.americancivicliteracy.org.

113. Derek Bok, *Our Underachieving Colleges: A Candid Look at How Much Students Learn and Why They Should Be Learning More* (Princeton, NJ: Princeton University Press, 2006), 38.

114. "The Alien and Sedition Acts," 1798, http://lexrex.com/enlightened/laws/alien_sedition.html.

115. Robert Bluey, "Congressman Strives for Intellectual Diversity on College Campuses," CNSNews.com, October 24, 2003, http://www.cnsnews.com/ViewPrint.asp?Page=/Nation/archive/200310/NAT20031024a.html.

116. Horowitz, "The Problem with America's Colleges and the Solution."

117. David Horowitz, "Missing Diversity on America's Campuses," FrontPageMagazine.com, September 3, 2002, http://www.frontpagemag.com/articles/readarticle.asp?ID=1003.

118. Horowitz, "The Battle for the Bill of Rights."

119. Mansour El-Kikhia, "Silencing Scholars a Sign of Intolerance," *San Antonio Express-News,* April 11, 2005, http://www.mysanantonio.com/opinion/columnists/melkikhia/stories/MYSA040805.07B.mansour.1b600a718.html.

120. Jim Rutenberg, "TV Program Canceled over Remarks on Gays," *New York Times,* July 8, 2003.

121. Wilson, "Interview with David Horowitz."

122. Jeff Schogol, "Horowitz Calls for Reformation at Lehigh University," *Express-Times* (Easton, PA), March 29, 2005.

123. David Horowitz, "Bowling Green Barbarians," FrontPageMagazine.com, April 4, 2005, http://www.frontpagemag.com/Articles/Read.aspx?GUID=366C52C2-BC42-4D38-AB72-69D0BD6E87A2.

124. Horowitz speech, Student Academic Freedom Conference, Washington, D.C., April 7, 2006.

125. Peggy Lowe, "The Man Behind War on Liberals," *Rocky Mountain News,* September 27, 2003, www.thefire.org/pdfs/4205_2506.pdf.

126. Ibid. See also Nate Carlisle, "Activist Prof under Investigation." *Columbia* (MO) *Daily Tribune,* April 25, 2003, http://www.frontpagemag.com/Articles/ReadArticle. asp?ID=7489.

127. Jack E. White, "A Real, Live Bigot." *TIME,* August 22, 1999, http://www.time.com/ time/magazine/article/0,9171,29787,00.html.

128. Horowitz, "The Campus Blacklist."

129. Ibid.

130. Robert Sanchez, "Students Assail 'Academic Bill of Rights,'" *Rocky Mountain News,* October 1, 2003, http://www.studentsforacademicfreedom.org/archive/2003/RMN100103. html.

131. David Horowitz speech, "Center for the Study of Popular Culture," Restoration Weekend, February 2006, http://rightalk.listenz.com/!ARCHIVES/9.DavidHorowitz.mp3.

132. Venuri Siriwardane, "David Horowitz Interview Transcript," *Temple News,* January 19, 2006.

133. Ibid.

134. Scott Jaschik, "$500 Fines for Political Profs," InsideHigherEd.com, February 19, 2007, http://www.insidehighered.com/news/2007/02/19/ariz; Arizona SB 1612, 2007, http://www.azleg.gov/FormatDocument.asp?inDoc=/legtext/48leg/1r/bills/sb1612p.htm.

135. Ibid.

136. Ibid.

137. David Horowitz, "The Arizona Bill Is Half Wrong," FrontPageMagazine.com, Monday, February 19, 2007, http://www.frontpagemag.com/Articles/Read.aspx?GUID={EDB896C8-9EA7-4A45-85BF-4F308F619D3C}.

138. Bill Zlatos, "CMU Newspaper Rejected Group's Ad," *Pittsburgh Tribune-Review,* December 27, 2004, http://www.studentsforacademicfreedom.org/archive/2005/January2005/ CMUnewspaperrejectsadtribunereview010505.htm.

139. Wilson, "Interview with David Horowitz."

140. David Horowitz blog, "Hot Time in Chicago," FrontPageMag.com, November 5, 2002, http://www.frontpagemag.com/Blog/Read.aspx?guid=6698696e-12e1-4c79-a78c-6f6e4177488e.

141. Maurice Isserman, "Whose Truth?" *Academe,* September–October 2005, 32–33, http://www.aaup.org/AAUP/pubsres/academe/2005/SO/Feat/isse.htm.

142. Ibid.

143. Jennifer Jacobson, "What Makes David Run?" *Chronicle of Higher Education,* May 6, 2005.

144. Kenneth Aaron, "Students Fight to Be Right," TimesUnion.com, May 2, 2005.

145. Horowitz, "The Campus Blacklist."

146. Siriwardane, "David Horowitz Interview Transcript."

147. Horowitz, "Missing Diversity on America's Campuses."

148. David Horowitz, "Bowling Green Barbarians." Frontpagemag.com, April 4, 2005, http://www.frontpagemag.com/Articles/Read.aspx?GUID=366C52C2-BC42-4D38-AB72-69D0BD6E87A2.

149. E-mail from Teri Sharp, media relations director, Bowling Green State University, July 5, 2005.

150. Speech at Duke University, March 7, 2006, http://inside.c-spanarchives.org:8080/ cspan/cspan.csp?command=dprogram&record=194694806; see also Wilson, "Interview with David Horowitz."

151. Scott Jaschik, "What You Do All Day," InsideHigherEd.com, December 22, 2005, http://insidehighered.com/news/2005/12/22/hours.

152. Center for the Study of Popular Culture IRS Form 990, 2005, http://www.guidestar. org/FinDocuments/2005/954/194/2005-954194642-029c30ec-9.pdf.

153. Dave Curtin, "Horowitz Defends Manifesto," *Denver Post,* October 1, 2003, http:// studentsforacademicfreedom.org/archive/2003/Denverpost100103.html.

154. David Horowitz, *The Campaign for Academic Freedom* (Los Angeles: Center for the Study of Popular Culture, 2005), 13–14.

155. Susan Lindt, "Is There Political Bias at State Colleges?" *Intelligencer Journal* (Lancaster, PA), March 23, 2006.

156. Rob Chaney, "Free Schools: David Horowitz Visits Montana," *The Missoulian*, December 3, 2003, http://www.studentsforacademicfreedom.org/archive/december/Missoulian120303.htm.

157. Horowitz, "Diversity, Not Quotas, for Faculties."

158. Students for Academic Freedom, "Indoctrination or Education?" 2004, http://www.studentsforacademicfreedom.org/literature/CSPC_BallState_ProofOnly.pdf, 12.

159. David Horowitz blog, "Send a Message to Al," Frontpagemag.com, November 30, 2004, http://www.frontpagemag.com/Blog/Read.aspx?guid=5f3e5761-f24d-4dd3-928d-cd51504e5ed4.

160. Students for Academic Freedom, "Indoctrination or Education?" 6.

161. Brett Mock, "Indoctrination in the Classroom," FrontPageMagazine.com, September 13, 2004, http://www.studentsforacademicfreedom.org/archive/September2004/BrettMockIndoctrinationatBSU091304.htm.

162. Students for Academic Freedom, "Indoctrination or Education?" 24.

163. Ibid., 27.

164. Ibid., 24.

165. Shawna Tsoumas, "SAF Posts Pamphlet about Peace Program," *Ball State Daily News*, December 8, 2004.

166. Seth Slabaugh, "BSU Urged to Back Political Diversity," *Muncie Star Press*, September 29, 2004.

167. Ball State University AAUP, "AAUP Supports Professors Alves and Wolfe," September 27, 2004, www.aaupatbsu.org.

168. Students for Academic Freedom, "Indoctrination or Education?" 27.

169. Slabaugh, "BSU Urged to Back Political Diversity."

170. Students for Academic Freedom, "Indoctrination or Education?" 28.

171. Slabaugh, "BSU Urged to Back Political Diversity."

172. Students for Academic Freedom, "Indoctrination or Education?" 33.

173. Ibid., 5.

174. David Horowitz, "'One Man's Terrorist Is Another Man's Freedom Fighter,'" FrontPageMagazine.com, November 8, 2004, http://www.frontpagemag.com/Articles/Read.aspx?GUID=D1DC0212-6060-4108-AD2A-A9D28D42E72D.

175. David Horowitz blog, "A Sad Commentary," FrontPageMag.com, October 5, 2004, http://www.frontpagemag.com/Blog/Read.aspx?guid=c038d61c-f6ce-4b36-9021-d6131ba76919.

176. David Horowitz, "The Political Attack on Our Universities" (Testimony to the Kansas legislature), FrontPageMagazine.com, March 15, 2006, http://www.frontpagemag.com/Articles/ReadArticle.asp?ID=21657.

177. Ibid.

178. Horowitz, *Indoctrination U.*, 66–67.

179. David Horowitz, "Steinberger vs. Horowitz, Part II," FrontPageMag.com, June 26, 2006, http://studentsforacademicfreedom.org/archive/2006/June2006/DHSteinbergerdebatePartII062606.htm.

180. Ibid.

181. Ibid.

182. Horowitz, "The Political Attack on Our Universities."

183. David Horowitz blog, "Historians' Hypocrisy," Frontpagemag.com, March 14, 2006.

184. Horowitz, "The Political Attack on Our Universities."

185. Cia Verschelden, "Social Welfare (Social Work 510/Sociology 510)," Kansas State University (Spring 2002), http://www.k-state.edu/socialwork/socwk510.htm.

186. Horowitz blog, "Historians' Hypocrisy."

Notes

187. Horowitz, *The Campaign for Academic Freedom,* 15.

188. John H. Morrow Jr., "I Don't Punish Students Who Disagree with Me," History News Network, September 13, 2004, http://hnn.us/articles/7342.html.

189. David Horowitz blog, "University Officials Investigate Georgia Professor," FrontPageMag.com, September 15, 2004, http://www.frontpagemag.com/Blog/Read. aspx?guid=c7db5a27-b8b7-4790-87e7-9e75916d9f44.

190. Ibid.

191. Morrow, "I Don't Punish Students Who Disagree with Me."

192. Ibid.

193. Letter from the National Campus Director, "UGA Professor Investigated for Classroom Diatribe," studentsforacademicfreedom.org, September 21, 2004.

194. Horowitz, "University Officials Investigate Georgia Professor."

195. David Horowitz blog, "A New Brock Slander Goes Round the Web," March 14, 2005.

196. Student comment posting, May 22, 2006, http://www.studentsforacademicfreedom. org/comp/viewComplaint.asp?complainId=652.

197. Student comment posting, September 8, 2004, http://studentsforacademicfreedom. org/comp/viewComplaint.asp?complainId=225.

198. Student comment posting, September 18, 2004, http://studentsforacademicfreedom. org/comp/viewComplaint.asp?complainId=236.

199. Student comment posting, September 18, 2004, http://studentsforacademicfreedom. org/comp/viewComplaint.asp?complainId=235.

200. Student comment posting, February 5, 2004, http://studentsforacademicfreedom. org/comp/viewComplaint.asp?complainId=53.

201. Student comment posting, February 27, 2004, http://studentsforacademicfreedom. org/comp/viewComplaint.asp?complainId=97.

202. Student comment posting, June 30, 2004, http://studentsforacademicfreedom. org/comp/viewComplaint.asp?complainId=202.

203. Student comment posting, February 20, 2004, http://studentsforacademicfreedom. org/comp/viewComplaint.asp?complainId=83.

204. Student comment posting, March 10, 2004, http://studentsforacademicfreedom. org/comp/viewComplaint.asp?complainId=111.

205. Russell Jacoby, "The New PC," *The Nation,* April 4, 2005, http://www.thenation. com/doc.mhtml?i=20050404&s=jacoby.

206. Jennifer Jacobson, "Pennsylvania Lawmakers Are Told That Complaints about Classroom Bias Are Rare," *Chronicle of Higher Education,* June 1, 2006.

207. Bill Toland, "Pitt Provost: Political Bias Not a Problem," *Pittsburgh Post-Gazette,* November 11, 2005.

208. Scott Jaschik, "Murderers, Video and Academic Freedom," InsideHigherEd.com, March 23, 2006, http://insidehighered.com/news/2006/03/23/academic; Mark Harper, "Bills Raise Debate on Academic Freedom," *Daytona News-Journal,* March 31, 2006, http://www. news-journalonline.com/NewsJournalOnline/News/EastVolusia/evlEAST01033106.htm.

209. Markus Kemmelmeier, Cherry Danielson, and Jay Basten, "What's in a Grade? Academic Success and Political Orientation," *Personality and Social Psychology Bulletin* 31, no. 10 (2005): 1386–1399.

210. Louis Uchitelle, "Students Are Leaving the Politics Out of Economics," *New York Times,* January 27, 2006; see also David Colander, *The Making of an Economist Redux* (Princeton, NJ: Princeton University Press, 2006), ch.2, 3. A similar version appeared in the *Journal of Economic Perspectives* (Summer 2005).

211. David Horowitz, *The Professors: The 101 Most Dangerous Academics in America* (New York: Regnery, 2006).

212. Wilson, "Interview with David Horowitz."

213. David Horowitz, "Article: E-mail Interview with Scott Jaschik, Editor of Inside HigherEd.com," *Professors,* May 10, 2006, http://theprofessors.org/2006_05_10_archive. html.

214. Curtin, "Horowitz Defends Manifesto."

215. Klein, "Worried on the Right and the Left," 21.

216. Speech by Robert Andringa, AAUP Annual Meeting, Washington, D.C., June 10, 2005.

217. Klein, "Worried on the Right and the Left," 21.

218. Colby Itkowitz, "Armstrong, Cutler Vie in GOP Primary," *Intelligencer Journal* (Lancaster, PA), May 11, 2006, http://local.lancasteronline.com/4/22633.

219. John Leo, "A Kick Where It's Needed," *U.S. News & World Report,* February 23, 2004.

220. Jamie Glazov, "Purging Conservatives from College Faculties," FrontPageMagazine. com. May 23, 2005.

221. Josh Gerstein, "Push Is On for Academic Bill of Rights to Protect against 'Political Pollution,'" *New York Sun,* February 9, 2005.

222. Lamar Alexander, "Five Steps to Establishing Academic Freedom," FrontPageMagazine. com, April 18, 2006.

223. David Beito, Robert K. C. Johnson, and Ralph E. Luker, "Who's Undermining Freedom of Speech on Campus Now?" History News Network, April 11, 2005, http://hnn. us/articles/11276.html.

224. David Beito, Ralph E. Luker, and Robert K. C. Johnson, "The AHA's Double Standard on Academic Freedom," *AHA Perspectives,* March 2006.

225. Editorial, "Academic Rights and Wrongs," *Wall Street Journal,* October 7, 2005, http://www.opinionjournal.com/taste/?id=110007369.

226. Jesse Walker, "Chilling Effects," *Reason,* September 17, 2003, http://reason.com/links/links091703.shtml.

227. Ibid.

228. Klein, "Worried on the Right and the Left."

229. Kyle Ellis, "David Horowitz Falsifies BSyou.net Editor's Work for FrontPage Magazine," BSYou.net, November 11, 2005; "Falsifying without Prejudice," Free Exchange on Campus, April 4, 2006, http://www.freeexchangeoncampus.org/index.php?option=com_content&task=view&id=69&Itemid=27.

230. Michael Russell, "Horowitz Misses the Point (Again)," *Dartmouth Review,* April 7, 2006, http://www.dartreview.com/archives/2006/04/07/horowitz_misses_the_point_again. php.

231. "Restoration Weekend Speakers," 2003, http://frontpagemagonline.com/onlinestore/restorationweekend/speakers.html; "Restoration Weekend Speakers," 2005, http://www.cspc.org/rw2005.

232. AAUP, "Joint Statement on Rights and Freedoms of Students," 1967, http://www.aaup.org/AAUP/pubsres/policydocs/stud-rights.htm.

233. Temple University, "Student and Faculty Academic Rights and Responsibilities, August 1, 2006, http://policies.temple.edu/getdoc.asp?policy_no=03.70.02; AAUP, "Joint Statement on Rights and Freedoms of Students."

234. Press Release, "Temple University Trustees Adopt Policy on Students' Academic Rights," July 20, 2006, http://www.studentsforacademicfreedom.org/archive/2006/July2006/TempleTrusteesAdoptPolicyPressRelease072106.htm.

235. Temple University, "Student and Faculty Academic Rights and Responsibilities." http://policies.temple.edu/getdoc.asp?policy_no03.70.02.

Notes to Chapter Four

1. Editorial, "There He Goes Again," *Wall Street Journal,* Sept. 19, 2003, http://www.opinionjournal.com/taste/?id=110004030.

2. Sara Hebel, "Patrolling Professors' Politics," *Chronicle of Higher Education,* February 13, 2004, http://chronicle.com/free/v50/i23/23a01801.htm.

3. John Leo, "A Kick Where It's Needed," *U.S. News & World Report,* February 16, 2004.

4. John Hawkins, "The David Horowitz Interview," http://rightwingnews.com/interviews/horowitz.php.

5. Jack Kingston and Walter Jones, "The Academic Bill of Rights Goes to Washington," FrontPageMagazine.com, October 22, 2003, http://www.frontpagemag.com/articles/Printable.asp?ID=10444.

6. "Restoration Weekend: The Future of Academia," FrontPageMagazine.com, December 30, 2003, http://www.frontpagemag.com/articles/readarticle.asp?ID=11509.

7. *Scarborough Country* interview, MSNBC, February 24, 2005.

8. David Horowitz and Eli Lehrer, "Political Bias in the Administrations and Faculties of 32 Elite Colleges and Universities," August 28, 2003, http://studentsforacademicfreedom.org/reports/lackdiversity.html.

9. Harvard Fact Book, 2005–2006, 18, http://vpf-web.harvard.edu/budget/factbook/current_facts/2006OnlineFactBook.pdf.

10. David Horowitz blog, "Back to School," September 3, 2003, http://www.frontpagemag.com/blog/printable.asp?ID=203.

11. David Horowitz, "The Battle for the Bill of Rights," FrontPageMagazine.com, October 15, 2003, http://www.frontpagemag.com/Articles/ReadArticle.asp?ID=10325.

12. Quoted in Rob Chaney, "Free Schools: David Horowitz Visits Montana," *The Missoulian,* December 2003, http://www.studentsforacademicfreedom.org/archive/december2003/Missoulian120303.htm.

13. Daniel Klein and Charlotta Stern, "How Politically Diverse Are the Social Sciences and Humanities? Survey Evidence from Six Fields," *Academic Questions,* http://www.ratio.se/pdf/wp/dk_ls_diverse.pdf.

14. John Tierney, "Republicans Outnumbered in Academia, Studies Find," *New York Times,* November 18, 2004; soon after writing this article, Tierney became the *Times*'s most conservative op-ed columnist.

15. *Rush Limbaugh show,* November 24, 2004.

16. Bartlett, Bruce, "No Republican Need Apply," Townhall.com, December 7, 2004.

17. Klein and Stern, "How Politically Diverse Are the Social Sciences and Humanities? Survey Evidence from Six Fields," 13.

18. Ibid., 6.

19. Calculated from table in ibid., 7, 9.

20. Ibid., 9.

21. Ibid., 5.

22. Bob Skolnik, "GOP Decries Slim Pickings in 3rd Dist. Race," *Riverside/Brookfield Landmark,* March 14, 2006, http://rblandmark.com/main.asp?SectionID=1&SubSectionID=1&ArticleID=1255&TM=76242.91.

23. Daniel Klein, "Ideology of Faculty in the Social Sciences and Humanities," 2, http://www.aei.org/docLib/200502141_klein.pdf, citing Ladd and Lipset, 1975, *The Divided Academy,* 62–64.

24. John F. Zipp and Rudy Fenwick, "Is the Academy a Liberal Hegemony? The Political Orientations and Educational Values of Professors," *Public Opinion Quarterly* 70, no. 3 (2006): 304–326, http://poq.oxfordjournals.org/cgi/content/full/70/3/304?ijkey=dVt13UcYfsj5AyF&keytype=ref#SEC3.

25. *Firing Line* debate, 1991, http://www.hu.mtu.edu/~tlockha/pcdebate.htm.

26. William F. Buckley Jr., "Dumb Bright Guys," Uexpress.com, November 19, 2004, http://www.uexpress.com/ontheright/?uc_full_date=20041119.

27. Daniel Klein speech, "A 'Liberal' Education: The Effects of Ideology in the Classroom," American Enterprise Institute conference, February 14, 2005, http://www.aei.org/events/filter.economic,eventID.993/transcript.asp.

28. Ibid.

29. Stanley Rothman, S. Robert Lichter, and Neil Nevitte, "Politics and Professional Advancement among College Faculty," *Forum* 3, no. 1 (2005), http://www.bepress.com/forum/vol3/iss1/art2.

30. Ibid.

31. Ibid.

32. Ibid., 4.

33. See "More on Political Bias in Academia," *Spartacus,* May 5, 2005, http://spartacus. blogs.com/spartacus/2005/05/more_on_academi.html.

34. Carnegie Foundation for the Advancement of Teaching, National Survey of Faculty, "1997 Survey of Faculty Members at a Stratified Random Sample of 306 U.S. Colleges and Universities," http://roperweb.ropercenter.uconn.edu/cgi-bin/hsrun.exe/roperweb/Catalog40/ Catalog40.htx;start=TopSummary_Link?Archno=USMISCHED1997-CARN-FAC.

35. Zipp and Fenwick, "Is the Academy a Liberal Hegemony?"

36. Higher Education Research Institute, UCLA, "Faculty Survey," 2004–05 survey, http://www.gseis.ucla.edu/heri/faculty.html.

37. Radford University, "Higher Education Research Institute, 2004–2005 Faculty Survey: National Comparison Report for Faculty Respondents," http://www.radford.edu/~assessmt/ Final%20Report_HERI05_Report_Faculty.pdf, 14; Radford University, "Higher Education Research Institute, 2004–05 Faculty Survey: National Comparison Report for Administrators," http://www.radford.edu/~assessmt/Final%20Report_HERI05_Report_Administration.pdf, 13.

38. Gary Tobin and Aryeh Weinberg, *A Profile of American College Faculty,* vol. 1, *Political Beliefs & Behavior* (San Francisco: The Institute for Jewish and Community Research, 2006), 9–10, http://www.jewishresearch.org/PDFs2/FacultySurvey_Web.pdf.

39. Peter Hart Research Associates, "Report Findings Based upon a Survey of American College Students." Panetta Institute, June 13, 2006, 6.

40. Rothman, Lichter, and Nevitte, "Politics and Professional Advancement among College Faculty."

41. Harris Press Release, "Harris Polls throughout 2005 Suggest Modest Gain by Democrats in Party Affiliation," January 18, 2006, http://www.harrisinteractive.com/harris_poll/ index.asp?PID=630.

42. Denise Glover and Basmat Parsad, "The Gender and Racial/Ethnic Composition of Postsecondary Instructional Faculty and Staff: 1992–98," *Education Statistics Quarterly* 4, no. 3 (2003), http://nces.ed.gov/programs/quarterly/vol_4/4_3/4_6.asp#Table-5A; U.S. Census Bureau, "Table DP-1: Profile of General Demographic Characteristics: 2000," http://www. census.gov/prod/cen2000/dp1/2kh00.pdf.

43. Ibid.

44. Anne Neal speech, "A 'Liberal' Education?" American Enterprise Institute conference, February 14, 2005, http://www.aei.org/events/filter.economic,eventID.993/transcript. asp; ACTA press release, "Survey Reveals Pervasive Political Pressure in the Classroom," November 30, 2004.

45. Editorial, "A Chill in the Classroom: Liberal Professors Routinely Harass Conservative Students," *Wall Street Journal,* December 3, 2004, http://www.opinionjournal.com/ taste/?id=110005976.

46. Ibid.

47. ACTA press release, "Survey Reveals Pervasive Political Pressure in the Classroom."

48. Zipp and Fenwick, "Is the Academy a Liberal Hegemony?"

49. Neal, "A 'Liberal' Education?"

50. Independent Women's Forum, "The Forgotten Generation: IWF Nationwide Survey of College Students," January 14, 2004, http://www.iwf.org/campuscorner/news/news_detail. asp?ArticleID=446.

51. A Harvard Institute on Politics poll in March 2006 of students nationwide found that 33 percent considered themselves liberal and only 19 percent conservative. See http://www. ksg.harvard.edu/iop/pdfs/survey/spring_poll_2006_topline.pdf.

52. Independent Women's Forum, "The Forgotten Generation: IWF Nationwide Survey of College Students."

53. Ibid.

54. Ibid.

55. David Horowitz blog, "The Politics of Personal Destruction," http://www.frontpagemag.com/Blog/Read.aspx?guid=60f3497e-ffd7-4cf4-b634-4cb195d90b80.

56. Andrew Jones, "The Fight for Academic Freedom at UCLA," UCLAprofs.com, June 21, 2006, http://www.uclaprofs.com/articles/uclaprofsbooklet.html.

57. Cindy Chang, "Conservative Alumnus Pulls Offer to Buy Lecture Tapes," *New York Times*, January 24, 2006.

58. "Election 2004," *Lawrence Journal-World*, http://ljworld.com/specials/election04.

59. David Horowitz and Eli Lehrer, "Representation of Political Perspectives in Law and Journalism Faculties," FrontPageMag.com, October 11, 2005, http://www.frontpagemag.com/media/pdf/JournalismandLawStudy.pdf; John Tierney, "Where Cronies Dwell," *New York Times*, October 11, 2005.

60. See Arthur Brooks, "The Fertility Gap," *Wall Street Journal*, August 22, 2006, http://www.opinionjournal.com/editorial/feature.html?id=110008831.

61. Letter, *Newsweek*, February 14, 2005, 17, http://www.msnbc.msn.com/id/6919082.

62. Fred Barnes speech, Collegiate Network 25th Anniversary dinner, Washington, D.C., December 2, 2004.

63. U.S. Department of Labor, *Bureau of Labor Statistics' Occupational Outlook Handbook 2006–07*, http://www.bls.gov/oco/ocos053.htm#earnings.

64. Julie Stolberg and Karen Hauptman, "Humanities Alumni Struggle to Find Jobs," *Duke Chronicle*, April 27, 2005.

65. James Monks, "The Relative Earnings of Contingent Faculty in Higher Education," December 2004, http://www.ilr.cornell.edu/cheri/wp/cheri_wp59.pdf.

66. Scott Jaschik, "Saving Higher Education in the Age of Money," InsideHigherEd.com, May 11, 2005, http://www.insidehighered.com/news/2005/05/11/engell.

67. Scott Jaschik, "The Eroding Faculty Paycheck," InsideHigherEd.com, April 24, 2006, http://insidehighered.com/news/2006/04/24/salaries.

68. Department of Education, "Table 234. Average base salary of full-time faculty and instructional staff in degree-granting institutions, by type and control of institution and field of instruction: Selected years, 1987–1988 through 2003–2004 [In 2004–05 dollars]," *Digest of Educational Statistics*, 2005, http://nces.ed.gov/programs/digest/d05/tables/dt05_234.asp.

69. *The Simpsons*, episode 355, "Home Away from Homer," http://www.answers.com/topic/home-away-from-homer.

70. Jeremy Beer, ed., *Choosing the Right College 2005: The Whole Truth about America's Top Schools* (Wilmington, DE: ISI Books, 2004), xxxi.

71. Arthur C. Brooks, "Right-Wing Heart, Left-Wing Heart," CBSNews.com, April 11, 2006, http://www.cbsnews.com/stories/2006/04/11/opinion/main1489914.shtml. See also Woessner and Kelly-Woessner, "Left Pipeline."

72. Robert G. Natelson, "Conservatives in a Liberal Landscape," *Chronicle of Higher Education Colloquy Live*, September 23, 2004, http://chronicle.com/colloquylive/2004/09/discrimination.

73. Kenneth Wagner, "Think Tanks: The Educational Counter-Establishment," NAS Online Forum, September 8, 2005, http://www.nas.org/forum.html.

74. Editorial, "Political Quotas in Higher Education?" *Rocky Mountain News*, September 9, 2003.

75. Ibid.

76. See Stephen Hegarty and Matthew Waite, "Teachers Do Not Vote in One Bloc," *St. Petersburg Times*, January 5, 2003.

77. U.S. Department of Labor, Bureau of Labor Statistics' Occupational Outlook Handbook 2006–07, http://www.bls.gov/oco/ocos069.htm#earnings.

78. See "United States Presidential Election, 2004," http://en.wikipedia.org/wiki/U.S._presidential_election%2C_2004_%28detail%29; because of the small number of Libertarians and the problems with Klein and Stern's dataset, this survey should not be regarded as definitive.

79. See Zipp and Fenwick, "Is the Academy a Liberal Hegemony?"

80. Roger Bowen speech, "A 'Liberal' Education? The Effects of Ideology in the Classroom," American Enterprise Institute conference, February 14, 2005, http://www.aei.org/events/filter.economic,eventID.993/transcript.asp.

81. Joseph Reisert, "Rethinking the Culture Wars—II," InsideHigherEd.com, August 22, 2006, http://insidehighered.com/views/2006/08/22/reisert.

82. Stephen Balch, "The Antidote to Academic Orthodoxy," *Chronicle of Higher Education*, April 23, 2004, at B7–B9; see also Klein, "A 'Liberal' Education?"

83. David Horowitz, "Ward Churchill Is Just the Beginning," *Rocky Mountain News*, February 9, 2005.

84. Figure calculated from the Rothman study, which found that a minimum of 11 percent of faculty are Republicans, out of the more than 1 million faculty members nationwide.

85. Gara LaMarche, "The Crisis of Democracy in America." OpenDemocracy.net, June 30, 2005, http://www.opendemocracy.net/globalization-institutions_government/democracy_2639.jsp.

86. Ibid.

Notes to Chapter Five

1. "Academic Freedom's Thin Line," *Black Issues in Higher Education*, March 11, 2004.

2. Jon Sanders, "Conservatives on Campus Speak Out against Ideological Intolerance," *Clarion Call* No. 185, December 13, 2002, http://www.johnlocke.org/news_columns/display_story.html?id=647.

3. Kenneth Aaron, "Students Fight to be Right," *Albany Times Union*, May 2, 2005.

4. John Miller, "Fear and Loathing," *National Review*, March 12, 2004.

5. Doug Giles, "Rebels with a Cause," Townhall.com, March 5, 2005, http://www.townhall.com/columnists/douggiles/dg20050305.shtml.

6. John Plecnik, "Hippies Lose Protest Movement to Campus Conservatives," Theconservativevoice.com, January 10, 2005.

7. John Colapinto, "The Young Hipublicans," *New York Times Magazine*, May 25, 2003.

8. Collegiate Network 25th Anniversary Dinner, Washington, D.C., December 3, 2004.

9. David Horowitz, "The Strange and Dishonest Campaign against Academic Freedom," FrontpageMag.com, April 29, 2005, http://www.studentsforacademicfreedom.org/archive/2005/April2005/DHStrangeandDishonestCampaign042905.htm.

10. Jeff Jacoby, "A Left-wing Monopoly on Campuses," *Boston Globe*, December 2, 2004.

11. R. Scott Moxley, "Campus Radicals," *OC Weekly* (Orange County, CA), May 9, 2003, 18.

12. Walter Williams, "America's Academic Tyrants," *Chattanooga Times Free Press*, September 7, 2003.

13. *Rush Limbaugh* show, June 1, 2004.

14. Ben Shapiro, *Brainwashed: How Universities Indoctrinate America's Youth* (Medford, OR: WND Books, 2004), xv.

15. Ibid., xvi.

16. Ibid., 6.

17. Ibid., 22.

18. Ibid., 23.

19. Ibid., 10.

20. Ibid., 100.

21. Ibid., 102.

22. Ibid., 84.

23. Ibid., 114.

24. Ibid., 115.

25. Ibid., 116.

26. Ibid., 179–180.

27. "Brainwashed: An Interview with Ben Shapiro," FrontPageMagazine. com, May 13, 2004, http://studentsforacademicfreedom.org/archive/May2004/ BenShapirofpageinterview051304.htm.

28. Sara Dogan, "A Pie Attack and More Hearings on the ABOR," April 12, 2005, studentsforacademicfreedom.org.

29. Horowitz blog, "Pied in Indiana," FrontPageMag.com, April 6, 2005.

30. Horowitz blog, "The President of Butler Apologizes and Takes a Stand for Academic Freedom," FrontPageMag.com, April 7, 2005.

31. Karen Rivedal, "'In the Eye Of The Storm,'" *Wisconsin State Journal,* February 24, 2005, http://www.madison.com/archives/read.php?ref=/wsj/2005/02/24/0502240023. php.

32. Brian C. Anderson, "On Campus, Conservatives Talk Back," *City Journal,* Winter 2005, http://www.city-journal.org/html/15_1_campus_conservatives.html.

33. Marissa Brookes, "Campus Right Unite? Are the Kids All Right?" *The Student Underground,* November 2004, 6–7.

34. Karen Paget, "Lessons of Right-Wing Philanthropy," *American Prospect,* September 1, 1998–October 1, 1998, http://www.prospect.org/print/V9/40/paget-k.html.

35. Lee Kaplan, "Palestinian Terror on Campus," FrontPageMagazine.com, November 23, 2004.

36. James Sullivan, "A Work of Art or a Harbinger of Violence?" *San Francisco Chronicle,* March 25, 2004, http://sfgate.com/cgi-bin/article.cgi?file=/c/a/2004/03/25/ MNGI85QTK11.DTL.

37. Heidi Benson, "Class Takes to Street to Protest Censorship," *San Francisco Chronicle,* April 8, 2004, http://www.sfgate.com/cgi-bin/article.cgi?f=/c/a/2004/04/08/ BAGNF61TM449.DTL&hw=Jan+Richman+Alan+Kaufman&sn=002&sc=541.

38. Rob Capriccioso, "Facebook Face Off," InsideHigherEd.com, February 14, 2006.

39. FIRE Press Release, "Student Wins Facebook.com Case at University of Central Florida," March 6, 2006.

40. Bucknell University Conservatives Club, "Bucknell Bars Rep. Pat Toomey," BucknellConservatives.org, April 5, 2004, http://www.frontpagemag.com/Articles/ ReadArticle.asp?ID=12858.

41. Charles Mitchell, "The Most Despicable Double Standard of 2005," Thefire.org, December 27, 2005.

42. Ibid.

43. Jim Brown and Jody Brown, "College Revamps Policy after Banning *The Passion.*" Agape Press, February 4, 2005; FIRE Press Release, "Victory for Free Speech at Indian River Community College," February 2, 2005, http://www.thefire.org/index.php/article/5211. html.

44. FIRE Press Release, "Major Victory for Free Speech at Cal Poly," May 6, 2004, http:// www.thefire.org/index.php/article/152.html.

45. "President Hamilton's Memo," March 13, 2001, http://www.thefire.org/index. php/article/4943.html.

46. Christina Littlefield, "Effort to Punish UNLV Professor Gains Exposure," *Las Vegas Sun,* February 8, 2005.

47. Ronald Radosh, "Purging Professors," *New York Sun,* November 26, 2002, http:// www.frontpagemag.com/Articles/Printable.asp?ID=4784; Robert David Johnson, Senate Committee Hearing, "Is Intellectual Diversity an Endangered Species on America's College Campuses," October 29, 2003, http://frwebgate.access.gpo.gov/cgi-bin/getdoc. cgi?dbname=108_senate_hearings&docid=90-304.

48. "Letter from the National Campus Director," studentsforacademicfreedom.org, October 5, 2004; James Miller, "Endangered Species: Enjoy Perilous Work? Try Being a Conservative on a College Campus in Massachusetts," *Forbes,* June 7, 2004.

49. Jamilah Evelyn, "Texas College Grants Tenure to Marxist Professor Despite Community Protests," *Chronicle of Higher Education,* March 27, 2002.

50. Nick Mamatas, "Take It from the Top," *Village Voice,* June 6, 2005, http://villagevoice. com/people/0523,interview,64691,24.html.

51. David Epstein, "Early Exit," InsideHigherEd.com, May 18, 2005, http://www. insidehighered.com/news/2005/05/18/yale.

52. Joshua Frank, "Without Cause: Yale Fires an Acclaimed Anarchist Scholar," *Counterpunch,* May 13, 2005, http://www.counterpunch.org/frank05132005.html; Andrej Grubacic, "In Support of David Graeber," *San Francisco Indymedia,* May 11, 2005, http://sf.indymedia. org/news/2005/05/1714403.php; Julie Post, "Graeber Appeals Decision," *Yale Daily News,* September 8, 2005.

53. AAUP, "Report on Academic Freedom and Tenure: Medaille College," http://www. aaup.org/Com-a/Institutions/archives/2004/04mc.htm.

54. Tina Dirmann, "Charges Fly at Riverside College over Suspension," *Los Angeles Times,* May 23, 2002.

55. Dan Atkinson, "COM Dean Baker, Film and TV Dept. Chair Lawson Forced Out of Positions," *Boston University Daily Free Press,* July 10, 2003, http://www.dailyfreepress.com/ home/index.cfm?event=displayArticlePrinterFriendly&uStory_id=8a93ff22-a866-4177-b0bd-6639dc31c2ef; see also John K. Wilson, *The Myth of Political Correctness: The Conservative Attack on Higher Education* (Durham, NC: Duke University Press, 1995).

56. Scott Smallwood, "Faculty Group Censures Benedict College Again, This Time over 'A for Effort' Policy," *Chronicle of Higher Education,* January 21, 2005, 11.

57. Thomas Bartlett, "Move to Fire 2 Professors Roils Campus in Mississippi," *Chronicle of Higher Education,* March 19, 2004, http://chronicle.com/subscribe/login?url=/weekly/ v50/i28/28a00101.htm.

58. Scott Smallwood, "2 Professors at U. of Southern Mississippi Settle for Pay Without Jobs," *Chronicle of Higher Education,* May 14, 2004, http://chronicle.com/subscribe/ login?url=/weekly/v50/i36/36a01402.htm; Rachel Quinlivan, "Faculty Supports 'No Confidence,'" *Hattiesburg American,* March 10, 2004, http://www.hattiesburgamerican.com/news/ stories/20040310/localnews/51372.html.

59. David French, "Conformity on Campus," *American Enterprise,* June 1, 2005.

60. Foundation for Individual Rights in Education, "FIRE's Spotlight," http://thefire. org/index.php/article/5826.html, as of October 2007.

61. Duke University, "Harassment Policy and Procedures," 2005, http://www.duke. edu/web/equity/har_policy.htm.

62. University of Pennsylvania, "Sexual Harassment Handbook," http://www.upenn. edu/affirm-action/introsh.html#3.

63. University of Pennsylvania, "Guidelines on Open Expression," http://www.vpul. upenn.edu/osl/openexp.html.

64. Dartmouth College, "The Academic Honor Principle," http://www.dartmouth. edu/~deancoll/documents/handbook/conduct/standards/honor.html; "Dartmouth Community Standards of Conduct," http://www.dartmouth.edu/~deancoll/documents/ handbook/conduct/standards/conduct.html.

65. Bucks County Community College Code of Conduct, http://www.bucks.edu/ catalog/concode.html.

66. Duke University, "Disorderly Conduct," http://judicial.studentaffairs.duke.edu/ policies/policy_list/disorderly_conduct.html.

67. Carnegie Mellon University, "Disorderly Conduct," 1999, http://www.cmu.edu/ policies/documents/Conduct.html.

68. University of Tennessee, "Standards of Conduct," http://web.utk.edu/~homepage/ hilltopics/HILLTOPICS2005-06.pdf#page=11, 12.

69. Dartmouth College *Handbook,* "Sponsored Visits of/by Political Candidates," http://www.dartmouth.edu/~deancoll/documents/handbook/rules-regs/spon-vis-pol-cand. html.

70. University of Pennsylvania, "Student Activities Council Funding Policies and Guidelines for Student Groups," http://www.vpul.upenn.edu/osl/fundpol.html; "Political Candidates" policy, http://www.vpul.upenn.edu/osl/polcand.html.

Notes

71. Washington & Lee University Student Handbook, 2006–2007, http://studentaffairs. wlu.edu/deanofstudents/Student%20Handbook.htm.

72. Cleveland State University, "Student Code of Conduct," 2004, http://www.csuohio. edu/studentlife/conduct/scc.html.

73. University of Nebraska, "Board of Regents Policies," http://www.nebraska.edu/ board/RegentPolicies.pdf, 116.

74. Elizabeth City State University Policies and Procedures Manual, June 14, 2005, http://www.ecsu.edu/forms/facultystaff/policymanual.pdf, 663.

75. Ibid., 646.

76. Ibid., 660–661.

77. Greg Lukianoff, "The Speech Code of the Month," Thefire.org, February 14, 2005.

78. Antioch College Sexual Harassment Policy, 1985, in *The Antioch Solution*, 2005–2006, http://www.antioch-college.edu/Academics/registrar/catalogs/CatalogDEC052006.pdf, at 25.

79. Antioch Civil Liberties Code, 1959, in *The Antioch Solution*, 23–24.

80. Rebecca McNulty, "N.Y. College Settles Lawsuit with Students Who Challenged Campus Speech Codes," Student Press Law Center, June 22, 2005.

81. Matthew Daneman, "College Settles Case, Will Revise Its Speech Code." *Rochester Democrat and Chronicle,* May 11, 2005.

82. Associated Press, "Georgia Tech Retracts Policy Banning Offensive Speech," August 17, 2006, http://www.firstamendmentcenter.org/news.aspx?id=17285.

83. Sara Dogan, "Speech Code Demolished at Georgia Tech," Students forAcademicFreedom.org, September 21, 2006, http://www.studentsforacademic freedom.org/letters/LettersAug-Dec2006/letter-RuthMalhotraGATechSpeechCode VIctory092106.htm.

84. Doug Lederman, "Freer Speech at Georgia Tech," InsideHigherEd.com, August 16, 2006, http://insidehighered.com/news/2006/08/16/speech.

85. Paul Fain, "Judge Dismisses UVA Free-Speech Case," *Chronicle of Higher Education,* April 6, 2007, http://chronicle.com/weekly/v53/i31/31a03403.htm.

86. Stuart Taylor Jr., "Failing the First Amendment," *Legal Times,* July 14, 2003.

87. Gerald A. Reynolds memo, Office of Civil Rights, July 28, 2003, http://www.thefire. org/pdfs/ocr_fire_072803.pdf.

88. Marissa Levy, "George Washington U. Officials Agree to Meet with Dismissed Sex Prof," *GW Hatchet,* September 26, 2005.

89. See AAUP, "Sexual Harassment: Suggested Policy and Procedures for Handling Complaints," 1995, http://www.aaup.org/AAUP/pubsres/policydocs/contents/sexharass. htm.

90. Associated Press, "UND 'Sioux' Tag Cited for 'Unwelcome' Environment," WCCO, October 3, 2007, http://wcco.com/sports/local_story_276105205.html.

91. Scott Jaschik, "Student Government in Exile," InsideHigherEd.com, July 7, 2006, http://www.insidehighered.com/news/2006/07/07/newpaltz.

92. Scott Jaschik, "George Carlin Need Not Apply," InsideHigherEd.com, March 8, 2006, http://insidehighered.com/news/2006/03/08/language.

93. Chris Branm, "Fayetteville: Professor Removed over Foul Language," *Arkansas Democrat-Gazette,* March 18, 2006, http://www.nwanews.com/adg/News/149002/.

94. Grayson Steinberg, "Offensive Assignment? Just Skip It," *ASU State Press,* March 6, 2006, http://www.statepress.com/issues/2006/03/06/news/696103.

95. Scott Jaschik, "Avoid Whatever Offends You," InsideHigher Ed.com, February 17, 2006, http://www.insidehighered.com/news/2006/02/17/ariz.

96. Bill Morrow and Mark Wyland, "California Campuses Majoring in Indoctrination," *North County Times* (Escondido, CA), April 1, 2005, http://www.nctimes.com/ articles/2005/04/01/opinion/commentary/23_13_113_31_05.txt.

97. Laura Youngs, "Academic Showdown in North Carolina," *Daily Tar Heel* (Chapel Hill, NC), April 4, 2005.

Notes

98. See Mick Swasko, "University Threatens Site with Possible Legal Action," *Daily Vidette,* March 23, 2005, http://www.dailyvidette.com/media/paper420/news/2005/03/23/News/University.Threatens.Site.With.Possible.Legal.Action-900703.shtml.

99. Diane Roberts, "Zoned Out," *New Republic,* May 13, 2002, http://www.thenewrepublic.com/doc.mhtml?i=20020513&s=roberts051302.

100. Melanie Yeager, "Tent City Comes Down at FSU," *Tallahassee Democrat,* July 17, 2002, http://www.tallahassee.com/mld/tallahassee/news/local/3676969.htm.

101. Margaret Kohn, *Brave New Neighborhoods: The Privatization of Public Space* (New York: Routledge, 2004), 40–41.

102. Jordan Green, "Student Arrest at UNCG Highlights Restrictive Assembly Policy," *Yes! Weekly* (Greensboro, NC), September 4, 2007, http://yesweekly.com/main.asp?Search=1&ArticleID=2788&SectionID=1&SubSectionID=&S=1.

103. Ibid.

104. "Bake Sale Creates Controversy at GVSU," WXMI.com, March 25, 2005.

105. John Leo, "Baking with Fire." *U.S. News & World Report,* April 18, 2005.

106. Charles Mitchell, "Liberating America's Intellectual Gulags," *Campus Magazine,* March 31, 2005, http://www.campusmagazine.org/articledetail.aspx?id=8950bdfc-efba-4482-b084-d88d4715d93d.

107. See the Illinois Public Accommodation law, 775 ILCS 5/5 101.

108. Associated Press, "Ohio State Cancels Hempfest," June 4, 2004, http://cannabisnews.com/news/18/thread18926.shtml; Matt Peiken, "College Cancels Marijuana Festival," *St. Paul Pioneer Press,* April 21, 2006, http://www.twincities.com/mld/pioneerpress/14394203.htm.

109. Fred Kelly, "Mock Bake Sale Ignites Racial Tension, Anger," *Charlotte Observer,* February 11, 2005.

110. See Cathy Young, "Under the Radar: Political Correctness Never Died," *Reason,* July 2004.

111. "Clinton Crowd Featured Again: Liberals Dominate Spring Commencement Exercises," Young America's Foundation, June 17, 2004, http://www.freerepublic.com/focus/f-news/1155574/posts.

112. Ibid. Since YAF made the attack in 2004, Yale invited Eleanor Holmes Norton, Anderson Cooper, and Fareed Zakaria as commencement speakers.

113. David Horowitz, "Study of Bias in the Selection of Commencement Speakers at 32 Elite Colleges and Universities," StudentsforAcademicFreedom.org, August 28, 2003, http://www.studentsforacademicfreedom.org/reports/liberalbias.html.

114. "From the Desk of David Horowitz," FrontpageMag.com, cached at http://web.archive.org/web/20040204010434/http://www.frontpagemag.com/Content/read.asp?ID=50.

115. David Horowitz blog, FrontPagemag.com, May 2, 2004.

116. PR Newswire, "PROFNET ROUND-UP: 2005 Commencement Speakers," April 26, 2005, http://www.advfn.com/news_PROFNET-ROUND-UP-2005-Commencement-Speakers_11108990.html.

117. *Chronicle of Higher Education,* "Commencement Speakers 2006," March 19, 2007, http://chronicle.com/free/speakers/index.php3?handler=search&Last_Name=&Institution=&State=&year=2006&order=&all=1.

118. Nat Hentoff, "Is Free Speech Un-American?" *Jewish World Review,* January 7, 2002, http://www.jewishworldreview.com/cols/hentoff010702.asp.

119. Brandon Keim, "The Jihad Against 'Jihad,'" Commondreams.org, June 7, 2002, http://www.commondreams.org/views02/0607-07.htm.

120. Greg Pierce, "Inside Politics," *Washington Times,* May 28, 2003, http://www.washtimes.com/national/20030528-120428-9461r.htm.

121. Peggy Noonan, "Doctorow's Malpractice: Hofstra Students Use Boos Responsibly," Opinionjournal.com, May 25, 2004.

122. Carrie Watters, "Speaker Disrupts RC Graduation," *Rockford Register Star,* May 20, 2003, http://www.rrstar.com/localnews/your_community/rockford/hedgescoverage.shtml.

123. Oliver North, "Campus Critics," FreedomAlliance.org, May 22, 2003, http://www.freedomalliance.org/view_article.php?a_id=272.

124. *Hannity and Colmes,* Fox News Channel, May 21, 2003.

125. Interview with Chris Hedges, *Democracy Now!* May 21, 2003, http://www.alternet.org/story/15982/.

126. Cathy Young, "The Tyranny of Hecklers," *Boston Globe,* June 2, 2003, www.thefire.org/pdfs/4186_2495.pdf.

127. Amy Argetsinger, "3 Students Face U-Md. Action for Shouting at Cheney Speech," *Washington Post,* April 5, 2004, http://www.washingtonpost.com/ac2/wp-dyn/A50129-2004 Apr4?language=printer.

128. Rachel Laskow, "Administration Does Not Approve Speaker," *Bucknellian,* October 11, 2002, http://www.thefire.org/index.php/article/4817.html?PHPSESSID=...http://www.campusconservatives.com/updates/000017.html.

129. Scott Jaschik, "Hate at Carnegie Mellon," InsideHigherEd.com, February 22, 2005, http://www.insidehighered.com/insider/hate_at_carnegie_mellon.

130. Avraham Sinensky, "Censorship, Polarization, and Torah U'Madda," *The Yeshiva Commentator,* May 19, 2004, http://www.yucommentator.com/home/index.cfm?event=displayArticlePrinterFriendly&uStory_id=db74fc21-38ca-4a84-9c60-5c69124d8a6b.

131. Glen Kissel, "University of Southern Indiana Turnaround," Campus Report Online, April 16, 2007, http://www.campusreportonline.net/main/articles.php?id=1614.

132. Matt Snyders, "Banning Desmond Tutu," *City Pages* (Minneapolis/St. Paul), October 3, 2007, http://articles.citypages.com/2007-10-03/news/banning-desmond-tutu.

133. Desmond Tutu, "Ending the Occupation," Boston, April 13, 2002, http://blogs.citypages.com/blotter/2007/10/a_transcript_of.php.

134. Snyders, "Banning Desmond Tutu."

135. Associated Press, "College Dumps Lecturer after Learning about His Beef with Beef," FreedomForum.org, August 31, 2001, http://www.freedomforum.org/templates/document.asp?documentID=14766.

136. Scott Jaschik, "Banned in Akron," InsideHigherEd.com, February 5, 2007, http://insidehighered.com/news/2007/02/05/akron.

137. Danny Postel, "Sidney Hook, an Intellectual Street Fighter, Reconsidered," *Chronicle of Higher Education,* November 8, 2002, http://chronicle.com/free/v49/i11/11a01801.htm.

138. Eliana Johnson, "Columbia Withdraws an Invitation to Ahmadinejad," *New York Sun,* September 22, 2006, http://www.nysun.com/article/40142.

139. Doug Lederman, "Watch Out Whom You Invite to Speak," InsideHigherEd.com, September 28, 2007, http://www.insidehighered.com/news/2007/09/28/hunter.

140. Andy Guess, "Slap on the Wrist at Columbia?" InsideHigherEd.com, March 28, 2007, http://www.insidehighered.com/news/2007/03/28/columbia.

141. Intercollegiate Study Institute, "2006 Campus Outrage Awards," http://www.campusmagazine.org/articledetail.aspx?id=490d8620-3158-4d55-9be6-9866fd1ceefb.

142. Intercollegiate Study Institute, "2005 Campus Outrage Awards," http://www.campusmagazine.org/articledetail.aspx?id=4ff8775f-04a8-45c7-b61c-e6a8f9f157a5.

143. Intercollegiate Study Institute, "2004 Campus Outrage Awards," http://www.isi.org/cn/pollys/polly04.aspx.

144. Intercollegiate Study Institute, "2003 Campus Outrage Awards," http://www.isi.org/cn/pollys/polly03.aspx.

145. Intercollegiate Study Institute, "2002 Campus Outrage Awards," http://www.isi.org/cn/pollys/polly02.aspx.

146. Intercollegiate Study Institute, "2001 Campus Outrage Awards," http://www.isi.org/cn/pollys/polly01.aspx.

147. *Board of Regents v. Southworth,* 529 U.S. 217 (2000); see http://www.campusspeech.org/southworth.html.

148. Press release, "Jones Joins the Battle to Remove Partisan Politics from Universities and Schools," October 20, 2003, http://jones.house.gov/html/release.cfm?id=136.

149. Sara Russo [Dogan], "Academic Bill of Rights Goes to Washington," FrontpageMag.com, October 23, 2003, http://www.frontpagemag.com/Content/read.asp?ID=66.

150. Editorial, "The Nutty Professor," *Investor's Business Daily*, February 2, 2005.

151. Dinesh D'Souza, *Letters to a Young Conservative* (New York: Basic Books, 2002), 135.

152. David Horowitz, *The Professors* (Washington, DC: Regnery, 2006), xviii.

153. Roger Custer, "Building an Existing Campus Organization," in Patrick Coyle and Ron Robinson, eds., *The Conservative Guide to Campus Activism*, 2d ed. (Herndon, VA: Young America's Foundation, 2005), 36.

154. David French, "Michael Moore and the Scandal of Student Fees," FrontPageMagazine.com, November 11, 2004.

155. Ibid.

156. Ben Shapiro, "Cleaning Up the College Republicans," Townhall.com, March 23, 2005.

157. Matt Anderson, "Victory for Academic Freedom at Middle Tennessee State U," MTSU Sidelines Online, March 17, 2005.

158. Jeremy Beer, ed., *Choosing the Right College 2005: The Whole Truth about America's Top Schools* (Wilmington, DE: ISI Books, 2004), 942.

159. Jason Mattera, "The Activist Mentality," in Coyle and Robinson, eds., *The Conservative Guide to Campus Activism*, 1–6.

160. Ibid.

161. Ibid.

Notes to Chapter Six

1. Jodi Mardesich, "Pass or Fail," *The Advocate*, September 25, 2001, http://www.findarticles.com/p/articles/mi_m1589/is_2001_Sept_25/ai_78682400.

2. Ibid.

3. Ibid.

4. Kirsten Stewart, "BYU Brass Suspend Two Gays," *Salt Lake Tribune*, March 29, 2001, http://www.lds-mormon.com/gays_byu.shtml?FACTNet.

5. John Hyde, "Gay Rights Group 'Soulforce' to Visit BYU to Protest," *NYU NewsNet*, March 24, 2006, http://nn.byu.edu/story.cfm/59044.

6. Elia Powers, "Column on Gay Marriage Prompts Dismissal," InsideHigherEd.com, June 15, 2006, http://insidehighered.com/news/2006/06/15/byu.

7. Shinika A. Sykes, "Former Worker Accuses BYU of Wrongful Firing," *Salt Lake Tribune*, March 24, 2006.

8. Daniel Golden, "Expelled Scholar of Mormon History Can't Find Work," *Wall Street Journal*, April 6, 2006, http://www.post-gazette.com/pg/06100/680357-84.stm.

9. Committee Report, AAUP, "Albertus Magnus College," http://www.aaup.org/publications/Academe/2000/00jf/JF00AlbM.htm.

10. James M. O'Neill, "Religious Colleges Walk a Fine Line," *Philadelphia Inquirer*, May 6, 2003.

11. Curtis Lawrence, "Teacher Says School Won't Hire Her Because She's Lesbian," *Chicago Sun-Times*, December 4, 2003.

12. "North Park University Statement to the Press," December 5, 2003, http://www.covchurch.org/cov/news/item3388.html.

13. Art Jester, "Baptist School Ousts Gay Student," *Herald-Leader* (Lexington, KY), April 8, 2006, http://www.kentucky.com/mld/kentucky/news/state/14294381.htm.

14. David Kushner, "Face to Face," *Rolling Stone*, April 20, 2006, 30.

15. Scott Jaschik, "Baylor Dismisses Gay Alumnus from Advisory Board," InsideHigherEd.com, November 10, 2005, http://insidehighered.com/news/2005/11/10/baylor.

16. Cardinal Newman Society, Catholic Higher Education Alert, February 18, 2005; "Med School That Banned Gay Group Can't Ce Cited by Human Hights Commission," *Newsday*, March 30, 2005; a similar group was later allowed to exist without "gay" in its name.

17. Elia Powers, "No Room for a Gay Group," InsideHigherEd.com, February 26, 2007, http://www.insidehighered.com/news/2007/02/26/hampton.

18. Scott Jaschik, "Recognition with Limits," InsideHigherEd.com, December 19, 2005. http://insidehighered.com/news/2005/12/19/duquesne.

19. Sarah Schweitzer, "Abortion Rights Group Causes Stir at BC," *Boston Globe*, March 2, 2006.

20. Sue Lindsey, "Gay Rights Activists Arrested at Jerry Falwell's University," *Duluth News Tribune*, March 10, 2006, http://www.duluthsuperior.com/mld/duluthsuperior/14068727.htm.

21. Kay Miller, "Compassion Crusader," *Minneapolis Star Tribune*, March 13, 2006.

22. David Epstein, "Journalism That Dare Not Speak Its Name," InsideHigherEd.com, April 11, 2006, http://insidehighered.com/news/2006/04/11/newspaper.

23. Frank E. Lockwood, "Putting Faith before Freedom," *Herald-Leader* (Lexington, KY), May 7, 2006, http://www.ohio.com/mld/kentucky/news/state/14520982.htm?source=rss&channel=kentucky_state.

24. Ibid.

25. Ibid.

26. Goldie Blumenstyk, "Back in the Saddle at Boston University," *Chronicle of Higher Education*, October 11, 2002, http://chronicle.com/free/v49/i07/07a02901.htm.

27. Nick Beadle, "Gay Book Ban Would Limit Theater," *Alabama Crimson White* (Tuscaloosa, AL), January 10, 2005, http://www.cw.ua.edu/vnews/display.v/ART/2005/01/10/41e250508a21d.

28. "Gay Book Ban Goal of State Lawmaker; Homosexual Subjects Targets of Bill," *Birmingham News*, December 1, 2004, http://www.washblade.com/blog/index.cfm?blog_id=239.

29. Gerald Allen, conference on "Censorship, Free Speech and Free Press in the University," University of Alabama, Tuscaloosa, October 14, 2005.

30. Eric Hoover, "Unfazed (and Unconverted) by Book on the Koran," *Chronicle of Higher Education*, September 6, 2002, http://chronicle.com/weekly/v49/i02/02a04801.htm.

31. Liza Porteus, "U. of Maryland Slammed for Freshmen Reading," FoxNews.com, September 19, 2002, http://www.foxnews.com/story/0,2933,63487,00.html.

32. *Hannity and Colmes*, Fox News Channel, August 27, 2002.

33. Scott Jaschik, "College and Baptists Split over Gay Issues," InsideHigherEd.com, April 8, 2005, http://www.insidehighered.com/news/2005/04/08/baptist.

34. John Blake, "Baptists Vote to End Mercer Ties; State Convention Cites Lack of 'Common Values,'" *Atlanta Journal-Constitution*, November 16, 2005.

35. Jaschik, "College and Baptists Split over Gay Issues."

36. Associated Press, "Florida College Could Lose State Funding over Gay-Christ Play," March 30, 2001, http://www.freedomforum.org/templates/document.asp?documentID=13564.

37. National Coalition Against Censorship, *Censorship News* 89, Spring 2003, http://www.ncac.org/censorship_news/20030418~cn089~The_Long_And_The_Short_Of_It.cfm.

38. *Linnemeir v. Purdue*, 260 F.3d 757 (7th Cir. 2001).

39. Marianne Combs, "The Pope, the Witch, the U and the Church," Minnesota Public Radio, March 1, 2007, http://minnesota.publicradio.org/display/web/2007/02/28/popeplay/?rsssource=1.

40. George Archibald, "'How to be Gay' Course Draws Fire at Michigan," *Washington Times*, August 18, 2003, http://www.washtimes.com/national/20030818-122317-3268r.htm.

41. Brian Charlton, "Rep. Works to Restrict Sexuality Curriculum," *MSU State News*, August 26, 2003, http://www.statenews.com/print.phtml?pk=18602.

42. Robert O'Neil, "Controversial Weblogs and Academic Freedom," *Chronicle of Higher Education*, January 16, 2004.

43. John Milburn, "Regents Approve Policy on Sexual Harassment, Content in Classroom," Associated Press, December 18, 2003; Associated Press, "Kansas Prof's Sexuality Class Methods Prompt State Policy," December 26, 2003, http://www.firstamendmentcenter.

org/news.aspx?id=12396; University of Kansas report on Dennis Dailey, http://www.ur.ku.edu/News/sw303/report.html.

44. Kristina Burlewbio, "LGBTA Expects Censoring of Safer Sex Cabaret," *Penn State Daily Collegian*, March 21, 2001, http://www.collegian.psu.edu/archive/2001/03/03-21-01tdc/03-21-01dnews-1.asp; "Lawmaker Upset by Campus Sex Faire Threatens to Withhold Funding from Penn State," Student Press Law Center, March 13, 2001, http://splc.org/newsflash.asp?id=245&year=2001.

45. Jeremy Beer, ed., *Choosing the Right College 2005: The Whole Truth about America's Top Schools* (Wilmington, DE: ISI Books, 2004), 654.

46. Dale Keiger, "Political Science," *Johns Hopkins Magazine*, November 2004, http://www.jhu.edu/~jhumag/1104web/polysci.html.

47. Benedict Carey, "Long after Kinsey, Only the Brave Study Sex," *New York Times*, November 9, 2004.

48. Union of Concerned Scientists, "Scientific Integrity in Policy Making: An Investigation into the Bush Administration's Misuse of Science," February 18, 2004, http://www.ucsusa.org/scientific_integrity/interference/reports-scientific-integrity-in-policy-making.html, p. 21.

49. Naomi Schaefer Riley, *God on the Quad: How Religious Colleges and the Missionary Generation Are Changing America* (New York: St. Martin's Press, 2005), 121, 199.

50. Leslie Baldacci, "Wheaton College Prof Fired for Converting," *Chicago Sun-Times*, January 10, 2006.

51. Wheaton College, "Community Covenant," http://www.wheaton.edu/welcome/cov/comcov.html.

52. Tara Sweeney, "Ashland University: No Objectivists Need Apply," TheFire.org, July 12, 2007, http://thefire.org/index.php/article/8226.html.

53. Emily Peters, "LC Faculty Opposes Textbook Policy," *TownTalk*, December 6, 2003, http://www.thetowntalk.com/html/00CAC79F-BE4D-4A00-9BBE-436ABF689AF3.shtml.

54. "Textbook Policy Rescinded as La. College Deals with Probation," Associated Press, March 16, 2005.

55. Bruce Nolan, "Baptist College Racked by Strife," *New Orleans Times-Picayune*, November 13, 2004.

56. Ibid.

57. Ted Olsen, "Censoring Christian Films," Christianity Today Weblog, January 13, 2003, http://www.christianitytoday.com/ct/2003/102/11.0.html.

58. Riley, *God on the Quad*.

59. Ibid., 188–189.

60. Ibid., 50.

61. Molly Hennessy-Fiske, "A Clash of Ideas at Evangelical College," *Los Angeles Times*, May 13, 2006, http://www.latimes.com/news/nationworld/nation/la-na-college13may13,1,2794204.story?coll=la-headlines-nation.

62. Thomas Bartlett, "Give Me Liberty or I Quit," *Chronicle of Higher Education*, May 19, 2006.

63. Hennessy-Fiske, "A Clash of Ideas at Evangelical College."

64. Charlie Jackson, "Debating the Fundamentals: Professors Leave PHC in Rift," *Leesburg* (VA) *Today*, May 12, 2006, http://www.leesburg2day.com/current.cfm?catid=5&newsid=12026.

65. Barb Galbincea, "Only Jews, Christians to Be Full-time Faculty at Ashland University," *Cleveland Plain Dealer*, November 9, 2004.

66. Beth McMurtrie, "Do Professors Lose Academic Freedom by Signing Statements of Faith?" *Chronicle of Higher Education*, May 24, 2002.

67. Ibid.

68. Beer, ed., *Choosing the Right College 2005*.

69. Rebecca Green, "Area Religious Colleges Wrestle with Orthodoxy," *Fort Wayne Journal Gazette*, May. 21, 2005.

70. Ibid.

71. McMurtrie, "Do Professors Lose Academic Freedom by Signing Statements of Faith?"

72. Gonzaga press release, "University Adopts Policy on Campus Speakers, Events," September 22, 2003.

73. Cardinal Newman Society, Catholic Higher Education E-Mail Alert, November 1, 2004.

74. Amy Argetsinger, "Catholic U. Ban on Contrary Speakers Protested," *Washington Post*, October 4, 2004, http://prorev.com/freedc.htm#cua.

75. Patrick Healy, "Holy Cross Speech by Church Critic Is Canceled," *Boston Globe*, October 26, 2002, http://www.boston.com/globe/spotlight/abuse/print3/102602_holycross.htm.

76. Tim Mooney, "Katherine Adam: Pro-Choice and Proud," *Boston College Heights*, May 3, 2007, http://media.www.bcheights.com/media/storage/paper144/news/2007/05/03/ActivistProfiles/Katherine.Adam.ProChoice.And.Proud-2893503.shtml.

77. Patrick J. Reilly, "Misinvitation," *National Review Online*, September 13, 2006, http://article.nationalreview.com/?q=ZjdjNDY4ZGM0Nzg2ZjdjMzVjOGY4YzVhZGZlOWViYmU=.

78. McMurtrie, "Do Professors Lose Academic Freedom by Signing Statements of Faith?"

79. Peter Slevin, "Battle on Teaching Evolution Sharpens," *Washington Post*, March 14, 2005, http://www.washingtonpost.com/wp-dyn/articles/A32444-2005Mar13.html.

80. See Timothy Noah, "George W. Bush, The Last Relativist," Slate.com, October 31, 2000, http://www.slate.com/id/1006378.

81. Glenn Collins, "An Evolutionist's Evolution," *New York Times*, November 7, 2005, http://www.nytimes.com/2005/11/07/nyregion/07darwin.html?ei=5090&en=804c21468338bc80&ex=1289019600&partner=rssuserland&emc=rss&pagewanted=print.

82. Ibid.

83. Scott Jaschik, "E-Mails Kill a Course," InsideHigherEd.com, December 2, 2005, http://insidehighered.com/news/2005/12/02/kansas.

84. Mike Hendricks, "Prof's Spite Inflames the Right," *Kansas City Star*, November 30, 2005.

85. "Threats by Religious Group Spark Probe at CU–Boulder," *Denver Post*, July 10, 2007, http://www.denverpost.com/headlines/ci_6336193.

86. Marilyn Rauber, "Creationists Try to Edge around Ban," *Richmond Times Dispatch*, December 5, 2004.

87. McMurtrie, "Do Professors Lose Academic Freedom by Signing Statements of Faith?"

88. Chris Mooney, *The Republican War on Science* (New York: Basic Books, 2005), 176–177.

89. Editorial, "Give Us Liberty," *Christianity Today*, July 8, 2002.

90. Ibid.

91. Ibid.

92. Jamilah Evelyn, "Adjunct Professor Sues Ohio College, Saying He Was Punished for Revealing His Faith in Class," *Chronicle of Higher Education*, July 7, 2004.

93. Jim Brown, "Ousted Christian Prof Optimistic, Sees God's Hand in His Firing," Agapepress.com, March 11, 2005.

94. Elia Powers, "Faith and Fairness," InsideHigherEd.com, July 24, 2007, http://www.insidehighered.com/news/2007/07/24/bcc.

95. *Locke v. Davey*, 540 U.S. 712 (2004), http://www.supremecourtus.gov/opinions/03pdf/02-1315.pdf.

96. Jim Brown, "Community College Changes Speech Policy, Will Allow Christian Club," Agapepress.org, March 19, 2003, http://headlines.agapepress.org/archive/3/192003f.asp.

97. Katie Zezima, "Rhode Island: Students Sue over Sign Removal," *New York Times*, December 5, 2006.

98. Associated Press, "Ex-Theater Student Urges Federal Appeals Panel to Revive Suit," November 20, 2002, http://www.firstamendmentcenter.org/news.aspx?id=3201&printer-friendly=y.

99. *Axson-Flynn v. Johnson,* 151 F. Supp. 2d 1326 (D. Utah 2001), http://www.kscourts.org/ca10/cases/2004/02/01-4176.htm; Mindy Sink, "University Changes Religious Policy," *New York Times,* July 15, 2004.

100. "GRCC Rapped for Choice of Movie," *Grand Rapid Press,* April 12, 2007.

101. Laurie Goodstein, "Air Force Chaplain Says She Was Removed for Being Critical," *New York Times,* May 15, 2005.

102. Editorial, "Chairman Shortell," *New York Sun,* May 18, 2005.

103. *Hannity and Colmes,* Fox News Network, June 3, 2005.

104. Scott Jaschik, "Academic Freedom or Intolerance of Faith?" InsideHigherEd.com, May 26, 2005.

105. Sheryl Gay Stolberg, "First Bush Veto Maintains Limits on Stem Cell Use," *New York Times,* July 20, 2006, http://www.nytimes.com/2006/07/20/washington/20bush.html?ex=1161057600&en=7a80e791aa756f1f&ei=5070.

106. Matthew Franck, "Missouri Senate Shelves Proposal for Ban," *St. Louis Post-Dispatch,* April 6, 2005, http://www.missouricures.com/news_040605SLPD.php.

107. David Epstein, "Doctrinal Differences." InsideHigherEd.com, August 18, 2005.

108. Felicia Lee, "Bishop Protests Notre Dame Films," *New York Times,* February 12, 2005.

109. Cardinal Newman Society, Catholic Higher Education Alert, e-mail, February 18, 2005.

110. John Jenkins, "Academic Freedom and Catholic Character: An Invitation to Reflection and Response," *South Bend Tribune,* January 23, 2006; Jodi Cohen, "Notre Dame Reins in Gay, Women's Events," *Chicago Tribune,* January 25, 2006.

111. Cardinal Newman Society, Catholic Higher Education Alert, e-mail, November 1, 2004; Cardinal Newman Society, Catholic Higher Education Alert, e-mail, February 18, 2005.

112. Scott Jaschik, "Quick Takes," *InsideHigherEd.com,* August 29, 2007, http://www.insidehighered.com/news/2007/08/29/qt.

113. Newman Society Catholic Campus News, May 9, 2003; Associated Press, "Bishops Bow Out of College Commencements," May 23, 2003, http://www.beliefnet.com/story/127/story_12726_1.html.

114. Dennis Coday, "Rites of Spring: Commencement Protests," *National Catholic Reporter,* May 21, 2004, http://findarticles.com/p/articles/mi_m1141/is_29_40/ai_n6062492.

115. Cardinal Newman Society e-mail update, May 12, 2005.

116. Ibid.

117. Ibid.

118. Cardinal Newman Society e-mail alert, May 19, 2005.

119. Katherine Mangan, "Duquesne Students Protest Speaker Ban," *Chronicle of Higher Education,* February 9, 2007, http://chronicle.com/weekly/v53/i23/23a02602.htm.

120. Associated Press, "Protests Force Women's College to Cancel Speaker," *Sioux City Journal,* May 18, 2007, http://www.siouxcityjournal.com/articles/2007/05/18/news/nebraska/6a06e316fb2fef2e862572df000cfaf8.txt.

121. Elizabeth Crawford and Megan Rooney, "Speechless," *Chronicle of Higher Education,* June 6, 2003, http://chronicle.com/weekly/v49/i39/39a00801.htm.

122. Kathryn Lopez, "Catholic Schools Need to Stand for Something," *National Review Online,* May 11, 2005.

123. Bonnie Miller Rubin, "Catholic Group Urging Loyola to Dump Speaker," *Chicago Tribune,* May 19, 2005.

124. Susan C. Thomson, "Herpes Vaccine Trial at St. Louis University Draws Fire from Catholic Group," *St. Louis Post-Dispatch,* February 26, 2003, http://www.bgnews.com/home/index.cfm?event=displayArticlePrinterFriendly&uStory_id=60df95c3-402e-4ae0-95ab-4dfb4316fb9a.

125. Tom Mead, "Catholic Colleges Urged to Cut Ties with Amnesty International," Cardinal Newman Society, July 2, 2007, http://www.cardinalnewmansociety.org/Home/tabid/36/ctl/Details/mid/435/ItemID/32/Default.aspx.

126. Ralph Ranalli and Michael Kranish, "Catholic Group Rips 3 at BC for Stance on Schiavo," *Boston Globe,* August 17, 2005.

127. Rachel Zoll, "Catholic Lawmaker Debate Ensnares Colleges," Associated Press, June 23, 2004, http://www.boston.com/news/nation/articles/2004/06/23/catholic_lawmaker_debate_ensnares_colleges.

128. Julia Duin, "Answer to a Prayer," *Washington Times,* September 8, 2003, http://washingtontimes.com/national/20030908-115633-3265r.htm.

129. "AMU's 'Climate of Fear,'" *Ave Maria Watch,* March 4, 2007, http://www.avewatch.org/files/2083fa77bcb7237009ca4b3f9432d8e3-33.html.

130. "Statement by Archbishop Myers on the Recent Awards Ceremony at Seton Hall Law School," April 19, 2004, http://www.rcan.org/news04/041904pr.htm.

131. Associated Press, "Bishop Calls on Catholics to Snub Pro-choice Speakers," *Topeka Capital-Journal,* February 20, 2004, http://www.freerepublic.com/focus/f-news/1081811/posts.

132. United States Conference of Catholic Bishops, "Catholics in Political Life," June 2004, http://www.usccb.org/bishops/catholicsinpoliticallife.shtml.

133. Cardinal Newman Society News Alert, "CNS Fights to Halt *Monologues* at 30 Colleges," February 8, 2005, http://www.wf-f.org/0205CNS_VMonologues.html.

134. Cardinal Newman Society, Catholic Higher Education E-Mail Alert, January 31, 2006; Cardinal Newman Society E-Mail Alert, "V-Monologues Performances Decline Again," March 8, 2007.

135. David O'Connell, "Statement to CUA's Student Newspaper," *Tower,* January 20, 2006.

136. Brian Shanley, Statement, January 19, 2006, www.providence.edu/Administration/Presidents+Office/Vagina+Monologues.htm.

137. Amy Guckeen, "Upstaged," *Marquette Tribune,* February 23, 2006, http://www.marquettetribune.org/4624253530182.bsp.

138. Associated Baptist Press, "Missouri Baptists Cut Funds for William Jewell College," November 7, 2003, http://www.biblicalrecorder.org/content/news/2003/11_7_2003/ne071103missouri.shtml; Jim Brown, "Missouri Baptists Hold Wm. Jewell College Accountable to Scripture," Agapepress.org, November 13, 2003, http://headlines.agapepress.org/archive/11/132003b.asp.

139. Mary Krones, "Sex Is Normal," *Indy* (Normal, IL), February 9, 2005.

140. Robert Heberle, "Ad Campaign Opposes 'Monologues' Performance," *Georgetown Hoya,* February 27, 2004, http://www.thehoya.com/news/022704/news10.cfm.

141. Bishop John M. D'Arcy, "Concerning a Presentation at Notre Dame," February 12, 2004, http://www.diocesefwsb.org/COMMUNICATIONS/monologues.htm.

142. John Jenkins, "Academic Freedom and Catholic Character: An Invitation to Reflection and Response," *South Bend Tribune,* January 23, 2006, http://www.southbendtribune.com/apps/pbcs.dll/article?AID=/20060123/News01/60123010/CAT=News01; Jodi Cohen, "Notre Dame Reins in Gay, Women's Events," *Chicago Tribune,* January 25, 2006.

143. Eileen Duffy, "Play Faces Constant Changes at ND," *Notre Dame Observer,* March 2, 2007, http://www.ndsmcobserver.com/home/index.cfm?event=displayArticlePrinterFriendly&uStory_id=1f8282c9-0f0f-4724-9e03-11694be582df.

144. Susan Jones, "Catholic Group Blasts Play as Glorification of Sexual Abuse," CNSNews.com, February 17, 2004, http://www.cnsnews.com/ViewPrint.asp?Page=/Culture/archive/200402/CUL20040217b.html.

145. "Faculty Senate Vote, Sept. 9, 2003," *Baylor Magazine,* http://www.baylormag.com/story.php?story=004639.

146. Hunter Baker, "Sloan's Struggle: What Baylor University Can Prove about Christian Scholarship," *National Review Online,* January 10, 2005. http://www.nationalreview.com/comment/baker200501101423.asp.

147. Beer, ed., *Choosing the Right College 2005,* 52, 55.

148. Ibid., 100.

149. Ibid., 202.

150. Ibid., 374.

151. Ibid., 405–410.

152. Berny Morson, "Firing of Prof at Colorado Christian Puts Focus on Christ and Capitalism," *Rocky Mountain News,* August 13, 2007, http://www.rockymountainnews.com/drmn/education/article/0,1299,DRMN_957_5670848,00.html.

153. InterVarsity Christian Fellowship, "About Us," http://www.intervarsity.org/aboutus/.

154. Julie Foster, "Tufts Shuts Out Christian Group," WorldNetDaily.com, April 25, 2000, http://www.worldnetdaily.com/news/article.asp?ARTICLE_ID=17864.

155. FIRE Press Release, "InterVarsity Multi-Ethnic Christian Fellowship Banned at Rutgers University," December 30, 2002, http://www.thefire.org/index.php/article/54.html.

156. Charles Mitchell, "Liberating America's Intellectual Gulags," *Campus Magazine,* March 31, 2005, http://www.campusmagazine.org/articledetail.aspx?id=8950bdfc-efba-4482-b084-d88d4715d93d.

157. Michael Paulson, "Campus Faith Groups Face Rebuke on Gay Rights," *Boston Globe,* April 29, 2000.

158. Madelaine Jerousek, "Ban of Gay Leader Divides Campus," *Des Moines Register,* November 5, 2002, http://www.dmregister.com/news/stories/c4780927/19653878.html.

159. "Gay Student Leader Asked to Leave Religious Group," *The Advocate,* November 6, 2002, http://www.advocate.com/news_detail_ektid13790.asp.

160. Jeremy Quittner, "Campus Crusade," *The Advocate,* December 10, 2002, http://www.keepmedia.com/pubs/TheAdvocate/2002/12/10/1377505.

161. Emmet Dennis, "Re: InterVarsity Christian Fellowship Lawsuit," January 13, 2003, http://www.dogstreetjournal.com/story/198.

162. FIRE Press Release, "Victory for Freedom of Conscience," April 2, 2003, http://www.thefire.org/index.php/article/44.html.

163. *Boy Scouts v. Dale,* 530 U.S. 640 (2000), http://supct.law.cornell.edu/supct/html/99-699.ZS.html.

164. Scott Jaschik, "A Win for Anti-Bias Policies," InsideHigherEd.com, April 20, 2006, http://www.insidehighered.com/news/2006/04/20/hastingsApril 20.

165. Thomas Bartlett, "Southern Ill. Settles With Christian Group," *Chronicle of Higher Education,* June 1, 2007, http://chronicle.com/weekly/v53/i39/39a02801.htm.

166. Associated Press, "UW-Superior Will Recognize Christian Group after All," *Lacrosse Tribune,* April 14, 2007, http://www.lacrossetribune.com/articles/2007/04/14/wi/05wissuperior14.txt.

167. *Rosenberger v. University of Virginia,* 515 U.S. 819 (1995), http://www.oyez.org/cases/1990-1999/1994/1994_94_329.

168. FIRE Press Release, "InterVarsity Multi-Ethnic Christian Fellowship Banned at Rutgers University," December 30, 2002, http://www.thefire.org/index.php/article/54.html/print.

169. FIRE, "Victory for Freedom of Association at UNC-Chapel Hill," March 7, 2005, www.thefire.org.

170. Scott Jaschik, "To Discriminate or Not?" InsideHigherEd.com, February 21, 2005, http://www.insidehighered.com/insider/to_discriminate_or_not.

171. Christian Legal Society, "Student Chapter Affiliation Materials," Appendix 2, http://www.clsnet.org/lsmPages/lsm_manual/2005-2006AffilMatls.pdf.

172. Editorial, "Diversity of Opinions," *Columbus Dispatch,* October 5, 2004.

173. Kathleen Murphy, "Can Religious Groups Exclude Non-believers?" *Chicago Tribune,* November 18, 2005.

174. Ibid.

175. FIRE Press Release, "Victory for Religious Liberty at Milwaukee School of Engineering," April 22, 2005, http://www.thefire.org/index.php/article/5561.html? PHPSESSID=.

Notes to Chapter Seven

1. "Victory for Freedom to Destroy the Press," *Indy*, April 16, 2003, http://indy.pabn.org/archives/225chatt.shtml.

2. Panel discussion on "ISUskanks.com," March 23, 2005, Illinois State University; fortunately, the administration dismissed the complaint.

3. "Poisoned Ivy," *Investor's Business Daily*, September 9, 2004.

4. Marnette Federis, "Texas Papers Stolen, Some Discovered on Fraternity House Lawn," Student Press Law Center, October 11, 2006, http://splc.org/newsflash_archives.asp?id=1349&year=2006.

5. Marnette Federis, "1,000 Newspapers Disappear from Racks at Weber State University," Student Press Law Center, November 8, 2006, http://splc.org/newsflash_archives.asp?id=1365&year=2006.

6. Marnette Federis, "Halloween Edition Newspapers Disappear from ASU at the West Campus," Student Press Law Center, November 13, 2006, http://splc.org/newsflash_archives.asp?id=1367&year=2006.

7. Marnette Federis, "Bryant U. Student Newspaper Editor Witnesses Thieves Taking Papers," Student Press Law Center, November 14, 2006, http://splc.org/newsflash_archives.asp?id=1370&year=2006.

8. Marnette Federis, "Kentucky Newspapers Stolen after Article Connected Recent Deaths to Alcohol," Student Press Law Center, November 15, 2006, http://splc.org/newsflash_archives.asp?id=1371&year=2006.

9. Marnette Federis, "UNC Fraternity Claims Responsibility for Theft of 10,000 Newspapers," Student Press Law Center, December 1, 2006, http://splc.org/newsflash_archives.asp?id=1380&year=2006.

10. Brian Hudson, "Rowan University Newspapers Stolen after Article Named Alleged Drug Distributors," Student Press Law Center, March 9, 2007, http://splc.org/newsflash_archives.asp?id=1461&year=2007.

11. Brian Hudson, "Newspapers at Truman State U. Stolen after Article on Campus Rape Printed," Student Press Law Center, March 22, 2007, http://splc.org/newsflash_archives.asp?id=1484&year=2007.

12. Brian Hudson, "Papers Stolen from UNC-Charlotte after Staff Neglects to Feature Presidential Candidate," Student Press Law Center, April 18, 2007, http://splc.org/newsflash_archives.asp?id=1508&year=2007.

13. Scott Sternberg, "Adviser Suspects Picture Prompted Newspaper Theft at Framingham State U.," Student Press Law Center, May 8, 2007, http://splc.org/newsflash_archives.asp?id=1514&year=2007.

14. Brian Hudson, "California Student Newspaper Has Rape Article Physically Cut Out," Student Press Law Center, January 31, 2007, http://splc.org/newsflash_archives.asp?id=1425&year=2007.

15. Marnette Federis, "Tulane Fraternity Gets Bill from Student Newspaper," Student Press Law Center, December 7, 2006, http://splc.org/newsflash_archives.asp?id=1387&year=2006.

16. Marnette Federis, "Vandals Steal Conservative Paper at University of Georgia," Student Press Law Center, September 29, 2006, http://splc.org/newsflash_archives.asp?id=1340&year=2006.

17. Brian Hudson, "Hundreds of Copies of Political Magazine Stolen from College of Staten Island," Student Press Law Center, April 17, 2007, http://splc.org/newsflash_archives.asp?id=1505&year=2007.

18. Scott Sternberg, "University of Southern Mississippi Newspapers Missing, Some Found in Trash," Student Press Law Center, November 7, 2006, http://splc.org/newsflash_archives.asp?id=1364&year=2006.

19. Brian Hudson, "Newspaper Thefts Level Off," *Student Press Law Center Report* (Spring 2007), http://splc.org/report_detail.asp?id=1334&edition=42.

20. Kim Peterson, "Four Face Charges for Stealing Student Papers," *Student Press Law enter Report* (Winter 2005–2006), http://www.splc.org/report_detail.asp?id= 1263& edition=38.

21. Jared Taylor, "Conservative Newspaper Editor Says Administrators Restricted Distribution Based on Content," Student Press Law Center, January 18, 2007, http://splc. org/newsflash_archives.asp?id=1404&year=2007.

22. Brian Hudson, "California Professor Says Administrators Censored Magazine," Student Press Law Center, January 18, 2007, http://splc.org/newsflash_archives. asp?id=1401&year=2007.

23. Jared Taylor, "Grambling State Paper Publishing Again, Subject to Prior Review," Student Press Law Center, January 26, 2007, http://splc.org/newsflash_archives. asp?id=1419&year=2007.

24. Marnette Federis, "BC Administrators Remove Orientation Guide from Racks," Student Press Law Center, September 22, 2006, http://splc.org/newsflash_archives. asp?id=1331&year=2006.

25. Marnette Federis, "College Paper Pulled from Stands for Faulty Headline," Student Press Law Center, September 28, 2006, http://splc.org/newsflash_archives. asp?id=1337&year=2006.

26. Paulette Perhach, "Students at Odds with President over Gargoyle." St. Augustine *Record,* April 12, 2007, http://staugustine.com/stories/041207/news_4524610.shtml.

27. Brian Hudson, "Central Connecticut State President Will Investigate Editorial Process after Controversial Rape Article," Student Press Law Center, February 15, 2007, http://splc.org/newsflash_archives.asp?id=1443&year=2007.

28. "Student Editors Asked to White Out Address of Student Suspect in On-campus Assault," Student Press Law Center, October 18, 2004, http://splc.org/newsflash_archives. asp?year=2004.

29. Rebecca McNulty, "N.C. College, Student Newspaper Reach Agreement to Grant Paper Independence," Student Press Law Center, June 13, 2005, http://splc.org/newsflash_archives.asp?id=1022&year=2005.

30. "Fla. College Officials Replace Disbanded Student Newspaper with New Publication," Student Press Law Center, October 15, 2004, http://splc.org/newsflash_archives. asp?id=855&year=2004.

31. "Hampton U. Paper Prints First Issue after Two-Week Delay," Student Press Law Center, October 14, 2004, http://splc.org/newsflash_archives.asp?id=885&year=2004.

32. Rebecca McNulty, "N.J. College Official Blocks Printing of Student Newspaper." Student Press Law Center, June 13, 2005, http://splc.org/newsflash_archives. asp?id=1025&year=2005.

33. "Wash. College Officials Will Not Fire Student Editors over Photo," Student Press Law Center, June 17, 2003, http://splc.org/newsflash.asp?id=623&year=2003.

34. Rebecca McNulty, "Student Officials at N.Y. College Lock Student Journalists Out of Newsroom." Student Press Law Center, June 14, 2005, http://splc.org/newsflash_archives. asp?id=1027&year=2005.

35. "Student Paper Sues Colo. University Board for Approving Cut in Student-Fee Allocation," Student Press Law Center, July 16, 2004, http://splc.org/newsflash_archives. asp?id=852&year=2004.

36. Brian Hudson, "Missouri Newspaper Threatens University with Lawsuit to Restore Funding," Student Press Law Center, February 14, 2007, http://splc.org/newsflash_archives. asp?id=1440&year=2007.

37. Rebecca McNulty, "Ariz. Budget Prohibits 'Appropriated' Money from Going to College Newspapers," Student Press Law Center, June 28, 2005, http://splc.org/newsflash_archives.asp?id=1047&year=2005.

38. Kate Campbell, "Ariz. Lawmaker Proposes Eliminating State Funds for Student Publications," Student Press Law Center, March 16, 2005, http://splc.org/newsflash_archives.asp?id=985&year=2005.

39. Ibid.

40. John Dougherty, "Religious Wrong," *Phoenix New Times,* March 17, 2005, http://www.phoenixnewtimes.com/issues/2005-03-17/news/dougherty.html.

41. "University President Threatens to Cut Newspaper Funding over Magazine Cover," Student Press Law Center, November 30, 2004, http://splc.org/newsflash_archives.asp?id=918&year=2004.

42. Campbell Roth, "'Stop Using Our Acronym,' Ariz. University Tells Student Newspaper," Student Press Law Center, March 3, 2005, http://splc.org/newsflash.asp?id=970.

43. Jason Mattera, "Censorship on a Rhode Island Campus," Studentsfor AcademicFreedom.org, October 9, 2003, http://www.studentsforacademicfreedom.org/archive/2003/JasonMatteraRWU101703.html.

44. "N.Y. College Paper Sues Student Government for Denying Funds," Student Press Law Center, June 16, 2003, http://splc.org/newsflash.asp?id=626&year=2003.

45. "Victory for Freedom of the Press at University of Oregon," TheFire.org, March 3, 2005, www.thefire.org, http://www.thefire.org/index.php/article/5383.html.

46. "Mo. College Paper Asked to Undergo Mediation with Group Offended by Cartoon," Student Press Law Center, March 1, 2004, http://www.splc.org/newsflash_archives.asp?id=760&year=2004.

47. "Copies of Alternative College Paper Stolen at Calif. University, Editor Says." Student Press Law Center, February 9, 2004, http://splc.org/newsflash.asp?id=738&year=2004.

48. E-mail to author from Ronald McGuire, February 6, 2003.

49. "Administrators Lock Door to Campus Publication's Office in Dispute over Confidential Files," Student Press Law Center, March 7, 2001, http://splc.org/newsflash.asp?id=244.

50. Marcella Bombardieri, "Harvard's Sexy *H Bomb Magazine* Drops," *Boston Globe,* May 25, 2004.

51. "Radio Station Cries Censorship after Fla. Student Government Cut Its Funding," Student Press Law Center, March 10, 2004, http://splc.org/newsflash.asp?id=772.

52. "University Asked to Sanction Student Newspaper for 'Hate-Filled' Column," Student Press Law Center, November 4, 2004, http://splc.org/newsflash_archives.asp?id=905&year=2004.

53. Isolde Raftery, "Sense and Censorship," *Chronicle of Higher Education,* June 18, 2004.

54. "Okla. University, Student Journalists Settle Lawsuit over Christian Newspaper," Student Press Law Center, April 22, 2004, http://splc.org/newsflash.asp?id=794.

55. "2 Penn. College Papers Pay the Price for Publishing April Fool's Day Editions," Student Press Law Center, April 7, 2004, http://splc.org/newsflash.asp?id=788.

56. *Aquinas,* May 13, 2004, 9:

57. "A Return to the Old," *Aquinas,* May 13, 2004, 4.

58. Aquinas Online, "Content Policy," October 10, 2002, http://academic.scranton.edu/organization/aquinas/about/content.html.

59. "Statement from President Robert B. Sloan Jr.," *Baylor Lariat,* March 2, 2004, http://www.baylor.edu/lariat/news.php?action=story&story=20065.

60. "Wedded Blitz," *New Yorker,* March 15, 2004, http://www.newyorker.com/talk/content/articles/040315ta_talk_hertzberg.

61. Scott Gold, "Student Stand on Gay Unions Roils Baylor," *Los Angeles Times,* March 3, 2004, see http://rhetorica.net/archives/002304.html.

Notes

62. Tad Walch, "BYU Newspaper Yanks T-Shirt Ad," *Deseret Morning News*, September 25, 2004.

63. "Va. College Officials Threaten to Confiscate Independent Student Newspaper," Student Press Law Center, October 22, 2004, http://splc.org/newsflash_archives.asp?id=898&year=2004.

64. Marnette Federis, "CMA Censures Oklahoma Baptist University after Adviser Contract Not Renewed," Student Press Law Center, October 5, 2006, http://splc.org/newsflash.asp?id=1346.

65. "Catholic U. Cuts Scholarships for Student Newspaper, Yearbook Editors," Student Press Law Center, March 3, 2005; Elizabeth Farrell, "Catholic U. Cancels Scholarships for Student Leaders of 3 Groups, Including the Campus Newspaper," *Chronicle of Higher Education*, February 28, 2005.

66. "Statement of Student Press Law Center Executive Director Mark Goodman Regarding *Lane v. Simon* and Student Press Censorship at Kansas State University," Student Press Law Center, July 21, 2004, http://splc.org/newsflash_archives.asp?id=855&year=2004.

67. "SPJ Members Issue Resolution Condemning Kan. Adviser's Firing," Student Press Law Center, October 6, 2004.

68. "Kan. College Drops Adviser Who Refused Demands to Censor Student Paper," Student Press Law Center, May 3, 2004, http://splc.org/newsflash.asp?id=803; Suzanne Bell, "Adviser Gets $130,000 in Settlement with College," Student Press Law Center, August 10, 2006, http://www.splc.org/newsflash_archives.asp?id=1309&year=2006.

69. Michael Weissenstein, "L.I. University Crackdown Sparks Journalism Ethics Debate," *Editor & Publisher*, March 11, 2004, http://www.editorandpublisher.com/eandp/news/article_display.jsp?vnu_content_id=1000460102; "N.Y. University Punishes Editor, Adviser for Publishing Student's Grades," Student Press Law Center, February 13, 2004, http://splc.org/newsflash.asp?id=747.

70. "Public Tenn. University Again Demands That Adviser Review Content Before Publication," Student Press Law Center, August 26, 2004, http://splc.org/newsflash_archives.asp?id=865&year=2004.

71. Diane Krauthamer, "Former Newspaper Adviser Sues Ind. University over Transfer," Student Press Law Center, February 17, 2005, http://splc.org/newsflash_archives.asp?id=954&year=2005; Barb Berggoetz, "University Newspaper Adviser Removed," *Indianapolis Star*, May 26, 2004.

72. Diane Krauthamer, "Wisc. University Fires Newspaper Adviser Following Series of Disagreements," Student Press Law Center, February 9, 2005, http://splc.org/newsflash_archives.asp?year=2005; Bruce Murphy, "Marquette Cans Adviser to Student Newspaper," *Milwaukee Journal-Sentinel,* February 6, 2005.

73. Campbell Roth, "Fla. Student Newspaper Avoids Newsroom Lockout," Student Press Law Center, December 20, 2004, http://splc.org/newsflash_archives.asp?id=931&year=2004.

74. Melinda McCrady, "Changes in Journalism Department Surrounded by Contention, Controversy," *Long Beach Union*, May 10, 2004, http://cache.zoominfo.com/cachedpage/?archive_id=0&page_id=688360044&page_url=%2f%2fwww.lbunion.com%2fcurrentissue%2fnewsreader.php%3ffocusissuedate%3d2004-05-10%26news_id%3d118&page_last_updated=5%2f12%2f2004+2%3a45%3a58+AM&firstName=William&lastName=Mulligan.

75. Rebecca McNulty, "Neb. College Fires Second Newspaper Adviser in Five Years," Student Press Law Center, July 19, 2005, http://splc.org/newsflash.asp?id=1051.

76. Ibid.

77. Ibid.

78. "Tough Calls," *Student Press Law Center Report* (Winter 2001–2002) 36, http://www.splc.org/report_detail.asp?id=793&edition=20.

79. Elizabeth Redden, "Stumbling upon Secure Data," InsideHigherEd.com, October 1, 2007, http://www.insidehighered.com/news/2007/10/01/oregon.

Notes

80. "Student Cameraman Arrested for Filming Student Being Cited," Student Press Law Center, November 18, 2004, http://splc.org/newsflash_archives.asp?id=912&year= 2004.

81. Diane Krauthamer, "Calif. Police Arrest Student Journalist for Photographing Alleged Crime," Student Press Law Center, February 15, 2005, http://splc.org/newsflash_archives.asp?year=2005.

82. "Student Reporters Arrested, Detained While Covering Protest," Student Press Law Center, September 21, 2004, http://splc.org/newsflash_archives.asp?id= 867&year=2004.

83. Diane Krauthamer, "SPLC: Journalists' Requests for Campus Crime Records Often Denied by Schools," Student Press Law Center, March 14, 2005, http://splc.org/newsflash_archives.asp?year=2005.

84. Don Russell, "Swarthmore Groups Told to Nix Links," Philadelphia Daily News, October 23, 2003, http://www.swarthmore.edu/news/inthenews/03/03.10.23.html; see also http://www.why-war.com/features/2003/10/diebold.html.

85. Allison Retka, "Student Challenges Colorado Criminal Libel Statute," Student Press Law Center, January 21, 2006, http://splc.org/newsflash.asp?id=1160.

86. David Epstein, "Cloaked in Cyberspace," InsideHigherEd.com, May 13, 2005, http://insidehighered.com/news/2005/05/13/lawrence.

87. "Fla. College Files Defamation Lawsuit Against Anonymous Web Site Contributors," Student Press Law Center, February 26, 2004, http://splc.org/newsflash.asp?id=757.

88. Greg Lukianoff, "UC Santa Barbara's Unlikely Claims," TheFire.org, February 8, 2005, http://splc.org/newsflash_archives.asp?id=981&year=2005.

89. Roth, "'Stop Using Our Acronym,' Ariz. University Tells Student Newspaper."

90. Diane Krauthamer, "Community College Official Institutes Prior Review of Student-Produced News Show," Student Press Law Center, March 23, 2005, http://splc.org/newsflash_archives.asp?year=2005.

91. Mike Robinson, "Court Fight Looms over College Paper," Associated Press, July 24, 2003, http://www.collegefreedom.org/gsuap.htm.

92. Jeffrey Young, "Censorship or Quality Control?" Chronicle of Higher Education, August 9, 2002, http://chronicle.com/free/v48/i48/48a03601.htm.

93. "Editors Sue University for First Amendment Violations," Student Press Law Center, March 30, 2001, http://www.splc.org/newsflash.asp?id=259&year=2001.

94. "Free Speech Groups Worry Hosty Ruling Will Scale Back Students' 1st Amendment Rights," Student Press Law Center, June 23, 2005, http://www.splc.org/newsflash.asp?id=1042&year=.

95. Hosty v. Carter, 412 F.3d 731 (7th Cir. 2005) (en banc), http://caselaw.lp.findlaw.com/data2/circs/7th/014155pv2.pdf.

96. Ibid.

97. Ibid.

98. Ibid.

99. Ibid.

100. Rosenberger v. University of Virginia, 515 U.S. 819 (1995).

101. University of Wisconsin v. Southworth, 529 U.S. 217 (2000).

102. Hosty v. Carter, 412 F.3d 731 (7th Cir. 2005) (en banc), http://caselaw.lp.findlaw.com/data2/circs/7th/014155pv2.pdf.

103. Charles Mitchell, "Ugh," TheFire.org, June 22, 2005, http://www.thefire.org/index.php/article/5812.html.

104. Diane Krauthamer, Britt Hulit, and Campbell Roth, "Study Reveals 'Disturbing' Results about High Schoolers and the First Amendment," Student Press Law Center, February 1, 2005, http://splc.org/newsflash_archives.asp?year=2005.

105. Chiras v. Miller, 2004 WL 1660388 (N.D. Tex. July 23, 2004), appeal docketed, No. 04-10998 (5th Cir. 2004).

106. Memo to California State University presidents from Christine Helwick, CSU General Counsel, June 30, 2005, http://splc.org/newsflash.asp?id=1064.

107. Ibid.

108. Evan Mayor, "California Governor Signs College Student Press Freedom Bill," Student Press Law Center, August 28, 2006, http://splc.org/newsflash.asp?id=1316.

109. Michael Beder, "Ill. Governor Approves College Press Protections," Student Press Law Center, September 4, 2007, http://splc.org/newsflash.asp?id=1597; Judy Wang, "Oregon Student Free Press Bill Signed into Law," Student Press Law Center, July 13, 2007, http://splc.org/newsflash.asp?id=1575.

Notes to Chapter Eight

1. Mark Clayton, "Part-time Profs Try to Strike a New Bargain," *Christian Science Monitor,* November 5, 2002.

2. AAUP, "The Devaluing of Higher Education," *Academe,* March–April 2006, 32; Xiangmin Liu and Liang Zhang, "What Determines Employment of Part-Time Faculty in Higher Education Institutions?" Cornell Higher Education Research Institute working paper, June 2007, 3, http://www.ilr.cornell.edu/cheri/wp/cheri_wp105.pdf.

3. Ibid., 29.

4. David Laurence, "The 1999 MLA Survey of Staffing in English and Foreign Language Departments," *Profession* (2001), 211–224.

5. See Ronald Ehrenberg, "Key Issues Facing Trustees of National Research Universities in the Decades Ahead," Working Paper, Cornell Higher Education Research Institute, December 13, 2005, p. 4, http://www.ilr.cornell.edu/cheri/wp/cheri_wp85.pdf; Clayton, "Part-time Profs Try to Strike a New Bargain."

6. Lesley Stedman Weidenbener, "Ex-professor at Ivy Tech Files Complaint," *Louisville Courier-Journal,* September 2, 2007.

7. See Ehrenberg, "Key Issues Facing Trustees."

8. Scott Jaschik, "The Shrinking Tenure Track," InsideHigherEd.com, May 19, 2005.

9. Jennifer Brown, "Prof's Firing Stirs Blog Debate," *Denver Post,* January 8, 2006.

10. Vladimir Kogan, "Art School Fires Lead Union Organizer," *Voice of San Diego,* June 6, 2007, http://www.voiceofsandiego.org/articles/2007/06/06/news/03arts060607.txt.

11. Gretchen Morgenson, "Some Things You Just Can't Teach," *New York Times,* May 15, 2005, http://www.nytimes.com/2005/05/15/business/yourmoney/15gret.html?ex=1273809600&en=c90646abe7be721f&ei=5088&partner=rssnyt&emc=rss.

12. Piper Fogg, "Presidents Favor Scrapping Tenure," *Chronicle of Higher Education,* November 4, 2005, http://chronicle.com/weekly/v52/i11/11a03101.htm.

13. Victor Davis Hanson, "Professors Won't Like This: Death to Lifetime Contracts," *Chicago Tribune,* May 13, 2005.

14. David Epstein, "A Smaller Tulane," InsideHigherEd.com, December 9, 2005, http://insidehighered.com/news/2005/12/09/tulane; Report of an AAUP Special Committee, "Hurricane Katrina and New Orleans Universities," *Academe,* May–June 2007, http://www.aaup.org/AAUP/protect/academicfreedom/investrep/2007/katrina.htm.

15. Berny Morson, "It's Tougher to Get Tenure Now," *Rocky Mountain News,* July 24, 2007, http://www.rockymountainnews.com/drmn/local/article/0,1299,DRMN_15_5642491,00.html.

16. Gary Rhoades and Sheila Slaughter, *Academic Capitalism and the New Economy: Markets, State, and Higher Education* (Baltimore: Johns Hopkins University Press, 2004), 266.

17. "Ex-Student Sues St. John's Over Contract for Nike Gear," *New York Times,* November 20, 1999; see also www.educatingforjustice.org.

18. Scott Smallwood, "The Man without a Department," *Chronicle of Higher Education,* February 27, 2004.

19. FIRE Press release, "University of Oklahoma Administration Plots to Punish Professor for Political Beliefs, Whistleblowing," TheFire.org, December 8, 2004.

20. Smallwood, "The Man without a Department."

Notes

21. Charles Burress, "Embattled UC Teacher Is Granted Tenure," *San Francisco Chronicle,* May 21, 2005, http://www.sfgate.com/cgi-bin/article.cgi?f=/c/a/2005/05/21/BAG8VCSGL41. DTL.

22. Michael Milstein, "Logging Study Sets Off Own Firestorm," *Oregonian,* January 20, 2006, http://www.oregonlive.com/metro/oregonian/index.ssf?/base/news/1137729313106480.xml&coll=7.

23. Associated Press, "BLM Suspends Its Funding for Controversial OSU Fire Study," February 7, 2006, http://www.newsreview.info/article/20060207/NEWS/102070087/-1/rss01; see David Epstein, "Scientific Discourse or Prior Restraint?" InsideHigherEd.com, January 24, 2006, http://www.insidehighered.com/news/2006/01/24/logging.

24. Editorial, "Drug Thugs," *USA Today,* June 8, 2007, http://blogs.usatoday.com/oped/2007/06/drug_thugs.html.

25. Kembrew McLeod, *Freedom of Expression®: Overzealous Copyright Bozos and Other Enemies of Creativity* (New York: Doubleday/Random House, 2005), 227.

26. Sheila Slaughter, "Professional Values and the Allure of the Market," *Academe,* September–October 2001, http://www.aaup.org/publications/Academe/2001/01SO/so01sla.htm.

27. Report of AAUP Committee A, "Academic Freedom and Tenure: Philander Smith College," http://www.aaup.org/AAUP/protectrights/academicfreedom/investrep/2004/Philand.htm?PF=1.

28. David Chircop, "Loose Lips: Academic Freedom Be Damned," *Merced Sun Star,* March 7, 2006, http://www.mercedsunstar.com/local/story/11901835p-12671177c.html.

29. Scott Jaschik, "BMW Professors," InsideHigherEd.com, August 25, 2006, http://insidehighered.com/news/2006/08/25/clemson.

30. Lynnley Browning, "Donation Gives BMW Influence at University," *International Herald-Tribune,* August 23, 2006, http://www.iht.com/articles/2006/08/23/business/bmw.php.

31. Karin Fischer, "N.C. Political Aide Sought to Cancel a Study by an Economist Who Had Criticized State Taxes," *Chronicle of Higher Education,* November 25, 2005.

32. "Howard U. Denies Endowed Chair to Critic of Alcohol Marketers." *Chronicle of Higher Education,* November 17, 2006.

33. Ibid.

34. Brittany Anas, "Officers: Academic Freedom Threatened," *Daily Camera* (Boulder, CO), October 9, 2006, http://www.dailycamera.com/bdc/buffzone_news/article/0,1713,BDC_2448_5055506,00.html.

35. Statement by the University of Colorado Chapter of the American Association of University Professors, "The Adrienne Anderson Case," April 7, 2007.

36. Henry Giroux, *The University in Chains: Confronting the Military-Industrial-Academic Complex* (Boulder, CO: Paradigm Publishers, 2007).

37. See "SolomonResponse.org," http://www.law.georgetown.edu/solomon/index.html.

38. John K. Wilson, "The Defense Department vs. Free Speech on Campus," InsideHigherEd.com, June 25, 2007, http://www.insidehighered.com/views/2007/06/25/wilson.

39. Ibid.

40. Victor Davis Hanson, "Topsy-Turvy," *National Review,* October 13, 2003.

41. Scott Jaschik, "Unusual Union Battle," InsideHigherEd.com, July 24, 2006, http://insidehighered.com/news/2006/07/24/quinnipiac.

42. Scott Jaschik, "Professors: Managers or Employees?" InsideHigherEd.com, August 2, 2006, http://insidehighered.com/news/2006/08/02/union.

43. Eliza Strickland, "Grad-Student Walkout: First Step to Getting a Union?" *Christian Science Monitor,* March 29, 2005.

44. *New York University,* 332 N.L.R.B. 111 (2000); *Brown University,* 342 N.L.R.B. 42 (2004), http://www.lawmemo.com/nlrb/vol/342/42.htm.

45. AAUP, "Statement on Graduate Students," 2000, http://aaup.org/statements/Redbook/Gradst.htm.

46. Daniel Duane, "Eggheads Unite," *New York Times,* May 4, 2003.

47. Scott Jaschik, "Pickets and Protests," InsideHigherEd.com, April 15, 2005, http://www.insidehighered.com/news/2005/04/15/labor.

48. John Beckman, "Graduate Students Are Students," InsideHigherEd.com, August 15, 2005, http://insidehighered.com/views/2005/08/15/beckman.

49. Scott Sherman, "Bitter Winter at NYU," *The Nation,* January 9, 2006, http://www.thenation.com/doc/20060109/sherman.

50. Recommendation from the NYU Faculty Advisory Committee on Academic Priorities, April 26, 2005, http://www.nyu.edu/provost/communications/ga/ap042605.pdf.

51. Sherman, "Bitter Winter at NYU."

52. Karen Arenson, "N.Y.U. Teaching Aides End Strike, with Union Unrecognized," *New York Times,* September 7, 2006, http://www.nytimes.com/2006/09/07/nyregion/07nyu.html?ref=education.

53. Scott Jaschik, "Contract Breakthrough," InsideHigherEd.com, February 28, 2005, http://insidehighered.com/insider/contract_breakthrough.

54. Gordon Lafer, "Graduate Student Unions Fight the Corporate University," *Dissent,* Fall 2001.

55. Jennifer Washburn, "Columbia Unbecoming," *Nation,* April 25, 2005, http://www.thenation.com/doc.mhtml?i=20050509&s=washburn.

56. Elizabeth Redden, "Inquiry or Indoctrination?" InsideHigherEd.com, May 3, 2007, http://www.insidehighered.com/news/2007/05/03/ucsd.

57. Joel Westheimer, "Tenure Denied: Union Busting in the Corporate University," *Workplace,* November 5, 2001, http://www.louisville.edu/journal/workplace/westheimer.html.

58. "NYU Settles Tenure Denial Case," *Academe,* September–October 2002, http://www.aaup.org/publications/Academe/2002/02so/02soNB.htm#8.

59. Ana Marie Cox, "Department Head Loses Post for Refusing to Discipline T.A.'s," *Chronicle of Higher Education,* June 8, 2001, http://chronicle.com/free/v47/i39/39a01201.htm.

60. Dave Newbart, "City Colleges Strike Leaves Part-Timers without Jobs," *Chicago Sun-Times,* November 15, 2004; Robert Becker and Jamie Francisco, "Colleges Target 140 for Firing," *Chicago Tribune,* January 12, 2005.

61. Jaschik, "Pickets and Protests."; Marcella Bombardieri, "Vote asks Emerson President to Resign," *Boston Globe,* May 5, 2005.

62. Shawn Vestal, "Teacher Says She Lost Job for Speaking Out," *Spokane Spokesman-Review,* February 21, 2006.

63. *Trimble v. West Virginia,* 549 S.E.2d 294 (W.Va. 2001).

64. "Illegal TA Strikers Let Off the Hook," *Wisconsin State Journal,* May 27, 2004.

65. Andy Furillo, "Governor Cuts Labor Institute Funding,"*Sacramento Bee,* December 20, 2003, http://laborcenter.berkeley.edu/press/sacbee_dec03.shtml.

66. Charles Proctor, "Labor Center Fights Threat of Erasure," *Daily Bruin,* January 18, 2005, http://www.dailybruin.ucla.edu/news/articles.asp?id=31509.

67. Ryan Foley, "Legislator Takes Aim at UW Programs," *Wisconsin State Journal,* July 25, 2007, http://www.madison.com/wsj/home/local/index.php?ntid=202688&ntpid=3.

68. Joshua Seiden, "Labor Studies Professor in Limbo," *University News* (Kansas City, MO), September 17, 2007, http://media.www.unews.com/media/storage/paper274/news/2007/09/17/News/Labor.Studies.Professor.In.Limbo-2973238.shtml.

69. Isaac Arnsdorf, "Student Threatened with Suspension for Passing Out Fliers on Campus," Student Press Law Center, June 18, 2007, http://www.splc.org/newsflash.asp?id=1550.

Notes to Conclusion

1. Don Feder, "Ward Churchill: Useful Idiot," FrontPageMagazine.com, February 11, 2005.

Notes

2. Erwin Chemerinsky, "Erwin Chemerinsky: Dumped over an Op-Ed," *Los Angeles Times*, September 14, 2007, http://www.latimes.com/news/opinion/la-oe-chemerinsky14sep14,0,1499542.story?coll=la-opinion-center.

3. Garrett Therolf and Richard C. Paddock, "UC Irvine Rehires Chemerinsky as Dean," *Los Angeles Times*, September 18, 2007, http://www.latimes.com/news/local/la-me-uci18sep18,0,3167475.story?coll=la-home-center.

4. Gara LaMarche, "The Crisis of Democracy in America," OpenDemocracy.net, June 30, 2005, http://www.opendemocracy.net/globalization-institutions_government/democracy_2639.jsp.

5. Charles Mitchell, "Liberating America's Intellectual Gulags," *Campus Magazine*, March 31, 2005, http://www.campusmagazine.org/articledetail.aspx?id=8950bdfc-efba-4482-b084-d88d4715d93d.

6. Jake Stanford, "Political Correctness Is the Anti-Solution," *Crimson White*, January 8, 2004.

7. Patrick Coyle and Ron Robinson, eds., *The Conservative Guide to Campus Activism*, 2d ed. (Herndon, VA: Young America's Foundation, 2005), 3.

8. Scott Jaschik, "Ward & Newt & Tenure," InsideHigherEd.com, February 28, 2005, http://insidehighered.com/insider/ward_newt_tenure.

9. Cal Thomas, "Liberal Bias in Colleges Bleeds into Classroom," Townhall.com, March 30, 2005.

10. See Brian Anderson, *South Park Conservatives* (Washington, DC: Regnery, 2005).

11. Jeremy Beer, ed., *Choosing the Right College 2005: The Whole Truth about America's Top Schools* (Wilmington, DE: ISI Books, 2004), 211–212; see also David Kirp's description of the event in his book, *Shakespeare, Einstein and the Bottom Line: The Marketing of Higher Education.* (Cambridge, MA: Harvard University Press, 2003).

12. Pam Chamberlain, "Deliberate Differences," Political Research Associates, 2004, http://www.publiceye.org/campus/pdf/deliberate_differences.pdf.

13. Scott Jaschik, "Pessimistic Views on Academic Freedom," *InsideHigherEd.com*, August 15, 2007, http://www.insidehighered.com/news/2007/08/15/freedom.

INDEX

᪐

AAUP. *See* American Association of
    University Professors
Abortion, 160–161, 162–163
Abu Ghraib, 36
Academia: as battleground for political
    future, 207–209; and campus
    newspapers. *See* Freedom of the press
    (campus media); and corporate
    antidisparagement clauses, 195–
    198; corporate model ("Wal-Mart
    University"), 191, 193, 195–198, 210;
    discouraging of political activism, 115;
    how to attract more conservatives,
    114; and military, 198–199; need for
    more political discussion, 115; and
    paternalism, 121–122; predominance
    of liberals at elite schools, 103–104;
    reasons for predominance of liberals,
    108–115; underrepresentation of
    minorities on college faculties, 105;
    and unions, 199–205; use of adjunct
    faculty as (unsuccessful) cost-cutting
    measure, 192–193
Academic Bill of Rights, 5, 61–62, 132:
    as basis for campus policy changes,
    63–64; as basis for conservative
    legislative proposals, 62–63, 69–70; on
    collective statements, 68–69; Colorado
    campaign, 70–72; conservatives
    against, 94–97; on "efforts to obstruct,"
    68; on expression of political views as
    indoctrination, 67–68; flaws of, 66–69;

and funding threats, 71; and grievance
    procedures, 76–77, 97; on intellectual
    pluralism, 68; and legislative funding
    threats, 73–74; and Ohio, 72–74;
    on plurality of perspectives, 66; on
    political and religious beliefs, 66–67;
    and political discussions, 77–78, 84;
    on provision of dissenting sources
    and viewpoints, 67; uncertainty of
    enforcement issues, 76–82
Academic freedom: as casualty of 9/11,
    1, 9–10, 38–41; commonality of
    conservatives and liberals, 206–207,
    208–211; conservative attack on,
    5–8; defined, 1–2; disputes about,
    2; as essential to free society, 7; and
    extramural utterances, 2; historical
    lack of in U.S. higher education, 2–3;
    importance of, 213–214; intolerance
    toward teaching tolerance, 21–23; and
    McCarthyism, 4–6; and PATRIOT
    Act, 27–28; for professors, 2; proposed
    new support organization, 212–213;
    and right to work, 40; and squelching
    of free speech after 9/11, 10–13; for
    students, 2; and World War I, 3–4. *See
    also* Free speech; Freedom of the press
    (campus media)
Academic Questions, 101
Academy of Art University, 121
ACTA. *See* American Council of Trustees
    and Alumni

ABOUT THE AUTHOR

٭

John K. Wilson is the author of *Barack Obama: This Improbable Quest* (Paradigm Publishers 2008), *How the Left Can Win Arguments and Influence People: A Tactical Manual for Pragmatic Progressives* (New York University Press 2001); *Newt Gingrich: Capitol Crimes and Misdemeanors* (Common Courage Press 1996); and *The Myth of Political Correctness: The Conservative Attack on Higher Education* (Duke University Press 1995). Wilson studied law under Barack Obama at the University of Chicago. He currently works and resides in Chicago and has watched Obama rise from state senator to U.S. Senator to presidential candidate.